Open-Book Testing: Why It Makes Sense

By Kay Burke, Ph.D.

Educators who allow students to take open-book tests are not teaching *for the test*; they are teaching *for understanding*. Most students agree that open-book tests are more challenging than traditional objective tests because they require high-order thinking skills rather than recall skills.

The greatest benefit from open-book testing may be that it encourages the type of thinking that will benefit students in the real world.

- Open-book tests focus on students learning important concepts rather than memorizing facts.

- They encourage students to utilize the lifelong learning skill of "accessing information" rather than memorizing data. In most jobs, people do not have to memorize formulas or discrete bits of data; they have to know how to find the important information they need in order to solve problems and complete projects.

- Open-book tests encourage students to highlight the text and organize their notes so they can find the information they need.

- Open-book tests encourage students to **apply** the information they have learned and **transfer** it to new situations, rather than just repeat the facts.

Sources:

Burke, K.B. *The mindful school: How to assess authentic learning*. Arlington Heights, IL. Skylight Professional Development.

Stiggins, R.J. (1985, October). *Improving assessment where it means the most: In the classroom*. Educational Leadership, pp. 69-74.

Wiggins, G. (1989, April). *Creating tests worth taking*. Educational Leadership, pp. 121-127

Wiggins, G., & McTighe, J. (1989). *Understanding by design*. Alexandria, VA: Association for Supervision and Curriculum Development.

Test Bank

for

Zimbardo, Johnson, Weber, and Gruber

Psychology

AP* Edition

prepared by

Laura Brandt
Adlai E. Stevenson High School, Lincolnshire, Illinois

Boston   New York   San Francisco
Mexico City   Montreal   Toronto   London   Madrid   Munich   Paris
Hong Kong   Singapore   Tokyo   Cape Town   Sydney

ISBN 0-13-173184-X

Printed in the United States of America

10 9 8 7 6 5 4 3 2   10 09 08 07

Contents

Chapter 1   Introduction and History of Psychology

Multiple Choice Questions

1) A formal definition of psychology is as the scientific study of
   - A) human nature.
   - B) theories and research methods.
   - C) the process of learning and modifying behavioral reflexes.
   - D) the behavior of individuals and their mental processes.
   - E) groups of people.

   Answer: D
   Diff: 1   Page Ref: 2
   Topic: What Are the Components of Thought?
   Skill: Conceptual

2) The word psychology has evolved from the words 'psyche' and '-ology' which together mean
   - A) study of the mind.
   - B) study of people.
   - C) science of behavior.
   - D) study of insanity.
   - E) science of people.

   Answer: A
   Diff: 1   Page Ref: 2
   Topic: What is Psychology – And What Is It Not?
   Skill: Factual

3) What does the story of Clever Hans teach current psychology students about the findings of psychological studies?
   - A) Horses can have cognition, just as people have cognition.
   - B) The horse's owner was purposely tricking people into believing that Clever Hans could count.
   - C) While animals are not able to speak, they can be trained to compute basic numbers.
   - D) Occasionally, phenomenal events will occur that cannot easily be explained but are nonetheless valid and reliable.
   - E) One should think critically about what they are being asked to believe.

   Answer: E
   Diff: 3   Page Ref: 2
   Topic: What is Psychology – And What Is It Not?
   Skill: Applied

4) Why was Pfungst hesitant to believe that Clever Hans could actually count?

    A) He knew that horses could not count.

    B) He believed that Hans owner was trying to trick people into believing that hans could count.

    C) He wanted objective, verifiable evidence before he would believe that Hans could count.

    D) He knew that Hans cognition could never be properly studied.

    E) He was angry about all of the attention Hans was receiving.

Answer: C

Diff: 2   Page Ref: 2

Topic: What is Psychology – And What Is It Not?

Skill: Applied

5) Empirical investigation is

    A) a study that makes logical sense.

    B) data gathered directly by an observer.

    C) based on random coding of data.

    D) biased by random procedures.

    E) always found to be accurate.

Answer: B

Diff: 2   Page Ref: 3

Topic: How Do Psychologists Develop New Knowledge?

Skill: Factual

6) Empirical research is important because it

    A) can eliminate the flaws of pseudoscience.

    B) tests theories by using good scientific practices.

    C) allows psychology to rely on more than just speculation.

    D) allows psychology to use data to drive it's conclusions.

    E) All of the above are correct.

Answer: E

Diff: 2   Page Ref: 3

Topic: What is Psychology – And What Is It Not?

Skill: Conceptual

7) Pseudopsychology is
   A) the scientific study of human and animal behavior.
   B) the study of the psyche.
   C) the study of how the perception and cognition.
   D) phony unscientific psychology masquerading as the real thing.
   E) Freud's method of analyzing patients.

Answer: D
Diff: 1   Page Ref: 4
Topic: What is Psychology – And What Is It Not?
Skill: Factual

8) The Confirmation Bias can be difficult when scientists conduct research, because
   A) once can never control for all of the extraneous variables that may interact with the study.
   B) they do not use random sampling.
   C) they only look for evidence that confirms their previous beliefs.
   D) they know which participants belong to which groups.
   E) they are too objective when reviewing the data.

Answer: C
Diff: 3   Page Ref: 4
Topic: What is Psychology – And What Is It Not?
Skill: Recall

9) Pseudoscience is harmful because
   A) unfounded psychological beliefs can waste time, money and talent.
   B) it can be a fertile land for fraud.
   C) by accepting pseudo psychologies claims, individuals risk depriving themselves of interesting and useful psychological insights.
   D) it diminishes public support for legitimate psychological science.
   E) All of the above

Answer: E
Diff: 1   Page Ref: 4–5
Topic: What is Psychology – And What Is It Not?
Skill: Recall

10) In initial studies regarding facilitated communication to treat autistic children results looked promising. Upon further research it was found that this only occurred because

    A) the "facilitator" was unknowingly guiding the student in their responses.

    B) the children really were communicating without any aide from others.

    C) the children were told the correct answers.

    D) parents wanted their children to become better.

    E) the researchers had "Coached" the children and facilitators before the experiment began.

Answer: A
Diff: 2   *Page Ref: 5*
Topic: What is Psychology – And What Is It Not?
Skill: Conceptual

11) Alfred works in a laboratory at The University of Freud, he runs rats through mazes to determine how long it will take them to form a cognitive map. Alfred is primarily working the the field of

    A) Applied Psychology.

    B) Industrial/Organizational Psychology.

    C) School Psychology.

    D) Experimental Psychology.

    E) Engineering Psychology.

Answer: D
Diff: 2   *Page Ref: 6–7*
Topic: What is Psychology – And What Is It Not?
Skill: Applied

12) Dr. Jones is an industrial/organizational (I/O) psychologist. Thus, she is most likely to do which of the following?

    A) help individuals who have eating disorders, such as anorexia nervosa

    B) conduct experiments to determine which studying strategies work best

    C) diagnose learning disabilities within a school district

    D) assist in the design of easy-to-use software for home computer usage

    E) help companies determine which questions to ask job candidates

Answer: E
Diff: 2   *Page Ref: 7*
Topic: What is Psychology – And What Is It Not?
Skill: Applied

13) Which of the following is a career path that would be unlikely for a psychologist?
   A) a therapist who works with clients with mental disorders
   B) an individual who works with motivating a professional sports team
   C) an individual who designs products that will help people to become more efficient
   D) an individual working at a school administering psychological tests.
   E) an individual who invests in real estate

Answer: E
Diff: 1   Page Ref: 7
Topic: What is Psychology – And What Is It Not?
Skill: Applied

14) Which of the following best illustrates the job of a Engineering psychologist?
   A) a person who designs wheelchairs that are easier to maneuver for those with physical restrictions
   B) a person who drives a train
   C) a person who produces personality tests
   D) a person who works in a hospital helping individuals who have been in an accident to recover
   E) a person who helps others perform to the best of their abilities while under pressure.

Answer: A
Diff: 1   Page Ref: 7
Topic: What is Psychology – And What Is It Not?
Skill: Factual

15) Which of the following professionals would be best suited for conducting a market research study?
   A) Engineering Psychologist
   B) Industrial–Organizational Psychologist
   C) Clinical Psychologist
   D) School Psychologist
   E) Sports Psychologist

Answer: B
Diff: 2   Page Ref: 7
Topic: What is Psychology – And What Is It Not?
Skill: Applied

16) A(n) _____ psychologist would be most likely to help individuals overcome their depression.

    A) clinical

    B) industrial/organizational (I/O)

    C) engineering

    D) school

    E) social

Answer: A

Diff: 2   Page Ref: 7

Topic: What is Psychology – And What Is It Not?

Skill: Applied

17) Psychologists who help design equipment that is easy to use are classified as

    A) humanistic psychologists.

    B) industrial/organizational (I/O) psychologists.

    C) behavioral psychologists.

    D) engineering psychologists.

    E) clinical psychologists.

Answer: D

Diff: 2   Page Ref: 7

Topic: What is Psychology – And What Is It Not?

Skill: Factual

18) Applied Psychology has many different fields. If one helps people who are recovering from addictions, s/he is likely to be a/an _____.

    A) counseling psychologist.

    B) clinical psychologist.

    C) Industrial/Organizational psychologist.

    D) engineering psychologist.

    E) rehabilitation psychologist.

Answer: E

Diff: 2   Page Ref: 7

Topic: What is Psychology – And What Is It Not?

Skill: Conceptual

19) One likely difference between a psychiatrist and psychologist is that a psychiatrist would tend to use more

    A) talk therapy when dealing with clients having difficulties.

    B) medicine to treat those suffering from mental illness.

    C) cognitive therapy when dealing with clients irrational thoughts.

    D) behavioral modification with their clients.

    E) research than psychologists.

Answer: B

Diff: 2   Page Ref: 8

Topic: The Difference Between a Psychologist and a Psychiatrist

Skill: Conceptual

20) Ross is a psychologist, whereas Rachel is a psychiatrist. Thus, which of the following is MOST likely to be true?

    A) Rachel has not earned a PhD degree.

    B) They both have earned MD degrees.

    C) They both can prescribe medicine to help people with psychological problems.

    D) Only Ross can treat people with psychological problems.

    E) Ross is more likely than Rachel to use a medical perspective to understand people.

Answer: A

Diff: 3   Page Ref: 8

Topic: The Difference Between a Psychologist and a Psychiatrist

Skill: Applied

21) Psychology is distinct from psychiatry and psychoanalysis in that it

    A) requires significantly less graduate training.

    B) is concerned with all behavior, not just abnormality and mental illness.

    C) is based on counseling therapy rather than medication.

    D) is less concerned with scientific method than the latter disciplines.

    E) is not considered to be a scientific field.

Answer: B

Diff: 2   Page Ref: 8

Topic: The Difference Between a Psychologist and a Psychiatrist

Skill: Conceptual

22) Noted Greek philosophers—such as Socrates, Plato, and Aristotle—believed that

    A) brain damage contributed to most mental disorders.

    B) emotions were caused by changes in brain chemistry.

    C) 'truth' was determined by careful testing procedures.

    D) 'truth' was determined by observation and 'expert' opinion.

    E) emotions were not worthy of scientific discussion.

Answer: D
Diff: 3   *Page Ref: 9*
Topic: What Are Psychology's Historical Roots?
Skill: Conceptual

23) Which of the following was not one of the fields of study towards which Aristotle was interested in developing theories?

    A) sensation

    B) problem-solving

    C) consciousness

    D) memory

    E) cognition

Answer: C
Diff: 3   *Page Ref: 9*
Topic: What Are Psychology's Historical Roots?
Skill: Factual

24) French philosopher Rene Descartes most likely would believe that individuals suffer from schizophrenia due to

    A) irrational ways of interpreting events in the world.

    B) unconscious conflicts involving sexuality and aggression.

    C) whether an individual lives in a destructive society.

    D) the upbringing of the person.

    E) unusual activity within the person's nervous system.

Answer: E
Diff: 3   *Page Ref: 10*
Topic: What Are Psychology's Historical Roots?
Skill: Conceptual

25) The individual who believed that consciousness is a " stream of ideas" rather than elements that should be broken into smaller parts was

    A) Wundt.   B) Plato.   C) Darwin.   D) James.   E) Hall.

Answer: D
Diff: 3   Page Ref: 10
Topic: What Are Psychology's Historical Roots?
Skill: Factual

26) The science that led early psychological research in an attempt to "break people into their most basic components", was

    A) chemistry.   B) botany.   C) biology.   D) sociology.   E) geology.

Answer: A
Diff: 2   Page Ref: 11
Topic: What Are Psychology's Historical Roots?
Skill: Factual

27) What individual initially conducted revolutionary research on animals that made suggestions about human behavior?

    A) Helmholtz   B) Darwin   C) Wundt   D) James   E) Hall

Answer: B
Diff: 2   Page Ref: 11
Topic: What Are Psychology's Historical Roots?
Skill: Factual

28) Structuralists were concerned with uncovering the basic units of

    A) the unconscious.

    B) the mind.

    C) the environment.

    D) culture.

    E) the family unit.

Answer: B
Diff: 2   Page Ref: 11
Topic: What Are Psychology's Historical Roots?
Skill: Factual

29) Wilhelm Wundt founded the
    A) notion of free will.
    B) approach of radical behaviorism.
    C) psychodynamic approach.
    D) first psychology laboratory.
    E) first therapy clinic.

Answer: D
Diff: 2   Page Ref: 11
Topic: What Are Psychology's Historical Roots?
Skill: Factual

30) The research technique of introspection
    A) measures people biologically by using tools such as an MRI or PET scan.
    B) studies groups of people interacting with one another.
    C) asks people to describe their sensory experiences.
    D) studies children rather than adolescents and adults.
    E) exposes people to a variety of stressful situations to determine how they will respond.

Answer: C
Diff: 2   Page Ref: 11
Topic: What Are Psychology's Historical Roots?
Skill: Applied

31) Functionalists were interested in the role of _____ in dealing with the problems of everyday living.
    A) family and friends
    B) consciousness
    C) stress reduction techniques
    D) biofeedback
    E) professional therapists

Answer: B
Diff: 2   Page Ref: 11
Topic: What Are Psychology's Historical Roots?
Skill: Conceptual

32) William James argued that consciousness is analogous to a(n)
   A) iceberg.
   B) winding road.
   C) marathon.
   D) stream.
   E) buffet dinner.

Answer: D
Diff: 1   *Page Ref: 11*
Topic: What Are Psychology's Historical Roots?
Skill: Factual

33) John Dewey is well-known for founding which of the following areas of study within psychology?
   A) learning by listening to lectures
   B) progressive education which emphasizes learning by "doing"
   C) memorization of facts
   D) Gestalt Psychology
   E) insight learning

Answer: B
Diff: 3   *Page Ref: 12*
Topic: What Are Psychology's Historical Roots?
Skill: Factual

34) Gestalt psychology argued that perception is
   A) altered by an evolutionary pressure to avoid being eaten.
   B) impossible to study using introspection.
   C) a process in which the whole is more than the sum of the parts.
   D) a process found in animals but not humans.
   E) a function of our unique streams of consciousness.

Answer: C
Diff: 2   *Page Ref: 12*
Topic: What Are Psychology's Historical Roots?
Skill: Factual

35) The primary area to which Gestalt principles are generally tied to is
    A) perception.
    B) learning.
    C) cognition.
    D) sensation.
    E) memory.

Answer: A
Diff: 2   Page Ref: 12
Topic: What Are Psychology's Historical Roots?
Skill: Recall

36) A cognitive psychologist has been studying aggression in teens. Which of the following is most likely to be the title of his latest study?
    A) "The Consequences Of Teen Violence"
    B) "The Family Dynamics Of Violent Teens"
    C) "Social Pressures hat Produce Violent Teens"
    D) "The Use of Medications To Control Aggression in Teens"
    E) "How teens perceive threatening situations and thus respond violently"

Answer: E
Diff: 3   Page Ref: 12
Topic: What Are the Perspectives Psychologists Use Today?
Skill: Applied

37) The school of thought that investigates the connection between stimuli and responses is
    A) psychodynamic.
    B) humanistic.
    C) behaviorism.
    D) cognition.
    E) sociocultural.

Answer: C
Diff: 2   Page Ref: 12
Topic: What Are the Perspectives Psychologists Use Today?
Skill: Conceptual

38) Behaviorists sought to

    A) analyze dreams.

    B) try and discover how people learn.

    C) discover how an individuals behavior changes when with others.

    D) use introspection to uncover the clients unselfish thoughts.

    E) make psychology more objective.

Answer: E

Diff: 3   Page Ref: 12

Topic: What Are the Perspectives Psychologists Use Today?

Skill: Conceptual

39) The _____ approach views behavior as driven by powerful inner forces and conflicts.

    A) biological

    B) sociocultural

    C) behavioristic

    D) psychodynamic

    E) humanistic

Answer: D

Diff: 2   Page Ref: 13

Topic: What Are the Perspectives Psychologists Use Today?

Skill: Conceptual

40) A _____ psychologist would be most likely to explain nail-biting behavior as resulting from an oral fixation and a hidden self-destructive tendency.

    A) structuralist

    B) psychodynamic

    C) biological

    D) engineering

    E) behavioral

Answer: B

Diff: 3   Page Ref: 13

Topic: What Are the Perspectives Psychologists Use Today?

Skill: Applied

41) The principles of psychodynamics were first outlined by
    A) William James.
    B) B.F. Skinner.
    C) Sigmund Freud.
    D) Aristotle.
    E) Jean Piaget.

Answer: C
Diff: 1   Page Ref: 13
Topic: What Are the Perspectives Psychologists Use Today?
Skill: Factual

42) Biological psychologists look for the cause of behavior to come from
    A) the nervous system.
    B) the brain.
    C) prior learning.
    D) unresolved childhood conflicts.
    E) our striving to become better people.

Answer: A
Diff: 1   Page Ref: 15
Topic: What Are the Perspectives Psychologists Use Today?
Skill: Recall

43) The Biological View is most closely associated with the discipline of
    A) Evolution.
    B) Chemistry.
    C) Development.
    D) Neuroscience.
    E) Natural Selection.

Answer: D
Diff: 1   Page Ref: 15
Topic: What Are the Perspectives Psychologists Use Today?
Skill: Factual

44) Which of the following psychological perspectives would be most likely to examine humans genetic makeup and how that may influence behavior?

    A) sociocultural

    B) biological

    C) psychodynamic

    D) behavioral

    E) cognitive

Answer: B

Diff: 1   Page Ref: 15

Topic: What Are the Perspectives Psychologists Use Today?

Skill: Applied

45) According to the evolutionary approach, behavioral and mental _____ should be a primary focus of psychology.

    A) observation

    B) growth

    C) conflicts

    D) adaptiveness

    E) structures

Answer: D

Diff: 1   Page Ref: 15

Topic: What Are the Perspectives Psychologists Use Today?

Skill: Conceptual

46) Which perspective looks at the interaction between our genes and the experiences presented by our environment?

    A) Cognitive View

    B) Humanistic View

    C) Developmental View

    D) Evolutionary View

    E) Biological View

Answer: C

Diff: 1   Page Ref: 16

Topic: What Are the Perspectives Psychologists Use Today?

Skill: Conceptual

47) How has the field of Developmental Psychology changed in recent years?

    A) Developmental psychologists focus primarily on childhood development.

    B) Developmental psychologists focus on developmental disorders.

    C) Developmental psychologists focus on how our culture influences our behavior.

    D) Developmental psychologists study the entire life span.

    E) Developmental psychologists focus on assisting children with cognitive deficits.

Answer: D
Diff: 2   *Page Ref: 16*
Topic: What Are the Perspectives Psychologists Use Today?
Skill: Factual

48) A scientist who studies the strategies involved in playing a game of chess is most likely to follow a(n) _____ approach to psychology.

    A) cognitive

    B) humanistic

    C) behavioristic

    D) evolutionary

    E) psychoanalytic

Answer: A
Diff: 2   *Page Ref: 16*
Topic: What Are the Perspectives Psychologists Use Today?
Skill: Applied

49) All of the following related to the field of Cognitive Psychology except

    A) learned responses.

    B) interpretations of given situations.

    C) evaluation of mental processes.

    D) connections between the mind and subsequent behavior.

    E) perception.

Answer: A
Diff: 2   *Page Ref: 16*
Topic: What Are the Perspectives Psychologists Use Today?
Skill: Recall

50) Jake has had a troubled past. He had a difficult time getting along with his parents as a child and today he still holds much hostility towards his parents. He thinks he might be holding a longstanding grudge against them, but he cannot remember what it is. What field of psychology would be most interested in Getting to the root of Jake's troubled childhood?

    A) Behavioral

    B) Cognitive

    C) Sociocultural

    D) Humanistic

    E) Psychodynamic

Answer: E

Diff: 2   *Page Ref: 16*

Topic: What Are the Perspectives Psychologists Use Today?

Skill: Applied

51) Ted is seeing a humanistic psychologist for therapy. His psychologist is most likely to focus on

    A) cultural guidelines that shaped Ted's personality.

    B) how Ted's parents shaped his behavior.

    C) striving for growth and developing potential.

    D) the conflict between personal desires and social restrictions.

    E) Ted's unconscious resentment of his siblings.

Answer: C

Diff: 2   *Page Ref: 16*

Topic: What Are the Perspectives Psychologists Use Today?

Skill: Applied

52) The humanistic approach toward psychology emphasizes

    A) the positive side of human nature.

    B) the deterministic nature of human environments.

    C) unconscious motivations.

    D) stimulus–response relationships in humans.

    E) our brain biochemistry.

Answer: A

Diff: 2   *Page Ref: 17*

Topic: What Are the Perspectives Psychologists Use Today?

Skill: Conceptual

53) One of the Founders of Humanistic Psychology was

    A) B.F. Skinner.

    B) Carl Rogers.

    C) Sigmund Freud.

    D) John Watson.

    E) Wilhelm Wundt.

Answer: B

Diff: 2   Page Ref: 17

Topic: What Are the Perspectives Psychologists Use Today?

Skill: Factual

54) A behavioral psychologist studying the causes of alcohol usage would most likely

    A) ask people why they consume alcohol.

    B) observe how people behave after consuming alcohol.

    C) measure brain changes following alcohol consumption.

    D) determine patterns of alcohol usage within different cultures.

    E) ask people how they feel while they are consuming alcohol.

Answer: B

Diff: 1   Page Ref: 17

Topic: What Are the Perspectives Psychologists Use Today?

Skill: Applied

55) The key feature of behaviorism that distinguishes it from other approaches to psychology is that

    A) consciousness is central to the study of the mind.

    B) only observable behavior is appropriate for study.

    C) mental abilities evolve just as physical characteristics do.

    D) a holistic view of a person is essential for understanding.

    E) groups, not individuals, should be the focus of study.

Answer: B

Diff: 2   Page Ref: 17

Topic: What Are the Perspectives Psychologists Use Today?

Skill: Conceptual

56) This individual claimed that we could not prove that the mind existed, therefore it would be much too subjective to study.

   A) Jean Piaget

   B) William James

   C) B. F. Skinner

   D) Sigmund Freud

   E) Wilhelm Wundt

Answer: C
Diff: 2   Page Ref: 17
Topic: What Are the Perspectives Psychologists Use Today?
Skill: Factual

57) A sociocultural psychologist would be most interested in which of the following?

   A) measuring how children respond after they are spanked

   B) asking parents why they spank their children

   C) comparing how often Americans and Canadians spank their children

   D) examining how spanking has served an evolutionary purpose throughout history

   E) determining whether mothers or fathers are more likely to spank their children

Answer: C
Diff: 2   Page Ref: 18
Topic: What Are the Perspectives Psychologists Use Today?
Skill: Conceptual

58) Sociocultural Psychology is a necessary part of psychology because

   A) we must understand all human beings, not just those from one culture.

   B) by studying different cultures, we are better able to see links between them.

   C) by studying different cultures we can see how customs can shape our expectations, values and morals.

   D) by examining other cultures we can become more tolerant and understanding of how the behave.

   E) All of the above

Answer: E
Diff: 2   Page Ref: 18
Topic: What Are the Perspectives Psychologists Use Today?
Skill: Conceptual

59) This school of thought believes that by studying changes in animals over time we can better understand similar changes in humans.
   A) Evolutionary
   B) Behaviorist
   C) Cognitive
   D) Trait
   E) Humanistic
   Answer: A
   Diff: 2   Page Ref: 18
   Topic: What Are Psychology's Historical Roots?
   Skill: Conceptual

60) This perspective looks at the long-standing personality characteristics of an individual, and how this may impact their affect, behaviors and cognition.
   A) sociocultural theory
   B) trait theory
   C) behavioral theory
   D) humanistic theory
   E) psychodynamic theory
   Answer: B
   Diff: 2   Page Ref: 19
   Topic: What Are Psychology's Historical Roots?
   Skill: Conceptual

61) A Trait Theorist would be most likely to be involved with
   A) memory tests.
   B) cognitive ability.
   C) underlying childhood problems.
   D) personality testing.
   E) the characteristics that are passed on through each generation.
   Answer: D
   Diff: 2   Page Ref: 19
   Topic: What Are Psychology's Historical Roots?
   Skill: Applied

62) The Trait view would argue that the 'Big Five' personality characteristics
   A) change frequently as one ages
   B) are entirely inherited from one's parents
   C) are different in every person
   D) can apply to all people regardless of where they live in the world
   E) change about every five years

   Answer: D
   Diff: 3   *Page Ref: 19*
   Topic: What Are the Perspectives Psychologists Use Today?
   Skill: Conceptual

63) How is psychology changing in recent years in terms of it's focus on certain theories?
   A) more of an emphasis on Freudian psychoanalytic techniques
   B) less of an emphasis on sociocultural psychology
   C) less of an emphasis on Psychiatry
   D) more of an emphasis on sociocultural psychology
   E) more of an emphasis on animal research

   Answer: D
   Diff: 2   *Page Ref: 20*
   Topic: What Are the Perspectives Psychologists Use Today?
   Skill: Conceptual

64) Mary Whiton Calkins did not receive her doctoral degree from Harvard because
   A) she did not complete all of the course work involved.
   B) she was a woman.
   C) she violated ethical standards of Harvard University.
   D) she was married at the time.
   E) she was awarded the degree by Harvard but decided not the accept it.

   Answer: B
   Diff: 2   *Page Ref: 20*
   Topic: Psychology as a Major
   Skill: Factual

65) A masters degree is psychology typically involves how many additional years of study once an individual has completed their undergraduate studies?
   A) 4 years   B) 3 years   C) 2 years   D) 6 years   E) 5 years

   Answer: C
   Diff: 1   *Page Ref: 21*
   Topic: Psychology as a Major
   Skill: Factual

Check Your Understanding Questions

1) Experiments showing facilitated communication to be effective were similar to the experiment that exposed Clever Hans. Specifically, what did both experimental procedures have in common?

   A) Neither the horse nor the autistic children could see the questions.

   B) Neither Von Osten nor the facilitators could see the questions.

   C) Both Hans and the autistic children were given incentives for producing correct answers.

   D) In both situations, correct answers were given about half of the time.

   E) They proved that someone was purposely trying to provide false results for the studies.

   Answer: B
   Diff: 3   Page Ref: 2
   Topic: Check Your Understanding
   Skill: Recall

2) Researchers nee to be aware of the Confirmation Bias to

   A) make sure that the are not being purposefully deceitful.

   B) make sure they are not giving the participants the answers.

   C) insure that they do not look only for information that reaffirms what they already know.

   D) make sure that they do not practice pseudoscience.

   E) assure that they are not involved in their own studies.

   Answer: C
   Diff: 3   Page Ref: 4
   Topic: Check Your Understanding
   Skill: Conceptual

3) Which of the following would be most likely to do research on learning or memory?

   A) an applied psychologist

   B) an I/O psychologist doing basic research

   C) a psychiatrist

   D) an experimental psychologist

   E) an engineering psychologist

   Answer: D
   Diff: 3   Page Ref: 6
   Topic: Check Your Understanding
   Skill: Recall

4) Which one would be considered an applied psychologist?

    A) an I/O psychologist

    B) a psychologist doing basic research

    C) a professor of Psychology at the University

    D) a psychiatrist

    E) an lab assistant

Answer: A

Diff: 3   Page Ref: 7

Topic: Check Your Understanding

Skill: Recall

5) Psychology is different from other disciplines, such as psychiatry, which deal with people because

    A) psychology focuses on mental disorder.

    B) psychology is a broader field, covering all aspects of behavior and mental processes.

    C) psychologists must have doctoral degrees.

    D) psychologists do research.

    E) psychologists have medical degrees.

Answer: B

Diff: 3   Page Ref: 8

Topic: Check Your Understanding

Skill: Understanding the Core Concept

6) The ancient Greeks' approach to psychology was not scientific because they

    A) failed to check their opinions against controlled observations.

    B) used the process in introspection to get at people's perceptions.

    C) believed that all truth was revealed in sacred texts given by their gods.

    D) lived in an age before precise measuring instruments had been developed.

    E) did not publish their results.

Answer: A

Diff: 3   Page Ref: 10

Topic: Check Your Understanding

Skill: Conceptual

7) Rene Descartes made a science of psychology possible when he suggested that
    A) science should be based entirely on common sense rather than on religion.
    B) replicability of results was essential.
    C) the elements of conscious experience could be arranged into a periodic table.
    D) psychology should be a branch of philosophy.
    E) sensations and perceptions are the result of activity in the nervous system.

Answer: E
Diff: 3   Page Ref: 10
Topic: Check Your Understanding
Skill: Factual

8) Taking their cue from the science of Chemistry, this school of psychological thought intended to identify the "elements of conscious experience".
    A) structuralists
    B) functionalists
    C) Gestalt psychologists
    D) behaviorists
    E) psychoanalysts

Answer: A
Diff: 3   Page Ref: 11
Topic: Check Your Understanding
Skill: Conceptual

9) The issue that Functionalists such as William James had with the ideas of Structuralism was that
    A) they did not want psychology to become a science.
    B) they did not believe that consciousness could be broken down into different elements, but rather that it should looked at as a "stream of consciousness".
    C) psychology should look only at observable behavior.
    D) psychology should investigate issues on metal thought processes and interpretation of different situations.
    E) psychology should look at the potential good in all human beings.

Answer: B
Diff: 2   Page Ref: 12
Topic: Check Your Understanding
Skill: Conceptual

10) Modern day psychology has evolved from all of the following field of thought except for
   A) Greek philosophy.
   B) biology.
   C) astrology.
   D) functionalism.
   E) structuralism.

Answer: C
Diff: 2   Page Ref: 10–14
Topic: Check Your Understanding
Skill: Recall

11) Which of the following approaches to psychology would say that the difference between the behavior of males and females are the result of different survival and reproduction issues faced by the sexes?
   A) psychoanalytic theory
   B) evolutionary psychology
   C) the trait view
   D) the sociocultural perspective
   E) the biological view

Answer: B
Diff: 2   Page Ref: 15
Topic: Check Your Understanding
Skill: Applied

12) If you were a teacher trying to understand how students learn, which of the following viewpoints would be most helpful?
   A) the cognitive view
   B) psychoanalytic theory
   C) evolutionary psychology
   D) the trait view
   E) the behavioral view

Answer: A
Diff: 2   Page Ref: 16
Topic: Check Your Understanding
Skill: Applied

13) Focus on observable events rather than unconscious forces would describe which two theories?

    A) cognitive vs. psychoanalytic

    B) psychoanalytic vs. evolutionary

    C) behavioral vs. psychoanalytic

    D) behavioral vs. cognitive

    E) behavioral vs. humanistic

Answer: C
Diff: 2   Page Ref: 17
Topic: Check Your Understanding
Skill: Recall

14) Which of the following sets of factors is ALL associated with the indicated perspective?

    A) memory, personality, environment; the behaviorist perspective

    B) changes through the life span, changes as the result of mental illness, changes as the result of social pressure; developmental perspective

    C) mental health, mental disorder, mental imagery; the trait perspective

    D) neuroscience, evolutionary psychology, genetics; the biological perspective

    E) sensation. perception. memory. the psychoanalytic perspective

Answer: D
Diff: 2   Page Ref: 15–21
Topic: Check Your Understanding
Skill: Understanding the Core Concept

True/False Questions

1) "Clever Hans" was actually able to count.

Answer: FALSE
Diff: 1   Page Ref: 2
Topic: What is Psychology – And What Is It Not?
Skill: Factual

2) Empirical data is carefully collected and observed and based on scientific research.

Answer: TRUE
Diff: 1   Page Ref: 3
Topic: What is Psychology – And What Is It Not?
Skill: Factual

3) The confirmation bias occurs when after a experiment has been completed, people say that they were already aware of the results.

Answer: FALSE
Diff: 1   *Page Ref: 4*
Topic: What is Psychology – And What Is It Not?
Skill: Conceptual

4) Pseudoscience allows individuals to find out more about "real" psychology.

Answer: FALSE
Diff: 1   *Page Ref: 4*
Topic: What is Psychology – And What Is It Not?
Skill: Conceptual

5) The three major classes of psychology are applied, experimental, and teaching of psychology.

Answer: TRUE
Diff: 2   *Page Ref: 6*
Topic: What is Psychology – And What Is It Not?
Skill: Factual

6) Many Industrial/Organizational Psychologists work in the business field.

Answer: TRUE
Diff: 2   *Page Ref: 7*
Topic: What is Psychology – And What Is It Not?
Skill: Factual

7) Sports psychology would be considered a specialty of applied psychology.

Answer: TRUE
Diff: 2   *Page Ref: 7*
Topic: What is Psychology – And What Is It Not?
Skill: Factual

8) Clinical Psychologists often deal with patients who are mentally ill.

Answer: TRUE
Diff: 2   *Page Ref: 7*
Topic: What is Psychology – And What Is It Not?
Skill: Factual

9) Psychologists hold a medical degree and are authorized to write prescriptions.

Answer: FALSE
Diff: 2   Page Ref: 8
Topic: The Difference Between a Psychologist and a Psychiatrist
Skill: Factual

10) Psychiatrists are the same as clinical psychologists, except that psychiatrists have also earned a medical degree.

Answer: FALSE
Diff: 2   Page Ref: 8
Topic: The Difference Between a Psychologist and a Psychiatrist
Skill: Factual

11) Psychiatrists are qualified to write prescriptions for medications.

Answer: TRUE
Diff: 2   Page Ref: 8
Topic: The Difference Between a Psychologist and a Psychiatrist
Skill: Factual

12) DesCartes argued that the nervous system controls human behavior.

Answer: TRUE
Diff: 2   Page Ref: 10
Topic: What Are Psychology's Historical Roots?
Skill: Factual

13) Structuralism intended to break individuals down into their most basic parts.

Answer: TRUE
Diff: 2   Page Ref: 10
Topic: What Are Psychology's Historical Roots?
Skill: Factual

14) Functionalism tried to discover the contents of the unconscious mind.

Answer: FALSE
Diff: 3   Page Ref: 11
Topic: What Are Psychology's Historical Roots?
Skill: Conceptual

15) Structuralism and functionalism argued that the focus of psychology should be on solving practical issues.

Answer: FALSE
Diff: 2   *Page Ref: 10–12*
Topic: What Are Psychology's Historical Roots?
Skill: Conceptual

16) Gestalt Psychology suggests that "The Whole is Larger than the Sum of the Parts".

Answer: TRUE
Diff: 1   *Page Ref: 12*
Topic: What Are Psychology's Historical Roots?
Skill: Factual

17) John B. Watson founded the first formal psychology laboratory.

Answer: FALSE
Diff: 2   *Page Ref: 12*
Topic: What Are Psychology's Historical Roots?
Skill: Factual

18) The Necker cube experience suggests that we perceive rather than sense the outside world.

Answer: TRUE
Diff: 3   *Page Ref: 13–14*
Topic: An Introspective Look at the Necker Cube
Skill: Conceptual

19) The Biological View explores how our environment affects our behavior.

Answer: FALSE
Diff: 3   *Page Ref: 15*
Topic: What Are the Perspectives Psychologists Use Today?
Skill: Conceptual

20) Evolutionary psychology looks at the traits that are most suited for survival.

Answer: FALSE
Diff: 1   *Page Ref: 15*
Topic: What Are the Perspectives Psychologists Use Today?
Skill: Conceptual

21) The cognitive view explores our healthy and unhealthy behaviors.

Answer: FALSE
Diff: 2   Page Ref: 15–16
Topic: What Are the Perspectives Psychologists Use Today?
Skill: Factual

22) The Humanistic View is pessimistic about human nature.

Answer: FALSE
Diff: 1   Page Ref: 17
Topic: What Are the Perspectives Psychologists Use Today?
Skill: Factual

23) According to the humanistic view, our actions are influenced by our self–concept.

Answer: TRUE
Diff: 2   Page Ref: 17
Topic: What Are the Perspectives Psychologists Use Today?
Skill: Factual

24) Sigmund Freud is the founder of the behaviorist Theory of Psychology.

Answer: FALSE
Diff: 2   Page Ref: 17
Topic: What Are the Perspectives Psychologists Use Today?
Skill: Factual

25) Behaviorists would only measure what they could see.

Answer: TRUE
Diff: 2   Page Ref: 17
Topic: What Are the Perspectives Psychologists Use Today?
Skill: Conceptual

26) The sociocultural view investigates culture, religion, and customs.

Answer: TRUE
Diff: 1   Page Ref: 18
Topic: What Are the Perspectives Psychologists Use Today?
Skill: Factual

27) Each year, women receive more new doctorates in psychology than do men.

Answer: TRUE
Diff: 3   Page Ref: 20
Topic: What Are the Perspectives Psychologists Use Today?
Skill: Factual

28) Mary Whiton Calkins received her doctoral degree from Harvard.

Answer: FALSE
Diff: 3   Page Ref: 20
Topic: Psychology as a Major
Skill: Factual

29) The American Psychological Association elected its first woman president, Marie Tisak, in 1987.

Answer: FALSE
Diff: 3   Page Ref: 20
Topic: What Are the Perspectives Psychologists Use Today?
Skill: Factual

30) To become a psychologist, one must graduate from medical school.

Answer: FALSE
Diff: 3   Page Ref: 21
Topic: Psychology as a Major
Skill: Factual

Short Answer Questions

1) What does the empirical approach to psychology mean?

Answer: a study conducted via careful observation and scientifically based research
Diff: 2   Page Ref: 3
Topic: What is Psychology – And What Is It Not?
Skill: Factual

2) Why is pseudo psychology a danger to "real" psychology?

Answer: The publicity of pseudopsychology causes individuals to be skeptical or good
        scientifically sound studies in the field.
Diff: 2   Page Ref: 4
Topic: What is Psychology – And What Is It Not?
Skill: Conceptual

3) What is the term for researchers who only look for evidence that supports their hypothesis?

Answer: Confirmation Bias
Diff: 2   Page Ref: 4
Topic: What is Psychology – And What Is It Not?
Skill: Conceptual

4) Which type of psychologist might work at Ford Motor Company to determine how to change the lighting and the assembly line, or to determine which questions to ask potential employees?

Answer: I/O (or, industrial/organizational)
Diff: 2   Page Ref: 7
Topic: What is Psychology – And What Is It Not?
Skill: Applied

5) Which type of psychologist would typically look at how different toys are built and how to most fully engage children in the toys?

Answer: an engineering psychologist
Diff: 2   Page Ref: 7
Topic: What is Psychology – And What Is It Not?
Skill: Applied

6) Which "school" in psychology was dedicated to uncovering the basic "structures of the mind"?

Answer: structuralism
Diff: 2   Page Ref: 10–11
Topic: What Are Psychology's Historical Roots?
Skill: Factual

7) What was the process that Wundt employed when he asked people to respond to a variety of stimuli?

Answer: introspection
Diff: 2   Page Ref: 11
Topic: What Are Psychology's Historical Roots?
Skill: Conceptual

8) Which approach would a psychologist studying alcoholism be likely to use to examine how the person acts when he or she consumes alcohol?

Answer: the behavioral approach
Diff: 2   Page Ref: 12
Topic: What Are the Perspectives Psychologists Use Today?
Skill: Applied

9) Which schools of psychology are the most and the least likely to study thoughts and mental processes?

Answer: cognitive psychology; behaviorism
Diff: 2   Page Ref: 12–16
Topic: What Are the Perspectives Psychologists Use Today?
Skill: Factual

10) Who was the founder of psychoanalysis?

Answer: Sigmund Freud
Diff: 1   *Page Ref: 13*
Topic: What Are the Perspectives Psychologists Use Today?
Skill: Factual

11) What is the idea that Evolutionary psychologists use for passing the best genes on to the next generation?

Answer: natural selection
Diff: 1   *Page Ref: 15*
Topic: What Are the Perspectives Psychologists Use Today?
Skill: Factual

12) What school of psychology believes that "The whole s larger than the sum of the parts"?

Answer: Gestalt psychology
Diff: 1   *Page Ref: 16*
Topic: What Are the Perspectives Psychologists Use Today?
Skill: Factual

13) How did Behaviorists seek to move away from Freud's Psychodynamic theory?

Answer: They wanted to study not the unconscious, but only those behaviors that could be observed.
Diff: 3   *Page Ref: 17*
Topic: What Are the Perspectives Psychologists Use Today?
Skill: Conceptual

14) How has the gender differences in psychology majors made this a unique science?

Answer: 2/3rds of majors are women
Diff: 3   *Page Ref: 20*
Topic: Psychology as a Major
Skill: Factual

Essay Questions

1) Explain why pseudopsychology can be dangerous to the science of psychology.

   Answer: Psychology should rely on good empirical data. Studies should be conducted in which data can be conducted and analyzed. All of us have ideas about why individuals behave they way they do, but we cannot with confidence say that we are correct without good empirical data. Pseudoscience relies on speculation and here say, the publication of this type of information can provide misleading ideas about human and animal behavior.

   Diff: 2   Page Ref: 3

   Topic: What is Psychology – And What Is It Not?

   Skill: Conceptual

2) Provide a specific example of how research psychologists, teachers of psychology and applied psychologists can all work together to help the human condition.

   Answer: A potential example could focus on how individuals learn.. Research psychologists would collect data an find out under which conditions individuals learn best. Applied Psychologist could work with individual clients to see if their learning had improved and finally, teachers of psychology could implement these techniques in the classroom to insure that each students was learning to the best of their abilities. A sufficient answer must stress the fact that the student understand that the research psychologists mostly work behind the scenes or in a lab. The Applied psychologists work directly with clients and the teachers of psychology both teach about what we know of psychology but also implement these strategies themselves.

   Diff: 2   Page Ref: 6–7

   Topic: What is Psychology – And What Is It Not?

   Skill: Applied

3) How did structuralism and functionalism contribute to the early beliefs of psychology?

   Answer: Students must mention the insistence of each approach on basing knowledge on scientific evidence. Further, they should explain the basic principles of each early perspective and the overlap with current psychological perspectives.

   Diff: 2   Page Ref: 10–11

   Topic: What Are Psychology's Historical Roots?

   Skill: Conceptual

4) Identify a major differences between how a cognitive and a behavioral psychologists would address the focus of their research.

   Answer: Students should note that the cognitive view focuses on thought and what is happening in the mind. The behavioral view studies people from the 'outside' by focusing on people's actions.

   Diff: 2   Page Ref: 12–16

   Topic: What Are the Perspectives Psychologists Use Today?

   Skill: Applied

5) Name and briefly discuss the seven major perspectives in psychology today, explaining the foundational assumptions and methods of each.

Answer: See Table 1.1 for a brief review of the biological, evolutionary, cognitive, behavioral, psychodynamic, humanistic, and sociocultural views.

Diff: 3   Page Ref: 12–19

Topic: What Are the Perspectives Psychologists Use Today?

Skill: Factual

6) Briefly describe the psychodynamic view.

Answer: The student must mention the importance of the role of the unconscious mind. Better answers may also mention irrational desires and conflicts, sexual and aggressive impulses, and the focus on treating mental disorders.

Diff: 2   Page Ref: 13

Topic: What Are the Perspectives Psychologists Use Today?

Skill: Factual

7) How has the incorporation of the sociocultural theory benefitted all of psychology?

Answer: The student should mention that the sociocultural perspective allows researchers to compare and contrast individuals living in various parts of the world.

Diff: 2   Page Ref: 18

Topic: What Are the Perspectives Psychologists Use Today?

Skill: Conceptual

8) Anhul has been having trouble at school lately. He cannot seem to get his work in on time and try as he might he cannot fit in at school. His family only adds to the pressure, he recently moved to Ohio form Pakistan and his family expects him to participate in cultural family functions. The pressure is getting to him, but he is trying to get everything to fall into place. Explain hoe each of the following views of psychology would seek to explain Anhul's behavior. Sociocultural, Psychodynamic, Behavioral, Humanistic, Cognitive and Trait

Answer: Refer to graph on page 19 that summarizes the different views of psychology. This question is intended to have student's apply what they have learned to real-life situations.

Diff: 3   Page Ref: 15–19

Topic: What Are the Perspectives Psychologists Use Today?

Skill: Applied

9) Explain How Structuralism and functionalism gave rise to the modern day perspectives in Psychology.

Answer: structuralism attempted to look at an individual by breaking them down into their most basic components. The Behavioral approach has kept components of this idea by looking at stimulus and response pairings. Primarily however functionalism gave rise to disciplines of today that attempt look at the whole individual rather than some small portion of them. many psychologists today employ and eclectic approach to analyzing individuals because this allows them to incorporate two or more of the current perspectives in order to better evaluate the individual from all possible viewpoints.

Diff: 3   Page Ref: 10–19

Topic: What Are the Perspectives Psychologists Use Today?

Skill: Applied

Chapter 2 Research Methods

Multiple Choice Questions

1) Yumi and Maria who conducted research on whether or not there were differences in body image between Japanese and American teenagers were using what theory discussed in chapter one as the inspiration for their research?

    A) sociocultural view

    B) behavioral view

    C) cognitive view

    D) humanistic view

    E) psychodynamic view

Answer: A

Diff: 3   *Page Ref: 27*

Topic: How Do Psychologists Develop New Knowledge?

Skill: Applied

2) How is psychology different from pseudoscience?

    A) Psychology is based on gullibility.

    B) Psychology is always based on medical science.

    C) Pseudoscience uses the scientific method.

    D) Psychology is based on mere speculation.

    E) None of the pseudoscience has survived trial by the scientific method.

Answer: E

Diff: 2   *Page Ref: 28*

Topic: How Do Psychologists Develop New Knowledge?

Skill: Recall

3) If a study is conducted through empirical investigation, this means

    A) it is conducted in a research laboratory.

    B) it is conducted only by a psychologists who is a trained Ph.D.

    C) it is based on careful measurements and direct experience.

    D) it is a theory.

    E) it is based a persons individual experience in the world.

Answer: C

Diff: 2   *Page Ref: 28*

Topic: How Do Psychologists Develop New Knowledge?

Skill: Conceptual

4) Which of the following is a question that could be best answered using the scientific method?

    A) Is homosexuality sinful?

    B) Do men drive faster than women?

    C) Is it cruel to spank your child?

    D) Can your cat read your mind?

    E) Was Elvis a great singer?

Answer: B
Diff: 3   Page Ref: 28
Topic: How Do Psychologists Develop New Knowledge?
Skill: Applied

5) In science, a theory

    A) is based on several hypothesis.

    B) always generates accurate findings.

    C) is an unverified idea or abstract concept.

    D) is diametrically opposed to empiricism.

    E) is a testable explanation for a set of observations.

Answer: E
Diff: 2   Page Ref: 28
Topic: How Do Psychologists Develop New Knowledge?
Skill: Factual

6) A theory and a hypothesis are different in that

    A) both a theory and a hypothesis must be testable.

    B) a hypothesis is often representative of a larger theory.

    C) a theory is often representative of a larger hypothesis.

    D) you can prove that both of them are true.

    E) a theory is based on scientific information whereas a hypothesis is based on speculation.

Answer: B
Diff: 3   Page Ref: 28–29
Topic: How Do Psychologists Develop New Knowledge?
Skill: Conceptual

7) Emily Rosa discovered that therapeutic touch (TT) practitioners

    A) are effective in treating many medical problems.

    B) cannot be tested to determine their effectiveness.

    C) accurately predicted which hand she held out less than half the time.

    D) must make physical contact with patients to cure their problems.

    E) rarely use their techniques in medical settings.

Answer: C
Diff: 3   Page Ref: 29
Topic: How Do Psychologists Develop New Knowledge?
Skill: Factual

8) Dr. Spinney provides students with different types of beverages and then measures their ability to drive a car. In this example, beverage type is the

    A) independent variable.

    B) dependent variable.

    C) control group.

    D) hypothesis.

    E) confounding variable.

Answer: A
Diff: 2   Page Ref: 29
Topic: How Do Psychologists Develop New Knowledge?
Skill: Applied

9) The term 'hypothesis' literally means

    A) prediction.

    B) knowledge derived from common sense.

    C) an informed hunch.

    D) little theory.

    E) belief system.

Answer: D
Diff: 2   Page Ref: 29
Topic: How Do Psychologists Develop New Knowledge?
Skill: Factual

10) In Emily Rosa's experiment on therapeutic touch, her hypothesis was

   A) if the participants could predict which hand Emily's was above less than half of the time (when they could not see it) then therapeutic touch works no better than chance.

   B) if the participants could determine which hand Emily's was over half of the time (when they could not see it) then therapeutic touch has a reasonable amount of credibility.

   C) therapeutic touch was a hoax.

   D) if participants could determine which hand Emily's was above (when they could not see it) then therapeutic touch was not valid.

   E) if the participants could determine which hand Emily's was above (when they could not see it) every single time, then therapeutic touch was valid.

Answer: A
Diff: 3   Page Ref: 29
Topic: How Do Psychologists Develop New Knowledge?
Skill: Factual

11) Based on his classroom experiences, Dr. McGinty believes that those students sitting in the front row of a classroom get higher grades than those sitting in rows further back. His belief is an example of a

   A) hypothesis.

   B) theory.

   C) independent variable.

   D) correlation coefficient.

   E) dependent variable.

Answer: A
Diff: 2   Page Ref: 29–30
Topic: How Do Psychologists Develop New Knowledge?
Skill: Applied

12) A hypothesis must

   A) define the independent and dependent variables.

   B) be testable and falsifiable.

   C) be proven true.

   D) reaffirm what has already been tested.

   E) identify the randomization process

Answer: B
Diff: 2   Page Ref: 30
Topic: How Do Psychologists Develop New Knowledge?
Skill: Conceptual

13) Jenna wants to learn whether men or women are better drivers. To determine this, she decides that she will measure driving ability by examining the number of automobile accidents people have been involved in as a driver. The number of accidents is the basis of

   A) her control group in this study.

   B) a theory of good driving.

   C) the independent variable in this study.

   D) the operational definition of driving ability.

   E) a case study examination of driving ability.

Answer: D

Diff: 3   Page Ref: 30

Topic: How Do Psychologists Develop New Knowledge?

Skill: Applied

14) Jenna wants to learn whether men or women are better drivers. To determine this, she decides that she will measure driving ability by examining the number of automobile accidents people have been involved in as a driver. Whether a person is male or female is the basis of

   A) her control group in this study.

   B) a theory of good driving.

   C) the independent variable in this study.

   D) the operational definition of driving ability.

   E) a case study examination of driving ability.

Answer: C

Diff: 3   Page Ref: 30

Topic: How Do Psychologists Develop New Knowledge?

Skill: Applied

15) The independent variable

   A) is what one is trying to measure in a study.

   B) must be testable.

   C) is the condition that the researcher manipulates.

   D) is the group that receives no treatment.

   E) is the group that receives treatment.

Answer: C

Diff: 1   Page Ref: 30

Topic: How Do Psychologists Develop New Knowledge?

Skill: Recall

16) A psychology teacher wants to determine whether computer-aided learning will produce higher standardized test scores than a usual lecture format. In this example, the independent variable is the

  A) individual students.

  B) students' previous grades in psychology.

  C) test scores.

  D) students' interest in psychology.

  E) method of instruction.

Answer: E
Diff: 2   Page Ref: 30
Topic: How Do Psychologists Develop New Knowledge?
Skill: Applied

17) The independent variable _____, while the dependent variable _____.

  A) is the measured outcome of the study; is the group that does not receive the treatment

  B) is the measured outcome of the study; is controlled by the researcher

  C) is controlled by the researcher; is the measured outcome of the study

  D) is the group that does receive the treatment; is the measured outcome of the study

  E) is the group that does receive the treatment; is the group that does not receive the treatment

Answer: C
Diff: 3   Page Ref: 30-31
Topic: How Do Psychologists Develop New Knowledge?
Skill: Conceptual

18) Gina wants to conduct a study of discrimination based on looks in hiring practices. Gina selects two candidates with equivalent qualifications, one extremely attractive and the other of average attractiveness. She sends them to interview for the same job. The dependent variable in Gina's experiment is

  A) the relative attractiveness of the two candidates.

  B) the qualifications of the two candidates.

  C) the type of job the candidates apply for.

  D) the response of the interviewer to each candidate.

  E) the number of candidates who interviewed for the job.

Answer: D
Diff: 3   Page Ref: 31
Topic: How Do Psychologists Develop New Knowledge?
Skill: Applied

19) Randomization

    A) ensures that studies can be replicated.

    B) is a good way to define the dependent variable.

    C) is difficult to achieve in research.

    D) must be used with great caution.

    E) reduces experimenter bias.

Answer: E
Diff: 3   Page Ref: 30
Topic: How Do Psychologists Develop New Knowledge?
Skill: Conceptual

20) In her experiment, Emily Rosa's did not simply alternate between hands to determine if her participants could determine where her hand was. Instead, she used a process by which she flipped a coin, thus determining which hand she would test. This was necessary because

    A) the outcome would be based on the dependent variable.

    B) the outcome would be based only on the experimental group.

    C) the outcome would be based only on the control group.

    D) the outcome would test the independent variable.

    E) All of the above are correct

Answer: D
Diff: 3   Page Ref: 30
Topic: How Do Psychologists Develop New Knowledge?
Skill: Conceptual

21) Some people believe that money can buy happiness. Dr. Goodwin wants to determine whether paying people plays a role in their happiness. The level of money given to a subject would be considered to be the

    A) experimental variable.

    B) confounding variable.

    C) dependent variable.

    D) independent variable.

    E) control variable.

Answer: D
Diff: 2   Page Ref: 30
Topic: How Do Psychologists Develop New Knowledge?
Skill: Applied

22) These must be stated in terms of how the concepts are to be measured and what techniques will be employed to produce them.

    A) Operational Definitions

    B) A theories

    C) independent variables

    D) dependent variables

    E) control groups

Answer: A

Diff: 2   Page Ref: 30

Topic: How Do Psychologists Develop New Knowledge?

Skill: Factual

23) In Emily Rosa's therapeutic touch experiment, the research subjects had to provide correct answers more than 50% of the time in order to substantiate their claim that they could detect a "human energy field." What was Emily's reason for setting this high standard of proof?

    A) to compensate for unintentional cues that she may have given her subjects

    B) to overcome her own bias against non-conventional treatment

    C) to outweigh any possible flaws in the research design and execution

    D) to ensure that the observed results reached the level above mere chance

    E) to provide a way of replicating her study

Answer: D

Diff: 3   Page Ref: 30

Topic: How Do Psychologists Develop New Knowledge?

Skill: Conceptual

24) In an experiment to test the impact a sports drink had on amount of energy, individuals were given either water or a sports drink. They were watched a television show about basketball for 30 minutes and then were assessed on a number of physical tasks. The independent variable is _____ and the dependent variable is _____.

    A) the amount of energy; the type of drink

    B) the water; the sports drink

    C) the sports drink; the water

    D) the type of drink; the amount of energy

    E) the television show; the amount of energy

Answer: D

Diff: 2   Page Ref: 30-31

Topic: How Do Psychologists Develop New Knowledge?

Skill: Applied

25) The values of the _____ variable is the result of changes in another variable.

  A) intervening

  B) predictor

  C) dependent

  D) independent

  E) randomized

Answer: C

Diff: 2   Page Ref: 31

Topic: How Do Psychologists Develop New Knowledge?

Skill: Factual

26) In an experiment to test how study time influences test results, one group in given an hour to study while to other group does not study at all. Both groups are assessed to measure how they perform on the test. The test scores represent the _____ in this experiment.

  A) control group

  B) dependent variable

  C) experimental group

  D) independent variable

  E) a confounding (extraneous variable)

Answer: B

Diff: 3   Page Ref: 31

Topic: How Do Psychologists Develop New Knowledge?

Skill: Factual

27) Some people believe that money can buy happiness. Dr. Goodwin wants to determine whether paying people plays a role in their happiness. The level of happiness would be considered to be the

  A) experimental variable.

  B) confounding variable.

  C) dependent variable.

  D) independent variable.

  E) control variable.

Answer: C

Diff: 2   Page Ref: 31

Topic: How Do Psychologists Develop New Knowledge?

Skill: Applied

28) To determine whether results are likely due to the independent variable (as opposed to mere chance), the results of an experiment must reach the level of

   A) clinical significance.

   B) importance.

   C) power.

   D) quantification.

   E) statistical significance.

   Answer: E
   Diff: 3   Page Ref: 31
   Topic: How Do Psychologists Develop New Knowledge?
   Skill: Conceptual

29) If a researcher find that there results are significantly significant, this means that

   A) the results are probably due to chance.

   B) the results are likely the result of manipulation by the independent variable.

   C) the results cannot be replicated.

   D) the results that the received are likely a result of manipulation of the dependent variable.

   E) the results occurred because of the manipulation of the control group.

   Answer: B
   Diff: 3   Page Ref: 31
   Topic: How Do Psychologists Develop New Knowledge?
   Skill: Conceptual

30) Concepts that are measured and expressed as numbers are said to be

   A) stratified.

   B) significant.

   C) quantified.

   D) experimental.

   E) controlled.

   Answer: C
   Diff: 1   Page Ref: 32
   Topic: How Do Psychologists Develop New Knowledge?
   Skill: Factual

31) Measurements that use numbers to show levels, size, intensity or amounts of a variable are known as
  A) quantification.
  B) experimentation.
  C) standardization.
  D) correlation.
  E) covariation.

Answer: A
Diff: 2   Page Ref: 32
Topic: How Do Psychologists Develop New Knowledge?
Skill: Factual

32) A scientist who is skeptical about a particular study can decide to run that study in their laboratory. This would represent _____ the original research study.
  A) reconfiguring
  B) rearranging
  C) reanalyzing
  D) replicating
  E) referencing

Answer: D
Diff: 3   Page Ref: 32
Topic: How Do Psychologists Develop New Knowledge?
Skill: Applied

33) Why is it important that studies are replicated, especially if we already know the outcome of the study?
  A) to insure that the results are valid
  B) to insure that the experimenter bias did not influence the initial study
  C) to allow for a double–blind study by someone who has nothing to gain regardless of the outcome of the study
  D) to insure that the results did not occur simply by chance
  E) All of the above

Answer: E
Diff: 2   Page Ref: 32
Topic: How Do Psychologists Develop New Knowledge?
Skill: Conceptual

34) Emily Rosa's experiment regarding Therapeutic Touch (TT) should be replicated because

    A) therapeutic touch really does work for all patients.

    B) Emily did not appropriately test her independent variable.

    C) even in a carefully designed study, Emily could have received her results by chance.

    D) Emily was too young to conduct scientific tests.

    E) All of the above

Answer: C
Diff: 3   Page Ref: 32
Topic: How Do Psychologists Develop New Knowledge?
Skill: Conceptual

35) A key aspect of an experiment is the requirement that researchers

    A) use correlational methods.

    B) control and manipulate all the conditions.

    C) replicate their findings.

    D) publish their results in a scientific journal.

    E) provide some sort of placebo.

Answer: B
Diff: 2   Page Ref: 33
Topic: How Do Psychologists Develop New Knowledge?
Skill: Factual

36) Researchers design good experiments to determine

    A) whether the independent variable causes a change in the dependent variable.

    B) whether people interpret events in different ways.

    C) whether some people are better at certain tasks than are others.

    D) whether people are able to improve their abilities with practice.

    E) how most people feel about a certain subject, such as sexuality.

Answer: A
Diff: 2   Page Ref: 33
Topic: How Do Psychologists Develop New Knowledge?
Skill: Conceptual

37) You would like to study the effects of sleep on attentiveness in class. Which of the following is NOT a control in the experiment to prevent extraneous variables from influencing the outcome of the experiment?

    A) test both the experimental and control group in the same place

    B) insure that all participants received almost the same amount of sleep

    C) insure that all of the participants are tested by the same individual

    D) place those who are more tired in the control group

    E) test both the control and experimental group at the same time of day

Answer: D

Diff: 2   *Page Ref: 33*

Topic: How Do Psychologists Develop New Knowledge?

Skill: Applied

38) How are a sample and the population in an experiment different from oe another?

    A) The sample is a smaller representation of the population.

    B) The population is a smaller representation of the sample.

    C) The population are the individuals actually participating in the experiment.

    D) The population must be chosen randomly.

    E) A sample is made up of a small number of individuals, the highest number of individuals in a sample is ten.

Answer: A

Diff: 2   *Page Ref: 33*

Topic: How Do Psychologists Develop New Knowledge?

Skill: Conceptual

39) Simply put, the difference between people in the experimental group and those in the control group is whether they

    A) are participating in the research.

    B) receive the special treatment.

    C) are measured by the researcher(s).

    D) receive the dependent variable.

    E) are in a double-blind study.

Answer: B

Diff: 1   *Page Ref: 34*

Topic: How Do Psychologists Develop New Knowledge?

Skill: Factual

40) Random assignment means that

    A) participants should not know to which group they belong.

    B) every other person is placed in the control group.

    C) all participants should have an equal chance of being placed in either the control or experimental group.

    D) participants can select which group they would like to join.

    E) All of the above

Answer: C
Diff: 2   Page Ref: 34
Topic: How Do Psychologists Explain Development?
Skill: Factual

41) A subject who is exposed to the special treatment is said to be in the _____ condition.

    A) control

    B) operational

    C) experimental

    D) blind

    E) correlational

Answer: C
Diff: 1   Page Ref: 34
Topic: How Do Psychologists Develop New Knowledge?
Skill: Conceptual

42) Some research questions cannot be answered using human experiments because

    A) some studies would be impractical or unethical.

    B) randomization is often hard to achieve.

    C) double-blind studies are usually dangerous to participants.

    D) researchers know that their results usually will not be published.

    E) they are not a very effective way to learn about cause and effect relationships.

Answer: A
Diff: 2   Page Ref: 34
Topic: How Do Psychologists Develop New Knowledge?
Skill: Conceptual

43) A outcome of a correlational study on attendance and grade point average could potentially conclude all of the following except

    A) there is a relationship between the number of days a student comes to school and their semester grade point average.

    B) coming to school causes individuals to get higher grades.

    C) there is a link between those with high attendance and high grades.

    D) there is a link between those with low attendance and low grades.

    E) for some individuals, as attendance goes down, grades actually go up.

Answer: B
Diff: 3   Page Ref: 34
Topic: How Do Psychologists Develop New Knowledge?
Skill: Conceptual

44) Which of the following is NOT a drawback to correlational studies?

    A) Researchers must give up some control of the research conditions.

    B) One can never ensure that groups are similar in every way.

    C) Subjects cannot be assigned randomly to the various conditions.

    D) The results may not hold true in the real world outside of the laboratory.

    E) It cannot be determined whether one variable caused a change in the other.

Answer: D
Diff: 3   Page Ref: 34
Topic: How Do Psychologists Develop New Knowledge?
Skill: Conceptual

45) The value of a correlation coefficient reflects the

    A) type of research conducted.

    B) relationship between two variables.

    C) number of groups (or individuals) studied.

    D) accuracy of the results.

    E) amount of change that occurred.

Answer: B
Diff: 2   Page Ref: 34
Topic: How Do Psychologists Develop New Knowledge?
Skill: Conceptual

46) If you could measure height of each student in your introductory psychology class and the amount of money that each person has in their pockets right now, you would expect to find

   A) a zero correlation.

   B) a positive correlation.

   C) a negative correlation.

   D) that taller people have more money.

   E) that shorter people have more money.

   Answer: A

   Diff: 2   Page Ref: 35

   Topic: How Do Psychologists Develop New Knowledge?

   Skill: Applied

47) If obese people tend to whistle less than skinny people, what kind of correlation would be expected between weight and the tendency to whistle?

   A) zero   B) positive   C) negative   D) random   E) minimal

   Answer: C

   Diff: 3   Page Ref: 34

   Topic: How Do Psychologists Develop New Knowledge?

   Skill: Applied

48) If a study finds that there is a negative correlation between exercise and blood pressure, this would most likely indicate that

   A) exercise could be dangerous in terms of our blood pressure.

   B) blood pressure changes alter our exercise patterns.

   C) the more we exercise, the higher our blood pressure becomes.

   D) exercise causes our blood pressure to rise.

   E) people who exercise more tend to have a lower blood pressure.

   Answer: E

   Diff: 3   Page Ref: 34

   Topic: How Do Psychologists Develop New Knowledge?

   Skill: Applied

49) If there is a positive correlation between the number of children a person has and their overall life satisfaction, we would find that people with more children

   A) consistently find less satisfaction with their lives.

   B) are less satisfied with their lives than are people with fewer children.

   C) are no more or less satisfied than those with fewer children.

   D) are more satisfied with their lives than are people with fewer children.

   E) are less satisfied with their lives than they were before they had children.

Answer: D
Diff: 2   Page Ref: 34
Topic: How Do Psychologists Develop New Knowledge?
Skill: Applied

50) If people tend to wear more layers of clothing as the weather gets colder, we would expect _____ between the variables of temperature and amount of clothing.

   A) a negative correlation

   B) no correlation

   C) a positive correlation

   D) statistical significance

   E) C and D are correct.

Answer: A
Diff: 2   Page Ref: 34
Topic: How Do Psychologists Develop New Knowledge?
Skill: Applied

51) Which of the following represents the strongest correlation coefficient?

   A) +.70   B) –.75   C) +.50   D) –.25   E) +.57

Answer: B
Diff: 2   Page Ref: 34
Topic: How Do Psychologists Develop New Knowledge?
Skill: Applied

52) Which of the following would be considered a true experiment?

   A) longitudinal study

   B) cross-sectional study

   C) naturalistic observation

   D) survey

   E) None of the above

Answer: E
Diff: 2   Page Ref: 35
Topic: How Do Psychologists Develop New Knowledge?
Skill: Factual

53) If a researcher wanted to find out college students political opinions, which of the following methods f research would be most appropriate to gather this information?

    A) experiment

    B) case study

    C) survey

    D) correlational study

    E) naturalistic observation

Answer: C
Diff: 1   Page Ref: 35
Topic: How Do Psychologists Develop New Knowledge?
Skill: Applied

54) Susan wants to see if pedestrians obey the cross walk lights that indicate when it is safe to cross or when they should wait on the sidewalk. Which of the following methods of research would be most appropriate for this study?

    A) self–report measures.

    B) naturalistic observation.

    C) conditioning.

    D) introspection.

    E) a double–blind study.

Answer: B
Diff: 2   Page Ref: 35
Topic: How Do Psychologists Develop New Knowledge?
Skill: Applied

55) Which types of research study would best be used to determine how aggressive children are while playing at a schoolyard during recess?

    A) confounding

    B) case study

    C) introspection

    D) naturalistic observation

    E) experiment

Answer: D
Diff: 1   Page Ref: 35
Topic: How Do Psychologists Develop New Knowledge?
Skill: Applied

56) If a researcher wanted to conduct a study to determine if people's intelligence remained the same over the course of their life span, which approach would be the most complete to use?

   A) survey

   B) cross-sectional study

   C) longitudinal study

   D) naturalistic observation

   E) cohort-sequential

Answer: C
Diff: 1   *Page Ref: 35*
Topic: How Do Psychologists Develop New Knowledge?
Skill: Applied

57) Why do many researchers prefer the experimental method over other types of quasi-experimental research?

   A) With an experiment, the researcher can be assured that there a no confounding variables in the study.

   B) An experiment is the only type of research that can provide useful data.

   C) An experiment is the only type of research that can prove that there is a link between two variables.

   D) An experiment is the only method of research that can prove cause and effect.

   E) An experiment can be used to collect nearly every type of data.

Answer: D
Diff: 3   *Page Ref: 35*
Topic: How Do Psychologists Develop New Knowledge?
Skill: Factual

58) This phenomena is much like the Confirmation bias in which an experimenter allows their preconceived notions about what "should" happen in an experiment into what they then see in the experiment.

   A) personal bias

   B) observer bias

   C) expectancy bias

   D) double-blind study

   E) confounding variable

Answer: C
Diff: 2   *Page Ref: 36*
Topic: How Do Psychologists Develop New Knowledge?
Skill: Conceptual

59) Dr. Dolin wants to test the effects his new "wonder drug" that he believes provides individuals with an abundance of memory ability. He gives 50 males the drug while 50 males receive a placebo. (Of course, he doesn't tell people which they are getting.) Then, he has one of his assistants use a test to measure the memory of all participants. This would be said to

    A) be a correlational study.

    B) be a double-blind study.

    C) be a study with no control group.

    D) have two independent variables.

    E) be difficult to replicate.

Answer: B
Diff: 3   Page Ref: 36
Topic: How Do Psychologists Develop New Knowledge?
Skill: Applied

60) Keeping subjects uninformed about the purpose of a study makes them

    A) less likely to experience unconscious motivation.

    B) less likely to perform to the researchers expectations.

    C) more likely to engage in introspection.

    D) more likely to use a psychoanalytic perspective.

    E) more likely to know why the research was done.

Answer: B
Diff: 2   Page Ref: 36
Topic: How Do Psychologists Develop New Knowledge?
Skill: Conceptual

61) All of the following will reduce the likelihood of confounding variables ability to influence the outcome of an experiment except

    A) random assignment.

    B) double-blind study.

    C) testing all participants under the same conditions.

    D) using an outside third party to conduct the experiment.

    E) telling the participants to which group they belong

Answer: E
Diff: 3   Page Ref: 36
Topic: How Do Psychologists Develop New Knowledge?
Skill: Factual

62) _____ variables are changeable factors that could distort the results of an experiment and be confused with the _____.

   A) Treatment; hypothesis

   B) Subject; dependent variables

   C) Confounding; dependent variable

   D) Confounding; independent variable

   E) Treatment; placebo control

Answer: D
Diff: 3   Page Ref: 33–36
Topic: How Do Psychologists Develop New Knowledge?
Skill: Conceptual

63) Dr. Suttman measures the blood pressure of 50 women. She has 25 women exercise three times a week for eight weeks. She instructs the other 25 women to not exercise. After the eight weeks, Dr. Suttman measures the blood pressure of all 50 women. She finds that blood pressure decreased for the exercising women, but not for the others. Which of the following could NOT be a confounding variable?

   A) the blood pressure at the end of the study

   B) the women's blood pressure at the start of the study

   C) the dietary habits of each woman during the study

   D) the amount of stress in each woman's life

   E) the age of each woman who participated

Answer: A
Diff: 3   Page Ref: 36
Topic: How Do Psychologists Develop New Knowledge?
Skill: Applied

64) The _____ variables should be eliminated or controlled by keeping them the same or constant in an experiment.

   A) dependent

   B) independent

   C) confounding

   D) correlational

   E) placebo

Answer: C
Diff: 3   Page Ref: 36
Topic: How Do Psychologists Develop New Knowledge?
Skill: Conceptual

65) What is the purpose of an Institutional Review Board (IRB)?

    A) to insure that an experiments hypothesis is proven true

    B) to insure that all research being conducted adheres to ethical guidelines

    C) to see if the independent variable is actually influencing the outcome of the study

    D) to make sure that animals are treated humanly

    E) None of the above

Answer: B
Diff: 3   *Page Ref: 37*
Topic: How Do Psychologists Develop New Knowledge?
Skill: Factual

66) A study in which participation is NOT voluntary and informed is said to involve

    A) a double-blind control.

    B) debriefing.

    C) deception.

    D) vivisection.

    E) counter conditioning.

Answer: C
Diff: 2   *Page Ref: 37*
Topic: How Do Psychologists Develop New Knowledge?
Skill: Conceptual

67) The American Psychological Association guidelines state that research participants must

    A) be paid (or rewarded) for their participation.

    B) never be deceived under any circumstances.

    C) never participate in blind research.

    D) be debriefed after the study if the research involves deception.

    E) waive their right to privacy if they volunteer for a study.

Answer: D
Diff: 2   *Page Ref: 37*
Topic: How Do Psychologists Develop New Knowledge?
Skill: Factual

68) _____ refers to providing each subject with a full and honest account of the true purposes and assumptions of the research study, if the study involved deception.

A) Informed consent

B) Deception

C) Debriefing

D) Risk/gain assessment

E) IRB approval

Answer: C

Diff: 3   Page Ref: 37

Topic: How Do Psychologists Develop New Knowledge?

Skill: Factual

69) The American Psychological Society (APS) was formed to

A) help therapists treat patients.

B) give a stronger voice to the concerns of academic psychologists.

C) determine ethical guidelines for clinical research.

D) evaluate the quality of psychological research.

E) help clinical psychologists compete with counseling psychologists.

Answer: B

Diff: 3   Page Ref: 39

Topic: How do We Make Sense of the Data?

Skill: Factual

70) What is the purpose of using a frequency distribution to examine the data?

A) It allows you to see if a link exists between the independent and dependent variables.

B) It allows you to better evaluate the data by organizing it and seeing how many times different data points appear.

C) It allows you to determine if the results are statistically significant.

D) By creating a bar graph of the information you can see patterns in the data.

E) It allows you to create a correlation coefficient.

Answer: B

Diff: 3   Page Ref: 44

Topic: How do We Make Sense of the Data?

Skill: Factual

71) All of the following are examples of descriptive Statistics except for

   A) mean.

   B) mode.

   C) statistical significance.

   D) median.

   E) range.

Answer: C
Diff: 3   Page Ref: 44
Topic: How do We Make Sense of the Data?
Skill: Factual

72) What method of data evaluation will allow you to determine how frequently each score in a data set occurs?

   A) mean

   B) standard deviation

   C) range

   D) frequency distribution

   E) median

Answer: D
Diff: 3   Page Ref: 44
Topic: How do We Make Sense of the Data?
Skill: Recall

73) All of the following are measures of central tendency except

   A) mean.

   B) median.

   C) correlation coefficient.

   D) range.

   E) mode.

Answer: C
Diff: 1   Page Ref: 45
Topic: How do We Make Sense of the Data?
Skill: Factual

74) In a given data set, N represents
    A) the number of participants in the data set.
    B) the correlation coefficient.
    C) the likelihood that the results occurred by chance.
    D) the mean.
    E) the median.

Answer: A
Diff: 3   *Page Ref: 45*
Topic: How do We Make Sense of the Data?
Skill: Recall

75) Which of the following measures of central tendencies would be most effected by extreme scores?
    A) mode
    B) mean
    C) range
    D) median
    E) correlation coefficient

Answer: B
Diff: 3   *Page Ref: 45*
Topic: How do We Make Sense of the Data?
Skill: Conceptual

76) What does the standard deviation represent in a set of data?
    A) the average distance of a set of scores from the mean
    B) the score that occurs with the most frequency in a set of data
    C) the middle score in a set of data
    D) whether or not the results of the data is likely to be due to chance
    E) whether or not the data that was collected is valid

Answer: A
Diff: 3   *Page Ref: 46*
Topic: How do We Make Sense of the Data?
Skill: Factual

77) If a set of data has a relatively low variability, this means that

    A) the scores in the data set have a negative correlation.

    B) the scores in the data set are extremely diverse.

    C) the scores in the data set have a zero correlation.

    D) the scores in the data set a closely clustered around the mean.

    E) the scores in the data set are statistically significant.

Answer: D
Diff: 3   Page Ref: 46
Topic: How do We Make Sense of the Data?
Skill: Factual

78) In a normal distribution (bell curve, what percentage of scores fall within one standard deviation from the mean?

    A) 95%   B) 68%   C) 99.7%   D) 50%   E) 43%

Answer: B
Diff: 3   Page Ref: 47
Topic: How do We Make Sense of the Data?
Skill: Factual

79) Inferential Statistics can be used to determine

    A) the mean of a set of data.

    B) if the results from a study a due to chance.

    C) the correlation coefficient of a set of data.

    D) if there is a normal distribution for a set of data.

    E) the range for a set of data.

Answer: B
Diff: 3   Page Ref: 48
Topic: How do We Make Sense of the Data?
Skill: Factual

80) If a study resulted in a $p < .50$, what could we generally say about the study

    A) the data that was collected was reliable.

    B) the date that was collected was valid.

    C) the results that we received in the study are not likely due to chance.

    D) there is a relatively large possibility that we received these results just by chance.

    E) All of the above

Answer: D
Diff: 3   Page Ref: 49
Topic: How do We Make Sense of the Data?
Skill: Applied

81) Why is it impossible to ever have a p=.00?
   A) There is always some correlation between two variables.
   B) We never really use a completely random sample.
   C) because a p–value of +1.0 is ideal
   D) Even the most thorough studies have a small likelihood of obtaining the results they did based on chance.
   E) None of the above

Answer: D
Diff: 3   Page Ref: 49
Topic: How do We Make Sense of the Data?
Skill: Applied

82) How can the use of statistics help politicians running for office?
   A) It can help them to determine the opinions of the voting public.
   B) It can help them to determine which types of advertisements voters would respond to.
   C) It can help them to determine what issues the voters feel passionate about.
   D) It can help to determine what message the voters want to hear from their candidates.
   E) All of the above

Answer: E
Diff: 1   Page Ref: 50
Topic: How do We Make Sense of the Data?
Skill: Conceptual

83) Why did Yumi and Maria chose a survey to collect their research of body image differences between Japanese and American teenagers?
   A) because the body image served as their independent variable
   B) because they were getting the teenagers opinions about themselves
   C) because their wanted to gather the information without having direct contact with their participants
   D) because they wanted to manipulate as many parts of the experiment as possible
   E) because they wanted to determine if the control group was actually different from the experimental group

Answer: B
Diff: 2   Page Ref: 50
Topic: How do We Make Sense of the Data?
Skill: Conceptual

84) What is correct order in which information should be presented in a academic psychological article?

A) abstract, method, results, discussion, introduction, references

B) introduction, method, results, discussion, abstract, references

C) introduction, method, discussion, results, abstract, references

D) abstract, introduction, method, results, discussion, references

E) abstract, introduction, method, results, references, discussion

Answer: D
Diff: 2   Page Ref: 51–53
Topic: How do We Make Sense of the Data?
Skill: Recall

Check Your Understanding Questions

1) A theory is

A) an unsupported opinion.

B) a testable explanation for the data.

C) the opposite of a fact.

D) a statement that has not been supported with facts.

Answer: B
Diff: 1   Page Ref: 28
Topic: Check Your Understanding
Skill: Recall

2) A scientific study should begin with

A) a controlled test.

B) a hypothesis.

C) data collection.

D) risk/gain assessment.

E) IRB proposal

Answer: B
Diff: 1   Page Ref: 29
Topic: Check Your Understanding
Skill: Recall

3) In a experiment, the factor that is controlled by the experimenter is the

    A) independent variable.

    B) control group.

    C) experimental group.

    D) dependent variable.

    E) hypothesis.

Answer: A
Diff: 2   Page Ref: 35
Topic: Check Your Understanding
Skill: Factual

4) Which of the following could be an operational definition of "fear"?

    A) an intense fear of terror and dread when thinking about some threatening situation

    B) panic

    C) a desire to avoid something

    D) moving away from a stimulus

    E) moving towards a stimulus

Answer: D
Diff: 3   Page Ref: 30
Topic: Check Your Understanding
Skill: Applied

5) Which is the only form of research that can demonstrate cause and effect?

    A) a case study

    B) a correlational study

    C) naturalistic observation

    D) an experimental study

    E) cohort-sequential study

Answer: D
Diff: 2   Page Ref: 35
Topic: Check Your Understanding
Skill: Recall

6) Random assignment of subjects to different experimental conditions is a method for controlling differences that may exist between
   A) the dependent variable and the independent variable.
   B) the experimental group and the control group.
   C) empirical data and subjective data.
   D) heredity and environment.
   E) the independent variable and the control group.

Answer: B
Diff: 3   Page Ref: 34
Topic: Check Your Understanding
Skill: Conceptual

7) In which type of research does the scientist have the most control over variables that might affect the outcome of the study?
   A) a case study
   B) a correlational study
   C) an experimental study
   D) naturalistic observation
   E) a longitudinal study

Answer: C
Diff: 2   Page Ref: 35
Topic: Check Your Understanding
Skill: Recall

8) Which one of the following correlations shows the strongest relationship between two variables?
   A) +0.4   B) +0.38   C) –0.7   D) 0.05   E) –0.64

Answer: C
Diff: 2   Page Ref: 35
Topic: Check Your Understanding
Skill: Conceptual

9) A Correlational studies finds a link between how tall someone is and their shoe size. The taller someone is, the larger their shoe size, this could be said to be a

  A) positive correlation.

  B) negative correlation.

  C) zero correlation.

  D) being tall cause large shoe sizes.

  E) None of the above

Answer: A

Diff: 2   Page Ref: 34

Topic: Check Your Understanding

Skill: Conceptual

10) Which of the following correlation coefficients would a statistician know, at first glance is a mistake?

  A) 0.0   B) +1.1   C) +1.0   D) –0.7   E) –0.2

Answer: B

Diff: 2   Page Ref: 48

Topic: Check Your Understanding

Skill: Analysis

11) Which of the following measures of central tendencies is most affected by extreme scores?

  A) mean

  B) correlation

  C) mode

  D) frequency distribution

  E) median

Answer: A

Diff: 2   Page Ref: 45

Topic: Check Your Understanding

Skill: Factual

12) To determine how varied a set of data is around the mean, what would be the best measure of analysis to use?

A) mean

B) mode

C) standard deviation

D) correlation

E) median

Answer: C

Diff: 2   Page Ref: 46

Topic: Check Your Understanding

Skill: Factual

13) Most psychologists accept a difference between groups as 'real', or significant, under which of the following conditions?

A) $p<.5$ B) $p<.3$ C) $p<.1$ D) $p<.05$ E) $p=0$

Answer: D

Diff: 2   Page Ref: 49

Topic: Check Your Understanding

Skill: Factual

True/False Questions

1) Astrology, graphology, palmistry and biorhythm analysis are all types of psychology based on good empirical science.

Answer: FALSE

Diff: 2   Page Ref: 28

Topic: How Do Psychologists Develop New Knowledge?

Skill: Conceptual

2) One can prove a theory is true.

Answer: FALSE

Diff: 3   Page Ref: 28

Topic: How Do Psychologists Develop New Knowledge?

Skill: Factual

3) The scientific method allows us to put a hypothesis to a pass–fail test.

Answer: TRUE

Diff: 1   Page Ref: 28

Topic: How Do Psychologists Develop New Knowledge?

Skill: Factual

4) In an experiment, it is assumed that changes in the independent variable will produce changes in the dependent variable.

Answer: TRUE
Diff: 2   Page Ref: 30
Topic: How Do Psychologists Develop New Knowledge?
Skill: Conceptual

5) An Operational Definition describes what will be.

Answer: FALSE
Diff: 2   Page Ref: 30
Topic: How Do Psychologists Develop New Knowledge?
Skill: Factual

6) Experimental research gives scientists more control over the variables in their studies than either correlational research or the case study method.

Answer: TRUE
Diff: 1   Page Ref: 30–34
Topic: How Do Psychologists Develop New Knowledge?
Skill: Applied

7) The Dependent Variable is the part of an experiment which the experimenter manipulates.

Answer: FALSE
Diff: 1   Page Ref: 31
Topic: How Do Psychologists Develop New Knowledge?
Skill: Factual

8) In an experiment, only the control group is controlled by the researcher.

Answer: FALSE
Diff: 2   Page Ref: 33
Topic: How Do Psychologists Develop New Knowledge?
Skill: Conceptual

9) If another researcher can replicate a study it means that the theory which it is based of of must be true.

Answer: FALSE
Diff: 1   Page Ref: 32
Topic: How Do Psychologists Develop New Knowledge?
Skill: Factual

10) Psychologists can overcome the effects of confounding variables by using control procedures.

Answer: TRUE
Diff: 2   Page Ref: 33
Topic: How Do Psychologists Develop New Knowledge?
Skill: Conceptual

11) In quasi-experiments, researchers have just as much control over the variables as they do in an experiment.

Answer: FALSE
Diff: 2   Page Ref: 35
Topic: How Do Psychologists Develop New Knowledge?
Skill: Factual

12) A survey is typically conducted to reveal individuals opinions about given topics.

Answer: TRUE
Diff: 1   Page Ref: 35
Topic: How Do Psychologists Develop New Knowledge?
Skill: Factual

13) Jane Goodall conducted naturalistic observation in her study on chimpanzee behavior.

Answer: TRUE
Diff: 2   Page Ref: 35
Topic: How Do Psychologists Develop New Knowledge?
Skill: Factual

14) In a longitudinal study, researchers study individuals of different ages at the same time and then compare the results on a given variable.

Answer: FALSE
Diff: 2   Page Ref: 35
Topic: How Do Psychologists Develop New Knowledge?
Skill: Factual

15) A double-blind study involves a researcher who is visually impaired.

Answer: FALSE
Diff: 2   Page Ref: 36
Topic: How Do Psychologists Develop New Knowledge?
Skill: Conceptual

16) An IRB board is created to insure that research that is conducted meets ethical standards.

Answer: TRUE
Diff: 2 *Page Ref: 37*
Topic: How Do Psychologists Develop New Knowledge?
Skill: Recall

17) Most psychologists believe that animal research should be banned.

Answer: FALSE
Diff: 1 *Page Ref: 38*
Topic: How Do Psychologists Develop New Knowledge?
Skill: Factual

18) A histogram is similar to a pie chart that provides percentages of data analysis.

Answer: FALSE
Diff: 2 *Page Ref: 44*
Topic: How Do Psychologists Develop New Knowledge?
Skill: Recall

19) In a data set, the mean is the most resistant to extreme scores.

Answer: FALSE
Diff: 2 *Page Ref: 45*
Topic: How Do Psychologists Develop New Knowledge?
Skill: Conceptual

20) Standard deviation shows the average variation in a data set.

Answer: TRUE
Diff: 2 *Page Ref: 46*
Topic: How Do Psychologists Develop New Knowledge?
Skill: Factual

21) If a study finds that a zero correlation exists between financial status and happiness, we can infer that wealthy individuals tend to be no more or less happy than those with less money.

Answer: TRUE
Diff: 2 *Page Ref: 47*
Topic: How Do Psychologists Develop New Knowledge?
Skill: Applied

22) A strong negative correlation implies that increases in one variable creates increases in another variable.

Answer: FALSE
Diff: 2   Page Ref: 47
Topic: How Do Psychologists Develop New Knowledge?
Skill: Conceptual

23) A representative sample is reflective of the population.

Answer: FALSE
Diff: 2   Page Ref: 49
Topic: How Do Psychologists Develop New Knowledge?
Skill: Factual

24) If the results from a study are statistically significant, the results are likely to have occurred by chance.

Answer: FALSE
Diff: 2   Page Ref: 49
Topic: How Do Psychologists Develop New Knowledge?
Skill: Conceptual

Short Answer Questions

1) In an experiment, which variable is controlled by the experimenter and which is measured by the experimenter?

Answer: independent variable; dependent variable
Diff: 2   Page Ref: 30–31
Topic: How Do Psychologists Develop New Knowledge?
Skill: Conceptual

2) Why is it important to replicate studies?

Answer: If a study can be replicated, it increases the likelihood that the results are valid and that experimenter bias did not influence the results in the original study. It also lends credibility to the study if the results can be duplicated under different conditions.
Diff: 2   Page Ref: 32
Topic: How Do Psychologists Develop New Knowledge?
Skill: Analysis

3) Provide two examples of how a researcher can control for extraneous variables.

Answer: Test all participants under the same conditions and insure that you have a representative sample.
Diff: 2   Page Ref: 33
Topic: How Do Psychologists Develop New Knowledge?
Skill: Applied

4) In an experiment, explain the difference between the population and the sample.

Answer: The population is everyone who fits the criteria to participate in your experiment. Since it is impossible to test every person who fits the criteria, the sample is the smaller group (who should be representative of the larger population) that you actually test in your study.

Diff: 3   Page Ref: 33

Topic: How Do Psychologists Develop New Knowledge?

Skill: Conceptual

5) Explain why researchers have a tendency to prefer the experimental method over other types of quasi-experimental research.

Answer: An experiment is the only type of research that can prove cause and effect between two variables. in an experiment, the researchers have a great deal more control over the study than they would in quasi-experimental research.

Diff: 2   Page Ref: 35

Topic: How Do Psychologists Develop New Knowledge?

Skill: Applied

6) Why is it important for researchers to conduct double-blind studies?

Answer: To insure that their own personal biases do not influence the outcome of the study.

Diff: 1   Page Ref: 36

Topic: How Do Psychologists Develop New Knowledge?

Skill: Analysis

7) What is the purpose of Institutional Review Boards?

Answer: to insure that all research that is conducted follows ethical guidelines created by the America Psychological Association (pa)

Diff: 2   Page Ref: 37

Topic: How Do Psychologists Develop New Knowledge?

Skill: Conceptual

8) Why is it preferable to provide a Likert scale (0–5 from strongly agree to strongly disagree) to individuals taking a survey, rather than simply giving an option of agree or disagree?

Answer: This allows the individual more choice, and makes it less likely that they simply agree with all of the statements, it also gives them a neutral option as a choice.

Diff: 2   Page Ref: 43

Topic: How Do Psychologists Develop New Knowledge?

Skill: Applied

9) What is an advantage to using the median when examining a set of data?

Answer: It is less resistant to extreme scores than the mean and more reflective of a set of data than the mode.

Diff: 2   Page Ref: 46

Topic: How do We Make Sense of the Data?

Skill: Factual

10) If there is a negative correlation between candy consumption and happiness, what would we expect to note in people who eat a lot of candy?

Answer: People who eat more candy are sadder than those people who eat less candy.

Diff: 2   Page Ref: 47

Topic: How Do Psychologists Develop New Knowledge?

Skill: Applied

11) What does the correlation coefficient demonstrate, and how is this displayed?

Answer: The strength of a relationship between two variables and it is displayed a (r) and can range from a -1.0 through $+1.0$

Diff: 2   Page Ref: 47–48

Topic: How Do Psychologists Develop New Knowledge?

Skill: Factual

12) As it is nearly impossible to get a completely random sample from the population, how can we get the best representation while still being practical?

Answer: We can sue a representative sample which represents the population on larger variables such as gender, age,etc (the gallup poll uses this method). Generally if the sample is collected randomly even a relatively small sample size will create an accurate idea of what the larger population looks like.

Diff: 2   Page Ref: 49

Topic: How do We Make Sense of the Data?

Skill: Applied

13) What does $p<.05$ mean?

Answer: This means that the probability that the results of this study occurred simple by chance are less that 5%. This means that the results of the study are likely due to the manipulation of the independent variable.

Diff: 3   Page Ref: 49

Topic: How do We Make Sense of the Data?

Skill: Conceptual

Essay Questions

1) You have been asked to create an experiment to determine whether exposure to violent television in teenagers has an impact on behavior. In creating the experiment, be sure to include the following characteristics.
Hypothesis
Description of Population
Description of Sample
independent Variable
Dependent variable
Control Group
Experimental Group
2 controls for potential extraneous variables

Answer: Hypothesis: The more violent television one is exposed to, the more violent behavior they will exhibit
Description of Population: All American teenagers
Description of the Sample: A random selection of all students in the local high school
Independent Variable: Type of television show (violent or non-violent)
Dependent Variable: Amount of aggressive behavior displayed
Control Group: Group not exposed to violent television
Experimental Group: the group that is exposed to violent television
2 controls for potential extraneous variables: test all participants under the same conditions and insure that the participants are randomly selected for the control and experimental groups.

Diff: 3   Page Ref: 33–34

Topic: How Do Psychologists Develop New Knowledge?

Skill: Applied

2) Explain at least on advantage and one disadvantage to the following types of research and include a brief description of when this type of research could be used.
   Survey
   Naturalistic Observation
   Longitudinal Study
   Cross-Sectional Study

   Answer: Survey Use: To gather information on one's political views
   Advantage: Simple, quick cheap
   Disadvantage: people can lie, can get a non-representative group to answer surveys
   Naturalistic Observation: To view individuals in their natural setting so they do not know they are being observed. To look at parenting techniques at a local park.
   Advantages: People will act naturally
   Disadvantages: Since there is no interaction with the participants, you must assume why they are behaving as they are.
   Longitudinal Study: Study intelligence over the life span.
   Advantages: Accurate, informative data
   Disadvantage: takes too long, too expensive, people die
   Cross-Sectional Study: study the different political opinions across different age groups
   Advantage: Get information more quickly than with a longitudinal study
   Disadvantage: May provide misleading results because of extraneous differences amongst groups.

   Diff: 3   Page Ref: 35

   Topic: How Do Psychologists Develop New Knowledge?

   Skill: Applied

3) You have just graduated from college, a company that you are considering working for claims that it's employees on average make $80,000 per year. You do some further investigation and discover that the CEO of the corporation makes $350,000 per year, but that most of the first year employees make $20,000 per year. When displaying this data using measures of central tendencies, explain how this data would influence the scores.

   Answer: The mean would be dramatically affected, the CEO's salary would dramatically pull up the average for all of the employees. The mode would be at $20,000 which for a new employee would better represent what they would earn, the median would be pulled up slightly.

   Diff: 2   Page Ref: 45

   Topic: How do We Make Sense of the Data?

   Skill: Applied

4) Explain what is involved in a correlational study and why such studies are sometimes performed instead of experiments. Describe several drawbacks to correlational studies.

Answer: Correlational studies are like experiments that have already occurred in the real world. They are performed in cases where conducting an experiment might be hazardous or unrealistic. The student should mention that there are several drawbacks to correlational studies. For example, one cannot be sure that the groups are similar. Also, researchers cannot control the independent variable or randomly assign people to the different conditions. Most important, we cannot claim that one factor causes a change in the other.

Diff: 2   *Page Ref: 47*

Topic: How Do Psychologists Develop New Knowledge?

Skill: Conceptual

Chapter 3 Biopsychology and the Foundations of Neuroscience

Multiple Choice Questions

1) Which of the following is true of nerve cell development?
   A) The brain has excess neurons at birth.
   B) The are about 100 billion nerve cells in the adult brain.
   C) Some nerve cells die during the first few years of life.
   D) Our brain can generate new nerve cells.
   E) All of the above are correct

   Answer: E
   Diff: 3   *Page Ref: 63*
   Topic: Biopsychology and the Foundations of Neuroscience
   Skill: Factual

2) Which of the following is true about neurons?
   A) There are only about 15 basic neuron types.
   B) Human neurons die only when you are very old.
   C) The total number of neurons remains relatively constant throughout life.
   D) Each type of neuron has its own distinct parts.
   E) Humans lose approximately 100 neurons per day.

   Answer: C
   Diff: 3   *Page Ref: 63*
   Topic: Biopsychology and the Foundations of Neuroscience
   Skill: Factual

3) The specialty in psychology that studies the interaction of biology, behavior, and mental processes.
   A) neuroscience
   B) biopsychology
   C) biology
   D) neurobiology
   E) cognition

   Answer: B
   Diff: 2   *Page Ref: 63*
   Topic: Biopsychology and the Foundations of Neuroscience
   Skill: Factual

4) _____ is the interdisciplinary field involving biologists, psychologists, computer scientists, and chemists.

   A) Psychiatry

   B) Eclecticism

   C) Human factors

   D) Evolutionology

   E) Neuroscience

Answer: E
Diff: 1   *Page Ref: 63*
Topic: How Are Genes And Behavior Linked?
Skill: Factual

5) Because the human brain is born already programmed for language, we can say that language is a(n) _____ behavioral tendency.

   A) learned   B) critical   C) innate   D) somatic   E) cerebral

Answer: C
Diff: 1   *Page Ref: 64*
Topic: How Are Genes And Behavior Linked?
Skill: Conceptual

6) _____ theory argues that organisms adapt over time to their unique environments.

   A) Evolution

   B) Cortical restructuring

   C) Adaptive realism

   D) Incremental functionalism

   E) Neuroscience

Answer: A
Diff: 1   *Page Ref: 64*
Topic: How Are Genes And Behavior Linked?
Skill: Factual

7) Darwin's theory of _____ argues that evolution favors those organisms that are best adapted to their environment.

  A) intelligent design

  B) bipedalism

  C) specialization

  D) natural selection

  E) creationism

Answer: D

Diff: 1   Page Ref: 64

Topic: How Are Genes And Behavior Linked?

Skill: Conceptual

8) Darwin's theory of evolution suggests that the only measure of success for a species is

  A) being the largest of the species.

  B) not competing with members of the same species.

  C) possessing the best coloring and shape of the species.

  D) the passing of genes along to succeeding generations.

  E) the uniqueness of the species.

Answer: D

Diff: 3   Page Ref: 64

Topic: How Are Genes And Behavior Linked?

Skill: Conceptual

9) Charles Darwin's theory of evolution proposes all of the following except

  A) those who are best suited to their environment are more likely to create offspring.

  B) those traits that best served a given species are the traits most likely to be passed on to future generations.

  C) humans evolved from monkeys.

  D) our genetic make-up can contribute to the overall quality of our life.

  E) humans and monkeys share a common ancestors millions of years ago.

Answer: C

Diff: 3   Page Ref: 65

Topic: How Are Genes And Behavior Linked?

Skill: Factual

10) Which of the following is NOT a way in which humans have demonstrated evolution?
   A) We are more likely to fear (have phobias) for those things like snakes and spiders that could potentially harm us.
   B) We are taller now that we were 100 years ago.
   C) There are certain foods (sweets and fats) that we are attracted to and others (bitter) that we generally dislike.
   D) Our desire to wear stylish clothing.
   E) Some of our organs such as the gallbladder and appendix have come to serve a less important function than they once did.

Answer: D
Diff: 3   Page Ref: 65
Topic: Biopsychology and the Foundations of Neuroscience
Skill: Applied

11) Why is it that identical twins can often look different?
   A) Sometimes identical twins do not share the same genetic make–up.
   B) The environment plays a role in how our genes are exhibited.
   C) Even though identical twins share the same genetic make–up, they can have different DNA.
   D) They may differ in the number of chromosomes that are contained in their hereditary make–up.
   E) All of the above

Answer: B
Diff: 3   Page Ref: 65
Topic: How Are Genes And Behavior Linked?
Skill: Applied

12) Which of the following is a characteristic that might be a part of your phenotype?
   A) your height and eye color
   B) the members of your family
   C) what you have learned in school
   D) the childhood diseases you have had
   E) your genetic make–up

Answer: A
Diff: 2   Page Ref: 66
Topic: How Are Genes And Behavior Linked?
Skill: Recall

13) Which of the following did you NOT inherit from your parents?
    A) falling in love with a certain individual
    B) facial features
    C) weight
    D) hair color
    E) height

Answer: A
Diff: 1   Page Ref: 66
Topic: How Are Genes And Behavior Linked?
Skill: Conceptual

14) The genetic structure you inherited from your parents is referred to as your
    A) genetic hardiness.
    B) genotype.
    C) genomic identity.
    D) phenotype.
    E) chromotype.

Answer: B
Diff: 2   Page Ref: 66
Topic: How Are Genes And Behavior Linked?
Skill: Factual

15) The long–complex molecule that encodes he directions for the inherited physical and mental characteristics of an organism is
    A) genotype.
    B) chromosomes.
    C) phenotype.
    D) DNA.
    E) nucleotides.

Answer: D
Diff: 2   Page Ref: 66
Topic: How Are Genes And Behavior Linked?
Skill: Factual

16) You and your brother have the same parents but look very different. The difference in your looks is an expression of your different

    A) genotypes.

    B) environmental selections.

    C) phenotypes.

    D) habitats.

    E) neurons.

Answer: C

Diff: 2   *Page Ref: 66*

Topic: How Are Genes And Behavior Linked?

Skill: Applied

17) Behavior consistently found in a species is likely to have a genetic basis that evolved because the behavior has been adaptive. Which of the following human behaviors illustrate this concept?

    A) driving a car

    B) eye color

    C) Down syndrome

    D) language

    E) All of the above

Answer: D

Diff: 2   *Page Ref: 66*

Topic: How Are Genes And Behavior Linked?

Skill: Understanding the Core Concept

18) Which of the following statements expresses the correct relationship?

    A) genes are made of chromosomes.

    B) DNA is made of chromosomes.

    C) nucleotides are made of genes.

    D) genes are made of DNA.

    E) DNA is made of genes

Answer: D

Diff: 2   *Page Ref: 66*

Topic: How Are Genes And Behavior Linked?

Skill: Recall

19) In purely evolutionary terms, which one would be a measure of your own success as an organism?

    A) your intellectual accomplishments

    B) the length of your life

    C) the number of children you have

    D) the contributions you made to the happiness of humanity

    E) the attractiveness of the individual you marry

Answer: C
Diff: 2   Page Ref: 66
Topic: How Are Genes And Behavior Linked?
Skill: Conceptual

20) The mechanism of genetic variation produces

    A) beneficial traits that work to the organism's advantage.

    B) maladaptive traits that work to the organism's disadvantage.

    C) both beneficial and maladaptive traits at random.

    D) more beneficial than maladaptive traits.

    E) more maladaptive than beneficial traits.

Answer: C
Diff: 3   Page Ref: 67–68
Topic: How Are Genes And Behavior Linked?
Skill: Conceptual

21) At the moment of conception, a male child receives _____ chromosomes from his mother and _____ from his father

    A) 23; 23   B) 24; 24   C) 23; 46   D) 46; 23   E) 2; 2

Answer: A
Diff: 2   Page Ref: 68
Topic: How Are Genes And Behavior Linked?
Skill: Factual

22) A male child inherits _____ from their fathers.

    A) no chromosomes

    B) an X chromosome

    C) a Y chromosome

    D) either an X or a Y chromosome

    E) both an X and a Y chromosome

Answer: C
Diff: 2   Page Ref: 68
Topic: How Are Genes And Behavior Linked?
Skill: Factual

23) Schizophrenia, a severe mental disorder, is thought to involve

    A) more than one chromosome.

    B) a single chromosome.

    C) a single gene.

    D) the deletion of genes from the 22nd chromosome.

    E) some missing chromosomes.

Answer: A
Diff: 3　　　Page Ref: 68
Topic: How Are Genes And Behavior Linked?
Skill: Factual

24) Which of the following is NOT characteristic of Down syndrome?

    A) impaired psychomotor development

    B) mental retardation

    C) behavior that is modifiable through training

    D) an missing chromosome in the 21st pair

    E) impaired physical development

Answer: D
Diff: 3　　　Page Ref: 69
Topic: How Are Genes And Behavior Linked?
Skill: Factual

25) A key goal of the Human Genome Project is to

    A) determine the complete human genetic code.

    B) create new genetic material in scientific laboratories.

    C) figure out how to destroy dangerous genetic material.

    D) uncover the causes of each person's genetic makeup.

    E) examine the degree of genetic similarity between humans and other animals.

Answer: A
Diff: 2　　　Page Ref: 69
Topic: Choosing Your Children's Genes
Skill: Conceptual

26) Cells that have not yet determined which type of tissue they will become are known as

    A) DNA.

    B) stem cells.

    C) chromosomes.

    D) nucleotides.

    E) genes.

Answer: B

Diff: 2   *Page Ref: 69*

Topic: How Are Genes And Behavior Linked?

Skill: Factual

27) _____ form the the body's two communication systems.

    A) The left and right hemispheres of the brain

    B) The dendrites and the axons

    C) The nervous system and the endocrine system

    D) Genetics and the environment

    E) Reflexes and controlled behavior

Answer: C

Diff: 1   *Page Ref: 71*

Topic: How Does the Body Communicate Internally?

Skill: Factual

28) All of the following are important messengers within the endocrine system except

    A) pituitary.

    B) thalamus.

    C) thyroid.

    D) adrenal glands.

    E) gonads.

Answer: B

Diff: 3   *Page Ref: 71*

Topic: How Does the Body Communicate Internally?

Skill: Factual

29) The _____ is the basic building block of the nervous system.

   A) soma

   B) neuron

   C) axon

   D) terminal button

   E) reflex

Answer: B
Diff: 1   Page Ref: 72
Topic: How Does the Body Communicate Internally?
Skill: Factual

30) _____ neurons carry messages to the central nervous system, and _____ neurons carry messages away from the central nervous system.

   A) Motor; sensory

   B) Sensory; motor

   C) Inter–; motor

   D) Sensory; inter–

   E) Inter–; sensory

Answer: B
Diff: 2   Page Ref: 72–73
Topic: How Does the Body Communicate Internally?
Skill: Factual

31) Place the following types of neurons in the correct order from a messages inception through a physical response.

   A) motor, inter–, sensory

   B) inter–, motor, sensory

   C) sensory motor, inter–

   D) sensory, inter–, motor

   E) motor, sensory, inter

Answer: D
Diff: 2   Page Ref: 72
Topic: How Does the Body Communicate Internally?
Skill: Recall

32) Afferent neurons

    A) are responsible for delivering messages from the CNS to the muscles and glands.

    B) transport messages between sensory neurons and motor neurons.

    C) are specialized sensory neurons that are sensitive to external stimuli.

    D) communicate directly with motor neurons in the peripheral nervous system.

    E) continuously monitor the routine operation of the body's internal functions.

Answer: C
Diff: 3   *Page Ref: 72*
Topic: How Does the Body Communicate Internally?
Skill: Factual

33) Which of the following is true about interneurons?

    A) Interneurons form complex circuits in the brain.

    B) There are 200,000 of them for every motor neuron.

    C) They are only found in the peripheral nervous system.

    D) They are not found in the brain and spinal cord.

    E) They relay messages between motor neurons.

Answer: A
Diff: 3   *Page Ref: 73*
Topic: How Does the Body Communicate Internally?
Skill: Conceptual

34) A dendrite does all of the following with the exception of

    A) carry messages to the terminal buttons.

    B) pick up messages from direct stimulation.

    C) pick up messages from other neurons.

    D) carry messages to the cell body.

    E) is branch like in structure.

Answer: A
Diff: 3   *Page Ref: 73–74*
Topic: How Does the Body Communicate Internally?
Skill: Conceptual

35) This is the area in a neuron that determines whether or not a given neuron will 'fire'.

    A) soma   B) dendrite   C) axon   D) myelin   E) synapse

Answer: A
Diff: 2   *Page Ref: 74*
Topic: How Does the Body Communicate Internally?
Skill: Factual

36) Neural signals travel along a neuron in what order?

    A) axon, dendrite, soma, terminal button

    B) terminal button, soma, dendrite, axon

    C) dendrite, soma, axon, terminal button

    D) dendrite, axon, soma, terminal button

    E) axon, soma, dendrite, terminal button

Answer: C
Diff: 2   Page Ref: 73–74
Topic: How Does the Body Communicate Internally?
Skill: Factual

37) Every one of your actions arises from

    A) neural impulses delivered from your sensory neurons to your brain.

    B) neural impulses from the brain delivered to your muscles.

    C) the imperatives of natural selection.

    D) the peripheral nervous system.

    E) sympathetic nervous system activity.

Answer: B
Diff: 2   Page Ref: 74
Topic: How Does the Body Communicate Internally?
Skill: Applied

38) During the process of synaptic communication,

    A) information is passed between the two cerebral hemispheres.

    B) is sent from the reticular formation to the cortex.

    C) a chemical message is sent across the synapse.

    D) a gland releases a hormone into the bloodstream.

    E) the neuron becomes silent.

Answer: C
Diff: 1   Page Ref: 74
Topic: How Does the Body Communicate Internally?
Skill: Conceptual

39) Why is it possible that some weak signals (such as a mosquito landing on your arm) go completely unnoticed?

    A) Only a few neurons a firing and they are too weak to detect.

    B) The mosquito is sending only inhibitory responses to our neurons.

    C) Neurons fire with an all–or–nothing response and the mosquito may not provide enough impulse fo a neuron to reach its threshold.

    D) The signal gets weaker as it moves down the axon.

    E) It is attempting to send the message through a motor neuron.

Answer: C

Diff: 3   Page Ref: 74

Topic: How Does the Body Communicate Internally?

Skill: Applied

40) Which of the following will cause a neuron to fire?

    A) activating the neurotransmitters held in the terminal buttons

    B) The excitatory signals outweigh the inhibitory signals received by the neuron.

    C) The inhibitory signals outweigh the excitatory signals received by the neuron.

    D) insuring that the axon is properly covered with myelin sheath

    E) if there is a positive charge inside of the neuron

Answer: B

Diff: 3   Page Ref: 74

Topic: How Does the Body Communicate Internally?

Skill: Conceptual

41) Which of the following is NOT true of neuron function?

    A) At rest, the nerve cell has a slight negative charge across the membrane.

    B) The action potential is due to positive ions flowing into the neuron.

    C) The action potential is a switch from negative to positive potential that moves along the axon membrane.

    D) A stimulus will either "fire" the neuron or it will fail to fire it.

    E) Nerve cells only use electrical signals to communicate with each other.

Answer: E

Diff: 3   Page Ref: 74–75

Topic: How Does the Body Communicate Internally?

Skill: Conceptual

42) During synaptic transmission, the _____ in the axon is converted into a(n) _____ that can traverse the synaptic gap.

   A) myelin sheath; chemical message

   B) electrical impulse; chemical message

   C) chemical message; electrical impulse

   D) myelin sheath; electrical impulse

   E) ionic impulse; electrical impulse

Answer: B
Diff: 2   Page Ref: 75
Topic: How Does the Body Communicate Internally?
Skill: Factual

43) The charge in the resting neuron is

   A) primarily a negative charge.

   B) primarily a positive charge.

   C) neither a negative or a positive charge.

   D) primarily effected by neurotransmitters.

   E) primarily effected by hormones.

Answer: A
Diff: 2   Page Ref: 74
Topic: How Does the Body Communicate Internally?
Skill: Recall

44) When an action potential moves down an axon, all of the following occur except

   A) an electrical message is taken down the axon.

   B) it moves like dominoes as it moves down the axon.

   C) the myelin sheath facilitates the quick movement of the message down the axon.

   D) a chemical message is taken along the axon.

   E) positive ions rush into the axon.

Answer: D
Diff: 3   Page Ref: 74
Topic: How Does the Body Communicate Internally?
Skill: Factual

45) This holds the neurotransmitters and eventually releases then into the synapse for transmittal to the next neuron.

   A) axon

   B) terminal buttons

   C) dendrites

   D) soma

   E) myelin sheath

Answer: B
Diff: 1   Page Ref: 74
Topic: How Does the Body Communicate Internally?
Skill: Recall

46) The process of reuptake involves

   A) neurotransmitters moving from the synapse into the postsynaptic receptor sites.

   B) the movement of positive ions to the outside of the axon.

   C) the movement of negative ions to the outside of the axon.

   D) the building up of the myelin sheath around the axon.

   E) neurotransmitters moving from the synapse back to the presynaptic terminal buttons.

Answer: E
Diff: 2   Page Ref: 75
Topic: How Does the Body Communicate Internally?
Skill: Recall

47) _____ are biochemical substances that are released into the synaptic cleft to stimulate or suppress other neurons.

   A) Receptors

   B) Hormones

   C) Neurotransmitters

   D) Interneurons

   E) Neurohormones

Answer: C
Diff: 2   Page Ref: 75
Topic: How Does the Body Communicate Internally?
Skill: Factual

48) Eddie has just stepped on a nail. There are pain messages moving through many of his neurons. Which of the following is the best summation of how that message will move from one neuron to the next?

    A) The terminal buttons will match up the response to the appropriate neurotransmitter.

    B) Neurotransmitters for pain will fit like a lock and key and carry to messages to receptor sites on the receiving neuron.

    C) Any neurotransmitters will allow the message to cross over the synapse to the receiving neuron.

    D) The process of reuptake will allow the message to move across the synapse.

    E) All of the above are true.

Answer: B
Diff: 3   Page Ref: 75
Topic: How Does the Body Communicate Internally?
Skill: Conceptual

49) Sam works as a bicycle messenger in lower Manhattan. As he moves between a car and a bus, he relies of his nervous system's production of _____, which carry information between _____, to enable him to swerve out of danger.

    A) hormones; glands

    B) hormones; nerve cells

    C) neurotransmitters; glands

    D) neurotransmitters; nerve cells

    E) neurons; axons

Answer: D
Diff: 2   Page Ref: 75
Topic: How Does the Body Communicate Internally?
Skill: Applied

50) Individuals who abuse Opiate such as heroin or morphine are artificially increasing levels of

    A) acetylcholine.

    B) endorphins.

    C) serotonin.

    D) dopamine.

    E) norepinephrine.

Answer: B
Diff: 3   Page Ref: 76
Topic: How Does the Body Communicate Internally?
Skill: Applied

51) Schizophrenia is thought to occur when a person has a higher–than–normal level of

A) serotonin.

B) endorphins.

C) dopamine.

D) acetylcholine.

E) GABA.

Answer: C

Diff: 3   Page Ref: 76

Topic: How Does the Body Communicate Internally?

Skill: Factual

52) Peter suffers damage to his left frontal lobe and loses the ability to speak, although he can still understand speech. Despite the permanence of this damage, he is able to recover some of his speech due to the ability of other parts of the brain to take over lost function. This phenomenon is known by neuroscientists as

A) flexibility.

B) adaptiveness.

C) plasticity.

D) compensation.

E) homeostasis.

Answer: C

Diff: 2   Page Ref: 76

Topic: How Does the Body Communicate Internally?

Skill: Applied

53) Individuals who suffer from Depression sometimes lack which of the following neurotransmitters?

A) dopamine

B) acetylcholine

C) serotonin

D) GABA

E) endorphins

Answer: C

Diff: 2   Page Ref: 76

Topic: How Does the Body Communicate Internally?

Skill: Applied

54) A person whose brain has an imbalance of serotonin would likely suffer from

    A) high blood pressure.

    B) epilepsy.

    C) Parkinson's disease.

    D) Alzheimer's disease.

    E) obsessive–compulsive disorder.

Answer: E
Diff: 3   Page Ref: 76
Topic: How Does the Body Communicate Internally?
Skill: Applied

55) Disturbances of the neurotransmitter _____ can produce memory problems.

    A) serotonin

    B) norepinephrine

    C) GABA

    D) acetylcholine

    E) glutamate

Answer: D
Diff: 3   Page Ref: 76
Topic: How Does the Body Communicate Internally?
Skill: Factual

56) Hallucinogenic drugs, such as LSD (lsergic acid diethylamide), produce their effects via an action on the neurotransmitter

    A) dopamine.

    B) GABA.

    C) endorphin.

    D) acetylcholine.

    E) serotonin.

Answer: E
Diff: 3   Page Ref: 76
Topic: How Does the Body Communicate Internally?
Skill: Factual

57) A four-year-old boy was accidentally shot in the head nearly his entire left hemisphere was removed but just three years later he was nearly completely normal. What term best explains the ability of the brain to 'rewire' itself, especially when we are young?

   A) plasticity

   B) reflexology

   C) reuptake

   D) expandibility

   E) refraction

Answer: A

Diff: 3   *Page Ref: 76*

Topic: How Does the Body Communicate Internally?

Skill: Applied

58) Multiple sclerosis is a disease that involves the degeneration of the

   A) dendrites.

   B) soma, or cell body.

   C) axon.

   D) myelin sheath.

   E) terminal buttons.

Answer: D

Diff: 2   *Page Ref: 77*

Topic: How Does the Body Communicate Internally?

Skill: Factual

59) Scientists now believe that glial cells play an important role in all of the following except

   A) motor skills.

   B) the production of myelin sheath.

   C) structural support for neurons.

   D) intelligence.

   E) helping to form new synapses.

Answer: A

Diff: 2   *Page Ref: 77*

Topic: How Does the Body Communicate Internally?

Skill: Conceptual

60) Marla is 76, she needs a walker to get around because even though she knows that she wants to walk she cannot get her body to cooperate with her. What might be happening within Marla's body.

    A) Her sensory neurons are not picking up the messages she wants to send.

    B) Her myelin sheath is beginning to break down.

    C) The charges inside of her neurons are not working properly.

    D) She is not producing enough of the neurotransmitter norepinephrine.

    E) Her sympathetic nervous system is acting inappropriately.

Answer: B
Diff: 2   Page Ref: 77
Topic: How Does the Body Communicate Internally?
Skill: Applied

61) The two major subsystems of the nervous system are the central nervous system and the

    A) autonomic nervous system.

    B) sympathetic nervous system.

    C) peripheral nervous system.

    D) parasympathetic nervous system.

    E) somatic nervous system.

Answer: C
Diff: 1   Page Ref: 78
Topic: How Does the Body Communicate Internally?
Skill: Factual

62) The central nervous system is comprised of all the neurons in the _____ and the _____.

    A) brain; spinal cord

    B) muscles; terminal buttons

    C) brain; skeletal muscles

    D) glands; spinal cord

    E) axons; dendrites

Answer: A
Diff: 1   Page Ref: 78
Topic: How Does the Body Communicate Internally?
Skill: Factual

63) Actor Christopher Reeve was paralyzed from the neck down because of accidental damage to his

A) peripheral nervous system.

B) cerebral cortex.

C) midbrain.

D) spinal cord.

E) sympathetic nervous system.

Answer: D

Diff: 2   *Page Ref: 78*

Topic: How Does the Body Communicate Internally?

Skill: Applied

64) Amy has an itch on her nose and would like to scratch it. What part of her nervous system will control the movement of her arm to scratch her nose?

A) somatic nervous system

B) sympathetic nervous system

C) parasympathetic nervous system

D) autonomic nervous system

E) central nervous system

Answer: A

Diff: 2   *Page Ref: 78–79*

Topic: How Does the Body Communicate Internally?

Skill: Applied

65) The peripheral nervous system is comprised of

A) the autonomic nervous system and the sympathetic division.

B) the autonomic nervous system and the central nervous system.

C) the somatic nervous system and the autonomic nervous system.

D) the somatic nervous system and the sympathetic division.

E) the parasympathetic nervous system and the central nervous system.

Answer: C

Diff: 2   *Page Ref: 79*

Topic: How Does the Body Communicate Internally?

Skill: Factual

66) "Fight or flight" behavior is associated with
   A) the parasympathetic division.
   B) central nervous system.
   C) the sympathetic division.
   D) the somatic nervous system.
   E) interneurons.

Answer: C
Diff: 2   *Page Ref: 79*
Topic: How Does the Body Communicate Internally?
Skill: Factual

67) The parasympathetic nervous system is a subdivision of
   A) the somatic nervous system.
   B) the sympathetic nervous system.
   C) the central nervous system.
   D) the autonomic nervous system.
   E) the limbic system.

Answer: D
Diff: 2   *Page Ref: 79*
Topic: How Does the Body Communicate Internally?
Skill: Factual

68) _____ is an example of a parasympathetic response.
   A) Promoting your sexual development
   B) Monitoring the operation of the body's routine functioning
   C) Preparing for a competitive dance competition
   D) Preparing yourself to fight an attacking dog
   E) Figuring out the answer to a difficult test question

Answer: B
Diff: 2   *Page Ref: 79*
Topic: How Does the Body Communicate Internally?
Skill: Applied

69) _____ is an example of a sympathetic response.
    A) Promoting your sexual development
    B) Monitoring the operation of the body's routine functioning
    C) Picking up a dime off the floor
    D) Preparing yourself to fight an attacking dog
    E) Figuring out the answer to a difficult test question

Answer: D
Diff: 2   Page Ref: 79
Topic: How Does the Body Communicate Internally?
Skill: Applied

70) All of the following are characteristic of an active sympathetic nervous system except
    A) dilated pupils.
    B) accelerated heartbeat.
    C) increased digestion.
    D) production od adrenaline.
    E) increase in saliva.

Answer: C
Diff: 2   Page Ref: 80
Topic: How Does the Body Communicate Internally?
Skill: Factual

71) Hormones are chemicals secreted into the bloodstream by
    A) axon terminals.
    B) neurotransmitters.
    C) endocrine glands.
    D) synapses.
    E) dendritic terminals.

Answer: C
Diff: 2   Page Ref: 80
Topic: How Does the Body Communicate Internally?
Skill: Factual

72) The sexual desire of a women is primarily determined by hormones produced by her
    A) thyroid.
    B) ovaries.
    C) posterior pituitary.
    D) adrenal glands.
    E) pancreas.

Answer: D
Diff: 3   Page Ref: 81
Topic: How Does the Body Communicate Internally?
Skill: Factual

73) Secretions from the thyroid gland control
    A) breast milk excretion.
    B) sperm production.
    C) stress reaction.
    D) metabolism.
    E) uterine contractions.

Answer: D
Diff: 3   Page Ref: 81
Topic: How Does the Body Communicate Internally?
Skill: Factual

74) The _____ produce female sex characteristics, while the _____ produce male sex characteristics.
    A) testes; ovaries
    B) thyroid; testes
    C) pituitary; thyroid
    D) ovaries; testes
    E) ovaries; thyroid

Answer: D
Diff: 3   Page Ref: 81
Topic: How Does the Body Communicate Internally?
Skill: Recall

75) The _____ is a limbic region that ultimately controls the endocrine system.

  A) hypothalamus

  B) pituitary gland

  C) reticular formation

  D) amygdala

  E) adrenal cortex

Answer: A

Diff: 2   Page Ref: 82

Topic: How Does the Body Communicate Internally?

Skill: Factual

76) The "master gland" is a term that refers to the

  A) thalamus.

  B) hypothalamus.

  C) pituitary gland.

  D) adrenal gland.

  E) thyroid gland.

Answer: C

Diff: 2   Page Ref: 82

Topic: How Does the Body Communicate Internally?

Skill: Factual

77) Prozac (fluoxetine) acts as a _____ for serotonin.

  A) agonist

  B) antagonist

  C) neurotransmitter

  D) hormone

  E) synapse

Answer: A

Diff: 3   Page Ref: 82

Topic: How Does the Body Communicate Internally?

Skill: Conceptual

78) A drug that mimics the effects of neurotransmitters, thus enhancing production is called a

    A) neurotransmitter.

    B) agonist.

    C) antagonist.

    D) hormone.

    E) endorphin.

Answer: B
Diff: 3   Page Ref: 82
Topic: How Does the Body Communicate Internally?
Skill: Conceptual

79) Which of the following is true of Prozac?

    A) Prozac elevates serotonin levels in the brain.

    B) Amphetamine is another name for Prozac.

    C) The effects of Prozac are specific to mood.

    D) Prozac is an antagonist for dopamine receptors.

    E) B and C are correct.

Answer: A
Diff: 3   Page Ref: 83
Topic: How Does the Body Communicate Internally?
Skill: Factual

80) A recording of brain waves using electrodes placed on the scalp is called a

    A) EEG.   B) PET.   C) GABA.   D) MRI.   E) RAS.

Answer: A
Diff: 2   Page Ref: 85
Topic: How Does the Brain Produce Behavior and Mental Processes?
Skill: Factual

81) The type of measure that would be most appropriate for revealing abnormalities in the brain waves such h as occurs in an epileptic seizure would be

    A) PET.   B) CT.   C) EEG.   D) MRI.   E) FMRI.

Answer: C
Diff: 2   Page Ref: 85
Topic: How Does the Brain Produce Behavior and Mental Processes?
Skill: Applied

82) Which scanning method produces a computerized image of X rays that have been passed through the brain at various angles?

    A) PET scanning

    B) CT scanning

    C) MRI scanning

    D) psychosurgery

    E) neurosurgery

Answer: B
Diff: 2   *Page Ref: 86*
Topic: How Does the Brain Produce Behavior and Mental Processes?
Skill: Factual

83) In the _____ procedure, a composite picture of neuron activity is produced by detecting atomic particles emitted by a radioactive dye.

    A) PET   B) CT   C) MRI   D) EEG   E) fMRI

Answer: A
Diff: 2   *Page Ref: 86*
Topic: How Does the Brain Produce Behavior and Mental Processes?
Skill: Conceptual

84) The scanning device that is best for distinguishing between closely related brain structures is the

    A) CT.   B) PET.   C) MRI.   D) EEG.   E) RAS.

Answer: C
Diff: 2   *Page Ref: 86*
Topic: How Does the Brain Produce Behavior and Mental Processes?
Skill: Factual

85) A unique feature of the fMRI is the capacity to

    A) detect cell activity throughout the brain.

    B) measure the magnetic fields in the brain.

    C) control brain activity by stimulating various brain regions.

    D) take a detailed X-ray of the brain while the person is conscious.

    E) distinguish more active tissues from less active ones.

Answer: E
Diff: 3   *Page Ref: 86*
Topic: How Does the Brain Produce Behavior and Mental Processes?
Skill: Factual

86) Which of the following is NOT a brain imaging technique?

    A) EEG   B) MRI   C) CT   D) PET   E) FMRI

Answer: A
Diff: 2   Page Ref: 85–86
Topic: How Does the Brain Produce Behavior and Mental Processes?
Skill: Analysis

87) All brain scanning techniques currently face weaknesses n terms of how they image the brain, which of the following would best explain the weakness of the PET scan?

    A) It cannot capture responses in the brain that are longer than a few seconds.

    B) It is not a good as the MRI in distinguishing fine detail of brain structure.

    C) It is not a color image.

    D) It is not very good at tracking brain activity.

    E) All of the above

Answer: B
Diff: 3   Page Ref: 86
Topic: How Does the Brain Produce Behavior and Mental Processes?
Skill: Conceptual

88) What is one of the benefits of using a FMRI?

    A) It tracks levels of glucose used by the brain to indicate levels of high brain activity.

    B) It provides the most detailed images of the brain to detect brain activity.

    C) It uses X ray passed through the brain at a number of different angels to detect a static image of the brain.

    D) It can provided information about brain wave activity.

    E) It provides an X-Ray type image of the brain.

Answer: B
Diff: 2   Page Ref: 86
Topic: How Does the Brain Produce Behavior and Mental Processes?
Skill: Applied

89) From an evolutionary perspective, which part of our brain is the oldest and looks much the same as any other lower order animal?
   A) cerebral cortex
   B) frontal lobe
   C) parietal lobe
   D) brain stem
   E) limbic system
   Answer: D
   Diff: 2   Page Ref: 87
   Topic: How Does the Brain Produce Behavior and Mental Processes?
   Skill: Factual

90) Our ability to breathe is controlled by the _____ which is located within the _____.
   A) medulla; brainstem
   B) thalamus; forebrain
   C) cerebellum; midbrain
   D) brain stem; medulla
   E) pons; forebrain
   Answer: A
   Diff: 2   Page Ref: 87–88
   Topic: How Does the Brain Produce Behavior and Mental Processes?
   Skill: Factual

91) Nerve fibers that interconnect the left side of the brain to the right side of the body (and vice versa) cross over the brain midline at the
   A) amygdala.
   B) brain stem.
   C) hypothalamus.
   D) thalamus.
   E) cerebrum.
   Answer: B
   Diff: 2   Page Ref: 88
   Topic: How Does the Brain Produce Behavior and Mental Processes?
   Skill: Factual

92) Sleep and dreaming is regulated by the

    A) the pons.

    B) amygdala.

    C) thalamus.

    D) pituitary gland.

    E) hippocampus.

Answer: A

Diff: 2   Page Ref: 88

Topic: How Does the Brain Produce Behavior and Mental Processes?

Skill: Factual

93) George is a swimmer, he made a bad turn during the last lab and his head and neck on the wall. He is now having trouble breathing, which of the following brain stem areas would be responsible for this function?

    A) pons

    B) reticular formation

    C) medulla

    D) cerebellum

    E) thalamus

Answer: C

Diff: 2   Page Ref: 88

Topic: How Does the Brain Produce Behavior and Mental Processes?

Skill: Applied

94) Arousal would be produced by _____ of the _____.

    A) inactivation; cerebral cortex

    B) inactivation; reticular activating system

    C) activation; reticular activating system

    D) activation; cerebellum

    E) inactivation; cerebellum

Answer: C

Diff: 2   Page Ref: 89

Topic: How Does the Brain Produce Behavior and Mental Processes?

Skill: Applied

95) You are sleeping and are suddenly startled by the fire alarm in your house going off, almost immediately you are awake and ready to find your family to help them outside. Which of the flowing areas of the brain stem would most likely be responsible for your speedy alert behavior?

    A) pons

    B) reticular formation

    C) brain stem

    D) medulla

    E) cerebellum

Answer: B

Diff: 3   Page Ref: 89

Topic: How Does the Brain Produce Behavior and Mental Processes?

Skill: Applied

96) Which sensory system does NOT relay information through the thalamus en route to the cortex?

    A) pain

    B) somatosensory

    C) audition

    D) vision

    E) smell

Answer: E

Diff: 2   Page Ref: 89

Topic: How Does the Brain Produce Behavior and Mental Processes?

Skill: Conceptual

97) Hearing a bird sing involves the transfer of auditory information from the ear through the spinal cord, then the reticular activating system, then to the _____ which will direct messages to the auditory cortex.

    A) the pons

    B) the hypothalamus

    C) the thalamus

    D) the auditory hemisphere

    E) Broca's area

Answer: C

Diff: 2   Page Ref: 89

Topic: How Does the Brain Produce Behavior and Mental Processes?

Skill: Applied

98) Some researchers suggest that individuals who suffer from schizophrenia may have a smaller _____ than other individuals, thus causing messages to be sent to incorrect areas of the brain potentially causing the idea of stimuli that are not really present.

  A) hypothalamus

  B) reticular formation

  C) pons

  D) thalamus

  E) hippocampus

Answer: D

Diff: 3   Page Ref: 89

Topic: How Does the Brain Produce Behavior and Mental Processes?

Skill: Conceptual

99) Which of the following structures is grouped into the brain stem, but is not actually part of the brain stem?

  A) reticular formation

  B) thalamus

  C) pons

  D) cerebellum

  E) medulla

Answer: D

Diff: 2   Page Ref: 89

Topic: How Does the Brain Produce Behavior and Mental Processes?

Skill: Factual

100) The _____ is important for the human ability to tap dance and walk on a tightrope.

  A) hypothalamus

  B) thalamus

  C) amygdala

  D) cerebellum

  E) hippocampus

Answer: D

Diff: 2   Page Ref: 89

Topic: How Does the Brain Produce Behavior and Mental Processes?

Skill: Applied

101) Research now suggests that which of the following brain stem functions plays a role in remembering sequential events, such as in a song?

A) cerebellum

B) thalamus

C) medulla

D) reticular formation

E) pons

Answer: A
Diff: 2   Page Ref: 89
Topic: How Does the Brain Produce Behavior and Mental Processes?
Skill: Recall

102) Which of the following animals would have a fully developed limbic system?

A) fish   B) elephant   C) duck   D) snake   E) bird

Answer: A
Diff: 2   Page Ref: 89
Topic: How Does the Brain Produce Behavior and Mental Processes?
Skill: Factual

103) Damage to the _____ would be expected to impair your ability to name three exciting news events that occurred after this damage to your brain.

A) hippocampus

B) reticular formation

C) corpus callosum

D) thalamus

E) hypothalamus

Answer: A
Diff: 3   Page Ref: 89–90
Topic: How Does the Brain Produce Behavior and Mental Processes?
Skill: Applied

104) A person who has has suffered damage to their hippocampus would be expected to have difficulty with

    A) remembering newer information.

    B) remembering events from his distant past.

    C) concentrating on complex tasks.

    D) controlling his temper.

    E) moving in a smooth manner.

Answer: A

Diff: 3   Page Ref: 89–90

Topic: How Does the Brain Produce Behavior and Mental Processes?

Skill: Applied

105) A stroke that damages parts of your amygdala would be expected to

    A) calm your angry disposition.

    B) stimulate an aggressive instinct.

    C) increase your sexual desire.

    D) erase important memories.

    E) make you feel hungry.

Answer: A

Diff: 3   Page Ref: 90

Topic: How Does the Brain Produce Behavior and Mental Processes?

Skill: Applied

106) Rhesus monkeys who had their _____ lesioned, changed from foul-tempered beings to docile creatures.

    A) hypothalamus

    B) hippocampus

    C) thalamus

    D) amygdala

    E) cerebellum

Answer: D

Diff: 3   Page Ref: 90

Topic: How Does the Brain Produce Behavior and Mental Processes?

Skill: Factual

107) Which of the following situations is NOT processed primarily by the limbic system?

    A) You remember how your grandmother's living room looked.

    B) You get angry and want to hit a person who has just bumped into you.

    C) You are feeling hungry because you have not eaten since yesterday.

    D) You are trying to reason through a logic problem in math class.

    E) You feel aroused by the good-looking person sitting next to you.

Answer: D
Diff: 3   Page Ref: 89–90
Topic: How Does the Brain Produce Behavior and Mental Processes?
Skill: Applied

108) The _____ is involved in the regulation of feeding, drinking, and sexual behavior.

    A) hippocampus

    B) amygdala

    C) hypothalamus

    D) thalamus

    E) medulla

Answer: C
Diff: 2   Page Ref: 91
Topic: How Does the Brain Produce Behavior and Mental Processes?
Skill: Factual

109) The _____ is that part of the limbic system that maintains homeostasis in body in terms of temperature, hunger and thirst.

    A) cerebellum

    B) reticular formation

    C) hypothalamus

    D) spinal cord

    E) hippocampus

Answer: C
Diff: 2   Page Ref: 91
Topic: How Does the Brain Produce Behavior and Mental Processes?
Skill: Factual

110) The limbic system contributes to the production of 'pleasure' in our brain. Which of the following neurotransmitters is linked to the activation of neural pathways that activate the limbic system?

    A) acetylcholine

    B) dopamine

    C) GABA

    D) norepinepherine

    E) adrenaline

Answer: B

Diff: 3   Page Ref: 91

Topic: How Does the Brain Produce Behavior and Mental Processes?

Skill: Applied

111) Place the following in the correct order regarding control of hormone production in the body.

    A) pituitary, hypothalamus, endocrine system

    B) endocrine system, pituitary, hypothalamus

    C) hypothalamus, endocrine system, pituitary

    D) hypothalamus, pituitary, endocrine system

    E) pituitary, endocrine system, hypothalamus

Answer: D

Diff: 3   Page Ref: 91

Topic: How Does the Brain Produce Behavior and Mental Processes?

Skill: Analysis

112) Which body structure was altered during the process of evolution which resulted in higher levels of cognitive functioning for humans?

    A) cerebrum

    B) cerebellum

    C) hypothalamus

    D) amygdala

    E) hippocampus

Answer: A

Diff: 2   Page Ref: 92

Topic: How Does the Brain Produce Behavior and Mental Processes?

Skill: Conceptual

113) The _____ controls functions such as reasoning, creating, and problem solving.
   A) brain stem
   B) cerebellum
   C) spinal cord
   D) cerebral cortex
   E) limbic system

Answer: D
Diff: 2   Page Ref: 92
Topic: How Does the Brain Produce Behavior and Mental Processes?
Skill: Factual

114) The _____ of the brain accounts for two-thirds of the brain's total mass.
   A) frontal lobes
   B) cerebrum
   C) corpus callosum
   D) limbic system
   E) brain stem

Answer: B
Diff: 2   Page Ref: 92
Topic: How Does the Brain Produce Behavior and Mental Processes?
Skill: Factual

115) _____ developed the concept of _____.
   A) B.F. Skinner; cerebral dominance
   B) Gustav Fritz; germ theory
   C) Wilder Penfield; cerebral dominance
   D) Franz Gall; localization of function
   E) Paul Broca; cortical processing styles

Answer: D
Diff: 3   Page Ref: 92
Topic: How Does the Brain Produce Behavior and Mental Processes?
Skill: Factual

116) The concept of phrenology suggested that

   A) the different hemispheres held different tasks.

   B) the brain had specific area that were responsible for certain functions, these were indicated by bumps on the skull.

   C) damage to the frontal lobe would create changes in personality.

   D) damage to the parietal lobe would create sensory changes.

   E) speech was held in our left hemisphere.

   Answer: B
   Diff: 2   Page Ref: 92
   Topic: How Does the Brain Produce Behavior and Mental Processes?
   Skill: Conceptual

117) German surgeons Fritsch and Hitzig, found that when they stimulated the exposed cortex on injured soldiers that the soldiers would occasionally move and arm or leg when a certain location was touched. Which are of the brain had Fritsch and Hitzig discovered?

   A) cerebellum

   B) somatosensory cortex

   C) motor cortex

   D) hippocampus

   E) Broca's area

   Answer: C
   Diff: 2   Page Ref: 92
   Topic: How Does the Brain Produce Behavior and Mental Processes?
   Skill: Factual

118) Damage to the _____ would impair our ability to plan and reason.

   A) autonomic nervous system

   B) cerebral cortex

   C) hypothalamus

   D) limbic system

   E) spinal cord

   Answer: B
   Diff: 2   Page Ref: 92
   Topic: How Does the Brain Produce Behavior and Mental Processes?
   Skill: Applied

119) Phineus Gage served as an example that an individual could experience extreme trauma to this area of their brain and live. However their personality would be drastically changed.

   A) central fissure

   B) frontal lobes

   C) lateral fissure

   D) parietal cortex

   E) temporal lobes

Answer: B

Diff: 2   Page Ref: 93

Topic: How Does the Brain Produce Behavior and Mental Processes?

Skill: Applied

120) The action of grabbing your keys with your right hand is controlled your

   A) right somatosensory cortex.

   B) left motor cortex.

   C) association cortex.

   D) frontal lobes.

   E) right motor cortex.

Answer: B

Diff: 2   Page Ref: 93

Topic: How Does the Brain Produce Behavior and Mental Processes?

Skill: Applied

121) You are holding an ice cube in your left hand. You touch it and find that it is hard and slick and cold. Soon the coldness becomes painful. Most of this information is processed by the _____, held in the _____ lobe.

   A) motor; frontal

   B) association; parietal

   C) somatosensory; parietal

   D) visual; occipital

   E) somatosensory; frontal

Answer: C

Diff: 3   Page Ref: 94

Topic: How Does the Brain Produce Behavior and Mental Processes?

Skill: Applied

122) The _____ would provide information about body position.

    A) motor cortex

    B) frontal lobe

    C) somatosensory cortex

    D) temporal lobe

    E) hippocampus

Answer: C

Diff: 2   Page Ref: 94

Topic: How Does the Brain Produce Behavior and Mental Processes?

Skill: Factual

123) Some boxers have permanent vision damage from their years of fighting, which of the lobes would incur damage to create this result?

    A) lateral   B) occipital   C) parietal   D) temporal   E) frontal

Answer: B

Diff: 2   Page Ref: 95

Topic: How Does the Brain Produce Behavior and Mental Processes?

Skill: Applied

124) Your temporal lobes are most important for processing of _____ signals.

    A) olfactory   B) visual   C) auditory   D) tactile   E) gustatory

Answer: C

Diff: 2   Page Ref: 95

Topic: How Does the Brain Produce Behavior and Mental Processes?

Skill: Factual

125) Some schizophrenics who claims to be experiencing auditory hallucinations have irregular activity where in their brain?

    A) temporal lobe

    B) occipital lobe

    C) frontal lobe

    D) parietal lobe

    E) association areas

Answer: A

Diff: 3   Page Ref: 95

Topic: How Does the Brain Produce Behavior and Mental Processes?

Skill: Applied

126) A task that is most likely coordinated by the Association Cortex is

    A) motor skills.

    B) speech production.

    C) decision making.

    D) sense of touch.

    E) emotions.

Answer: C

Diff: 2   Page Ref: 96

Topic: How Does the Brain Produce Behavior and Mental Processes?

Skill: Applied

127) _____ concluded that language production depended on the functioning of structures in a specific region of the left hemisphere.

    A) Rene Descartes

    B) Paul Broca

    C) Phineas Gage

    D) Charles Darwin

    E) Roger Sperry

Answer: B

Diff: 2   Page Ref: 96

Topic: How Does the Brain Produce Behavior and Mental Processes?

Skill: Factual

128) Spatial orientation appears to be a function of the brain's _____ hemisphere., while speech is located in _____ hemisphere.

    A) right; left

    B) left; right

    C) visual; frontal

    D) temporal; parietal

    E) central; left

Answer: A

Diff: 2   Page Ref: 97

Topic: How Does the Brain Produce Behavior and Mental Processes?

Skill: Factual

129) _____ refers to the tendency for each hemisphere of the brain to take control of different functions.

   A) Neurotransmission

   B) Homeostasis

   C) Cortical transmission

   D) Cerebral dominance

   E) Spatial orientation

Answer: D

Diff: 1   Page Ref: 97

Topic: How Does the Brain Produce Behavior and Mental Processes?

Skill: Factual

130) In most people, _____ of the brain is(are) most involved in visual–spatial activities.

   A) the right side

   B) the left side

   C) neither side

   D) the lower surface

   E) rear aspect

Answer: A

Diff: 2   Page Ref: 98

Topic: How Does the Brain Produce Behavior and Mental Processes?

Skill: Factual

131) The _____ interconnects the two hemispheres of the cerebrum.

   A) cerebellum

   B) limbic system

   C) cerebral cortex

   D) corpus callosum

   E) pituitary

Answer: D

Diff: 2   Page Ref: 98

Topic: How Does the Brain Produce Behavior and Mental Processes?

Skill: Factual

132) A surgical procedure that attempts to prevent violent electrical rhythms from crossing from one hemisphere to another involves

    A) stimulating the cerebellum.

    B) rearranging the cerebrum.

    C) inactivating the cerebral cortex.

    D) severing the corpus callosum.

    E) stimulating the hypothalamus.

Answer: D
Diff: 2   *Page Ref: 98*
Topic: How Does the Brain Produce Behavior and Mental Processes?
Skill: Applied

133) Sperry and Gazzaniga found in their research on split-brained patients, that when patients were presented with a spoon to their right field of vision, they could

    A) identify it spatially but not say what it was.

    B) say what is was but not identify it spatially.

    C) had no problems identifying it spatially or naming it.

    D) pick it up, but not name it.

    E) neither name it or locate it spatially.

Answer: B
Diff: 3   *Page Ref: 99*
Topic: How Does the Brain Produce Behavior and Mental Processes?
Skill: Applied

Check Your Understanding Questions

1) Which of the following processes are involved in natural selection, the driving force behind evolution?

    A) Individuals best adapted to the environment have a survival advantage.

    B) Some individuals reproduce more successfully than others.

    C) The offspring of some individuals survive in greater numbers than do those of others.

    D) Individuals that are poorly adapted tend to have fewer offspring.

    E) Al l are correct

Answer: E
Diff: 2   *Page Ref: 64–65*
Topic: Check Your Understanding
Skill: Recall

2) Which of the following is a characteristic that might be a part of your phenotype?

    A) your height and eye color

    B) the members of your family

    C) what you have learned in school

    D) the childhood diseases you have had

    E) your genetic makeup

Answer: A

Diff: 2   Page Ref: 66

Topic: Check Your Understanding

Skill: Factual

3) Which of the following statements expresses the correct relationship?

    A) Genes are made of chromosomes.

    B) DNA is made of chromosomes.

    C) Nucleotides are made of genes.

    D) Genes are made of DNA.

    E) Phenotype dictates genotype.

Answer: D

Diff: 3   Page Ref: 66–67

Topic: Check Your Understanding

Skill: Recall

4) In purely evolutionary terms, which one would be a measure of your own success as an organism?

    A) your intellectual accomplishments

    B) the length of your life

    C) the number of children you have

    D) the contributions that you make to the happiness of humanity

    E) your ability to find food and water

Answer: C

Diff: 3   Page Ref: 64

Topic: Check Your Understanding

Skill: Analysis

5) All of the following are examples of evolution except
    A) finches with larger beaks for catching fish are likely to have offspring with similar characteristics.
    B) giraffes with longer necks have a greater chance of procreating because they can reach higher branches of trees.
    C) reptiles who are better able to blend into their environment are more likely to live longer by eluding prey and thus able to reproduce.
    D) humans who are more intelligent will always be able to reproduce more than others.
    E) All of the above are examples of evolution

Answer: D
Diff: 3   Page Ref: 64–65
Topic: Check Your Understanding
Skill: Applied

6) Which of the following statements is true?
    A) Our genes always influence our environment.
    B) The environment will always influence how our genes display themselves.
    C) According to an evolutionary psychologist, nurture is mor important that nature.
    D) The is no way for parents to select the gender of their future child.
    E) Humans have evolved from monkeys.

Answer: B
Diff: 2   Page Ref: 63–64
Topic: Check Your Understanding
Skill: Understanding the Core Concept

7) Which of the following might carry a neural message across the synapse?
    A) an electrical charge
    B) dopamine
    C) the blood
    D) the cerebrospinal fluid
    E) an axon

Answer: B
Diff: 2   Page Ref: 74
Topic: Check Your Understanding
Skill: Recall

8) Which part of the brain communicates directly with the "master gland" of the endocrine system?

A) the cortex

B) the brainstem

C) the cerebellum

D) the hypothalamus

E) the pituitary

Answer: D

Diff: 2   Page Ref: 82

Topic: Check Your Understanding

Skill: Recall

9) As you are sleeping, the fire alarm in your house goes off, immediate you are wide awake an helping your family to escape from your house. Which part of the nervous system produces this response?

A) the somatic nervous system

B) the sympathetic nervous system

C) the parasympathetic nervous system

D) the spinal cord

E) the midbrain

Answer: B

Diff: 2   Page Ref: 79

Topic: Check Your Understanding

Skill: Applied

10) Select the parts of neural transmission that are presented in the correct order.

A) soma, dendrites, axon, neurotransmitters, terminal buttons

B) dendrites, soma, axon, terminal buttons, neurotransmitters

C) axon, soma, dendrites, terminal buttons, neurotransmitters

D) terminal buttons, dendrites, soma, axon, neurotransmitters

E) dendrites, axon, soma, terminal buttons, neurotransmitters

Answer: B

Diff: 2   Page Ref: 74

Topic: Check Your Understanding

Skill: Factual

11) Select in order the types of neurons that will transmit a message from it's inception through your response.

    A) motor, inter, sensory

    B) inter, motor, sensory

    C) sensory, motor, inter

    D) sensory, inter, motor

    E) motor, sensory, inter

Answer: D
Diff: 2   *Page Ref: 72-73*
Topic: Check Your Understanding
Skill: Recall

12) Which technique for studying the brain relies on the brain's electrical activity?

    A) EEG   B) MRI   C) PET   D) CT   E) X-Ray

Answer: A
Diff: 2   *Page Ref: 85*
Topic: Check Your Understanding
Skill: Recall

13) A brain tumor in the limbic system is most likely to produce changes in a person's

    A) coordination.

    B) vision.

    C) sleep patterns.

    D) emotions.

    E) hearing.

Answer: D
Diff: 2   *Page Ref: 89-90*
Topic: Check Your Understanding
Skill: Recall

14) In the split-brain operation, what part of the brain is severed?

    A) the left hemisphere

    B) the right hemisphere

    C) the corpus callosum

    D) the occipital lobe

    E) the parietal lobe

Answer: C
Diff: 2   *Page Ref: 98*
Topic: Check Your Understanding
Skill: Recall

15) Which of the following according to an Evolutionary Psychologist is the oldest to newest portion of the brain in the correct order?

    A) limbic system, cerebral cortex, brain stem

    B) brain stem, cerebral cortex, limbic system

    C) brain stem, limbic system, cerebral cortex

    D) cerebral cortex, limbic system, brain stem

    E) limbic system, brain stem, cerebral cortex

Answer: C
Diff: 2   *Page Ref: 87–94*
Topic: Check Your Understanding
Skill: Applied

True/False Questions

1) We are born with all of the nerve cells that we will ever have.

Answer: FALSE
Diff: 2   *Page Ref: 63*
Topic: Biopsychology and the Foundations of Neuroscience
Skill: Factual

2) The newly devised science of genetics was the basis that allowed Darwin to propose the concept of natural selection.

Answer: FALSE
Diff: 3   *Page Ref: 64*
Topic: How Are Genes And Behavior Linked?
Skill: Conceptual

3) Neuroscience allows us to study the brain's role in physiological responses.

Answer: TRUE
Diff: 1   *Page Ref: 63*
Topic: How Are Genes And Behavior Linked?
Skill: Factual

4) Darwin suggested that humans evolved from apes.

Answer: FALSE
Diff: 1   *Page Ref: 64–65*
Topic: How Are Genes And Behavior Linked?
Skill: Factual

5) Natural selection suggests that those who are most well suited to their environment will be the most likely to pass their genes onto the next generation.

Answer: TRUE
Diff: 2   Page Ref: 65
Topic: How Are Genes And Behavior Linked?
Skill: Factual

6) One's genotype relates to the physical characteristics one displays, while one's genotype relates to one's genetic makeup.

Answer: FALSE
Diff: 2   Page Ref: 66
Topic: How Are Genes And Behavior Linked?
Skill: Recall

7) Our genes contain the instructions that control the expression of our phenotypic traits.

Answer: TRUE
Diff: 2   Page Ref: 66
Topic: How Are Genes And Behavior Linked?
Skill: Factual

8) Disease, stress, and nutrition can alter a person's phenotype.

Answer: TRUE
Diff: 2   Page Ref: 66
Topic: How Are Genes And Behavior Linked?
Skill: Conceptual

9) The complete genetic code for an individual is contained in the nucleus of every cell in an organism's body.

Answer: TRUE
Diff: 2   Page Ref: 67
Topic: How Are Genes And Behavior Linked?
Skill: Factual

10) Each persons genes contain 46 chromosomes organized into 23 pairs.

Answer: TRUE
Diff: 2   Page Ref: 68
Topic: How Are Genes And Behavior Linked?
Skill: Factual

11) At this point in time it is impossible for future parents to select the gender of their child.

Answer: FALSE
Diff: 2   *Page Ref: 69*
Topic: How Are Genes And Behavior Linked?
Skill: Recall

12) Afferent neurons carry sensory messages to the brain and spinal cord.

Answer: TRUE
Diff: 2   *Page Ref: 72*
Topic: How Does the Body Communicate Internally?
Skill: Factual

13) Interneurons determine whether or not a given impulse is reflexive or whether it must be sent to the brain for further analysis.

Answer: TRUE
Diff: 3   *Page Ref: 73*
Topic: How Does the Body Communicate Internally?
Skill: Conceptual

14) Neurotransmitters are held on the receptor sites on dendrites until an action potential is sent.

Answer: FALSE
Diff: 2   *Page Ref: 74*
Topic: How Does the Body Communicate Internally?
Skill: Factual

15) The action potential in a neuron involves the rush of negative ions to the inside of the axon.

Answer: FALSE
Diff: 3   *Page Ref: 74*
Topic: How Does the Body Communicate Internally?
Skill: Factual

16) Messages that are sent through neurons are electrical while message sent between neurons are chemical.

Answer: TRUE
Diff: 2   *Page Ref: 74-75*
Topic: How Does the Body Communicate Internally?
Skill: Factual

17) Glial cells are believed to play a role in learning.

Answer: TRUE
Diff: 2   Page Ref: 77
Topic: How Does the Body Communicate Internally?
Skill: Conceptual

18) The peripheral nervous system relays information directly from the outside world to the brain.

Answer: TRUE
Diff: 2   Page Ref: 78
Topic: How Does the Body Communicate Internally?
Skill: Factual

19) The peripheral nervous system is composed of all the neurons in the brain and spinal cord.

Answer: FALSE
Diff: 1   Page Ref: 78
Topic: How Does the Body Communicate Internally?
Skill: Factual

20) The endocrine system works more slowly than does the nervous system.

Answer: TRUE
Diff: 1   Page Ref: 71
Topic: How Does the Body Communicate Internally?
Skill: Factual

21) When you attempt to dance you are using your somatic nervous system.

Answer: TRUE
Diff: 1   Page Ref: 79
Topic: How Does the Body Communicate Internally?
Skill: Applied

22) The pituitary gland can either stimulate or inhibit the release of hormones from a gland.

Answer: TRUE
Diff: 2   Page Ref: 82
Topic: How Does the Body Communicate Internally?
Skill: Factual

23) The EEG process reveals whether brain cells are functioning normally by scanning their response to pulses of magnetic energy.

Answer: FALSE
Diff: 2   Page Ref: 85
Topic: How Does the Brain Produce Behavior and Mental Processes?
Skill: Factual

24) The FMRI provides the most detailed image of the brain by examining cells response to a high–intensity magnetic field.

Answer: TRUE
Diff: 2   Page Ref: 86
Topic: How Does the Brain Produce Behavior and Mental Processes?
Skill: Factual

25) The limbic system was the first brain layer to develop during human evolution.

Answer: FALSE
Diff: 2   Page Ref: 87
Topic: How Does the Brain Produce Behavior and Mental Processes?
Skill: Conceptual

26) The medulla is responsible for sleeping and dreaming.

Answer: FALSE
Diff: 2   Page Ref: 88
Topic: How Does the Brain Produce Behavior and Mental Processes?
Skill: Factual

27) A person whose hippocampus was removed in 1966 would be surprised to be told that george W. Bush is President of the United States.

Answer: TRUE
Diff: 3   Page Ref: 89–90
Topic: How Does the Brain Produce Behavior and Mental Processes?
Skill: Applied

28) Surgical removal of the amygdala will increase aggression in humans.

Answer: FALSE
Diff: 2   Page Ref: 90
Topic: How Does the Brain Produce Behavior and Mental Processes?
Skill: Factual

29) When rats had the opportunity to activate 'pleasure centers' in the brain, they would even endure painful shocks in order to gain the feelings of 'pleasure'.

Answer: FALSE
Diff: 2   Page Ref: 91
Topic: How Does the Brain Produce Behavior and Mental Processes?
Skill: Factual

30) The pituitary gland controls the hypothalamus.

Answer: FALSE
Diff: 2   Page Ref: 91
Topic: How Does the Brain Produce Behavior and Mental Processes?
Skill: Factual

31) Localization of function asserts that different functions are controlled by different brain regions.

Answer: TRUE
Diff: 2   Page Ref: 92
Topic: How Does the Brain Produce Behavior and Mental Processes?
Skill: Conceptual

32) The motor cortex is found in the parietal lobe.

Answer: FALSE
Diff: 2   Page Ref: 93
Topic: How Does the Brain Produce Behavior and Mental Processes?
Skill: Factual

33) The parietal lobe processes incoming sensory information related to temperature.

Answer: TRUE
Diff: 2   Page Ref: 94
Topic: How Does the Brain Produce Behavior and Mental Processes?
Skill: Factual

34) When you are humming a song in your head, you are activating your temporal lobe.

Answer: TRUE
Diff: 2   Page Ref: 95
Topic: How Does the Brain Produce Behavior and Mental Processes?
Skill: Applied

35) The Association Cortex connects the two hemispheres.

Answer: FALSE
Diff: 2   Page Ref: 96
Topic: How Does the Brain Produce Behavior and Mental Processes?
Skill: Factual

36) For most people, the motor speech area lies only in the right hemisphere.

Answer: FALSE
Diff: 2   Page Ref: 98
Topic: How Does the Brain Produce Behavior and Mental Processes?
Skill: Factual

37) The right cerebral hemisphere is important t for musical ability.

Answer: TRUE
Diff: 2   Page Ref: 98
Topic: How Does the Brain Produce Behavior and Mental Processes?
Skill: Factual

38) Severing of the corpus callosum is intended to reduce the severity of epilepsy.

Answer: TRUE
Diff: 2   Page Ref: 98–99
Topic: How Does the Brain Produce Behavior and Mental Processes?
Skill: Factual

Short-Answer Questions

1) Which specialty aims to explain how the nervous system and the endocrine system cooperate to produce all human action and the field that focuses on the brain and it's role in psychological processes?

Answer: Biopsychology and Neuroscience
Diff: 1   Page Ref: 63
Topic: Biopsychology and the Foundations of Neuroscience
Skill: Conceptual

2) Briefly explain the theory behind Natural Selection.

Answer: Natural selection contends that some members of a species tend to produce more offspring than others because the natural environmental conditions are more conducive to that species.
Diff: 2   Page Ref: 65
Topic: How Are Genes And Behavior Linked?
Skill: Conceptual

3) Briefly explain how genotype and phenotype affect each of us.

Answer: Genotype describes an organism's genetic makeup while phenotype describes an organism's physical characteristics.

Diff: 2   Page Ref: 66

Topic: How Are Genes And Behavior Linked?

Skill: Conceptual

4) Explain how our parents influence our chromosomes and how chromosomes organize themselves.

Answer: Our 46 chromosomes are arranged in 23 pairs. One in each pair is contributed by each of your parents.

Diff: 2   Page Ref: 68

Topic: How Are Genes And Behavior Linked?

Skill: Factual

5) Describe the process of synaptic transmission.

Answer: Action potentials cause a formerly negatively charged ion to become positive. When the message arrives at the axon terminal, it releases neurotransmitters into the cleft; which in turn activate receptors on the adjacent neuron if it fits like a lock and key.

Diff: 2   Page Ref: 74

Topic: How Does the Body Communicate Internally?

Skill: Factual

6) Provide examples of four different types of neurotransmitters and briefly explain their responsibilities.

Answer: Dopamine is responsible for producing sensations of pleasure. serotonin is responsible in regulating sleep, mood and pain. Norepinephrine is used by the autonomic nervous system. Acetylcholine is responsible for learning and memory.

Diff: 2   Page Ref: 76

Topic: How Does the Body Communicate Internally?

Skill: Factual

7) Briefly explain how the sympathetic and parasympathetic nervous systems work together to help us respond the events appropriately.

Answer: The parasympathetic nervous system is in use for normal days activities, if an emergency arises the sympathetic nervous system kicks into gear to prepare for the emergency response. When the emergency has passed, the parasympathetic nervous system again brings the body back to a normally functioning state.

Diff: 2   Page Ref: 79

Topic: How Does the Body Communicate Internally?

Skill: Applied

8) List the structures found in a neuron and the order in which a response will experience each.

Answer: dendrites, cell body, axon/myelin sheath, terminal buttons, neurotransmitters
Diff: 2   Page Ref: 74
Topic: How Does the Body Communicate Internally?
Skill: Factual

9) Jimmy has recently dissected a turtle in biology and is fascinated with the animal's brain. Jimmy is trying to determine how his own brain might be similar and different than the turtles. Using the three layers described by the text (brain stem, limbic system and cerebral cortex) explain which parts would be the same and which parts different.

Answer: Brain stem, since this area provides basic functioning of the brain it would look essentially the same. The limbic system would be different since only mammals have fully developed limbic systems. Finally the cerebral cortex would be different as humans have much more surface area allowing for more folds and thus more neural networks to aid in higher order thinking.
Diff: 3   Page Ref: 87–94
Topic: How Does the Brain Produce Behavior and Mental Processes?
Skill: Analysis

10) Provide two examples of the specialization of the right and left hemispheres respectively.

Answer: The left hemisphere controls language and memory for words and numbers, the right hemisphere controls memory for shapes and music and the recognition of faces.
Diff: 2   Page Ref: 98
Topic: How Does the Brain Produce Behavior and Mental Processes?
Skill: Factual

11) Briefly explain the difference between a EEG and a MRI and and advantage and disadvantage to using each.

Answer: EEG records brain waves, is not very detailed in terms of the picture of the brain because only a few dozen electrodes are placed on the scalp, but it works well for recording abnormalities in brain waves especially in diseases such as epilepsy. The MRI uses highly powerful electronic energy to determine where there is high activity in the brain. his provides a much better picture and allows researchers to see brain structure, but it cannot record very quick responses such as the startle response.
Diff: 2   Page Ref: 85–86
Topic: How Does the Brain Produce Behavior and Mental Processes?
Skill: Applied

12) Ricky's baseball team is not having a very good season. In their last game, they had a number of errors that resulted in some major injuries for the team. There was a collision between the first base man and a runner that resulted in the first base man "seeing stars" and the runner not being able to walk in a straight line. Later in the inning, the right fielder lept for a ball, but instead landed on his head, he has temporarily lost his hearing ability. The coach fed up with all of the nonsense fell asleep on the bench. For the following individuals name the area of the brain that is either damaged or that is regulating the current behavior of the individual.
first base man
runner
right fielder
coach

Answer: first base man: occipital lobe
runner: cerebellum
right fielder: temporal lobe
coach: pons

Diff: 3   *Page Ref: 87–94*

Topic: How Does the Brain Produce Behavior and Mental Processes?

Skill: Factual

Essay Questions

1) How does Down syndrome occur and what are the repercussions of the disorder?

Answer: It is caused by an extra 21st chromosome fragment. The disorder involves impairment in both psychomotor and physical development, as well as mental retardation. Currently, there is no cure for Down syndrome. Persons with Down syndrome are capable of considerable learning if given life skills training.

Diff: 2   *Page Ref: 69*

Topic: How Are Genes And Behavior Linked?

Skill: Applied

2) Explain how Darwin's theory of natural selection can relate to humans.

Answer: Humans just like animals are more likely to pass on genes that are most well adapted to their environment. Organs such a s our appendix and gallbladder have come to be essentially useless. e have become gradually taller and those who are more well adjusted are more likely to have offspring who will share those same strong characteristics.

Diff: 2   *Page Ref: 64*

Topic: How Are Genes And Behavior Linked?

Skill: Applied

3) Explain the influence that parents have on their children's genetic makeup and how nature and nurture relate to genotype and phenotype.

Answer: Each child will have 46 chromosomes arranged into 23 pairs. For each of these pairs, the mother and father will each contribute one chromosome. Two of these chromosomes are the sex chromosomes, in these, the mother will contribute a X chromosome and the father will contribute either a X (female) or a Y (male) to determine the gender of the child. Even though we inherit our genes from our parents our genetic makeup as represented by our genotype can be influenced by our environment. Our genes may display themselves in different ways based on their interaction with the environment especially very early in life. Thus our physical display of our genetic makeup (phenotype) is malleable and can be modified, thus creating a constant interaction between nature and nurture.

Diff: 3   Page Ref: 66–68

Topic: How Are Genes And Behavior Linked?

Skill: Applied

4) Briefly discuss five different neurotransmitters as well as the effect that too much or too little of that neurotransmitter may cause on the body.

Answer: Dopamine produces sensation of pleasure and rewards too much may result in schizophrenia and too little may result in Parkinson's. serotonin regulate sleep, mood and pain too little may result in depression while too much may result in anxiety disorders such as OCD. Acetylcholine plays a role in learning and memory. Too little may result in Alzheimer's disease. Endorphins reduce pain and promote pleasure. lower levels may result from opiate addictions.

Diff: 3   Page Ref: 76

Topic: How Does the Body Communicate Internally?

Skill: Conceptual

5) Explain how the nervous system is broken down into subdivisions and the function of each.

Answer: The nervous system is broken down into the central nervous system which is made up of the brain and spinal cord. The brain can be further broken down into the hindbrain, midbrain and forebrain. The other portion of the nervous system is the peripheral nervous system, which carries messages to and from the central nervous system. The peripheral nervous system can be broken down into the autonomic nervous system which is responsible for involuntary activities. The next portion of the peripheral nervous system in the somatic nervous system which controls the skeletal muscles or voluntary activities.The autonomic nervous system can then be broken down into the sympathetic nervous system which prepares the body for an emergency situation and the parasympathetic nervous system which brings the body back to normal.

Diff: 2   Page Ref: 78

Topic: How Does the Body Communicate Internally?

Skill: Applied

6) Explain how an action potential influences a neuron. Be sure to include the different portions of the neuron the message must pass through and how ions and neurotransmitters play a role in neural transmissions.

Answer: Dendrites pick up the message from the initial stimulus, it then passes the message onto the soma (cell body) which determines if the impulse has reached the threshold. If it has reached the threshold, the neuron will completely fire. The action potential causes the positive charges held on the outside of the axon to rush inside on the axon, thus pushing the message down the axon. When reaching the end of the axon (axon terminals), the neurotransmitters are released into the synapse. These will fit like a lock and key and carry the message to the next neuron.

Diff: 2   Page Ref: 74

Topic: How Does the Body Communicate Internally?

Skill: Analysis

7) Explain how psychoactive drugs work in brain and explain why each drug has important side effects.

Answer: Psychoactive drugs generally interact with neuron signalling pathways. Such drugs can increase the release of transmitter molecules into the cleft or can block transmitter reuptake (both of which will increase the synaptic transmitter level). A second mechanism involves the drug directly activating/inactivating postsynaptic receptors. Because a single transmitter may be used in multiple brain pathways, a drug that passes throughout the brain may generate multiple behavioral effects.

Diff: 2   Page Ref: 57

Topic: How Does the Body Communicate Internally?

Skill: Conceptual

8) Dr. Lee has been given the task of creating an artificial being that is as human like as possible. Unfortunately, his university is severely under funded. He will still need to create his "creature" but the being will not be able to have all of his brain parts as this is the most expensive portion of the project. Help Dr. Lee in making his decision regarding what parts of the brain to leave out by discussing in which of the three layers of the following structures are located and the function of each.
Pons
Cerebellum
Hypothalamus
Parietal lobe
thalamus
Hippocampus

Answer: The pons, thalamus and cerebellum are located in the brain stem. The pons are responsible for sleep and dreaming and the cerebellum is responsible for posture and balance, the thalamus is responsible for motoring the incoming sensory messages and outgoing motor messages. it serves as the "traffic officer" of the brain. The hypothalamus and the hippocampus are part of the limbic system. The hypothalamus plays a role in motivation and is responsible for basic biological needs such as hunger and thirst. The hippocampus plays a role in encoding new memories. The Parietal Lobe is part of the cerebral cortex and is important for sensory information such as temperature, body position and sense of touch.

Diff: 3   *Page Ref: 87–91*

Topic: How Does the Brain Produce Behavior and Mental Processes?

Skill: Applied

9) Discuss the phenomenon of cerebral dominance and contrast the specialized functions of each of the two cerebral hemispheres.

Answer: The student should note that although the two hemispheres (halves) of the brain appear to be mirror–images, each has specialized functions. For example, vocabulary, memory for words and numbers, anxiety and emotion, and movement sequences are mainly controlled by the left hemisphere. Conversely, the right hemisphere controls such tasks as facial recognition, music and shape memory, and emotional responsiveness.

Diff: 2   *Page Ref: 96–101*

Topic: How Does the Brain Produce Behavior and Mental Processes?

Skill: Conceptual

Chapter 4 Sensation and Perception

Multiple Choice Questions

1) Jonathan I. developed _____ after sustaining brain injury.
   A) loss of hearing
   B) cerebral achromatsopia
   C) an inability to write words
   D) a change in personality
   E) phantom pains

   Answer: B
   Diff: 3   Page Ref: 109
   Topic: How Does Stimulation Become Sensation?
   Skill: Factual

2) Which of the following was NOT an adaptation that Jonathan I. was able to make following his unique visual loss?
   A) He became a night person.
   B) He reinterpreted his loss as a gift.
   C) He began painting in black and white.
   D) He used more vivid colors in his paintings.
   E) He began sculpting.

   Answer: D
   Diff: 3   Page Ref: 109–110
   Topic: How Does Stimulation Become Sensation?
   Skill: Factual

3) The case of Jonathan I. dramatically illustrates the fact that
   A) loss of color vision always accompanies amnesia.
   B) the world of color is not just a construction of the sensory and perceptual processes of the brain.
   C) colors do not objectively exist "out there" in objects.
   D) loss of color vision leads to persistent depression.
   E) loss of color vision is usually a temporary condition.

   Answer: C
   Diff: 2   Page Ref: 109–110
   Topic: How Does Stimulation Become Sensation?
   Skill: Conceptual

4) Jonathon eventually began to see his cerebral achromatopsia as a gift. Jonathon noticed that he benefitted from all of the following except

  A) he could read license plates from four blocks away.

  B) the ability to distinguish between very close colors of red.

  C) he was no longer 'distracted' by colors.

  D) he was better able to focus on shape and form.

  E) he was better able to focus on content.

Answer: B
Diff: 3   Page Ref: 110
Topic: How Does Stimulation Become Sensation?
Skill: Recall

5) The process by which sensory receptors produce neural impulses which are then sent to the brain.

  A) transduction

  B) perception

  C) photoreception

  D) sensation

  E) olfaction

Answer: D
Diff: 1   Page Ref: 110
Topic: How Does Stimulation Become Sensation?
Skill: Factual

6) Through the process of _____, we are able to interpret incoming sensory patterns.

  A) sensation

  B) kinesthesias

  C) transduction

  D) gustation

  E) perception

Answer: E
Diff: 1   Page Ref: 111
Topic: How Does Stimulation Become Sensation?
Skill: Conceptual

7) _____ is heavily influenced by an individual's expectations.
    A) Perception
    B) Neural networks
    C) Sensation
    D) Transduction
    E) Sensory receptors

Answer: A
Diff: 1   Page Ref: 111
Topic: How Does Stimulation Become Sensation?
Skill: Conceptual

8) Seeing a face is to sensation as recognizing a friend's face is to _____.
    A) kinesthesia
    B) olfaction
    C) transduction
    D) sensation
    E) perception

Answer: E
Diff: 2   Page Ref: 111
Topic: How Does Stimulation Become Sensation?
Skill: Applied

9) Tasting a carrot is _____ remembering that you hate the taste of carrots is _____.
    A) sensation; sensation
    B) perception; perception
    C) sensation; perception
    D) perception; sensation
    E) None of the above

Answer: C
Diff: 2   Page Ref: 111
Topic: How Does Stimulation Become Sensation?
Skill: Applied

10) Neurons cannot

    A) convert an external stimulus into a nerve impulse.

    B) carry information to the cerebral cortex.

    C) transmit light or sound waves directly to the brain.

    D) transform stimuli into diverse sensations.

    E) code sensory information.

Answer: C

Diff: 3   Page Ref: 111

Topic: How Does Stimulation Become Sensation?

Skill: Conceptual

11) When considering how a message travels from it's inception to it's evaluation, select which of the following places the processes involved in the correct order.

    A) transduction–stimulation–sensation–perception

    B) stimulation–sensation–transduction–perception

    C) stimulation–transduction–sensation–perception

    D) stimulation–sensation–perception–transduction

    E) sensation–stimulation–transduction–perception

Answer: C

Diff: 3   Page Ref: 112

Topic: How Does Stimulation Become Sensation?

Skill: Analysis

12) In the visual system, how far does light travel from an external stimulus before it is converted to a neural message.

    A) the optic nerve

    B) the lens

    C) the back of the eye

    D) the occipital lobe

    E) the visual cortex

Answer: C

Diff: 3   Page Ref: 112

Topic: How Does Stimulation Become Sensation?

Skill: Factual

13) The process of _____ is responsible for the conversion of physical energy to neural impulses.

    A) transduction

    B) plasticity

    C) absolute threshold

    D) psychophysics

    E) adaptation

Answer: A

Diff: 2   Page Ref: 112

Topic: How Does Stimulation Become Sensation?

Skill: Conceptual

14) Phosphenes are

    A) visual images caused by stimulating the visual system with a small amount of pressure.

    B) odors that spontaneously occur with no known source.

    C) cells that connect the rods and cones to the optic nerve.

    D) the sense of pressure, temperature and other sensory information when none is actually present.

    E) different types of taste receptors.

Answer: A

Diff: 3   Page Ref: 113

Topic: How Does Stimulation Become Sensation?

Skill: Factual

15) Nerve impulses that carry information travel along _____ to specialized processing areas in the brain.

    A) vestibular canals

    B) nerve endings

    C) sensory pathways

    D) olfactory epithelium

    E) photoreceptors

Answer: C

Diff: 2   Page Ref: 113

Topic: How Does Stimulation Become Sensation?

Skill: Factual

16) Our sensory receptors play a key role in detecting _____ in the external world.

   A) comparisons

   B) similarities

   C) adaptations

   D) changes

   E) receptors

Answer: D

Diff: 1   *Page Ref: 113*

Topic: How Does Stimulation Become Sensation?

Skill: Recall

17) Robbie is has been sitting in a hot tub for 30 minutes. He emerges and immediately jumps into the nearby pool. Robbie screams because he feels that the pool water is freezing. What phenomena has caused Robbie's surprise?

   A) sensory overload

   B) sensory adaptation

   C) sensory deprivation

   D) transduction

   E) absolute thresholds

Answer: B

Diff: 2   *Page Ref: 113*

Topic: How Does Stimulation Become Sensation?

Skill: Applied

18) _____ refers to the loss of responsiveness in receptor cells due to constant stimulation.

   A) Absolute threshold

   B) Sensory adaptation

   C) Signal detection

   D) Weber's law

   E) Equilibrium

Answer: B

Diff: 2   *Page Ref: 113*

Topic: How Does Stimulation Become Sensation?

Skill: Conceptual

19) The fact that the great smell of baked goods is more powerful when you first enter a bakery than when you have been there for awhile is because of

   A) sensory adaption.

   B) the just noticeable difference.

   C) Weber's law.

   D) closure.

   E) subliminal messaging.

   Answer: A

   Diff: 2   *Page Ref: 113*

   Topic: How Does Stimulation Become Sensation?

   Skill: Applied

20) The _____ refers to the smallest amount of physical energy needed to produce a sensory experience.

   A) difference threshold

   B) signal detection

   C) absolute threshold

   D) equilibrium constant

   E) transduction threshold

   Answer: C

   Diff: 2   *Page Ref: 114*

   Topic: How Does Stimulation Become Sensation?

   Skill: Recall

21) Elana can hear the radio even at a much lower setting than her mother. At a given setting Elana can detect that there is music playing about half of the time. At the same setting, her mother cannot hear anything. Elana could be said to have a _____, _____ than he mother.

   A) higher; absolute threshold

   B) higher; difference threshold

   C) lower; absolute threshold

   D) lower; difference threshold

   E) lower; just noticeable difference

   Answer: C

   Diff: 3   *Page Ref: 114*

   Topic: How Does Stimulation Become Sensation?

   Skill: Applied

22) If you are able to taste one teaspoon of salt in a bucketful of hot buttered popcorn, this amount is above your

A) difference threshold.

B) equilibrium.

C) vestibular sense.

D) olfaction.

E) absolute threshold.

Answer: E

Diff: 2   Page Ref: 114

Topic: How Does Stimulation Become Sensation?

Skill: Applied

23) A(n) _____ refers to the smallest change in physical energy between two stimuli that is recognized as different.

A) a difference threshold

B) an absolute threshold

C) signal detection

D) sensorimotor threshold

E) supraliminal threshold

Answer: A

Diff: 2   Page Ref: 114

Topic: How Does Stimulation Become Sensation?

Skill: Applied

24) Weber's law states that _____ are a function of the initial stimulus intensity.

A) absolute thresholds

B) signal detection

C) difference thresholds

D) false alarms

E) sensorimotor thresholds

Answer: C

Diff: 2   Page Ref: 115

Topic: How Does Stimulation Become Sensation?

Skill: Conceptual

25) Benji often lifts weights, if he lifts a ten pound weight he has to add two pounds to the weight to detect the difference. According to Weber's Law, what would Benji have to add to the weight to detect the difference if he was lifting 100 pounds of weight?

    A) 20 pounds   B) 8 pounds   C) 12 pounds   D) 14 pounds   E) 18 pounds

Answer: A
Diff: 3   Page Ref: 115
Topic: How Does Stimulation Become Sensation?
Skill: Applied

26) Annie is working on a new perfume. her perfume has hints of lavender and rose. She has just added some more lavender, there is just enough for her to detect the change. This is an example of a

    A) Fechner's Law.

    B) absolute threshold.

    C) just noticeable difference.

    D) sensory receptors.

    E) transduction.

Answer: C
Diff: 3   Page Ref: 115
Topic: How Does Stimulation Become Sensation?
Skill: Applied

27) Susan is listening to the radio, she notices that when she initially turned on the radio and changed the volume only slightly she noticed a large difference. Now, the music is louder and if she changes the radio by the same amount as she originally did, she can hardly detect the change at all. What phenomena best explains what Susan is currently experiencing?

    A) Weber's Law

    B) Fechner's law

    C) Absolute Threshold

    D) Difference Threshold

    E) Just Noticeable Difference

Answer: B
Diff: 3   Page Ref: 115
Topic: How Does Stimulation Become Sensation?
Skill: Applied

28) Weber's law states that the higher the intensity of the stimulus, the _____ it will have to be _____ to result in a noticeable difference in sensory experience.

   A) more; changed
   B) less; reduced
   C) less; increased
   D) faster; reduced
   E) faster; removed

   Answer: A
   Diff: 3   Page Ref: 115
   Topic: How Does Stimulation Become Sensation?
   Skill: Conceptual

29) This explains when we are likely to detect weak signals.

   A) absolute threshold
   B) signal detection theory
   C) difference threshold
   D) Weber's law
   E) just noticeable difference

   Answer: B
   Diff: 2   Page Ref: 116
   Topic: How Does Stimulation Become Sensation?
   Skill: Factual

30) The principle that predict when parents of newborn's hear their children crying but siblings sleep through the night.

   A) absolute threshold
   B) Weber's law
   C) sensory adaptation
   D) signal detection theory
   E) difference threshold

   Answer: D
   Diff: 3   Page Ref: 116
   Topic: How Does Stimulation Become Sensation?
   Skill: Applied

31) Signal detection theory suggests that differences in absolute thresholds between different people reflect

    A) signal strength.

    B) sensory processes.

    C) human judgment.

    D) absolute thresholds.

    E) sensory adaptation.

Answer: C

Diff: 2   Page Ref: 115

Topic: How Does Stimulation Become Sensation?

Skill: Conceptual

32) A subliminal stimulus

    A) is well above the absolute threshold.

    B) is at or below the absolute threshold.

    C) is not strong enough to alter our sensory system.

    D) can be reliably detected 50% of the time.

    E) can dramatically alter buying behavior.

Answer: B

Diff: 2   Page Ref: 116

Topic: A Critical Look at Subliminal Persuasion

Skill: Factual

33) Scientific studies of subliminal messages have thus far shown

    A) significant changes, especially when influencing purchasing habits.

    B) little to no effect on behavior.

    C) effective to help people stop smoking.

    D) effective to help self-esteem.

    E) effective to prevent shoplifting.

Answer: B

Diff: 2   Page Ref: 116-117

Topic: A Critical Look at Subliminal Persuasion

Skill: Conceptual

34) Which of the following explains why subliminal persuasion has failed to work in practice?

    A) Absolute thresholds occur at different levels in different people.

    B) There is no absolute proof that subliminal messages can influence one's behavior.

    C) The concept of subliminal manipulation by advertisers is unacceptable to the public.

    D) People do not respond to stimuli presented below the absolute threshold.

    E) All of the correct

Answer: E
Diff: 3   Page Ref: 117
Topic: A Critical Look at Subliminal Persuasion
Skill: Conceptual

35) The most complex and highly developed sense for humans is

    A) hearing.   B) sight.   C) pain.   D) touch.   E) taste.

Answer: B
Diff: 1   Page Ref: 119
Topic: How Are the Senses Alike?
Skill: Factual

36) Visual transduction occurs within the

    A) fovea.   B) cornea.   C) iris.   D) retina.   E) pupil.

Answer: D
Diff: 2   Page Ref: 119
Topic: How Are the Senses Alike?
Skill: Factual

37) Rods are photoreceptors that allow us to perceive _____, while cones would allow us to see _____.

    A) a bagful of jelly beans; our way to the bathroom when we wake up in the middle of the night

    B) a glass of grape Kool-Aid; shades of grey in the evening

    C) both will allow us to see anything we would like

    D) the stars at night; a yellow car during the day

    E) a small butterfly; a rainbow

Answer: D
Diff: 1   Page Ref: 119-120
Topic: How Are the Senses Alike?
Skill: Applied

38) We are able to perceive color and fine detail when a visual scene stimulates _____ within the _____.

   A) rods; retina

   B) cones; fovea

   C) photoreceptors; lens

   D) ganglion cells; iris

   E) bipolar cells; cornea

Answer: B

Diff: 2   Page Ref: 120

Topic: How Are the Senses Alike?

Skill: Conceptual

39) Place the following in the correct order regarding transmission of a visual stimulus from it's arrival at the retina until it travels towards the brain.

   A) bipolar cells, ganglion cells, rods/cones, optic nerve

   B) ganglion cells, bipolar cells, rods/cones, optic nerve

   C) rods/cones, ganglion cells, bipolar cells, optic nerve

   D) rods.cones; bipolar cells, ganglion cells, optic nerve

   E) rods/cones, optic nerve, bipolar cells, ganglion cells

Answer: D

Diff: 3   Page Ref: 120

Topic: How Are the Senses Alike?

Skill: Applied

40) What is the purpose of the bipolar cells?

   A) to collect impulses from the ganglion cells and send them to the optic nerve

   B) to collect impulses from the rods and cones and send them to the ganglion cells

   C) to collect impulses from the rods and cones and send them to the optic nerve

   D) to collect impulses from the fovea and send them to the rods and cones

   E) to collect impulses from the ganglion cells and send them to the brain

Answer: B

Diff: 3   Page Ref: 120

Topic: How Are the Senses Alike?

Skill: Factual

41) As Jenny reads her psychology textbook, she notices that the words that she is looking directly at are in focus, while those in her peripheral vision are more fuzzy. What would explain this phenomena?

    A) The words in the peripheral vision are focused on her blind spot.

    B) The words in the center are focused on her fovea.

    C) The words in the center are activating rods.

    D) The words in the periphery are activating cones.

    E) The words in her peripheral vision are not activating rods or cones.

Answer: B
Diff: 2   Page Ref: 120
Topic: How Are the Senses Alike?
Skill: Applied

42) The fovea

    A) holds only rods.

    B) holds both rods and cones.

    C) is part of the blind spot.

    D) holds only cones.

    E) cannot see very clearly during the day.

Answer: D
Diff: 2   Page Ref: 120
Topic: How Are the Senses Alike?
Skill: Factual

43) The blind spot refers to the region of the eye at which the _____ exit the eye.

    A) blood vessels

    B) icones

    C) optic nerve

    D) retina

    E) bipolar cells

Answer: C
Diff: 1   Page Ref: 121
Topic: How Are the Senses Alike?
Skill: Factual

44) When you look at a green, yellow and black flag for one minute and then look at a neutral surface and see a red, white and blue flag, you are experiencing a

   A) positive afterimage.

   B) phosphene.

   C) Negative afterimage.

   D) activation of the blind spot.

   E) trichromatic theory of light.

Answer: C

Diff: 3   Page Ref: 121

Topic: How Are the Senses Alike?

Skill: Conceptual

45) The visual cortex is located within the

   A) cerebellum.

   B) parietal lobe.

   C) frontal lobe.

   D) occipital lobe.

   E) thalamus.

Answer: D

Diff: 1   Page Ref: 121

Topic: How Are the Senses Alike?

Skill: Factual

46) Why is it that we do not see a 'black hole' in the area where our blind spot exists?

   A) Not everyone has a blind spot.

   B) Rods and Cones still exists at the blind spot.

   C) The blind spot in located in the fovea therefore we are able to see quite well.

   D) Neurons do not take visual information to the blind spot.

   E) What we miss with one eye we will catch with our other eye.

Answer: E

Diff: 2   Page Ref: 121

Topic: How Are the Senses Alike?

Skill: Applied

47) The perception of _____ is related to the intensity of light

A) movement

B) afterimages

C) brightness

D) color

E) distance

Answer: C

Diff: 1   Page Ref: 121

Topic: How Are the Senses Alike?

Skill: Conceptual

48) If you look at a tree with your left eye, the image will go to

A) the right hemisphere of your brain.

B) the left hemisphere of your brain.

C) the right visual field will go to the left hemisphere, while the left visual field will go to the right visual field.

D) the left visual field will go to the left hemisphere, while the right visual field will go to the right hemisphere.

E) None of the above

Answer: C

Diff: 1   Page Ref: 122

Topic: How Are the Senses Alike?

Skill: Applied

49) The sky appears to be blue because it reflects _____ wavelengths of light., while a rose appears red because it reflects _____ wavelengths of light.

A) subliminal, long

B) short, long

C) medium; long

D) long; short

E) long; medium

Answer: B

Diff: 2   Page Ref: 123

Topic: How Are the Senses Alike?

Skill: Conceptual

50) Wavelength translates into _____ while intensity will affect the _____ of what we see.

   A) brightness; color

   B) amplitude; color

   C) color; brightness

   D) amplitude; brightness

   E) None of the above

   Answer: C

   Diff: 2   Page Ref: 123

   Topic: How Are the Senses Alike?

   Skill: Conceptual

51) Wavelengths within this range usually fall within humans spectrum of visible light.

   A) 400–700   B) 300–900   C) 100–600   D) 100–1000   E) 300–400

   Answer: A

   Diff: 2   Page Ref: 124

   Topic: How Are the Senses Alike?

   Skill: Factual

52) If you stare at a blue square fo one minute and then look at a neutral surface, you will likely see

   A) red.   B) yellow.   C) green.   D) white.   E) pink.

   Answer: B

   Diff: 2   Page Ref: 124

   Topic: How Are the Senses Alike?

   Skill: Applied

53) A person who has the most common form of color blindness will probably have the hardest time distinguishing between

   A) red and green.

   B) yellow and blue.

   C) tan and pink.

   D) yellow and red.

   E) orange and red.

   Answer: A

   Diff: 2   Page Ref: 124

   Topic: How Are the Senses Alike?

   Skill: Applied

54) Snapping your fingers causes the surrounding air to
    A) move in circles.
    B) lose heat.
    C) vibrate.
    D) gain moisture.
    E) implode.

Answer: C
Diff: 1   Page Ref: 125
Topic: How Are the Senses Alike?
Skill: Applied

55) The sound that is produced when you strike a tuning fork has the physical properties of
    A) timbre and pitch.
    B) frequency and amplitude.
    C) volume and wavelength.
    D) loudness and speed.
    E) key and intensity.

Answer: B
Diff: 3   Page Ref: 125
Topic: How Are the Senses Alike?
Skill: Conceptual

56) In terms of sound waves, frequency refers to the
    A) peak-to-valley height of the wave.
    B) number of vibrations the wave completes in a given time.
    C) physical strength of the wave as determined by the listener.
    D) relative complexity of the wave form.
    E) loudness of the sound.

Answer: B
Diff: 1   Page Ref: 126
Topic: How Are the Senses Alike?
Skill: Conceptual

57) The hammer, anvil, and stirrup transmit sound waves from the _____ to the _____.
   A) middle ear; cochlea
   B) outer ear; cochlea
   C) retina; frontal cortex
   D) cochlea; auditory cortex
   E) retina; basilar membrane

Answer: B
Diff: 2   Page Ref: 126
Topic: How Are the Senses Alike?
Skill: Factual

58) When discussing hearing, the process of transduction occurs in the _____.
   A) tympanic membrane
   B) hammer anvil, stirrup
   C) auditory nerve
   D) cochlea
   E) semicircular canals

Answer: D
Diff: 3   Page Ref: 126
Topic: How Are the Senses Alike?
Skill: Conceptual

59) Place the following in the correct order concerning how a message travels through the ear.
   A) tympanic membrane, hammer/anvil/stirrup, basilar membrane, cochlea, auditory nerve
   B) tympanic membrane, hammer/anvil/stirrup, cochlea, basilar membrane, auditory nerve
   C) hammer/anvil/stirrup, tympanic membrane, cochlea, basilar membrane, auditory nerve
   D) cochlea, basilar membrane, tympanic membrane, hammer/anvil/stirrup, auditory nerve
   E) tympanic membrane, cochlea, hammer/anvil/stirrup, basilar membrane, auditory nerve

Answer: B
Diff: 3   Page Ref: 126
Topic: How Are the Senses Alike?
Skill: Analysis

60) The basilar membrane

    A) is located in the middle ear.

    B) is part of the semicircular canals.

    C) is fluid in the cochlea.

    D) surrounds the hammer/anvil and stirrup.

    E) holds the cochlea.

Answer: C
Diff: 1   *Page Ref: 126*
Topic: How Are the Senses Alike?
Skill: Factual

61) Auditory signals are processed in the

    A) association areas of frontal cortex.

    B) vestibular cortex of the frontal lobes.

    C) somatosensory cortex of the parietal lobes.

    D) auditory cortex of the cerebellum.

    E) auditory cortex of the temporal lobes.

Answer: E
Diff: 2   *Page Ref: 127*
Topic: How Are the Senses Alike?
Skill: Conceptual

62) Whether a sound has a high or low _____ refers to the frequency of the sound.

    A) tone   B) amplitude   C) pitch   D) gigahertz   E) timbre

Answer: C
Diff: 2   *Page Ref: 127*
Topic: How Are the Senses Alike?
Skill: Factual

63) Place theory argues that sounds of different frequencies induce vibration in different areas of the

    A) hammer.

    B) basilar membrane.

    C) auditory nerve.

    D) temporal lobe.

    E) tympanic membrane.

Answer: B
Diff: 2   *Page Ref: 128*
Topic: How Are the Senses Alike?
Skill: Conceptual

64) Frequency theory ALONE would best describe how a person can hear pitches of
    A) 8300 Hz.   B) 5200Hz.   C) 2200 Hz.   D) 890 Hz.   E) 4800 Hz.

Answer: D
Diff: 3   *Page Ref: 128*
Topic: How Are the Senses Alike?
Skill: Conceptual

65) Loudness is determined by sound
    A) pitch.
    B) quality.
    C) amplitude.
    D) frequency.
    E) speed.

Answer: C
Diff: 2   *Page Ref: 128*
Topic: How Are the Senses Alike?
Skill: Factual

66) Most sounds in the real world
    A) have the same amplitude but different frequencies.
    B) are comprised of complex tones.
    C) consist of frequencies that are narrow in range, but vary greatly in amplitude.
    D) usually have only one frequency and one amplitude.
    E) combine amplitudes and frequencies in basically the same way.

Answer: B
Diff: 2   *Page Ref: 128*
Topic: How Are the Senses Alike?
Skill: Factual

67) The _____ is the unit of measurement for loudness.
    A) amplitude
    B) pounds per square inch
    C) hertz
    D) decibel
    E) pitch

Answer: D
Diff: 1   *Page Ref: 128*
Topic: How Are the Senses Alike?
Skill: Factual

68) The _____ of sound allows us to distinguish a guitar note from a saxophone note.
   A) timbre
   B) kinesthesis
   C) harmonics
   D) auditory diffusion
   E) absolute thresholds

Answer: A
Diff: 2   Page Ref: 128
Topic: How Are the Senses Alike?
Skill: Applied

69) When sounds waves cannot be converted to nerve energy, one has
   A) conduction deafness.
   B) color blindness.
   C) nerve deafness.
   D) damaged hammer.anvil and or stirrup.
   E) All of the above are possible

Answer: A
Diff: 2   Page Ref: 129
Topic: How Are the Senses Alike?
Skill: Factual

70) A hearing aid generally helps with
   A) damage to the auditory nerve.
   B) conduction deafness.
   C) nerve deafness.
   D) damage to the temporal lobe.
   E) damage to the basilar membrane.

Answer: B
Diff: 2   Page Ref: 129
Topic: How Are the Senses Alike?
Skill: Applied

71) All of the senses must do the following.

   A) reduce the intensity of incoming stimuli

   B) transmit incoming stimuli directly to the brain in it's original form

   C) convert physical to neural information

   D) determine the significance of incoming stimuli

   E) All of the above

Answer: C
Diff: 2   *Page Ref: 129*
Topic: How Are the Senses Alike?
Skill: Conceptual

72) The _____ sense allows us to orient our body with respect to gravity.

   A) gustatory

   B) vestibular

   C) olfactory

   D) kinesthetic

   E) analgesic

Answer: B
Diff: 2   *Page Ref: 129*
Topic: How Are the Senses Alike?
Skill: Factual

73) The receptors for body position and movement are located

   A) in parietal cortex.

   B) in the inner ear.

   C) in the outer layer of the skin.

   D) within the corpus callosum.

   E) within the spinal cord.

Answer: B
Diff: 2   *Page Ref: 130*
Topic: How Are the Senses Alike?
Skill: Factual

74) A person with damage to the _____ would be clumsy and uncoordinated.

    A) frontal lobe

    B) hippocampus

    C) olfactory bulb

    D) temporal lobes

    E) kinesthetic receptors

Answer: E
Diff: 2   Page Ref: 130
Topic: How Are the Senses Alike?
Skill: Applied

75) Fred is a basketball player, his _____ will provide him with information regarding his body position and where he is on the court at any given time.

    A) temporal lobe

    B) pheromones

    C) kinesthetic sense

    D) basilar membrane

    E) motor strip

Answer: C
Diff: 2   Page Ref: 130
Topic: How Are the Senses Alike?
Skill: Applied

76) The sense of smell is adaptive in that

    A) it aids in the location of food.

    B) it allows us to detect decaying flesh.

    C) it signals sexual receptivity in some mammals.

    D) smell can mark the boundaries of a territory.

    E) All of the above are correct

Answer: E
Diff: 2   Page Ref: 130
Topic: How Are the Senses Alike?
Skill: Conceptual

77) _____ are chemical signals that often influence animals sexual responses, alerts animals to danger and territorial boundaries

A) Phosphenes

B) Pheromones

C) Olfaction

D) Semicircular canals

E) Hormones

Answer: B

Diff: 2   Page Ref: 130

Topic: How Are the Senses Alike?

Skill: Conceptual

78) The sense of taste is known as

A) gustation.

B) gesticulation.

C) gestation.

D) gastrulation.

E) gentrification.

Answer: A

Diff: 2   Page Ref: 131

Topic: How Are the Senses Alike?

Skill: Factual

79) Which of the following is NOT one of the five taste qualities?

A) bitter   B) sour   C) umami   D) spicy   E) salty

Answer: D

Diff: 2   Page Ref: 131

Topic: How Are the Senses Alike?

Skill: Conceptual

80) Which of the following can produce a loss of taste reactivity?

A) aging

B) reduced density of papillae on the tongue

C) smoking

D) over consumption of hot spicy foods

E) All of the above are correct

Answer: E

Diff: 2   Page Ref: 131

Topic: How Are the Senses Alike?

Skill: Factual

81) Supertasters have an advantage over non–tasters because

    A) they are more sensitive to tastes such as broccoli.

    B) they are more sensitive to tastes like diet cola.

    C) they can more easily detect foods that might be potentially harmful.

    D) they cannot detect foods that are bitter.

    E) None of the above

Answer: C
Diff: 2   Page Ref: 131
Topic: How Are the Senses Alike?
Skill: Conceptual

82) Sensory information related to the skin senses is processed within the

    A) frontal lobes.

    B) semicircular canals.

    C) hairs of the basilar membrane.

    D) somatosensory cortex.

    E) reticular activating system.

Answer: D
Diff: 2   Page Ref: 132
Topic: How Are the Senses Alike?
Skill: Factual

83) Which of the following is true of pain?

    A) Signals from damaged sensory endings generate phantom pain.

    B) Pain is mal adaptive.

    C) Pain stimuli can damage your body.

    D) Pain may result from intense sensory stimulation.

    E) C and D are correct.

Answer: E
Diff: 3   Page Ref: 133
Topic: The Experience of Pain
Skill: Conceptual

84) Intense pain stimulation generates signals that are carried by

    A) the PAG.

    B) fast fibers.

    C) slow fibers.

    D) efferent fibers.

    E) the anterior frontal cortex.

Answer: C
Diff: 2   Page Ref: 133
Topic: The Experience of Pain
Skill: Factual

85) Damage to the _____ would be expected to diminish the perception of pain.

    A) superior colliculus

    B) amygdala

    C) tympanic membrane

    D) hippocampus

    E) anterior cingulate cortex

Answer: E
Diff: 3   Page Ref: 133
Topic: The Experience of Pain
Skill: Applied

86) If a new pain medication is tested against a placebo and both the experimental ad the control groups experience the same benefits, the new pain medication could be said to be

    A) a very effective medication.

    B) not a very effective medication.

    C) also a placebo.

    D) just as good as current pain medication.

    E) None of the above

Answer: B
Diff: 2   Page Ref: 134
Topic: The Experience of Pain
Skill: Applied

87) The capacity of a placebo treatment to reduce pain perception is due to

    A) release of endorphins in brain.

    B) inactivation of cells in the occipital cortex.

    C) the release of naloxone in the spinal cord.

    D) damage by needles to skin receptors.

    E) B and D are correct.

Answer: A
Diff: 2   Page Ref: 134
Topic: The Experience of Pain
Skill: Factual

88) A(n) percept consists of _____ in combination with _____.

    A) sensation; associated meaning

    B) stimulus; a receptor

    C) receptor; a sensory pathway

    D) afterimage; a motor response

    E) phosgene; associated meaning

Answer: A
Diff: 2   Page Ref: 135
Topic: What is the Relationship Between Sensation and Perception?
Skill: Factual

89) _____ are specialized cells dedicated to the detection of specific stimuli such as length, color, and boundaries.

    A) Sensory receptors

    B) Sensory organs

    C) Feature detectors

    D) Tranducers

    E) Monocular cues

Answer: C
Diff: 2   Page Ref: 136
Topic: What is the Relationship Between Sensation and Perception?
Skill: Factual

90) _____ refers to the fact that we do not know how the brain combines features into a single percept. What do we call this lack of knowledge.

A) Gestalt perception

B) Combinatory confusion

C) Sensorimotor flux

D) The uncertainty principle

E) The binding problem

Answer: E

Diff: 2   Page Ref: 136

Topic: What is the Relationship Between Sensation and Perception?

Skill: Factual

91) In bottom-up processing, the resulting percept is determined by

A) stimulus features.

B) our expectations.

C) our current emotions.

D) what others tell us.

E) other environmental stimuli.

Answer: A

Diff: 2   Page Ref: 136

Topic: What is the Relationship Between Sensation and Perception?

Skill: Conceptual

92) What type of processing takes sensory data into the system through receptors and then sends the data to the brain for analysis of information?

A) top-down processing

B) integrative processing

C) distinction-extraction processing

D) bottom-up processing

E) serial combinatorial processing

Answer: D

Diff: 2   Page Ref: 136

Topic: What is the Relationship Between Sensation and Perception?

Skill: Conceptual

93) Your dog has been lost for three days.,and you cannot stop thinking about him. When you hear a bark, you assume that it is Fuzzy because of

    A) location constancy.

    B) closure.

    C) the law of common fate.

    D) bottom-up processing.

    E) top-down processing.

Answer: E
Diff: 2   Page Ref: 136
Topic: What is the Relationship Between Sensation and Perception?
Skill: Applied

94) Top-down processing emphasizes all of the following EXCEPT

    A) stimulus features.

    B) experience.

    C) cultural background.

    D) knowledge.

    E) memory.

Answer: A
Diff: 2   Page Ref: 136
Topic: What is the Relationship Between Sensation and Perception?
Skill: Conceptual

95) Top-down processing is also known as _____ processing.

    A) stimulus-driven

    B) data-driven

    C) conceptually-driven

    D) feature-driven

    E) time-driven

Answer: C
Diff: 2   Page Ref: 136
Topic: What is the Relationship Between Sensation and Perception?
Skill: Conceptual

96) As a bird flies towards you, you do not perceive it as growing larger. This is primarily due to

    A) perceptual constancy.

    B) conservation.

    C) recognition.

    D) perceptual ambiguity.

    E) the law of Pragnanz.

Answer: A

Diff: 2   *Page Ref: 137*

Topic: What is the Relationship Between Sensation and Perception?

Skill: Conceptual

97) Perceptual constancy reflects the understanding of the perceiver that

    A) objects remain the same despite changes in their appearance.

    B) most objects readily change their shape, but not color.

    C) our brain is readily fooled by sensory input.

    D) images can be interpreted in more than one way.

    E) perceived boundaries are not a function of the stimulus.

Answer: A

Diff: 2   *Page Ref: 137*

Topic: What is the Relationship Between Sensation and Perception?

Skill: Factual

98) The concept of _____ explains why a shirt looks the same shade of orange when it looks darker in dim light or brighter while outside on a sunny day.

    A) closure

    B) the law of proximity

    C) the placebo effect

    D) color constancy

    E) olfaction

Answer: D

Diff: 2   *Page Ref: 137*

Topic: What is the Relationship Between Sensation and Perception?

Skill: Applied

99) The concept of _____ explain why we do not see people morphing in shape as they walk past us and we see them from a different perspective.

    A) shape constancy

    B) color constancy

    C) size constancy

    D) sensation

    E) bottom-up processing

Answer: A
Diff: 2   Page Ref: 137
Topic: What is the Relationship Between Sensation and Perception?
Skill: Applied

100) Illusions are more likely when

    A) familiar patterns are absent.

    B) the stimulus is unclear.

    C) elements are combined in unusual ways.

    D) information is missing.

    E) All of the above are correct

Answer: E
Diff: 2   Page Ref: 138
Topic: What is the Relationship Between Sensation and Perception?
Skill: Recall

101) When most people look at the black–and–white Hermann Grid illusion,

    A) they see other colors where there are none.

    B) the inhibiting process causes them to see gray areas.

    C) the boxes blur together and it is difficult to determine boundaries.

    D) the black boxes are seen as white, and the white lines are seen as black.

    E) they see two alternating patterns appear and disappear.

Answer: B
Diff: 3   Page Ref: 138
Topic: What is the Relationship Between Sensation and Perception?
Skill: Applied

102) A Necker cube is an example of a(n)

    A) ambiguous figure.

    B) Gestalt creation.

    C) mental set.

    D) pheromone.

    E) phosphene.

Answer: A

Diff: 2   *Page Ref: 139*

Topic: What is the Relationship Between Sensation and Perception?

Skill: Applied

103) if you were presented with a picture of a vase and then presented with the ambiguous image of he faces and vases, you would be more likely to see the vase first. In this case the initial image of a vase served as a _____.

    A) sensory modality

    B) perceptual set

    C) bottom-up processing

    D) sensory receptor

    E) innate judgement about what you would see

Answer: B

Diff: 3   *Page Ref: 139*

Topic: What is the Relationship Between Sensation and Perception?

Skill: Applied

104) Many individuals perceive one of the lines in the Muller-Lyer illusion to be distorted because

    A) The inside corner appears to recede into the distance while the outside corner appears to be coming towards the viewer.

    B) railroad tracks converge in the distance.

    C) parallel lines appear to bend towards one another.

    D) the inside circle appears to be surrounded by larger circles thus making the inter circle appear smaller.

    E) None of the above are correct

Answer: A

Diff: 3   *Page Ref: 139*

Topic: What is the Relationship Between Sensation and Perception?

Skill: Conceptual

105) Interior designers use the principle of illusions to create 'space' in an otherwise small room by
    A) placing much furniture in the room to give it a cozy feeling.
    B) painting it in dark colors.
    C) using many decorative accessories.
    D) painting it in light colors.
    E) hanging draperies the same colors as the walls to make the walls appear longer.

Answer: D
Diff: 3   *Page Ref: 140-141*
Topic: What is the Relationship Between Sensation and Perception?
Skill: Applied

106) Learning–based inference is to nurture as _____ is to nurture.
    A) Pavlovian theory
    B) gene therapy
    C) artificial intelligence
    D) environmental theory
    E) Gestalt theory

Answer: E
Diff: 2   *Page Ref: 141*
Topic: What is the Relationship Between Sensation and Perception?
Skill: Conceptual

107) "The whole is more than the sum of its parts" is a statement reflecting
    A) experience–based inference.
    B) the artificial intelligence approach.
    C) environmental adaptation.
    D) Gestalt psychology.
    E) top–down processing.

Answer: D
Diff: 2   *Page Ref: 142*
Topic: What is the Relationship Between Sensation and Perception?
Skill: Conceptual

108) When you see the word su–k–r outside of a candy store. even though some of the letters are missing, you are still able to perceive the word as saying 'sucker'. You are using

    A) figure–ground distinctions.

    B) subjective contour.

    C) perceptual grouping.

    D) closure.

    E) common fate.

Answer: D

Diff: 2   Page Ref: 143

Topic: What is the Relationship Between Sensation and Perception?

Skill: Applied

109) As you view an abstract painting, you eventually see the red as the people and the black as the background, this demonstrates

    A) proximity.

    B) illusory contour.

    C) figure–ground.

    D) ambiguity.

    E) continuity.

Answer: C

Diff: 2   Page Ref: 143

Topic: What is the Relationship Between Sensation and Perception?

Skill: Applied

110) When you walk through the cafeteria at lunch, you see many people seated at tables you perceive those individuals who are sitting near each other as being friends with one another. You are demonstrating which of the following?

    A) law of proximity

    B) law of common fate

    C) law of similarity

    D) law of Pragnanz

    E) law of continuity

Answer: A

Diff: 2   Page Ref: 144

Topic: What is the Relationship Between Sensation and Perception?

Skill: Applied

111) according to the Gestalt principle of _____, even when we see a line take a 90 degree turn, we still see it as the same line.

   A) proximity

   B) similarity

   C) figure–ground

   D) continuity

   E) law of common fate

Answer: D

Diff: 2   Page Ref: 144

Topic: What is the Relationship Between Sensation and Perception?

Skill: Applied

112) The law of Pragnanz is also known as the

   A) minimum principle of perception.

   B) law of common fate.

   C) grouping perception.

   D) principle of least resistance.

   E) just noticeable difference.

Answer: A

Diff: 2   Page Ref: 145

Topic: What is the Relationship Between Sensation and Perception?

Skill: Factual

113) Proofreading is a task that is made difficult because of the Gestalt principle known as the law of

   A) continuity.

   B) proximity.

   C) Pragnanz.

   D) common fate.

   E) similarity.

Answer: C

Diff: 2   Page Ref: 145

Topic: What is the Relationship Between Sensation and Perception?

Skill: Applied

114) The visual cliff created by Gibson and Walk was designed to test infants on
   A) motor abilities.
   B) gestalt principles.
   C) depth perception.
   D) sensory adaptation.
   E) sensory overload.

Answer: C
Diff: 2   Page Ref: 145
Topic: What is the Relationship Between Sensation and Perception?
Skill: Recall

115) experimenters have found by using virtual reality goggles that children as young as _____ may show evidence of depth perception.
   A) 2 years   B) 2 months   C) 6 months   D) 2 weeks   E) 12 months

Answer: D
Diff: 2   Page Ref: 145
Topic: What is the Relationship Between Sensation and Perception?
Skill: Recall

116) Sammy works in a high rise, he can see the buildings that surround his own, but those further in the distance appear fuzzy and hazy. Sammy is experiencing
   A) relative size.
   B) interposition.
   C) light and shadow.
   D) atmospheric perspective.
   E) All of the above are correct

Answer: D
Diff: 2   Page Ref: 146
Topic: What is the Relationship Between Sensation and Perception?
Skill: Applied

117) An aircraft pilot with only eye is able to guide the plane during takeoff and landing using the depth cues of

   A) relative size.

   B) interposition.

   C) light and shadow.

   D) atmospheric perspective.

   E) All of the above are correct

Answer: E
Diff: 3   Page Ref: 146
Topic: What is the Relationship Between Sensation and Perception?
Skill: Conceptual

118) Hermann von Helmholtz was a proponent of which perceptual theory?

   A) Gestalt principles

   B) learning–based inference

   C) environmental adaptation

   D) artificial intelligence approach

   E) the absolute threshold theory

Answer: B
Diff: 3   Page Ref: 146
Topic: What is the Relationship Between Sensation and Perception?
Skill: Factual

119) The learning perspective suggests that the most important factors in determining our ability to identify a percept are

   A) time, weather, and day of the week.

   B) our eyes, our ears, and our brain.

   C) the object, its environment, and the presence of distractors.

   D) the laws of continuity, similarity, and proximity.

   E) context, expectation, and perceptual sets.

Answer: E
Diff: 3   Page Ref: 147
Topic: What is the Relationship Between Sensation and Perception?
Skill: Conceptual

120) It may take your favorite teacher a few seconds to recognize you when you see her in the grocery store. This experience illustrates the importance of

   A) perceptual sets.

   B) context.

   C) closure.

   D) contiguity.

   E) common fate.

Answer: B
Diff: 2   Page Ref: 147
Topic: What is the Relationship Between Sensation and Perception?
Skill: Applied

121) If you are listening to music backwards in the hopes of hearing an interesting message (there is little evidence that you will have any luck) and you hear nothing until a friend suggests that he hears something. One he suggests that the song played backwards says, "get the slippers" you also hear it. Your friend has created

   A) a proximal stimuli.

   B) a perceptual set.

   C) bottom–up processing.

   D) a difference threshold.

   E) a phosphene.

Answer: B
Diff: 2   Page Ref: 148
Topic: What is the Relationship Between Sensation and Perception?
Skill: Applied

122) Shannon reads Jason the words 'folk,' 'soak,' and 'joke.' Then she asks him, "What do you call the white of an egg?" He replies by saying, "Yolk," when the correct answer is albumen (or simply, egg white). Jason gave an incorrect answer due to

   A) bottom–up processing.

   B) a perceptual illusion.

   C) closure.

   D) a perceptual set.

   E) the law of common fate.

Answer: D
Diff: 2   Page Ref: 148
Topic: What is the Relationship Between Sensation and Perception?
Skill: Applied

123) The tendency of adults from the mainland United States to be tricked by the Ponzo illusion, whereas Guam citizens are often not fooled by it, can be explained by

A) Gestalt psychology.

B) learning–based inference.

C) heredity.

D) the law of continuity.

E) the law of Pragnanz.

Answer: B

Diff: 2   *Page Ref: 149*

Topic: What is the Relationship Between Sensation and Perception?

Skill: Conceptual

Check Your Understanding Questions

1) The sensory pathways carry information

A) from the brain to the muscles.

B) from the sense organs to the brain.

C) from the brain to the sense organs.

D) from the central nervous system to the autonomic nervous system.

E) from the muscles to the brain.

Answer: B

Diff: 2   *Page Ref: 118*

Topic: Check Your Understanding

Skill: Recall

2) Which one refers to the least amount of stimulation that your perceptual system can detect about half of the time?

A) the stimulus threshold

B) the difference threshold

C) the absolute threshold

D) the action potential

E) Weber's law

Answer: C

Diff: 2   *Page Ref: 118*

Topic: Check Your Understanding

Skill: Recall

3) Which of the following would involve sensory adaptation?
   A) The water in a pool seems warmer after you have been in for a while than when you first jumped in.
   B) The flavor of a spicy salsa on your taco seems hot by comparison with the blandness of the sour cream.
   C) You are unaware of a priming stimulus flashed on the screen at 1/100 of a second.
   D) You prefer the feel of silk to the feel of velvet.
   E) You can determine the difference between a very low sound and a slightly louder sound.

   Answer: A
   Diff: 2   Page Ref: 118
   Topic: Check Your Understanding
   Skill: Applied

4) Which of the following best explains why when preparing a meal we have to add more spice to an already spicy dish to detect the difference
   A) absolute threshold.
   B) difference threshold.
   C) sensory adaptation.
   D) Weber's law.
   E) sensory overload.

   Answer: D
   Diff: 2   Page Ref: 118
   Topic: Check Your Understanding
   Skill: Recall

5) When you hear the sound of a tree falling in the forest, the brain has received nothing but
   A) sound waves from the air.
   B) neural activity in the sensory pathways.
   C) the vibration of the eardrums.
   D) sound waves traveling through the sensory pathways.
   E) the sense of air rushing by you.

   Answer: B
   Diff: 2   Page Ref: 118
   Topic: Check Your Understanding
   Skill: Understanding the Core Concept

6) The eyes have two distinct types of photoreceptor: the rods, which which detect _____, and the cones, which detect _____.

    A) low intensity light; wavelengths corresponding to colors

    B) motion; shape

    C) bright light; dim light

    D) stimuli in consciousness; unconscious stimuli

    E) color; brightness

Answer: A
Diff: 2   Page Ref: 135
Topic: Check Your Understanding
Skill: Recall

7) The wavelength of light causes _____, while the intensity of light causes sensations of _____.

    A) motion; shape

    B) color; brightness

    C) primary colors; secondary vision

    D) depth; color

    E) bright light; dim light

Answer: B
Diff: 2   Page Ref: 135
Topic: Check Your Understanding
Skill: Recall

8) The frequency theory best explains _____ sounds, while the place theory explains _____ sounds.

    A) low pitched; high–pitched

    B) loud; soft

    C) pitch; timbre

    D) simple; complex

    E) tonal; atonal

Answer: A
Diff: 2   Page Ref: 135
Topic: Check Your Understanding
Skill: Recall

9) Which sense makes use of electromagnetic energy?

   A) hearing   B) taste   C) pain   D) vision   E) olfaction

Answer: D
Diff: 1   *Page Ref: 135*
Topic: Check Your Understanding
Skill: Recall

10) Different senses give us different sensations mainly because

   A) they involve different stimuli.

   B) they activate different sensory regions of the brain.

   C) they have different intensities.

   D) we have different memories associated with them.

   E) they exist in different forms in the environment.

Answer: B
Diff: 2   *Page Ref: 135*
Topic: Check Your Understanding
Skill: Understanding the Core Concept

11) Which of the following is an example of the kind of information that top-down processing contributes to perception?

   A) looking for a friend's face in the crowd

   B) having to wait for your eyes to adjust to the dark in a theatre

   C) hearing a painfully loud noise

   D) feeling a pinprick

   E) constructing an object from memory

Answer: A
Diff: 2   *Page Ref: 151*
Topic: Check Your Understanding
Skill: Recall

12) Which of the following is NOT a monocular cue for depth perception?

   A) relative size

   B) retinal disparity

   C) relative height

   D) interposition

   E) relative motion

Answer: B
Diff: 2   *Page Ref: 151*
Topic: Check Your Understanding
Skill: Recall

13) The Gestalt theory proposes that many of our perceptions are determined by
    A) bottom-up processing.
    B) illusions.
    C) ambiguity.
    D) innate factors.
    E) top-down factors.

Answer: D
Diff: 2   Page Ref: 151
Topic: Check Your Understanding
Skill: Recall

14) The faces/vase image (Fig 5.17A) illustrates
    A) similarity.
    B) closure.
    C) figure and ground.
    D) attention as a gateway to consciousness.
    E) interposition.

Answer: C
Diff: 2   Page Ref: 151
Topic: Check Your Understanding
Skill: Recall

15) When two close friends are talking, other people may not be able to follow their conversation because it has many gaps, which the friends can mentally fill in from their shared experience. Which Gestalt principle is illustrated by the friends' ability to fill in these conversational gaps?
    A) similarity
    B) proximity
    C) closure
    D) common fate
    E) ambiguity

Answer: C
Diff: 2   Page Ref: 151
Topic: Check Your Understanding
Skill: Applied

16) Which of the following best illustrates the idea that perception is not an exact internal copy of the world, but also based on one's experience in the world?

    A) the sound of a familiar tune

    B) the Ponzo illusion

    C) a bright light

    D) jumping in response to a pinprick

    E) bottom–up processing

Answer: B
Diff: 2   Page Ref: 151
Topic: Check Your Understanding
Skill: Understanding the Core Concept

True/False Questions

1) Our sense organs transform physical stimuli into neural impulses.

Answer: TRUE
Diff: 2   Page Ref: 111
Topic: How Does Stimulation Become Sensation?
Skill: Factual

2) The brain receives information from the outside world.

Answer: FALSE
Diff: 2   Page Ref: 111
Topic: How Does Stimulation Become Sensation?
Skill: Factual

3) Sensory receptors convert physical energy into neural energy.

Answer: TRUE
Diff: 2   Page Ref: 112
Topic: How Does Stimulation Become Sensation?
Skill: Factual

4) Transduction refers to the process of converting neural impulses into neural energy that the brain can process.

Answer: TRUE
Diff: 3   Page Ref: 112
Topic: How Does Stimulation Become Sensation?
Skill: Factual

5) Sensation is heavily influenced by detecting changes in the environment.

Answer: TRUE
Diff: 2   Page Ref: 113
Topic: How Does Stimulation Become Sensation?
Skill: Conceptual

6) An absolute threshold measures the difference made in a stimulus.

Answer: FALSE
Diff: 2   Page Ref: 114
Topic: How Does Stimulation Become Sensation?
Skill: Factual

7) A difference threshold measures the smallest noticeable difference in a stimulus.

Answer: TRUE
Diff: 2   Page Ref: 114
Topic: How Does Stimulation Become Sensation?
Skill: Factual

8) Weber's law suggest that changes in a stimulus must always remain the same for then to be detected.

Answer: FALSE
Diff: 2   Page Ref: 115
Topic: How Does Stimulation Become Sensation?
Skill: Factual

9) Judgement is an important component to the signal detection theory.

Answer: TRUE
Diff: 2   Page Ref: 116
Topic: How Does Stimulation Become Sensation?
Skill: Conceptual

10) Our buying habits are controlled by subliminal stimuli.

Answer: FALSE
Diff: 2   Page Ref: 117
Topic: How Does Stimulation Become Sensation?
Skill: Factual

11) The cones in the eye help you distinguish red from blue in good light.

Answer: TRUE
Diff: 1   *Page Ref: 120*
Topic: How Are the Senses Alike?
Skill: Factual

12) Bipolar cells connect rods and cones to the Optic nerve.

Answer: FALSE
Diff: 2   *Page Ref: 120*
Topic: How Are the Senses Alike?
Skill: Factual

13) Physical information from the environment stimulates the optic nerve directly.

Answer: FALSE
Diff: 2   *Page Ref: 120*
Topic: How Are the Senses Alike?
Skill: Factual

14) The blind spot holds neither rods nor cones.

Answer: TRUE
Diff: 2   *Page Ref: 121*
Topic: How Are the Senses Alike?
Skill: Factual

15) All of the information that is taken in by the left eye will go to the right hemisphere in order to be processed.

Answer: TRUE
Diff: 2   *Page Ref: 122*
Topic: How Are the Senses Alike?
Skill: Factual

16) The difference between visible light and other forms of electromagnetic energy is wavelength.

Answer: TRUE
Diff: 2   *Page Ref: 124*
Topic: How Are the Senses Alike?
Skill: Factual

17) The most common form of color blindness involves a difficulty in distinguishing red from green.

Answer: TRUE
Diff: 2   Page Ref: 124
Topic: How Are the Senses Alike?
Skill: Factual

18) The eardrum is also known as the tympanic membrane.

Answer: TRUE
Diff: 1   Page Ref: 126
Topic: How Are the Senses Alike?
Skill: Factual

19) Sound waves with larger amplitudes are softer than those with smaller amplitudes.

Answer: FALSE
Diff: 2   Page Ref: 126
Topic: How Are the Senses Alike?
Skill: Conceptual

20) The basilar membrane is located in the cochlea.

Answer: TRUE
Diff: 2   Page Ref: 126
Topic: How Are the Senses Alike?
Skill: Factual

21) Pitch is determined by the frequency of a sound wave.

Answer: TRUE
Diff: 2   Page Ref: 127
Topic: How Are the Senses Alike?
Skill: Factual

22) Nerve deafness usually means that there has been damage to the auditory nerve or one of the higher auditory processing areas.

Answer: TRUE
Diff: 2   Page Ref: 129
Topic: How Are the Senses Alike?
Skill: Factual

23) Kinesthetic and vestibular information is processed in the brain's parietal lobes.

Answer: TRUE
Diff: 2   Page Ref: 130
Topic: How Are the Senses Alike?
Skill: Factual

24) From an evolutionary perspective, smell is the oldest sense.

Answer: FALSE
Diff: 2   Page Ref: 130
Topic: How Are the Senses Alike?
Skill: Conceptual

25) We lose the ability to taste as well as we age.

Answer: TRUE
Diff: 2   Page Ref: 131
Topic: How Are the Senses Alike?
Skill: Factual

26) Taste buds can regenerate themselves.

Answer: TRUE
Diff: 2   Page Ref: 131
Topic: How Are the Senses Alike?
Skill: Factual

27) Regardless of where you feel a given sense of your body, you will feel the same sensation because you have the same amount to sensory receptors all over your body.

Answer: FALSE
Diff: 2   Page Ref: 132
Topic: How Are the Senses Alike?
Skill: Factual

28) People born with a congenital insensitivity to pain are more likely to live a long life than those who are sensitive to it.

Answer: FALSE
Diff: 2   Page Ref: 133
Topic: How Are the Senses Alike?
Skill: Conceptual

29) In top–down processing, expectations and memories can influence the interpretation of a stimulus or event.

Answer: TRUE
Diff: 2   Page Ref: 136
Topic: What is the Relationship Between Sensation and Perception?
Skill: Conceptual

30) When we see a door opening, we see it's shape gradually changing.

Answer: FALSE
Diff: 1   Page Ref: 137
Topic: What is the Relationship Between Sensation and Perception?
Skill: Conceptual

31) When we experience an illusion, we are seeing the effect of our expectations interfere with what we are actually perceiving.

Answer: TRUE
Diff: 2   Page Ref: 138
Topic: What is the Relationship Between Sensation and Perception?
Skill: Conceptual

32) The is always a 'correct ' way to see an ambiguous figure.

Answer: FALSE
Diff: 1   Page Ref: 139
Topic: What is the Relationship Between Sensation and Perception?
Skill: Factual

33) Gestalt theories of perception argue that how we perceive the world is based in large part on innate characteristics.

Answer: TRUE
Diff: 1   Page Ref: 141
Topic: What is the Relationship Between Sensation and Perception?
Skill: Conceptual

34) Gestalt theory argues that our brains are innately set up to organize sensory input into meaningful patterns.

Answer: TRUE
Diff: 2   Page Ref: 141–142
Topic: What is the Relationship Between Sensation and Perception?
Skill: Factual

35) In looking at ambiguous illusions, generally one figure will appear to be the figure and the other will temporarily fade into the background.

Answer: TRUE
Diff: 2   Page Ref: 143
Topic: What is the Relationship Between Sensation and Perception?
Skill: Conceptual

36) If we see the word c–tch at a baseball game we are likely to realize that it says catch based on the gestalt principle of proximity.

Answer: FALSE
Diff: 2   Page Ref: 144
Topic: What is the Relationship Between Sensation and Perception?
Skill: Applied

37) If all of the players on a given team are wearing the same uniforms, we are likely to view them as one unit using the Gestalt principle of similarity.

Answer: FALSE
Diff: 2   Page Ref: 144
Topic: What is the Relationship Between Sensation and Perception?
Skill: Applied

38) Most children up to the age of 2 would crawl over the visual cliff.

Answer: FALSE
Diff: 2   Page Ref: 145
Topic: What is the Relationship Between Sensation and Perception?
Skill: Factual

39) Retinal Disparity is a type of monocular cue.

Answer: FALSE
Diff: 2   Page Ref: 145
Topic: What is the Relationship Between Sensation and Perception?
Skill: Factual

40) The idea of introspection proposes that objects that are covered up by other objects will appear further in the distance than the object covering it.

Answer: TRUE
Diff: 2   Page Ref: 146
Topic: What is the Relationship Between Sensation and Perception?
Skill: Factual

41) Even when keeping the stimulus the same, by changing one's perceptual set, you can change what they perceive.

Answer: TRUE
Diff: 2   Page Ref: 148
Topic: What is the Relationship Between Sensation and Perception?
Skill: Conceptual

Short Answer Questions

1) How are sensation and perception different?

Answer: Sensation deals with incoming information and the transduction of physical to neural information in order to interpret our environment. Perception deals with the interpretation of that environment that deals with expectations and previous experience.
Diff: 2   Page Ref: 110–111
Topic: How Does Stimulation Become Sensation?
Skill: Conceptual

2) Explain Difference thresholds and Weber's law.

Answer: A difference threshold is the smallest detectable change in a stimulus, while Weber's Law states that the change must be in direct proportion to the size of the original stimulus.
Diff: 3   Page Ref: 114–115
Topic: How Does Stimulation Become Sensation?
Skill: Analysis

3) The minimal amount of stimulus change that is still noticeable half the time is the _____.

Answer: difference threshold or just noticeable difference (JND)
Diff: 2   Page Ref: 114
Topic: How Does Stimulation Become Sensation?
Skill: Conceptual

4) This predicts when we will detect a weak signal.

Answer: signal detection theory
Diff: 2   Page Ref: 116
Topic: How Does Stimulation Become Sensation?
Skill: Factual

5) Briefly discuss the research findings regarding subliminal messages.

Answer: James Vicary claimed that by playing subliminal messages in movie theatres he influenced buying habits of individuals, he later admitted that this was a hoax. Subliminal message tapes for the cessation of smoking or the improve self-esteem have little evidence to suggest that they work. While the scientific evidence may be shaky, the placebo effect may be playing a role in why these individuals feel better.

Diff: 3   Page Ref: 117

Topic: A Critical Look at Subliminal Persuasion

Skill: Analysis

6) Vision is at its sharpest in the _____, the very center of the _____ where cone-shaped photoreceptors are concentrated.

Answer: fovea; retina

Diff: 2   Page Ref: 120

Topic: How Are the Senses Alike?

Skill: Factual

7) These cells are responsible from connecting rods and cones to the optic nerve.

Answer: bipolar and ganglion cells

Diff: 2   Page Ref: 120

Topic: How Are the Senses Alike?

Skill: Factual

8) Explain how a message that comes in through your left eye will be sent to your brain.

Answer: The information from the right visual field will be sent to the left hemisphere while the information from the left visual field will be sent to the right visual field.

Diff: 3   Page Ref: 122

Topic: How Are the Senses Alike?

Skill: Factual

9) Visible light occupies only a tiny segment of the _____ spectrum. Humans can generally see light with wavelengths that fall between _____.

Answer: electromagnetic; 400–700

Diff: 2   Page Ref: 123

Topic: How Are the Senses Alike?

Skill: Factual

10) If you look at a red square for a minute and then remove it and replace it with a neutral stimulus, you will likely see _____. This is known as _____.

Answer: green; negative afterimage

Diff: 2   Page Ref: 124

Topic: How Are the Senses Alike?

Skill: Conceptual

11) Briefly explain the difference between nerve and conduction deafness.

Answer: Nerve deafness usually is a result on damage to the auditory nerve or a higher processing center, while conduction deafness involves a disruption in the ways in which sounds waves are convert to nerve energy.

Diff: 3   *Page Ref: 129*

Topic: How Are the Senses Alike?

Skill: Applied

12) The detection of body position is involved in the _____ sense, which is controlled by _____.

Answer: vestibular; semicircular canals

Diff: 2   *Page Ref: 130*

Topic: How Are the Senses Alike?

Skill: Conceptual

13) Impulses from nerve cells convey odor information to _____ bulbs located just below the frontal lobes, this is the only sense that does not travel through the _____.

Answer: olfactory; thalamus

Diff: 3   *Page Ref: 130*

Topic: How Are the Senses Alike?

Skill: Conceptual

14) How is a very sensitive sense of taste (super tasters) adaptive?

Answer: Supertasters can more easily detect foods that might be harmful and they are more sensitive to tastes such as bitter that from an evolutionary perspective may be poisonous.

Diff: 3   *Page Ref: 131*

Topic: How Are the Senses Alike?

Skill: Conceptual

15) Briefly explain how the Gat–Control theory of pain explains how pain messages occur.

Answer: The slow fibers that carry messages to the brain but lack myelin sheath, conduct pain messages. The fast fibers which contain much myelin sheath can block these messages by closing a "spinal gate" that will not allow pain messages to move up the spinal cord.

Diff: 3   *Page Ref: 133*

Topic: The Experience of Pain

Skill: Applied

16) Stimulus driven processing is known as _____, while conceptually driven processing is known as _____.

Answer: bottom–up processing; top–down processing
Diff: 2   Page Ref: 136
Topic: What is the Relationship Between Sensation and Perception?
Skill: Factual

17) Briefly explain why as a door opens we do not perceive it as morphing into something other than a door.

Answer: We experience perceptual constancies in order to more efficiently evaluate the world in which we live, therefore a door opening would remain the same in it's shape size and color.
Diff: 2   Page Ref: 137
Topic: What is the Relationship Between Sensation and Perception?
Skill: Applied

18) Briefly explain the differences in how Gestalt and learning-based inferences may influence our perception.

Answer: Gestalt believes that it is innately learned while learning based inferences suggest that it is nurture or learning in our given environment that allows us to perceive the word as we do.
Diff: 2   Page Ref: 141–146
Topic: What is the Relationship Between Sensation and Perception?
Skill: Analysis

19) What does Gestalt mean?

Answer: The whole is larger than the sum of the parts.
Diff: 2   Page Ref: 142
Topic: What is the Relationship Between Sensation and Perception?
Skill: Conceptual

20) The Gestalt principle of _____ makes you see incomplete figures as complete and supplies the missing edges beyond gaps and barriers.

Answer: closure
Diff: 2   Page Ref: 143
Topic: What is the Relationship Between Sensation and Perception?
Skill: Conceptual

21) If I see members of a baseball team waiting for their game to start all wearing the same uniforms and huddled together talking to one another. I am likely to use the Gestalt principles of _____ and _____ to see them as part of the same team.

Answer: similarity; proximity
Diff: 2   Page Ref: 144
Topic: What is the Relationship Between Sensation and Perception?
Skill: Applied

22) The visual cliff created by experimenters Gibson and Walk, demonstrates children's ability to detect.

Answer: depth
Diff: 2   Page Ref: 145
Topic: What is the Relationship Between Sensation and Perception?
Skill: Factual

23) If I see two houses that are the same size, the one that is actually further away will be perceived to be _____ than the other house.

Answer: larger
Diff: 2   Page Ref: 146
Topic: What is the Relationship Between Sensation and Perception?
Skill: Applied

24) When someone tells you that you have been singing to wrong words to a song and actually tells you what the correct words are, the next time that you hear the song you are likely to hear the correct words. What has your friend created for you?

Answer: a perceptual set
Diff: 2   Page Ref: 148
Topic: What is the Relationship Between Sensation and Perception?
Skill: Applied

Essay Questions

1) Explain how a message is transformed in order to be read properly by the brain, and how sensation and perception play a role in this process.

Answer: The physical information that exists in the world cannot be read by the brain, therefore sensory receptors change this information into neural information which can be read by the brain. The physical information then only gets as far as our sensory receptors. Stimulation occurs first, then transduction, followed by sensation and finally the interpretation of this information which is perception.
Diff: 3   Page Ref: 110–113
Topic: How Does Stimulation Become Sensation?
Skill: Analysis

2) Discuss the how the absolute and difference thresholds are different. Also explain how Weber's law and Signal Detection Theory influence when we will detect a stimulus

Answer: An absolute threshold is the amount of the stimulus necessary to be detected about 50 % of the time. A difference threshold is a change in a stimulus that is already present. in an absolute threshold there is initially no stimulus present in a difference threshold there is. Weber's law states that a change in the original stimulus must be in direct proportion to the size of the original stimulus. signal detection theory states that we are likely to detect weak signals when they are significant and meaningful to us.

Diff: 3   Page Ref: 114–117

Topic: How Does Stimulation Become Sensation?

Skill: Applied

3) Briefly explain how a message of a red ball you view during the day would travel from the retina to it's proper location in the brain. Be sure to include the importance of all of the areas which the message must pass through as well as to mention where is the visual process transduction occurs.

Answer: The message will reach cones in the retina because cones pick up color messages. the process of transduction occurs while the message is still in the retina and from here on out will be conveyed as a neural message. The message will then pass from bipolar to ganglion cells. The ganglion cells axons will combine to form the optic nerve. Were the optic nerve leaves the eyeball there are no visual receptors and this is known ad the blind spot When he message ultimately makes it to the brain it will wind up in the visual cortex in the occipital lobe.

Diff: 3   Page Ref: 120

Topic: How Are the Senses Alike?

Skill: Analysis

4) Contrast the two major views of color vision theory, and explain what happens if one of these systems fail.

Answer: One view is the trichromatic theory which argues that three classes of photoreceptors detect color, with each color representing a mixture of activation of the receptors. This view cannot account for negative color afterimages. In contrast, opponent process theory argues that for a system in which red light may activate a cell in the visual system, while green light inhibits that cell. individuals who do not have fully functional color vision systems may experience color blindness the most common type being the inability to distinguish between red and green.

Diff: 2   Page Ref: 124

Topic: How Are the Senses Alike?

Skill: Conceptual

5) Describe the four-step process by which sound vibrations are turned into auditory sensations.

Answer: First, sound waves must be relayed to the inner ear after reaching the eardrum first. Next, the cochlea must focus the vibrations on the basilar membrane. Then, this basilar membrane will transform the vibrations into neural impulses. Finally, these impulses will reach the auditory cortex in the temporal lobes for higher-order processing.

Diff: 2   *Page Ref: 125-127*

Topic: How Are the Senses Alike?

Skill: Applied

6) Name and describe the two competing theories that attempt to explain perception. Provide an example for how each theory might explain a percept.

Answer: The learning-based inference claims that prior learning determines our perceptions. The Gestalt theory claims that the brain is designed to seek out patterns. Thus, this theory believes that nature is the key determinant of what we perceive. As for the examples, the student's examples must reflect prior learning for the learning-based inference (for example, seeing B0Y as 'b-o-y' rather than 'b-zero-y').

Diff: 2   *Page Ref: 141-146*

Topic: What is the Relationship Between Sensation and Perception?

Skill: Conceptual

7) Imagine that you are attending a dance performance. there are hundreds of dancers performing over the course of the evening. Frequently, there are 20-30 dancers in each number. Using the following Gestalt principles of grouping, explain how these would fit into your evening allowing you to make more sense of the dancers you are viewing.
figure-ground
closure
similarity
proximity
continuity

Answer: Figure-ground (figure is seen as closer than background) could be seen as the dancers moving around against the set once the dancers move they 'pop out as the figures while the stagnant features become the background. Closure (we mentally 'fill in' missing elements). If the dancers are creating patterns and shapes by where they are standing on the stage, we perceive the shapes as being complete. The law of similarity (we mentally group similar things together). If the dancers for a given performance are wearing the same outfits we would view them as being together. The law of proximity (we mentally group items that are nearby one another together). If a group of dancers is standing near each other between performances we would tend to see them as being part of the same dance or perhaps as being friends with one another because they are close o one another. The law of continuity (we prefer smoothly connected figures), even if the dancers or doing complicated moves we will see their motion as continuous and flowing.

Diff: 3   *Page Ref: 141-144*

Topic: What is the Relationship Between Sensation and Perception?

Skill: Applied

8) Imagine you are drawing a landscape. You want to try to create an image that is as lifelike as possible. Using the following monocular cues, create elements of the picture that will seem to give the painting depth.
relative height
relative size
atmospheric perspective
interposition
linear perspective

Answer: For relative height, mountains that are further away should appear higher on the canvas. For relative size, the mountain that are further away should also appear to be smaller in size. For atmospheric perspective, the tops of the distant mountains would appear covered in haze or clouds. For interposition, those mountains that were further away would in large part b covered u by the mountains which were closer. For linear perspective, a river that is relatively wide at the front of the picture would gradually converge as it meanders away into the mountains in the distance.

Diff: 3   Page Ref: 146

Topic: What is the Relationship Between Sensation and Perception?

Skill: Applied

Chapter 5 States of Consciousness

Multiple Choice Questions

1) The process by which the brain creates a model of internal and external experience is defined as
   - A) unconsciousness.
   - B) pre consciousness.
   - C) consciousness.
   - D) non consciousness.
   - E) semiconsciousness.

   Answer: C
   Diff: 1   Page Ref: 158
   Topic: How is Consciousness Related to Other Mental Processes?
   Skill: Recall

2) Folk wisdom attributes consciousness to our _____, which is a spirit or inner life force.
   - A) thanatos
   - B) animus
   - C) anima
   - D) eros
   - E) None of the above

   Answer: C
   Diff: 3   Page Ref: 158
   Topic: How is Consciousness Related to Other Mental Processes?
   Skill: Factual

3) Structuralism used the technique of _____ to study consciousness.
   - A) psychoanalysis
   - B) experimentation
   - C) anima
   - D) naturalistic observation
   - E) introspection

   Answer: E
   Diff: 2   Page Ref: 159
   Topic: How is Consciousness Related to Other Mental Processes?
   Skill: Conceptual

4) A person who fervently believes in the writings of John B. Watson would be expected to believe or do all of of the following EXCEPT which one?

    A) emphasizes the direct observation of behavior

    B) focuses solely on external behavior

    C) dismisses introspection as unscientific

    D) claims that consciousness is merely a by-product of behavior

    E) attempts to search for the mental processes which cause behavior

Answer: E
Diff: 2   *Page Ref: 159*
Topic: How is Consciousness Related to Other Mental Processes?
Skill: Applied

5) _____ was an early psychologist who dismissed introspection as too subjective to be scientifically useful.

    A) Watson   B) Freud   C) Titchner   D) James   E) Helmholtz

Answer: A
Diff: 2   *Page Ref: 159*
Topic: How is Consciousness Related to Other Mental Processes?
Skill: Factual

6) Which type of psychologist is most likely to believe that the conscious mind is a natural process occurring in the nerve cells of the brain that can be studied through objective scientific inquiry?

    A) humanistic psychologists

    B) behavioral geneticists

    C) cognitive neuroscientists

    D) experiential psychologists

    E) clinical psychologists

Answer: C
Diff: 2   *Page Ref: 159*
Topic: How is Consciousness Related to Other Mental Processes?
Skill: Conceptual

7) From approximately the 1920s through the 1960s, the _____ view was the dominant popular approach to psychology.

   A) psychodynamic

   B) behavioristic

   C) humanistic

   D) sociocultural

   E) deterministic

Answer: B

Diff: 2   Page Ref: 159

Topic: How is Consciousness Related to Other Mental Processes?

Skill: Factual

8) Which of the following is NOT a general function of consciousness?

   A) constructing personal realities

   B) recognizing new information

   C) organizing thoughts

   D) restricting attention

   E) responding with impulses

Answer: E

Diff: 1   Page Ref: 159

Topic: How is Consciousness Related to Other Mental Processes?

Skill: Conceptual

9) _____ is an example of a conscious process.

   A) Breathing

   B) Trying to choose the best answer to this question

   C) Regulating your blood pressure

   D) Scratching an itch

   E) Blinking every few seconds

Answer: B

Diff: 1   Page Ref: 159

Topic: How is Consciousness Related to Other Mental Processes?

Skill: Applied

10) All of the following fields are related to cognitive neuroscience, except
    A) chemistry.
    B) neurology.
    C) biology.
    D) computer science.
    E) linguistics.

Answer: A
Diff: 2   *Page Ref: 159*
Topic: How is Consciousness Related to Other Mental Processes?
Skill: Recall

11) A cognitive neuroscientist would be most likely to have subjects _____ to determine which brain areas are active during different mental tasks.
    A) discuss their most recent dreams
    B) utilize a technique called "priming"
    C) undergo MRI, PET or EEG testing
    D) take psychoactive drugs
    E) report on their ideas by using introspection

Answer: C
Diff: 2   *Page Ref: 159*
Topic: How is Consciousness Related to Other Mental Processes?
Skill: Applied

12) Which of the following functions would be considered a non conscious process?
    A) studying for your psychology exam
    B) telling your Mother you love her
    C) digesting the cheeseburger you ate for lunch
    D) painting a picture of a landscape
    E) All of the above are non conscious processes

Answer: C
Diff: 2   *Page Ref: 160*
Topic: How is Consciousness Related to Other Mental Processes?
Skill: Applied

13) The body's monitoring of biological functioning such as digestion and breathing are examples of
  A) preconscious processes.
  B) subconscious awareness.
  C) conscious awareness.
  D) non conscious processes.
  E) semiconscious processes.

Answer: D
Diff: 2   Page Ref: 160
Topic: How is Consciousness Related to Other Mental Processes?
Skill: Conceptual

14) According the the findings of Shepard and Metzler (1971) volunteers in an experiment demonstrated
  A) it did not take them any longer to respond when asked to rotate an object in space.
  B) when they were asked to recall details about a given object, it took them a very long time to respond.
  C) If the participants had seen an object before, they could rotate it quickly in their mind.
  D) that it took them longer to rotate objects in their mind.
  E) None of the above

Answer: D
Diff: 3   Page Ref: 160
Topic: How is Consciousness Related to Other Mental Processes?
Skill: Recall

15) According to the work of Stephen Kosslyn, he found that when participants were asked about objects
  A) they took longer to respond as the details asked for became smaller.
  B) they took the same amount of time to respond regardless of how large or small the detail asked for was.
  C) it took them longer to rotate objects in space.
  D) it took tem no longer to respond regardless of whether or not they had to rotate and object.
  E) most individuals are easily hypnotizable.

Answer: A
Diff: 3   Page Ref: 161
Topic: How is Consciousness Related to Other Mental Processes?
Skill: Conceptual

16) Which of the following are components of William James' stream of consciousness?

    A) perceptions

    B) memories

    C) feelings

    D) sensations

    E) All of the above are components of Jame's theory of consciousness.

Answer: E
Diff: 1   Page Ref: 162
Topic: How is Consciousness Related to Other Mental Processes?
Skill: Recall

17) Freud believed that the vast majority of our motivation arose from our

    A) altered states of consciousness.

    B) preconscious.

    C) conscious.

    D) unconscious.

    E) non conscious.

Answer: D
Diff: 2   Page Ref: 162
Topic: How is Consciousness Related to Other Mental Processes?
Skill: Conceptual

18) How is the conscious mind different from the unconscious mind?

    A) The conscious mind holds our vast hidden desires.

    B) The conscious mind restricts our attention by setting limits of what we can thin about.

    C) The conscious mind in not under our waking control.

    D) The conscious mind holds repressed memories.

    E) None of the above

Answer: B
Diff: 2   Page Ref: 163
Topic: How is Consciousness Related to Other Mental Processes?
Skill: Conceptual

19) Preconscious memories are thought to

    A) function in the background until they are needed.

    B) detect changes in biological functioning and regulate them without conscious awareness.

    C) involve automatic cognitive processing of information.

    D) stem from the need to repress traumatic memories or taboo desires.

    E) cannot be brought to conscious memory because they are 'buried' too deep.

Answer: A

Diff: 2   Page Ref: 164

Topic: How is Consciousness Related to Other Mental Processes?

Skill: Conceptual

20) Dr. Gruber asked Pamela to say the words "folk," "soak," and "joke." Then, he asked her, "What do you call the white of an egg?" If her reply was "The yolk," rather than the right answer (the albumen, or egg white), this answer would be evidence for

    A) selective attention.

    B) hypnotizability.

    C) priming.

    D) functionalism.

    E) cataplexy.

Answer: C

Diff: 3   Page Ref: 164

Topic: How is Consciousness Related to Other Mental Processes?

Skill: Applied

21) According to Freud, which of the following is likely to be found in one's unconscious?

    A) threatening impulses

    B) a person's internment at a P.O.W. camp

    C) powerfully negative memories from childhood

    D) sexual urges

    E) All of the above are examples of thoughts Freud would suggest we hold in our unconscious.

Answer: E

Diff: 1   Page Ref: 164–165

Topic: How is Consciousness Related to Other Mental Processes?

Skill: Conceptual

22) According to Freud, if you become aware of your unconscious thoughts
    A) there would be too much information for you to process.
    B) you would experience physical symptoms of illness.
    C) it would cause you extreme anxiety.
    D) you could function in a more healthy manner.
    E) you would become quite violent.

Answer: C
Diff: 2   Page Ref: 164
Topic: How is Consciousness Related to Other Mental Processes?
Skill: Conceptual

23) Which of the following is NOT true of daydreams?
    A) They magnify unwanted thoughts or obsessions.
    B) They help us to creatively confront and solve problems.
    C) They are under our control.
    D) They are most common in young adults.
    E) They occur more often in those with fantasy prone personalities.

Answer: A
Diff: 3   Page Ref: 166
Topic: What Cycles Occur in Everyday Consciousness?
Skill: Conceptual

24) Individual's desire to take a 'siesta' in the afternoon is driven by
    A) what they ate for lunch.
    B) biological rhythms.
    C) stage 1 of sleep.
    D) sleep spindles.
    E) sleep deprivation.

Answer: B
Diff: 1   Page Ref: 166–167
Topic: What Cycles Occur in Everyday Consciousness?
Skill: Conceptual

25) The pattern of human physiological processes seems to be controlled by an internal "biological clock" that is

    A) unaffected by the world's daylight–dark cycles.

    B) coordinated by neurons in the hypothalamus.

    C) set on a 12–hour cycle.

    D) identical for all people.

    E) unrelated to work schedules and travel.

Answer: B

Diff: 3   Page Ref: 167

Topic: What Cycles Occur in Everyday Consciousness?

Skill: Conceptual

26) Changes that occur daily in our consciousness that contribute to how alert we are at any given time during the day are controlled by

    A) our interests.

    B) biological tides.

    C) circadian rhythms.

    D) daydreaming.

    E) our genotypes.

Answer: C

Diff: 2   Page Ref: 167

Topic: What Cycles Occur in Everyday Consciousness?

Skill: Conceptual

27) Circadian rhythms are NOT disrupted by

    A) shifting work schedules.

    B) sleep and wake routines.

    C) eating regular meals.

    D) flying from West to East.

    E) changes in the light–dark cycle.

Answer: C

Diff: 1   Page Ref: 167

Topic: What Cycles Occur in Everyday Consciousness?

Skill: Conceptual

28) "Jet lag" is primarily a result of

    A) anxiety-producing unconscious processes.

    B) upset circadian rhythms.

    C) hangover due to drinking alcohol before flying.

    D) sensory isolation due to flying in an enclosed airplane for a long time.

    E) flying directly north to south.

Answer: B
Diff: 2   *Page Ref: 167*
Topic: What Cycles Occur in Everyday Consciousness?
Skill: Factual

29) The most severe cases of "jet lag" occur when we travel

    A) west.

    B) north.

    C) east.

    D) south.

    E) short distances.

Answer: C
Diff: 2   *Page Ref: 167*
Topic: What Cycles Occur in Everyday Consciousness?
Skill: Factual

30) All of the following are characteristic of REM sleep except

    A) rapid eye movement.

    B) vivid cognitions.

    C) voluntary muscles are immobile.

    D) it is a deep sleep.

    E) sleep paralysis.

Answer: D
Diff: 2   *Page Ref: 168*
Topic: What Cycles Occur in Everyday Consciousness?
Skill: Conceptual

31) While in the REM phase of sleep,

    A) your mental activity focuses on ordinary daily events.

    B) you are likely to act out your dreams.

    C) your voluntary muscles are immobilized in sleep paralysis.

    D) you may sleep walk and sleep talk.

    E) you experience sleep spindles.

Answer: C

Diff: 2   Page Ref: 168

Topic: What Cycles Occur in Everyday Consciousness?

Skill: Conceptual

32) How does the evolutionary view account for the presence of sleep paralysis during REM sleep?

    A) Sleep paralysis promotes brain development.

    B) Sleep paralysis allows us to focus our mental energy on problem solving.

    C) Our energy stores are recharged more rapidly during sleep paralysis.

    D) Sleep paralysis allows use to avoid predators at night.

    E) All of the above are correct

Answer: D

Diff: 2   Page Ref: 168

Topic: What Cycles Occur in Everyday Consciousness?

Skill: Conceptual

33) Which of the following does not happen during REM sleep?

    A) dreams

    B) vivid images and thoughts

    C) sleep paralysis

    D) sleep walking

    E) All of the above occur in REM sleep

Answer: D

Diff: 2   Page Ref: 168

Topic: What Cycles Occur in Everyday Consciousness?

Skill: Recall

34) The deepest point in the sleep cycle, when brain waves activity is the slowest, occurs in

    A) Stage 1, about three hours after falling asleep.

    B) REM sleep, about one hour after falling asleep.

    C) Stage 4, about a half hour after falling asleep.

    D) Stage 4, about two hours before waking up.

    E) REM sleep, about one hour before waking up.

Answer: C
Diff: 2   Page Ref: 168
Topic: What Cycles Occur in Everyday Consciousness?
Skill: Factual

35) Which of the following best describes a characteristic of stage 2 for sleep?

    A) sleep walking

    B) sleep spindles

    C) sleep talking

    D) dreaming

    E) sleep paralysis

Answer: B
Diff: 2   Page Ref: 168
Topic: What Cycles Occur in Everyday Consciousness?
Skill: Conceptual

36) Which of the following describes the sleep waves of stages 1,2 and 4?

    A) theta, sleep spindles, delta

    B) delta, theta, sleep spindles

    C) theta, delta, sleep spindles

    D) sleep spindles, delta, theta

    E) sleep spindles, theta, delta

Answer: A
Diff: 2   Page Ref: 168
Topic: What Cycles Occur in Everyday Consciousness?
Skill: Conceptual

37) Your alarm clock is set to wake you up two hours before you would normally arise. After a few days of this, you shut off your alarm clock and go to sleep. We would now expect to show

    A) even less REM sleep than usual.

    B) more REM sleep than usual.

    C) no REM sleep.

    D) the same REM sleep as usual.

    E) only REM sleep.

Answer: B

Diff: 2   Page Ref: 169

Topic: What Cycles Occur in Everyday Consciousness?

Skill: Applied

38) A characteristic of sleep as we grow closer to the morning is

    A) it gets gradually deeper.

    B) we spend more time in REM sleep.

    C) we spend more time in stages 3 and 4 of sleep.

    D) our brain waves become slower and deeper.

    E) All of the above are true

Answer: B

Diff: 2   Page Ref: 169

Topic: What Cycles Occur in Everyday Consciousness?

Skill: Conceptual

39) Deprivation of REM sleep for results in _____ during the next evening's sleep.

    A) REM rebound

    B) reduced problem solving

    C) reduced REM sleep

    D) reduced coordination

    E) All of the above are correct

Answer: A

Diff: 2   Page Ref: 169

Topic: What Cycles Occur in Everyday Consciousness?

Skill: Factual

40) The _____ argues that we sleep in order to conserve energy.
   A) clinical psychology view
   B) Freudian view
   C) evolutionary theory
   D) activation–synthesis theory
   E) homeostatic

Answer: C
Diff: 2   Page Ref: 169
Topic: What Cycles Occur in Everyday Consciousness?
Skill: Factual

41) Which of the following is an explanation of why we sleep?
   A) Sleep allows us to conserve energy.
   B) Sleep promotes memory.
   C) Sleep clears the brain of useless information.
   D) Sleep helps us to avoid nocturnal predators.
   E) All of the above are correct.

Answer: E
Diff: 2   Page Ref: 169–170
Topic: What Cycles Occur in Everyday Consciousness?
Skill: Conceptual

42) Sean is nervous and creative, whereas Jennifer is energetic and introverted. Based on research into sleep and personality, we can expect that
   A) Sean and Jennifer sleep about the same amount.
   B) Jennifer tends to sleep longer than most people.
   C) Jennifer tends to sleep longer than Sean.
   D) Sean tends to sleep more than Jennifer, but both sleep more than most people.
   E) Sean tends to sleep more than Jennifer.

Answer: E
Diff: 3   Page Ref: 170
Topic: What Cycles Occur in Everyday Consciousness?
Skill: Applied

43) Strenuous physical activity during the day is most likely to affect _____.

   A) Stage 2 sleep spindles

   B) Stage 1 sleep

   C) Stage 4 deep sleep

   D) REM sleep

   E) dream content

   Answer: C

   Diff: 3   Page Ref: 170

   Topic: What Cycles Occur in Everyday Consciousness?

   Skill: Factual

44) Who sleeps the least?

   A) newborns

   B) adolescents

   C) young adults

   D) the elderly

   E) children

   Answer: D

   Diff: 2   Page Ref: 171

   Topic: What Cycles Occur in Everyday Consciousness?

   Skill: Factual

45) If you live in a dark room without interruption, we would expect to sleep _____ hours per night.

   A) 8.5   B) 5   C) 10   D) 11   E) 12

   Answer: A

   Diff: 2   Page Ref: 171

   Topic: What Cycles Occur in Everyday Consciousness?

   Skill: Factual

46) A recent research study suggests that the cognitive deficit produced by sleep deprivation is similar to that of

   A) a short sleeper.

   B) a legally drunk person.

   C) a long sleeper.

   D) a 90 year old.

   E) C and D are correct.

   Answer: B

   Diff: 2   Page Ref: 172

   Topic: What Cycles Occur in Everyday Consciousness?

   Skill: Factual

47) Which of the following decreases when one had not had enough sleep?
    A) motor functioning
    B) work efficiency
    C) cognitive functioning
    D) immune system efficiency
    E) All of the above are correct

Answer: E
Diff: 2   *Page Ref: 172*
Topic: What Cycles Occur in Everyday Consciousness?
Skill: Applied

48) According to Freud, the two main functions of dreams are to
    A) release electrical discharges and aid in the growth of the brain.
    B) conserve energy and restore neuron function.
    C) help people rest and relax.
    D) reduce psychic tensions and work through unconscious desires.
    E) facilitate memory and clean out old memories.

Answer: D
Diff: 1   *Page Ref: 172*
Topic: What Cycles Occur in Everyday Consciousness?
Skill: Factual

49) _____ was the author of *The Interpretation of Dreams* (1900).
    A) Darwin   B) Hall   C) James   D) Freud   E) Broca

Answer: D
Diff: 1   *Page Ref: 172*
Topic: What Cycles Occur in Everyday Consciousness?
Skill: Factual

50) According the Freud, the two main function of dreams were
    A) wish fulfillment and physical restoration.
    B) physical restoration and flushing of the preconscious.
    C) to guard sleep and wish fulfillment.
    D) to guard sleep and provide physical restoration.
    E) wish fulfillment and random neural firing.

Answer: C
Diff: 2   *Page Ref: 172*
Topic: What Cycles Occur in Everyday Consciousness?
Skill: Conceptual

51) A therapist who analyzes your dreams is most likely to have been trained according to the _____ school of psychology.

    A) behaviorism

    B) cognitive

    C) humanistic

    D) psychoanalytic

    E) neuroscience

Answer: D
Diff: 2   *Page Ref: 173*
Topic: What Cycles Occur in Everyday Consciousness?
Skill: Applied

52) According to Freud, the manifest content of a dream refers to

    A) the setting of the dream.

    B) the story line of the dream.

    C) whether the dream is in color or black and white.

    D) the emotional tone of the dream.

    E) the symbolic meaning of the dream.

Answer: B
Diff: 2   *Page Ref: 173*
Topic: What Cycles Occur in Everyday Consciousness?
Skill: Factual

53) According to Freud, the latent content of a dream refers to

    A) the setting of the dream.

    B) the story line of the dream.

    C) whether the dream is in color or black and white.

    D) the emotional tone of the dream.

    E) the symbolic meaning of the dream.

Answer: E
Diff: 2   *Page Ref: 173*
Topic: What Cycles Occur in Everyday Consciousness?
Skill: Factual

54) Which of the following is true of dreams?

    A) Men are equally likely to dream of children than are women.

    B) Men dream about men twice as often as they dream of women.

    C) Americans seldom dream of being naked in public.

    D) Male dreams are more likely to feature friendly exchanges rather than hostility.

    E) Adults are more likely than children to dream of large, threatening animals.

Answer: B
Diff: 3   Page Ref: 173
Topic: What Cycles Occur in Everyday Consciousness?
Skill: Conceptual

55) Your last dream of the night is likely to

    A) have the weakest connection to events of the previous day.

    B) have the strongest connection to events of the previous day.

    C) anticipate the events of the coming day.

    D) be the hardest to remember.

    E) occur about two hours before you awaken.

Answer: A
Diff: 2   Page Ref: 174
Topic: What Cycles Occur in Everyday Consciousness?
Skill: Conceptual

56) _____ is the view that the mind makes a coherent story out of spontaneous brain stem discharges.

    A) The psychoanalytic perspective

    B) The activation–synthesis dream model

    C) The humanistic model

    D) The behavioristic approach

    E) The homeostatic approach

Answer: B
Diff: 2   Page Ref: 174
Topic: What Cycles Occur in Everyday Consciousness?
Skill: Conceptual

57) All of the following are examples of modern explanations about why we dream except

    A) activation–synthesis model.

    B) it allows us to predict the future.

    C) REM sleep furnishes the brain with an internal source of needed stimulation.

    D) A source of creative insights.

    E) All of the above are examples of modern explanations of why we dream.

Answer: B
Diff: 2   Page Ref: 174
Topic: What Cycles Occur in Everyday Consciousness?
Skill: Conceptual

58) Which of the following is true of insomnia? It

    A) involves frequent daytime sleeping.

    B) affects about one in ten adults.

    C) rarely affects American adults.

    D) occurs when breathing stops while sleeping.

    E) is the most common sleep disorder.

Answer: E
Diff: 1   Page Ref: 175
Topic: Sleep Disorders
Skill: Factual

59) All of the following can be helpful in treating insomnia except

    A) using cognitive–behavioral therapy to get to sleep faster.

    B) associating one's bedroom with sleeping only (not studying, watching television, etc.).

    C) having parents of newborn infants go about their normal day instead of trying not to make any noise while the child is sleeping.

    D) trying to reduce levels of stress on a daily basis.

    E) All of the above would be useful in reducing insomnia

Answer: E
Diff: 2   Page Ref: 175
Topic: What Cycles Occur in Everyday Consciousness?
Skill: Applied

60) Sleep apnea is
    A) common in premature infants.
    B) associated with high blood oxygen levels.
    C) a lower respiratory sleep disorder.
    D) a surgical technique that can prevent loud snoring.
    E) a common cause of insomnia.

Answer: A
Diff: 2   *Page Ref: 176*
Topic: Sleep Disorders
Skill: Conceptual

61) Sleep apnea can be dangerous for adults because it
    A) can reduce heart rate.
    B) can cause a migraine.
    C) elevates blood pressure, which in turn stresses the heart.
    D) causes a loss of muscle tone.
    E) causes lower back pain.

Answer: C
Diff: 3   *Page Ref: 176*
Topic: Sleep Disorders
Skill: Factual

62) Which of the following is a common cause of insomnia?
    A) extra skin in the throat temporarily blocking breathing pathways
    B) early morning exercise
    C) inappropriate use of sleeping pills
    D) eating a large meal at dinner
    E) collapse of the airways to the lungs

Answer: C
Diff: 2   *Page Ref: 176*
Topic: Sleep Disorders
Skill: Factual

63) _____ is treated using a device that pumps air into his lungs and keeps the airway open during sleep.

    A) Narcolepsy

    B) Cataplexy

    C) Sleep paralysis

    D) Insomnia

    E) Sleep apnea

Answer: E
Diff: 1   Page Ref: 176
Topic: Sleep Disorders
Skill: Applied

64) Which of the following is true of night terrors?

    A) Night terrors occur primarily in children.

    B) Night terrors occur during Non–REM sleep.

    C) Night terrors involve anxiety and panic.

    D) Night terrors usually disappear by adulthood.

    E) Night terrors seem to be real.

Answer: E
Diff: 2   Page Ref: 176
Topic: Sleep Disorders
Skill: Factual

65) The occurrence of daytime sleep attacks is a symptom of

    A) sleep paralysis.

    B) narcolepsy.

    C) insomnia.

    D) daytime sleepiness.

    E) sleep apnea.

Answer: B
Diff: 1   Page Ref: 176–177
Topic: Sleep Disorders
Skill: Applied

66) The frequency of narcolepsy can be reduced by

    A) medication.

    B) regular exercise.

    C) psychotherapy.

    D) mid–afternoon naps.

    E) herbal therapy.

Answer: A

Diff: 2   *Page Ref: 176*

Topic: Sleep Disorders

Skill: Factual

67) What is the loss of muscle control often preceding a narcoleptic episode?

    A) apnea

    B) cataplexy

    C) catatonia

    D) incontinent

    E) None of the above

Answer: B

Diff: 2   *Page Ref: 177*

Topic: Sleep Disorders

Skill: Factual

68) The capacity of hypnosis to reduce pain is termed

    A) hypnotic amnesia.

    B) autohypnosis.

    C) hypnotic analgesia.

    D) hypnotic meditation.

    E) hypnotic aphasia.

Answer: C

Diff: 3   *Page Ref: 179*

Topic: What Other Forms Can Consciousness Take?

Skill: Applied

69) Which of the following is true of hypnosis?

    A) Hypnosis is a form of REM sleep.

    B) Hypnosis is accompanied by delta wave activity of the brain.

    C) Hypnosis is a state of awareness associated with relaxation and susceptibility.

    D) Hypnosis is a form of non-REM sleep.

    E) Hypnotic analgesia is blocked by naloxone.

Answer: C
Diff: 2   Page Ref: 179
Topic: What Other Forms Can Consciousness Take?
Skill: Factual

70) A person who is highly susceptible to hypnosis

    A) are not likely to experience a perceptual distortion.

    B) are resistant to self-hypnosis.

    C) have very high IQ scores.

    D) can actively resist hypnotic commands.

    E) is more susceptible to hypnotic analgesia.

Answer: E
Diff: 3   Page Ref: 179
Topic: What Other Forms Can Consciousness Take?
Skill: Factual

71) Experiments have shown that the _____ effect of hypnosis _____ mediated by the release of endorphins in the brain.

    A) analgesic; is

    B) relaxation; is

    C) euphoric; is not

    D) catatonic; is

    E) analgesic; is not

Answer: E
Diff: 3   Page Ref: 179
Topic: What Other Forms Can Consciousness Take?
Skill: Factual

72) All of the following are true about hypnosis except

    A) hypnotized participants have a heightened sense of motivation.

    B) hypnotized participants are in a trance.

    C) hypnosis in large part depends on the participants suggestibility.

    D) hypnosis can involve laying a role in order to please the hypnotist.

    E) they may be a "hidden observer' as they watch themselves perform different behaviors.

Answer: B

Diff: 2   Page Ref: 179

Topic: What Other Forms Can Consciousness Take?

Skill: Conceptual

73) Which of the following would hypnosis be useful in treating?

    A) relieving some of the pain in natural childbirth

    B) temporary relief of anxiety

    C) treating phobias

    D) eliminating negative behaviors such as smoking

    E) Hypnosis can be useful in treating all of the above

Answer: E

Diff: 1   Page Ref: 180

Topic: What Other Forms Can Consciousness Take?

Skill: Applied

74) _____ involves controlled breathing while assuming certain body positions and minimizing external stimuli.

    A) Hypnosis

    B) Meditation

    C) Consciousness

    D) Dichotic listening

    E) Cataplexy

Answer: B

Diff: 2   Page Ref: 181

Topic: What Other Forms Can Consciousness Take?

Skill: Applied

75) Mediation can cause all of the following purposes except

    A) changes in brain wave patterns in experienced mediators.

    B) frontal lobe changes.

    C) and increase in positive emotions.

    D) reduction of various signs of bodily arousal.

    E) a highly suggestible state.

Answer: E
Diff: 2   Page Ref: 181
Topic: What Other Forms Can Consciousness Take?
Skill: Applied

76) Widely abused illegal drugs such as cocaine, heroin, and amphetamines are attractive to users because

    A) they stimulate the brain's "reward circuits."

    B) they helped our ancestors survive and reproduce.

    C) they suppress REM sleep.

    D) they slow down mental and physical activity.

    E) they produce hallucinations and delusions.

Answer: A
Diff: 2   Page Ref: 181–182
Topic: What Other Forms Can Consciousness Take?
Skill: Conceptual

77) The ability of a drug to act as a hallucinogen involves an interaction with _____ neurons.

    A) psilocybin

    B) melatonin

    C) serotonin

    D) phencyclidine

    E) norepinephrine

Answer: C
Diff: 3   Page Ref: 182
Topic: What Other Forms Can Consciousness Take?
Skill: Factual

78) Which of the following is NOT classified as a hallucinogen?

    A) psilocybin   B) angel dust   C) LSD   D) cocaine   E) cannabis

Answer: D
Diff: 2   Page Ref: 182
Topic: What Other Forms Can Consciousness Take?
Skill: Factual

79) The psychoactive effect of smoking cannabis is due to an action of _____ on the brain.

    A) codeine   B) THC   C) valium   D) PCP   E) opium

Answer: B
Diff: 2   Page Ref: 183
Topic: What Other Forms Can Consciousness Take?
Skill: Factual

80) Which of the following people would be most likely to benefit from using cannabis?

    A) Wayne, who is trying to remember the name of his second grade teacher

    B) Brad, who is driving home after watching the 11 o'clock news

    C) Colin, who is trying to lose 50 pounds in the next six months

    D) Ryan, who is nauseous from receiving chemotherapy

    E) Drew, a pilot, who is about to fly a 757 to Detroit

Answer: D
Diff: 2   Page Ref: 183
Topic: What Other Forms Can Consciousness Take?
Skill: Applied

81) cannabis can produce all of the following except

    A) altered perception.

    B) abundance of energy.

    C) pain relief.

    D) failure in memory.

    E) reduction in motor coordination.

Answer: B
Diff: 2   Page Ref: 183
Topic: What Other Forms Can Consciousness Take?
Skill: Applied

82) The positive effects of cannabis, such as sedation, mild euphoria, altered perception, pain relief, and distortions of space and time, have been found by recent research to be similar in some respects to that of

    A) tranquilizers.

    B) heroin.

    C) alcohol.

    D) cocaine.

    E) daydreams.

Answer: B
Diff: 2   Page Ref: 183
Topic: What Other Forms Can Consciousness Take?
Skill: Factual

83) The psychoactive effect of THC may reflect the capacity of THC to cause the release of
    A) serotonin.
    B) endorphins.
    C) benzodiazepines.
    D) dopamine.
    E) GABA.

Answer: D
Diff: 3   Page Ref: 184
Topic: What Other Forms Can Consciousness Take?
Skill: Factual

84) Morphine, heroin, and codeine are derived from
    A) the opium poppy.
    B) cannabis.
    C) peyote buttons.
    D) tea leaves.
    E) tobacco plants.

Answer: A
Diff: 2   Page Ref: 184
Topic: What Other Forms Can Consciousness Take?
Skill: Factual

85) The _____ are highly addictive drugs that suppress physical sensation and responsiveness to stimulation.
    A) opiates
    B) depressants
    C) hallucinogens
    D) stimulants
    E) amphetamines

Answer: A
Diff: 3   Page Ref: 184
Topic: What Other Forms Can Consciousness Take?
Skill: Factual

86) The capacity of morphine and codeine to provide excellent pain relief occurs because these drugs

    A) inhibit the uptake of serotonin.

    B) cause the loss of physical sensation.

    C) exert analgesic properties that resemble those of the body's endorphins.

    D) increase central nervous system activity.

    E) cause temporary failure within the cerebrum.

Answer: C
Diff: 3   Page Ref: 184
Topic: What Other Forms Can Consciousness Take?
Skill: Conceptual

87) Because addicts steal to support their habit, _____ addiction is blamed for the high proportion of property crime in cities worldwide.

    A) alcohol

    B) heroin

    C) barbiturates

    D) amphetamines

    E) LSD

Answer: B
Diff: 2   Page Ref: 184
Topic: What Other Forms Can Consciousness Take?
Skill: Factual

88) _____ drugs inhibit the central nervous system and thus slow mental and physical activity.

    A) Depressant

    B) Stimulant

    C) Opiate

    D) Hallucinogenic

    E) Amphetamine-like

Answer: A
Diff: 1   Page Ref: 184
Topic: What Other Forms Can Consciousness Take?
Skill: Conceptual

89) depressants cause

    A) inhibition of transmission of messages in the central nervous system.

    B) individuals to feel clinically depressed.

    C) individuals to feel euphoric and excited.

    D) anxiety.

    E) All of the above

Answer: A
Diff: 2   *Page Ref: 184*
Topic: What Other Forms Can Consciousness Take?
Skill: Conceptual

90) _____ is a benzodiazepine drug that is useful in the treatment of anxiety.

    A) Psilocybin   B) Valium   C) Morphine   D) Prozac   E) Lithium

Answer: B
Diff: 2   *Page Ref: 185*
Topic: What Other Forms Can Consciousness Take?
Skill: Applied

91) _____ is classified as a _____ and was one of the first psychoactive substances used by humans.

    A) Nicotine; depressant

    B) Barbiturate; stimulant

    C) Morphine; antipsychotic

    D) Heroin; stimulant

    E) Alcohol; depressant

Answer: E
Diff: 2   *Page Ref: 185*
Topic: What Other Forms Can Consciousness Take?
Skill: Factual

92) Overdoses of benzodiazepines can cause

    A) poor muscle coordination.

    B) slurred speech.

    C) muscle twitching.

    D) irritability.

    E) All of the above

Answer: E
Diff: 2   *Page Ref: 185*
Topic: What Other Forms Can Consciousness Take?
Skill: Factual

93) In general, the body breaks down alcohol at the rate of

   A) 1 once per hour.

   B) 5 ounces per hour.

   C) 10 ounces per hour.

   D) 4 ounces per hour.

   E) it takes up to three hours for the body to break down an ounce of alcohol.

Answer: A
Diff: 2   *Page Ref: 185*
Topic: What Other Forms Can Consciousness Take?
Skill: Factual

94) The leading cause of mental retardation is related to a mother's use of _____.

   A) alcohol

   B) opium

   C) sleeping pills

   D) caffeine

   E) cocaine

Answer: A
Diff: 1   *Page Ref: 186*
Topic: What Other Forms Can Consciousness Take?
Skill: Factual

95) Stimulants

   A) increase attention problems in ADHD children.

   B) are often prescribed to reduce anxiety.

   C) can effectively treat narcolepsy.

   D) slow central nervous system activity.

   E) reduce energy levels for most people.

Answer: C
Diff: 3   *Page Ref: 186*
Topic: What Other Forms Can Consciousness Take?
Skill: Conceptual

96) Crack cocaine is a psychoactive drug of the _____ class.

    A) opiate

    B) hallucinogen

    C) stimulant

    D) cannabis

    E) depressant

Answer: C

Diff: 1   Page Ref: 186

Topic: What Other Forms Can Consciousness Take?

Skill: Factual

97) Individuals may be drawn to stimulants for their euphoric capabilities, however they side effects of stimulants may include

    A) high addiction rates.

    B) dehydration.

    C) decreased memory.

    D) convulsions.

    E) All of the above

Answer: E

Diff: 2   Page Ref: 186

Topic: What Other Forms Can Consciousness Take?

Skill: Factual

98) The drug _____ has a greater negative effect on health than does all the other psychoactive drugs combined.

    A) heroin   B) PCP   C) nicotine   D) alcohol   E) LSD

Answer: C

Diff: 2   Page Ref: 187

Topic: What Other Forms Can Consciousness Take?

Skill: Factual

99) _____ is(are) the leading cause of preventable disease.

    A) Smoking

    B) Alcohol abuse

    C) Risky sexual practices

    D) Barbiturate overdose

    E) Morphine addiction

Answer: A

Diff: 2   Page Ref: 187

Topic: What Other Forms Can Consciousness Take?

Skill: Factual

100) Addiction refers to

    A) increased drug effect with repeated use.

    B) the loss of withdrawal symptoms when the drug use is stopped.

    C) maintained drug effect with repeated use.

    D) a situation where drug use continues despite adverse consequences to the user.

    E) augmented drug reward.

Answer: D

Diff: 2   Page Ref: 188

Topic: What Other Forms Can Consciousness Take?

Skill: Conceptual

101) The phenomenon by which a constant drug dose produces smaller effects with repeated administration is termed

    A) physiological dependence.

    B) tolerance.

    C) activation–synthesis.

    D) psychological dependence.

    E) drug withdrawal.

Answer: B

Diff: 2   Page Ref: 188

Topic: What Other Forms Can Consciousness Take?

Skill: Conceptual

102) After binging the entire week of Spring Break, Virginia has not had alcohol for a week, she is trembling, nauseous, perspiring, and begging for alcohol. Virginia is probably suffering from

    A) alcohol intolerance.

    B) a painful illusion.

    C) sensory deprivation.

    D) withdrawal symptoms.

    E) cataplexy analgesia.

Answer: D

Diff: 2   Page Ref: 188

Topic: What Other Forms Can Consciousness Take?

Skill: Applied

103) Katie is constantly craving alcohol and its effects. Katie is definitely experiencing

    A) physiological dependence.

    B) alcohol intolerance.

    C) psychological dependence to alcohol.

    D) hallucinations.

    E) addiction.

Answer: C
Diff: 2   *Page Ref: 188*
Topic: What Other Forms Can Consciousness Take?
Skill: Applied

104) Psychological dependence

    A) occurs primarily with the use of opiates.

    B) can occur with any drug.

    C) causes intense withdrawal symptoms.

    D) can only occur in conjunction with physiological dependence.

    E) is basically the same thing as addiction.

Answer: B
Diff: 2   *Page Ref: 188*
Topic: What Other Forms Can Consciousness Take?
Skill: Conceptual

Check Your Understanding Questions

1) Who objected most strenuously to defining psychology as the science of consciousness?

    A) the cognitive psychologists

    B) the behaviorists

    C) the humanists

    D) the neurologists

    E) the Freudians

Answer: B
Diff: 2   *Page Ref: 165*
Topic: Check Your Understanding
Skill: Recall

2) According to cognitive neuroscience,

    A) consciousness does not exist.

    B) creativity arises from altered states of consciousness.

    C) consciousness is a product of the brain.

    D) the consciousness mind has little access to the larger world of mental activity in the unconscious.

    E) consciousness has no relation to the brain.

Answer: C
Diff: 2   Page Ref: 165
Topic: Check Your Understanding
Skill: Recall

3) Suppose you wanted to sample the contents of preconscious in a group of volunteers. What technique would be most appropriate?

    A) give them MRI scans

    B) ask them to recall specific memories to consciousness

    C) do a priming experiment

    D) have them undergo psychoanalysis

    E) ask them to evaluate a dream

Answer: B
Diff: 2   Page Ref: 165
Topic: Check Your Understanding
Skill: Applied

4) Which of the following is a definition of consciousness suggested by the Core Concept of this section?

    A) Consciousness processes information serially.

    B) Consciousness allows us to respond reflexively, without thinking.

    C) Consciousness controls the autonomic nervous system.

    D) Consciousness makes us more alert.

    E) All levels of consciousness are essentially the same.

Answer: A
Diff: 2   Page Ref: 165
Topic: Check Your Understanding
Skill: Understanding the Core Concept

5) Research completed by Shepard and Metzler showed that
    A) individuals take longer to respond the images that have to be rotated in space.
    B) individuals can easily and quickly rotate objects in space.
    C) if we have ever seen a given object before, we do not have to mentally rotate the object since we are already aware of what is looks like from all angles.
    D) the more specific details we ask a participant to recall about a given object, the longer it will take them to respond.
    E) All of the above are correct

Answer: A
Diff: 3   Page Ref: 165
Topic: Check Your Understanding
Skill: Conceptual

6) Which of the following is true of daydreaming?
    A) Most people can easily suppress unwanted thoughts.
    B) Most people dream every day.
    C) Daydreams usually serve as an escape from the concerns of real life.
    D) Daydreams are usually more vivid than night dreams.
    E) Daydreams help focus your attention.

Answer: B
Diff: 2   Page Ref: 177
Topic: Check Your Understanding
Skill: Recall

7) Which of the following is the correct order of a cycle of sleep?
    A) 1,2,3,4,3,2,1,REM
    B) 1,2,3,4,REM,3,2,1
    C) REM, 1,1,3,4,3,2,1
    D) 1,2,3,4,3,2,REM
    E) 1,2,3,4,3,REM,2,1

Answer: D
Diff: 2   Page Ref: 177
Topic: Check Your Understanding
Skill: Recall

8) Suppose that you are working in a sleep laboratory where you are monitoring a subject's sleep recording during the night. As the night progresses, you would expect that

A) the four–stage cycle gradually lengthens.

B) REM periods become longer.

C) Stage 3 and Stage 4 sleep periods lengthen.

D) dreaming becomes less frequent.

E) Stage 1 continuously appears.

Answer: B

Diff: 2   Page Ref: 177

Topic: Check Your Understanding

Skill: Recall

9) According to the activation–synthesis theory, dreams are

A) replays of events during the previous day.

B) an attempt by the brain to make sense of random activity in the brain stem.

C) a story–like episode that provides clues about problems in the unconscious mind.

D) wish fulfillment.

E) working on problems that occur during the course of the day.

Answer: B

Diff: 2   Page Ref: 177

Topic: Check Your Understanding

Skill: Recall

10) Which of the following symptoms suggests the presence of a sleep disorder?

A) a brief cessation of breathing once or twice a night

B) a REM period at the beginning of sleep

C) needing nine hours of sleep each night in order to feel rested

D) not remembering your dreams

E) napping during the day

Answer: B

Diff: 2   Page Ref: 177

Topic: Check Your Understanding

Skill: Applied

11) Our Core Concept states that consciousness changes in cycles that normally correspond to our
    A) circadian rhythms
    B) consciousness
    C) REM rebound
    D) sleep stages
    E) cataplexy

Answer: A
Diff: 2   *Page Ref: 177*
Topic: Check Your Understanding
Skill: Understanding the Core Concept

12) Hypnosis can be used to
    A) aid in memory.
    B) induce amnesia after the hypnotic episode.
    C) create hallucinations.
    D) help women have a less painful experience with natural childbirth.
    E) All of the above

Answer: E
Diff: 2   *Page Ref: 189*
Topic: Check Your Understanding
Skill: Recall

13) Psychoactive drugs usually create their effects by _____ in the brain.
    A) disabling dendrites
    B) stimulating reward circuits
    C) causing delayed stress reactions
    D) altering memories
    E) rewiring neural pathways

Answer: B
Diff: 2   *Page Ref: 189*
Topic: Check Your Understanding
Skill: Recall

14) Which of the following statements is true?

    A) Research has proven conclusively that addiction is a disease.

    B) Most public health professional view addiction as a character weakness.

    C) Some psychologists suggest that treating addiction as a disease ignores the social and economic factors that surround the problem.

    D) The cycle of addiction is most efficiently broken with a combination of of punishment for relapses and drugs that counteract the effects of psychoactive drugs.

    E) The reinforcing nature of drugs ensures low addiction rates.

Answer: C
Diff: 2   Page Ref: 121
Topic: Check Your Understanding
Skill: Recall

15) Which of the following groups of drugs have the opposite effects on the brain?

    A) hallucinogens and stimulants

    B) opiates and sedatives

    C) stimulants and depressants

    D) depressants and opiates

    E) hallucinogens and sedatives

Answer: C
Diff: 2   Page Ref: 121
Topic: Check Your Understanding
Skill: Applied

16) An altered state of consciousness occurs when some aspect of normal consciousness is modified by mental, behavioral, or chemical means. This suggests that

    A) some states of consciousness are mystical phenomena that cannot ever be explained.

    B) all states of consciousness are controlled by unconscious needs.

    C) altered states of consciousness are the primary source of creativity.

    D) psychologists can study altered states of consciousness with scientific methods.

    E) consciousness is immutable.

Answer: D
Diff: 2   Page Ref: 189
Topic: Check Your Understanding
Skill: Understanding the Core Concept

17) Which of the following statements is true regarding addiction?

   A) Research has proven conclusively that addiction is a brain disease.

   B) The reinforcing nature of drugs ensures low addiction rates.

   C) Some psychologists suggest that treating addiction as a disease ignores the social and economic factors that surround the problem.

   D) The cycle of addiction is most efficiently broken with a combination of punishment for relapses.

   E) Most public health professionals view addiction as a character weakness.

   Answer: C
   Diff: 2   Page Ref: 189
   Topic: Check Your Understanding
   Skill: Factual

True/False Questions

   1) We are aware of everything in our consciousness.

   Answer: TRUE
   Diff: 1   Page Ref: 158
   Topic: How is Consciousness Related to Other Mental Processes?
   Skill: Factual

   2) Structuralism used the method of introspection to study consciousness.

   Answer: TRUE
   Diff: 1   Page Ref: 159
   Topic: How is Consciousness Related to Other Mental Processes?
   Skill: Factual

   3) John Watson believed that we must study the mind if we were ever to fully understand human behavior.

   Answer: FALSE
   Diff: 2   Page Ref: 159
   Topic: How is Consciousness Related to Other Mental Processes?
   Skill: Conceptual

   4) Cognitive neuroscientists believe that the brain acts like a biological computing device.

   Answer: TRUE
   Diff: 2   Page Ref: 159
   Topic: How is Consciousness Related to Other Mental Processes?
   Skill: Conceptual

5) Both conscious and nonconscious information must be processes serially.

Answer: FALSE
Diff: 3   Page Ref: 160
Topic: How is Consciousness Related to Other Mental Processes?
Skill: Factual

6) According to Shepard and Metzler (1971), individuals take longer to identify objects that they have to rotate in space.

Answer: TRUE
Diff: 3   Page Ref: 160
Topic: How is Consciousness Related to Other Mental Processes?
Skill: Conceptual

7) Stephen Kosslyn's research suggests that it takes equally as long for an individual to respond to any detail of an object regardless of how large or small that detail is.

Answer: FALSE
Diff: 3   Page Ref: 161
Topic: How is Consciousness Related to Other Mental Processes?
Skill: Conceptual

8) William James used the metaphor of an iceberg to represent our different levels of consciousness.

Answer: FALSE
Diff: 2   Page Ref: 162
Topic: How is Consciousness Related to Other Mental Processes?
Skill: Factual

9) Freud argued that unconscious associations and reminders of repressed trauma can shape our behavior even though we have no awareness of these thoughts.

Answer: TRUE
Diff: 1   Page Ref: 162–163
Topic: How is Consciousness Related to Other Mental Processes?
Skill: Factual

10) Information in our preconscious can be easily pulled into our consciousness simply by giving it our attention.

Answer: TRUE
Diff: 1   Page Ref: 164
Topic: How is Consciousness Related to Other Mental Processes?
Skill: Factual

11) Our unconscious can work on problems in our live without our current awareness.

Answer: TRUE
Diff: 1   Page Ref: 164
Topic: How is Consciousness Related to Other Mental Processes?
Skill: Factual

12) When Robert tells his girlfriend that he will pick her up at "sex O'Clock". He is surprised by what he has said. This is known as a Freudian Slip.

Answer: TRUE
Diff: 1   Page Ref: 165
Topic: How is Consciousness Related to Other Mental Processes?
Skill: Applied

13) Our daydreams typically can create future experiences.

Answer: FALSE
Diff: 2   Page Ref: 166
Topic: How is Consciousness Related to Other Mental Processes?
Skill: Conceptual

14) Forbidding your mind to daydream about an unwanted feeling or thought will erase that thought from your mind.

Answer: FALSE
Diff: 1   Page Ref: 166
Topic: What Cycles Occur in Everyday Consciousness?
Skill: Factual

15) If we were not guided by light an dark, we would most likely having a normal circadian rhythm of 27 hours.

Answer: FALSE
Diff: 2   Page Ref: 167
Topic: What Cycles Occur in Everyday Consciousness?
Skill: Factual

16) Jet travel in an eastward direction produces more fatigue (lag) than does westward travel.

Answer: TRUE
Diff: 2   Page Ref: 167
Topic: What Cycles Occur in Everyday Consciousness?
Skill: Factual

17) The deepest point in the sleep cycle is in REM sleep, which occurs about three hours after falling asleep.

Answer: FALSE
Diff: 2   Page Ref: 168
Topic: What Cycles Occur in Everyday Consciousness?
Skill: Factual

18) Sleep spindles generally occur in stage 4 of sleep.

Answer: FALSE
Diff: 2   Page Ref: 168
Topic: What Cycles Occur in Everyday Consciousness?
Skill: Factual

19) Alpha waves are characteristic of stages 3 and 4 of sleep.

Answer: FALSE
Diff: 2   Page Ref: 168
Topic: What Cycles Occur in Everyday Consciousness?
Skill: Factual

20) The amount of time spent in REM sleep increases with each sleep cycle of the night.

Answer: TRUE
Diff: 2   Page Ref: 169
Topic: What Cycles Occur in Everyday Consciousness?
Skill: Factual

21) If individuals miss REM sleep one evening, they will spend more time in REM the following night.

Answer: TRUE
Diff: 2   Page Ref: 169
Topic: What Cycles Occur in Everyday Consciousness?
Skill: Recall

22) Short sleepers tend to be energetic and extroverted.

Answer: TRUE
Diff: 2   Page Ref: 170
Topic: What Cycles Occur in Everyday Consciousness?
Skill: Factual

23) If adults are allowed to sleep as long as they would like (without suffering from sleep deprivation) most of them will fall into a cycle in which they sleep for about 10 hours a night.

Answer: FALSE
Diff: 2   *Page Ref: 171*
Topic: What Cycles Occur in Everyday Consciousness?
Skill: Factual

24) According to Freud, the manifest content of a dream refers to its symbolic meaning.

Answer: FALSE
Diff: 2   *Page Ref: 172*
Topic: What Cycles Occur in Everyday Consciousness?
Skill: Factual

25) The activation–synthesis theory claims that dreams serve as sources of wish-fulfillment.

Answer: FALSE
Diff: 2   *Page Ref: 174*
Topic: What Cycles Occur in Everyday Consciousness?
Skill: Conceptual

26) Individuals who suffer from sleep apnea generally are groggy and lethargic during the day.

Answer: TRUE
Diff: 2   *Page Ref: 176*
Topic: Sleep Disorders
Skill: Factual

27) Patients with narcolepsy fall rapidly into a deep sleep.

Answer: TRUE
Diff: 3   *Page Ref: 176*
Topic: Sleep Disorders
Skill: Factual

28) Information gained under a hypnotic state can never be trusted.

Answer: FALSE
Diff: 2   *Page Ref: 179*
Topic: What Other Forms Can Consciousness Take?
Skill: Factual

29) An intravenous heroin user experiences euphoria, without any major changes in cognitive abilities.

Answer: TRUE
Diff: 2   Page Ref: 116
Topic: What Other Forms Can Consciousness Take?
Skill: Factual

30) Everyone can be hypnotized.

Answer: FALSE
Diff: 2   Page Ref: 179
Topic: What Other Forms Can Consciousness Take?
Skill: Recall

31) Endorphins may account for pain relief during hypnotic analgesia.

Answer: FALSE
Diff: 2   Page Ref: 180
Topic: What Other Forms Can Consciousness Take?
Skill: Conceptual

32) Buddhists believe that meditation can help individuals have a more accurate view of reality.

Answer: TRUE
Diff: 2   Page Ref: 181
Topic: What Other Forms Can Consciousness Take?
Skill: Recall

33) Anti drug educational programs are especially effective in reducing drug use.

Answer: FALSE
Diff: 2   Page Ref: 182
Topic: What Other Forms Can Consciousness Take?
Skill: Conceptual

34) The caffeine in coffee and the nicotine in cigarettes are in the same category of addictive drugs as crack cocaine.

Answer: TRUE
Diff: 2   Page Ref: 183
Topic: What Other Forms Can Consciousness Take?
Skill: Factual

35) Depressants slow the mental and physical activity of the body by inhibiting activity in the central nervous system.

Answer: TRUE
Diff: 2   Page Ref: 184
Topic: What Other Forms Can Consciousness Take?
Skill: Factual

36) Scientists classify alcohol as a stimulant because people using alcohol can become talkative and extroverted.

Answer: FALSE
Diff: 2   Page Ref: 186
Topic: What Other Forms Can Consciousness Take?
Skill: Conceptual

37) If a person is psychologically addicted to a drug, they must also be physically addicted to the drug.

Answer: FALSE
Diff: 2   Page Ref: 187
Topic: What Other Forms Can Consciousness Take?
Skill: Factual

38) In the addiction literature, withdrawal is defined as the pervasive desire to obtain and use a drug.

Answer: FALSE
Diff: 2   Page Ref: 188
Topic: What Other Forms Can Consciousness Take?
Skill: Factual

Short Answer Questions

1) Briefly explain William James' idea of the Stream of Consciousness.

Answer: This is the awareness both of ourselves and of stimulation for our environment.
Diff: 2   Page Ref: 162
Topic: How is Consciousness Related to Other Mental Processes?
Skill: Conceptual

2) What metaphor did Freud use for consciousness and what are the different levels.

Answer: An iceberg —the conscious is the small part just above the surface that involves what we are aware of, the preconscious is just below the surface and can easily be brought into our awareness by focusing on the information and the the unconscious which is the large portion hidden beneath the water that holds our unwanted thoughts and desires and is difficult to bring.to our awareness.

Diff: 2   *Page Ref: 164*

Topic: How is Consciousness Related to Other Mental Processes?

Skill: Conceptual

3) Briefly explain a Freudian Slip.

Answer: This is information that is held in the unconscious, but is not fully repressed. According to Freud, these are mostly sexual or aggressive in nature and is reflective of what is happening in the unconscious mind of the individual.

Diff: 1   *Page Ref: 164*

Topic: How is Consciousness Related to Other Mental Processes?

Skill: Applied

4) Place the stages of sleep in the correct order through the first REM period.

Answer: Stage 1, Stage 2, Stage 3, Stage 4, stage 3, Stage 2, REM

Diff: 2   *Page Ref: 168–169*

Topic: What Cycles Occur in Everyday Consciousness?

Skill: Factual

5) Describe the evolutionary explanation of the function of sleep.

Answer: REM paralysis keeps us away from predators.

Diff: 3   *Page Ref: 169*

Topic: What Cycles Occur in Everyday Consciousness?

Skill: Factual

6) Briefly explain Freud's idea of the manifest and Latent content f dreams.

Answer: The manifest content is the actual storyline of the dream, whereas the latent content is the underlying meaning of the dream.

Diff: 3   *Page Ref: 173*

Topic: What Cycles Occur in Everyday Consciousness?

Skill: Recall

7) Explain why night terrors seem to be so real.

Answer: Generally the occur in children and their body is telling them that this is not a dream so the event seems to be real.

Diff: 2   *Page Ref: 176*

Topic: What Cycles Occur in Everyday Consciousness?

Skill: Conceptual

8) Briefly explain Narcolepsy.

Answer: Narcolepsy occurs when individuals fall rapidly into a deep sleep, it can be dangerous for driving as it is difficult to predict the onset of these "attacks".
Diff: 2   Page Ref: 175

Topic: Sleep Disorders

Skill: Factual

9) _____ is an induced state of awareness characterized by deep relaxation and heightened suggestibility.

Answer: Hypnosis
Diff: 2   Page Ref: 179

Topic: What Other Forms Can Consciousness Take?

Skill: Conceptual

10) How do opiates suppress pain?

Answer: These drugs interact with the endogenous opiate system (which naturally suppresses pain).
Diff: 2   Page Ref: 184

Topic: What Other Forms Can Consciousness Take?

Skill: Conceptual

11) Barbiturates and benzodiazepines belong to the category of psychoactive drugs known as _____ and are used for _____.

Answer: depressants; helping people get to sleep
Diff: 3   Page Ref: 184–185

Topic: What Other Forms Can Consciousness Take?

Skill: Factual

12) _____ refers to the condition in which a drug's effectiveness is reduced due to repeated usage.

Answer: Tolerance
Diff: 2   Page Ref: 187

Topic: What Other Forms Can Consciousness Take?

Skill: Conceptual

13) Briefly explain the difference between physical and psychological dependence on drugs.

Answer: Physical dependence refers to the process by which the body adjusts to, and comes to need a drug for everyday functioning. Psychological dependence is a desire to obtain of use the drug even thought there is no physical dependence.
Diff: 2   Page Ref: 187–188

Topic: What Other Forms Can Consciousness Take?

Skill: Conceptual

Essay Questions

1) Define conscious, preconscious, subconscious, and unconscious thought and provide examples of thoughts that might have been in each level of consciousness.

   Answer: Preconscious thoughts are memories accessed after something calls attention to them (like what you had for dinner last night). Subconscious thoughts are things in our current environment that we 'pick up' without them being consciously attended to (like the sound of the fan in the classroom). Unconscious thoughts include threatening memories and thoughts blocked from conscious thought (like the belief that one's mother is sexy).

   Diff: 2   Page Ref: 158–165

   Topic: How is Consciousness Related to Other Mental Processes?

   Skill: Applied

2) Contrast the physiological events that occur during Non–REM and REM sleep.

   Answer: The brain wave activity differs between the 2 states. In non–REM sleep, there is a presence of slow-waves, and especially delta waves during stages 3 and 4 of non–REM sleep. In REM sleep, the body is mostly paralyzed and the brain wave pattern is that present (beta waves) when we are awake. Dream type also differs between the two states.

   Diff: 2   Page Ref: 168–169

   Topic: What Cycles Occur in Everyday Consciousness?

   Skill: Factual

3) Explain three models researchers have proposed for the purpose of dreaming.

   Answer: Freud believed that dreams were reflective of wish fulfillment and the unconscious revealing itself. The Activation-Synthesis model suggests that dreams attempt to make sense of the random neural firings in our brain. Dreams reflect daily events in our lives.

   Diff: 2   Page Ref: 172–174

   Topic: What Cycles Occur in Everyday Consciousness?

   Skill: Conceptual

4) Contrast the sleep disorders of insomnia, sleep apnea, and narcolepsy with regard to key symptoms, known causes, and treatments for each.

   Answer: The three disorders include insomnia (which involves repeated difficulty in falling or staying asleep, usually due to stress), sleep apnea (which involves breathing stoppages while sleeping due to the collapse of the airway), and narcolepsy (which involves sudden sleep attacks during the daytime due to genetic abnormalities in the brain stem). Insomnia can be treated using sleeping pills; sleep apnea may require a device to keep the airways open, while certain stimulants can treat narcolepsy.

   Diff: 2   Page Ref: 175–176

   Topic: What Cycles Occur in Everyday Consciousness?

   Skill: Conceptual

5) Explain the effects of opiates (Include information about drugs in this category, reasons why they are used, their effects, and the likelihood of addiction.)

Answer: Morphine, heroin, and codeine are all within this class of drugs that are often used as painkillers because their chemical properties are similar to endorphins. These drugs also have been known to suppress coughing. These drugs are all derived from the opium poppy and are highly addictive except when under medical supervision. The drugs produce pleasurable, euphoric sensations that override all worries of bodily needs, however, they do not really affect cognitive ability.

Diff: 2   Page Ref: 184

Topic: What Other Forms Can Consciousness Take?

Skill: Applied

6) Describe the general class of drugs known as stimulants and explain their action within the brain.

Answer: Stimulants increase central nervous system activity. Examples of drugs in this class are caffeine, nicotine, amphetamine, and cocaine. The euphoric/reinforcing property of stimulants is thought to be related to their ability to facilitate the release of dopamine within the brain reward circuits.

Diff: 2   Page Ref: 186

Topic: What Other Forms Can Consciousness Take?

Skill: Conceptual

7) Hypnosis has often been regarded as pseudoscience. Explain how hypnosis is believed to work and how it may be used productively.

Answer: Hypnosis works by employing a heightened sense of suggestibility. It can be effectively employed to help relieve pain, to help aid in memory and to eliminate unwanted behaviors such as smoking.

Diff: 2   Page Ref: 178–181

Topic: What Other Forms Can Consciousness Take?

Skill: Applied

Chapter 6 Learning

Multiple Choice Questions

1) Learning always occurs as a result of
   A) changing our emotions.
   B) experience.
   C) changes in the environment.
   D) classical conditioning.
   E) internal changes.

Answer: B
Diff: 2   *Page Ref: 196*
Topic: Introduction
Skill: Conceptual

2) Which of the following would NOT be an example of learning?
   A) A newborn infant sucks on a nipple filled with milk.
   B) A teenager falls asleep after staying awake for 96 hours.
   C) A rat presses a lever to obtain a food pellet.
   D) You wince when you see a long needle similar to the one that hurt you during a drug injection last week.
   E) A and B are correct.

Answer: E
Diff: 2   *Page Ref: 196*
Topic: Introduction
Skill: Conceptual

3) While walking down a dark alley, you jump at a loud noise. This would not be considered learning because
   A) it is not a behavior.
   B) jumping is only done for survival purposes.
   C) not everyone would jump in this situation.
   D) jumping is merely a reflex.
   E) jumping is a difficult skill, biologically speaking.

Answer: D
Diff: 2   *Page Ref: 196*
Topic: Introduction
Skill: Applied

4) A dog rattles a chain by the door to indicate that he wants to go out, his owner is thrilled an thinks that her dog is brilliant. The dog however has not yet proven learning because

    A) the change must be lasting.

    B) he may have accidentally bumped to chain.

    C) he must demonstrate that he has associated the chain with going out through prior experience.

    D) he must repeat the behavior.

    E) All of the above

Answer: E

Diff: 2   Page Ref: 196

Topic: Introduction

Skill: Applied

5) Jenna walks into her science class laboratory, and she immediately feels queasy. Today is the day her class is dissecting frogs and she is sickened by the smell of the formaldehyde. However, after an hour Jenna is no longer sickened because of

    A) classical conditioning.

    B) habituation.

    C) operant conditioning.

    D) her reflexes.

    E) spontaneous recovery.

Answer: B

Diff: 3   Page Ref: 197

Topic: Introduction

Skill: Applied

6) When you start doing your own grocery shopping, you notice that you often buy the same brands that your mom bought when you lived at home rather than trying something new this can be the result of

    A) the mere exposure effect.

    B) habituation.

    C) continuous reinforcement.

    D) shaping.

    E) classical conditioning.

Answer: A

Diff: 3   Page Ref: 197

Topic: Introduction

Skill: Applied

7) The two main types of behavioral learning are
    A) reflexive responses and shaping.
    B) insight learning and operant conditioning.
    C) classical conditioning and operant conditioning.
    D) social learning and observational learning.
    E) reinforcement and insight learning.

Answer: C

Diff: 2   *Page Ref: 198*

Topic: Introduction

Skill: Conceptual

8) _____ was a dietician be training, but during an experiment testing the salivary gland of dogs, he discovered _____ conditioning.
    A) Skinner; operant
    B) Watson; observational
    C) Pavlov; classical
    D) Pavlov; operant
    E) Bandura; insight

Answer: C

Diff: 3   *Page Ref: 198*

Topic: What Sort of Learning Does Classical Conditioning Explain?

Skill: Factual

9) In Pavlov's original experiment, the key that the dogs had learned something was that
    A) they blinked when they were fed.
    B) they salivated to the food.
    C) they salivated to the footsteps of those that would feed them.
    D) they did not salivate to the food.
    E) None of the above are correct

Answer: C

Diff: 2   *Page Ref: 198*

Topic: What Sort of Learning Does Classical Conditioning Explain?

Skill: Factual

10) An eye blink is an example of

    A) introspection.

    B) an environmental event.

    C) a reflex.

    D) an operant.

    E) shaping.

Answer: C

Diff: 1   Page Ref: 199

Topic: What Sort of Learning Does Classical Conditioning Explain?

Skill: Conceptual

11) If you salivate when your mother tells you about the lemon cake she is baking, we can attribute your reaction to

    A) classical conditioning.

    B) observational learning.

    C) stimulus generalization.

    D) olfactory hallucinations.

    E) operant conditioning.

Answer: A

Diff: 2   Page Ref: 199

Topic: What Sort of Learning Does Classical Conditioning Explain?

Skill: Factual

12) You are sitting in a class when your professor holds up a large white feather. We could guess that most people would not really respond in any important way to the feather, because the feather is a(n)

    A) primary reinforcer.

    B) negative punisher.

    C) unconditioned response.

    D) neutral stimulus.

    E) extinct event.

Answer: D

Diff: 2   Page Ref: 199

Topic: What Sort of Learning Does Classical Conditioning Explain?

Skill: Applied

13) A(n) _____ refers to the behavior elicited by the unconditioned stimulus.

   A) conditioned stimulus

   B) conditioned response

   C) unconditioned response

   D) reflex

   E) neutral response

Answer: C
Diff: 2   Page Ref: 199
Topic: What Sort of Learning Does Classical Conditioning Explain?
Skill: Conceptual

14) An unconditioned stimulus is any stimulus that

   A) triggers a learned response.

   B) is based upon its association with another unconditioned stimulus.

   C) provides positive or negative reinforcement.

   D) naturally elicits a reflexive behavior.

   E) inhibits previously learned behavior.

Answer: D
Diff: 2   Page Ref: 199
Topic: What Sort of Learning Does Classical Conditioning Explain?
Skill: Conceptual

15) The initial learning stage in classical conditioning in which the neutral stimulus is repeatedly paired with the unconditioned stimulus is known as

   A) prompting.

   B) trial–and–error learning.

   C) acquisition.

   D) insight learning.

   E) shaping.

Answer: C
Diff: 2   Page Ref: 200
Topic: What Sort of Learning Does Classical Conditioning Explain?
Skill: Factual

16) In order for the UCS to cause a UCR, there must be

   A) that the person must be hungry.

   B) the individual must receive either punishment or reinforcement.

   C) a critical impact of insight.

   D) no learning.

   E) that the dog salivates at the sound of the bell.

   Answer: D
   Diff: 2   Page Ref: 200
   Topic: What Sort of Learning Does Classical Conditioning Explain?
   Skill: Conceptual

17) For Pavlov, a tone is to food as

   A) an unconditioned stimulus (UCS) is to an unconditioned response (UCR).

   B) an orienting response (OR) is to a conditioned stimulus (CS).

   C) a conditioned stimulus (CS) is to an unconditioned stimulus (UCS).

   D) a conditioned response (CR) is to an operant stimulus (OS).

   E) a neutral stimulus (NS) is to an conditioned response (CR).

   Answer: C
   Diff: 3   Page Ref: 200
   Topic: What Sort of Learning Does Classical Conditioning Explain?
   Skill: Conceptual

18) After acquisition of classical conditioning, the _____ now has the ability to elicit a response the resembles the UCR.

   A) operant response

   B) conditioned stimulus

   C) unconditional stimulus

   D) orienting stimulus

   E) independent stimulus

   Answer: B
   Diff: 1   Page Ref: 200
   Topic: What Sort of Learning Does Classical Conditioning Explain?
   Skill: Conceptual

19) After having some bad barbecue pork in the cafeteria, your stomach gets a bit woozy each time you enter. The cafeteria is the _____ and your stomach feeling woozy is the _____.
   A) unconditioned response; unconditioned stimulus
   B) conditioned response; conditioned stimulus
   C) conditioned stimulus; conditioned response
   D) unconditioned stimulus; unconditioned response
   E) conditioned stimulus; unconditioned response

   Answer: C
   Diff: 2   Page Ref: 200
   Topic: What Sort of Learning Does Classical Conditioning Explain?
   Skill: Applied

20) You are trying to eat fewer sweets, your friends taunt you with their candy and even though you are not eating any candy, when you see them eat your favorite treat "lemonheads" you find yourself salivating. Your reaction could be labelled a
   A) conditioned response.
   B) unconditioned response.
   C) conditioned stimulus.
   D) unconditioned stimulus.
   E) neutral stimulus.

   Answer: A
   Diff: 2   Page Ref: 200
   Topic: What Sort of Learning Does Classical Conditioning Explain?
   Skill: Applied

21) Burt had never been afraid of spiders, but at camp last summer he woke up and there was a spider on his face. Since this event, he cries in fear every time that he sees a multilegged creatures. For Burt, before the incident spiders had been a _____, after the incident, spiders are a _____.
   A) conditioned stimulus; conditioned response
   B) neutral stimulus; conditioned response
   C) unconditioned stimulus; unconditioned response
   D) neutral stimulus; conditioned stimulus
   E) conditioned stimulus; unconditioned stimulus

   Answer: D
   Diff: 2   Page Ref: 200
   Topic: What Sort of Learning Does Classical Conditioning Explain?
   Skill: Applied

22) _____ refers to a procedure in classical conditioning where a CR no longer occurs in the presence of the CS due to the absence of the UCS.

   A) Extinction

   B) Spontaneous recovery

   C) Inhibition

   D) Discrimination

   E) Generalization

Answer: A

Diff: 3   Page Ref: 201

Topic: What Sort of Learning Does Classical Conditioning Explain?

Skill: Conceptual

23) If Pavlov's dogs had been adopted by a nice family after the experiments ended and they eventually stopped salivating to a bell, but then suddenly when the door bell rang they began salivating again they would be demonstrating

   A) stimulus discrimination.

   B) extinction.

   C) spontaneous recovery.

   D) an unconditioned response.

   E) a neutral response.

Answer: C

Diff: 3   Page Ref: 201

Topic: What Sort of Learning Does Classical Conditioning Explain?

Skill: Applied

24) One of Pavlov's dogs had stopped salivating at the sound of the tone. The next day the tone was presented again and the dog began salivating. Pavlov referred to this as

   A) shaping.

   B) spontaneous extinction.

   C) stimulus generalization.

   D) spontaneous recovery.

   E) higher-order conditioning.

Answer: D

Diff: 1   Page Ref: 201

Topic: What Sort of Learning Does Classical Conditioning Explain?

Skill: Conceptual

25) Robert's dog, Fuzzy, runs to Robert when he says, "Come." If one day, Fuzzy comes running when Robert says, "Dumb," we might say that Fuzzy has demonstrated

    A) spontaneous recovery.

    B) social learning.

    C) insight learning.

    D) intermittent reinforcement.

    E) stimulus generalization.

Answer: E

Diff: 3   Page Ref: 202

Topic: What Sort of Learning Does Classical Conditioning Explain?

Skill: Applied

26) Merideth is a expert of wine. In a fine restaurant she orders a glass of Santa Margarita pinot grigio, when the wine comes out she tastes it and claims that she received Mezzacorona pinot grigio instead. Merideth is demonstrating

    A) stimulus generalization.

    B) stimulus discrimination.

    C) spontaneous recovery.

    D) extinction.

    E) an unconditioned response.

Answer: B

Diff: 3   Page Ref: 202

Topic: What Sort of Learning Does Classical Conditioning Explain?

Skill: Applied

27) As discrimination tasks with unpleasant stimuli become increasingly more difficult we can expect

    A) better learning to occur due to generalization.

    B) agitation due to experimental neurosis.

    C) extinction due to extreme confusion.

    D) appetitive conditioning due to shaping.

    E) intermittent reinforcement due to prompting.

Answer: B

Diff: 2   Page Ref: 202

Topic: What Sort of Learning Does Classical Conditioning Explain?

Skill: Factual

28) A serious problem with Watson and Rayner's testing with Little Albert is the danger that

    A) operant conditioning can modify behavior.

    B) the fear response may generalize to other stimuli.

    C) taste aversions can be formed in young children.

    D) counterconditioning is difficult.

    E) spontaneous recovery can occur at the wrong time.

Answer: B

Diff: 2   Page Ref: 203

Topic: What Sort of Learning Does Classical Conditioning Explain?

Skill: Conceptual

29) For Little Albert, his fear of _____ was interpreted as an instance of _____.

    A) John Watson; a sensible response

    B) a white laboratory rat; conditioned fear

    C) his mother; childhood psychosis

    D) Santa Claus mask; experimental psychosis

    E) a white laboratory rat; operant conditioning

Answer: B

Diff: 3   Page Ref: 203

Topic: What Sort of Learning Does Classical Conditioning Explain?

Skill: Conceptual

30) In the "Little Albert" experiment the rat when presented with the loud noise was the _____ and the noise was the _____.

    A) conditioned stimulus; conditioned response

    B) unconditioned stimulus; conditioned response

    C) conditioned response; unconditioned stimulus

    D) unconditioned stimulus; unconditioned response

    E) unconditioned stimulus; neutral stimulus

Answer: D

Diff: 3   Page Ref: 203

Topic: What Sort of Learning Does Classical Conditioning Explain?

Skill: Applied

31) One of the best therapy strategies for eliminating conditioned fears involves combining
_____ in a process known as _____, first described by Mary Cover Jones.

 A) negative and positive reinforcement; aversion

 B) arousal and stress reduction; shaping

 C) conditioned and unconditioned responses; discrimination

 D) primary and secondary reinforcers; social learning

 E) extinction and relaxation; counterconditioning

Answer: E
Diff: 2   Page Ref: 203
Topic: What Sort of Learning Does Classical Conditioning Explain?
Skill: Conceptual

32) If you had an intense fear of high spaces and were asked to climb to the top of a high tower.
As you ascended you therapist told you to relax and gave you positive feedback on how you
were doing, eventually you made it to the top. This therapeutic technique is known as

 A) flooding.

 B) counterconditioning.

 C) classical conditioning.

 D) operant conditioning.

 E) aversive conditioning.

Answer: B
Diff: 2   Page Ref: 203
Topic: What Sort of Learning Does Classical Conditioning Explain?
Skill: Applied

33) The factor that makes a food aversion different from most types of classical conditioning is that

 A) other people can cause us to develop the connection the CS and the UCS.

 B) once the conditioning is established, it cannot be eliminated.

 C) the conditioned response often occurs before the unconditioned response.

 D) there can be a long time delay between the CS and the UCS.

 E) conditioning may not always involve a change in the person's response.

Answer: D
Diff: 3   Page Ref: 203–204
Topic: What Sort of Learning Does Classical Conditioning Explain?
Skill: Conceptual

34) Judy has cancer and is receiving chemotherapy at a local hospital. Her parents notice that she now rejects food that she willingly ate last week (before chemotherapy). Through the process of _____, the food is now acting as _____.

   A) operant conditioning; negative reinforcer

   B) negative reinforcement; conditioned stimulus

   C) aversive conditioning; conditioned stimulus

   D) appetitive conditioning; conditioned stimulus

   E) conditioned reinforcement; unconditioned response

Answer: C
Diff: 3   Page Ref: 203–204
Topic: What Sort of Learning Does Classical Conditioning Explain?
Skill: Applied

35) The fact that taste aversions _____ poses a problem for classical conditioning theory.

   A) are difficult to measure

   B) not consistent

   C) learned through observation

   D) generalizable

   E) part of our biological make-up

Answer: E
Diff: 3   Page Ref: 204
Topic: What Sort of Learning Does Classical Conditioning Explain?
Skill: Conceptual

36) In John Garcia's study on taste aversion towards coyotes, the goal was to create a situation in which sheep became the _____ so that coyotes would not attack them.

   A) conditioned stimulus

   B) unconditioned stimulus

   C) conditioned response

   D) unconditioned response

   E) neutral stimulus

Answer: A
Diff: 3   Page Ref: 204
Topic: What Sort of Learning Does Classical Conditioning Explain?
Skill: Conceptual

37) To avoid conditioned taste aversions, cancer patients are now given _____ during chemotherapy.

    A) morphine

    B) naloxone

    C) a familiar food

    D) unusually flavored candies or ice cream

    E) psychotherapy

Answer: D

Diff: 3   Page Ref: 205

Topic: What Sort of Learning Does Classical Conditioning Explain?

Skill: Factual

38) In operant conditioning, behavioral change is brought about by the manipulation of

    A) reflexes.

    B) goals.

    C) consequences.

    D) motives.

    E) thoughts.

Answer: C

Diff: 2   Page Ref: 206

Topic: How Do We Learn New Behaviors by Operant Conditioning?

Skill: Conceptual

39) Operant Conditioning explains how new behaviors can be learned while Classical Conditioning refers only to _____ behaviors.

    A) reflexive

    B) voluntary

    C) cognitive

    D) insightful

    E) All of the above

Answer: A

Diff: 2   Page Ref: 206

Topic: How Do We Learn New Behaviors by Operant Conditioning?

Skill: Recall

40) Operant behaviors are different from those in Classical Conditioning, because in classical conditioning the behaviors are

   A) voluntary.

   B) cognitive.

   C) involuntary.

   D) observed.

   E) reinforced.

Answer: C

Diff: 2   Page Ref: 206

Topic: How Do We Learn New Behaviors by Operant Conditioning?

Skill: Conceptual

41) _____ are consequences that alter the likelihood of behaviors.

   A) Conditioned and unconditioned reflexes

   B) Successive approximations

   C) Rewards and punishments

   D) Conditioned and unconditioned stimuli

   E) Discrimination and generalization

Answer: C

Diff: 2   Page Ref: 206

Topic: How Do We Learn New Behaviors by Operant Conditioning?

Skill: Conceptual

42) Which of the following is NOT an example of an operant?

   A) A dog salivates after seeing a bowl of meat.

   B) One-month-old Jamie sucks on a nipple in order to hear her mother's voice.

   C) A rat presses a lever to receive a food pellet.

   D) Sam tells a joke that has previously evoked much laughter.

   E) Abe repeatedly presses a button on a toy, because he likes the loud sound it makes.

Answer: A

Diff: 3   Page Ref: 206

Topic: How Do We Learn New Behaviors by Operant Conditioning?

Skill: Applied

43) B.F. Skinner was a radical behaviorist who refused to
    A) conduct research with animals other than humans.
    B) believe that observation tells us anything about human nature.
    C) understand how it was possible for people to change.
    D) accept that individuals can change over time.
    E) speculate about what happens inside an organism.

Answer: E
Diff: 2   Page Ref: 206
Topic: How Do We Learn New Behaviors by Operant Conditioning?
Skill: Conceptual

44) Much f B.F Skinner's early work was inspired by the "Law of Effect" which was created by
    A) John Watson.
    B) Edward Thorndike.
    C) Ivan Pavlov.
    D) Albert Bandura.
    E) Mary Cover Jones.

Answer: B
Diff: 2   Page Ref: 206
Topic: How Do We Learn New Behaviors by Operant Conditioning?
Skill: Factual

45) As a result of Thorndike's work, we could expect that if Rebecca has learned calculus,
    A) she should be a great student in her Spanish class.
    B) she should be able to explain calculus to her friend Lauren.
    C) she will desire to learn even more about the field of mathematics.
    D) it will be difficult for her to learn to play tennis.
    E) it will have little effect on her ability to succeed in German history.

Answer: E
Diff: 2   Page Ref: 206
Topic: How Do We Learn New Behaviors by Operant Conditioning?
Skill: Applied

46) Negative and positive reinforcers are similar in that these always _____ the likelihood of ensuing responses.

    A) decrease

    B) increase

    C) extinguish

    D) eliminate

    E) have no effect on

Answer: B
Diff: 2   *Page Ref: 207*
Topic: How Do We Learn New Behaviors by Operant Conditioning?
Skill: Conceptual

47) The term "reinforcer" refers to any condition that _____ a response.

    A) precedes and causes

    B) strengthens or weakens

    C) weakens or eliminates

    D) follows and strengthens

    E) causes or eliminates

Answer: D
Diff: 2   *Page Ref: 207*
Topic: How Do We Learn New Behaviors by Operant Conditioning?
Skill: Factual

48) Negative reinforcement involves

    A) the learning of a new response.

    B) the removal of an aversive stimulus.

    C) decreasing the likelihood of certain future behaviors.

    D) providing an unpleasant stimulus periodically during the day.

    E) pairing an old reflex with a new stimulus.

Answer: B
Diff: 2   *Page Ref: 207*
Topic: How Do We Learn New Behaviors by Operant Conditioning?
Skill: Conceptual

49) When your alarm clock rings loudly until you turn it off, it is acting as a
   A) positive reinforcer.
   B) positive punishment.
   C) negative punishment.
   D) negative reinforcement.
   E) unconditioned stimulus.

Answer: D
Diff: 2   Page Ref: 207
Topic: How Do We Learn New Behaviors by Operant Conditioning?
Skill: Applied

50) A Positive reinforcer seeks to _____ desired behavior. A negative reinforcer seeks to
   _____ desired behavior.
   A) decrease;increase
   B) increase; increase
   C) increase; decrease
   D) decrease; decrease
   E) none of the above

Answer: B
Diff: 2   Page Ref: 207
Topic: How Do We Learn New Behaviors by Operant Conditioning?
Skill: Conceptual

51) The descriptors "positive" and "negative," when used in reference to reinforcers, are synonyms
   for
   A) "add" and "remove."
   B) "conditioned" and "unconditioned."
   C) "increase" and "decrease."
   D) "voluntary" and "involuntary."
   E) "new" and "familiar."

Answer: A
Diff: 2   Page Ref: 207
Topic: How Do We Learn New Behaviors by Operant Conditioning?
Skill: Conceptual

52) The operant chamber which has come to be known as a Skinner box was designed so that
    A) he could punish his daughter, Deborah.
    B) rats could eliminate painful stimuli.
    C) animals could press a lever to receive food.
    D) gerbils could make their way through a maze to a food pellet in the box.
    E) cats could pull a string to open the door to the box.

Answer: C
Diff: 2   *Page Ref: 207*
Topic: How Do We Learn New Behaviors by Operant Conditioning?
Skill: Factual

53) _____ is a procedure for changing behavior by reinforcing responses that approach the desired goal.
    A) Molding
    B) Shaping
    C) Natural selection
    D) Behavioral analysis
    E) Counterconditioning

Answer: B
Diff: 2   *Page Ref: 208*
Topic: How Do We Learn New Behaviors by Operant Conditioning?
Skill: Factual

54) Professors who offer only a final exam grade for the entire semester grade are forgetting the operant conditioning principle that
    A) a single test may not assess what an individuals knows about a given subject.
    B) contingencies of reinforcement must occur with more frequency to motivate behavior.
    C) students may learn become conditioned to fear an exam because it causes anxiety.
    D) students cognitive abilities should be studies more deeply.
    E) All of the above are correct

Answer: B
Diff: 3   *Page Ref: 208*
Topic: How Do We Learn New Behaviors by Operant Conditioning?
Skill: Applied

55) The best strategy to teach an organism a new response is to use

   A) continuous reinforcement.

   B) secondary reinforcement.

   C) negative reinforcement.

   D) intermittent reinforcement.

   E) extinction.

Answer: A

Diff: 2   *Page Ref: 208*

Topic: How Do We Learn New Behaviors by Operant Conditioning?

Skill: Conceptual

56) As a marine biologist, you are trying to teach a dolphin to jump over a bar. At first, you reward the dolphin every time it swims near the bar. Then, you only reward her when she emerges from the water near the bar. Eventually, you reward the dolphin each time she jumps out of the water. Then, you only reward the dolphin when she jumps over the bar. This technique is an example of

   A) classical conditioning.

   B) spontaneous recovery.

   C) discrimination.

   D) shaping.

   E) positive punishment.

Answer: D

Diff: 2   *Page Ref: 208*

Topic: How Do We Learn New Behaviors by Operant Conditioning?

Skill: Applied

57) Intermittent reinforcement is particularly effective for maintaining behavior because such reinforcement

   A) has popularity and generosity.

   B) produces resistance to extinction.

   C) has frequency and generalizability.

   D) has discriminability and consistency.

   E) has predictability and physicality.

Answer: B

Diff: 2   *Page Ref: 208*

Topic: How Do We Learn New Behaviors by Operant Conditioning?

Skill: Conceptual

58) I want my dog Fuzzy to fetch the paper for me in the morning. When first teaching Fuzzy how to fetch the paper I should reward her _____. After she has learned the behavior, I should change to a _____ schedule of reinforcement, if I want her to continue to fetch the paper.

   A) variable-ratio; variable interval

   B) continuous; fixed ratio

   C) fixed ratio; fixed-interval

   D) continuous; variable-ratio

   E) fixed-ratio; variable-ratio

Answer: D
Diff: 2   Page Ref: 209
Topic: How Do We Learn New Behaviors by Operant Conditioning?
Skill: Applied

59) In operant conditioning, extinction involves

   A) unpredictable reinforcement.

   B) consistent, unpleasant punishments.

   C) withholding reinforcement.

   D) adding new punishments.

   E) an increase in negative reinforcement.

Answer: C
Diff: 2   Page Ref: 209
Topic: How Do We Learn New Behaviors by Operant Conditioning?
Skill: Conceptual

60) The key difference between a ratio and a interval schedule of reinforcement is whether

   A) reinforcers are given or removed.

   B) reinforcement occurs often or rarely.

   C) the behaviors will increase or decrease in frequency.

   D) a person can control the consequences of the reinforcement.

   E) reinforcement is determined by time or by number of responses.

Answer: E
Diff: 2   Page Ref: 209
Topic: How Do We Learn New Behaviors by Operant Conditioning?
Skill: Conceptual

61) A telemarketer who tries to sell as many magazine subscriptions as possible is working according to a _____ schedule of reinforcement.

A) fixed ratio

B) variable ratio

C) fixed interval

D) variable interval

E) continuous

Answer: B

Diff: 2   Page Ref: 209

Topic: How Do We Learn New Behaviors by Operant Conditioning?

Skill: Applied

62) A television producer who receives a monthly check is working according to a _____ schedule of reinforcement.

A) fixed ratio

B) variable ratio

C) fixed interval

D) variable interval

E) continuous

Answer: C

Diff: 2   Page Ref: 209

Topic: How Do We Learn New Behaviors by Operant Conditioning?

Skill: Applied

63) If Tyler is given an allowance of $5.00 on every Friday for doing his chores, we should expect that he will

A) work hard consistently throughout the week.

B) never know when he will be rewarded.

C) not do many chores until just before allowance time.

D) do his chores to prevent punishment by his parents.

E) keep doing his chores, even when he no longer receives allowance.

Answer: C

Diff: 3   Page Ref: 209–210

Topic: How Do We Learn New Behaviors by Operant Conditioning?

Skill: Applied

64) Food, sex, and water are considered examples of

    A) primary reinforcers.

    B) secondary reinforcers.

    C) continuous reinforcers.

    D) intermittent reinforcers.

    E) conditioned stimuli.

Answer: A
Diff: 2   *Page Ref: 210*
Topic: How Do We Learn New Behaviors by Operant Conditioning?
Skill: Applied

65) The key advantage of using a variable ratio schedule of reinforcement is that

    A) the person will be rewarded often.

    B) it is very predictable.

    C) it is easy to extinguish.

    D) it prevents the extinction of the desired response.

    E) the individual is usually content.

Answer: D
Diff: 2   *Page Ref: 239*
Topic: How Do We Learn New Behaviors by Operant Conditioning?
Skill: Conceptual

66) During summer camp, campers get a sticker each time they demonstrate good sportsmanship. When they have earned 10 stickers, they may select a candy bar. This represents an example

    A) negative reinforcement.

    B) primary shaping.

    C) classical conditioning.

    D) reward generalization.

    E) a token economy.

Answer: E
Diff: 2   *Page Ref: 210*
Topic: How Do We Learn New Behaviors by Operant Conditioning?
Skill: Conceptual

67) Your family goes on a fishing trip for vacation. While you are fishing you are working on a
_____ schedule of reinforcement.

   A) continuous

   B) fixed ratio

   C) variable ratio

   D) fixed interval

   E) variable interval

Answer: E

Diff: 2   Page Ref: 210

Topic: How Do We Learn New Behaviors by Operant Conditioning?

Skill: Applied

68) Using the Premack principle, once you have finished studying for your next biology test you
should

   A) not study for at least two hours.

   B) study for a different test.

   C) work on your biology homework assignment.

   D) teach the biology material to a friend or classmate.

   E) do something you enjoy.

Answer: E

Diff: 2   Page Ref: 210-211

Topic: How Do We Learn New Behaviors by Operant Conditioning?

Skill: Applied

69) If you use money to buy ham the money is a _____, while the food is a _____.

   A) primary reinforcer; secondary reinforcer

   B) aversive stimulus; primary reinforcer

   C) aversive stimulus; secondary reinforcer

   D) secondary reinforcer; aversive stimulus

   E) secondary reinforcer; primary reinforcer

Answer: E

Diff: 2   Page Ref: 210

Topic: How Do We Learn New Behaviors by Operant Conditioning?

Skill: Applied

70) The Premack principle states that

    A) a preferred activity can be used to reinforce a less preferred one.

    B) in order to be effective, reinforcement must be unpredictable.

    C) reinforcement is more effective than punishment.

    D) punishment must be used consistently and immediately.

    E) using two types of punishment works better than using only one.

Answer: A
Diff: 2   *Page Ref: 210–211*
Topic: How Do We Learn New Behaviors by Operant Conditioning?
Skill: Factual

71) A punisher is an aversive consequence that

    A) weakens the behavior it follows.

    B) is withheld to increase the probability of the response over time.

    C) decreases the probability of shaping by successive approximations.

    D) withholds negative reinforcers.

    E) occurs on a consistent and predictable basis.

Answer: A
Diff: 2   *Page Ref: 211*
Topic: How Do We Learn New Behaviors by Operant Conditioning?
Skill: Conceptual

72) A punisher _____ the probability of a response while a negative reinforcer _____ the probability of a response.

    A) decreases; decreases

    B) increases; increases

    C) decreases; increases

    D) does not alter; decreases

    E) increases; decreases

Answer: C
Diff: 2   *Page Ref: 211*
Topic: How Do We Learn New Behaviors by Operant Conditioning?
Skill: Conceptual

73) The similarity of positive reinforcement and positive punishment is that each involves

    A) decreasing the likelihood of certain events.

    B) increasing the likelihood of certain events.

    C) desireable events or stimuli.

    D) removing a stimulus.

    E) adding a stimulus.

Answer: E

Diff: 2   Page Ref: 211

Topic: How Do We Learn New Behaviors by Operant Conditioning?

Skill: Conceptual

74) Negative punishment is sometimes referred to as _____.

    A) an aversive stimulus

    B) negative reinforcement

    C) positive reinforcement

    D) omission training

    E) premack principle

Answer: D

Diff: 2   Page Ref: 211

Topic: How Do We Learn New Behaviors by Operant Conditioning?

Skill: Factual

75) Punishment is an effective means to control someone's behavior only if

    A) you use a good amount of reinforcement too.

    B) learned helplessness occurs.

    C) the punishments are administered unpredictably.

    D) you can control the environment all of the time.

    E) the person receiving punishment acts with aggression.

Answer: D

Diff: 1   Page Ref: 212

Topic: How Do We Learn New Behaviors by Operant Conditioning?

Skill: Factual

76) Punishment must be administered _____ in order to be effective.

    A) on a schedule of partial reinforcement

    B) immediately and consistently

    C) intermittently

    D) after a cooling-off period

    E) by providing pleasant stimuli

Answer: B
Diff: 2   Page Ref: 212
Topic: How Do We Learn New Behaviors by Operant Conditioning?
Skill: Conceptual

77) Which of the following is true of punishment?

    A) Punishment may involve the application of an aversive stimulus.

    B) Punishment must be used consistently in order to be effective.

    C) Aggression is produced by punishment.

    D) Punishment interferes with the learning of new and better behaviors.

    E) All of the above are correct

Answer: E
Diff: 2   Page Ref: 213-214
Topic: How Do We Learn New Behaviors by Operant Conditioning?
Skill: Factual

78) The most effective form of punishment usually involves

    A) intense physical pain.

    B) penalties, such as loss of privileges.

    C) psychological pain.

    D) attacks on character.

    E) delayed and inconsistent consequences.

Answer: B
Diff: 3   Page Ref: 214-215
Topic: How Do We Learn New Behaviors by Operant Conditioning?
Skill: Conceptual

79) Which of the following is NOT a key difference between operant and classical conditioning?

    A) the order of stimulus and response

    B) whether they are voluntary

    C) whether they are based on reflex responses

    D) whether behavior is based on past stimulation or future conditions

    E) They are based on the behaviorist theory.

Answer: E
Diff: 2   Page Ref: 215
Topic: How Do We Learn New Behaviors by Operant Conditioning?
Skill: Conceptual

80) Which of the following is true of the difference between operant and classical conditioning?

    A) Food is presented before the response in classical conditioning.

    B) Food is presented after the response in classical conditioning.

    C) Classical conditioning requires a stimulus that follows the UCR.

    D) Classical conditioning is used to learn new useful behaviors.

    E) Operant conditioning involves the modification of an old reflex.

Answer: A
Diff: 3   Page Ref: 215
Topic: How Do We Learn New Behaviors by Operant Conditioning?
Skill: Conceptual

81) Negative reinforcement works best when the aversive stimulus

    A) is an operant.

    B) imposes physical pain.

    C) is controlled by the person to be punished.

    D) is imposed by natural or impersonal conditions.

    E) is on a variable ratio schedule.

Answer: D
Diff: 2   Page Ref: 217
Topic: How Do We Learn New Behaviors by Operant Conditioning?
Skill: Applied

82) The cognitive view would argue that learning

    A) always changes both behavior and thinking.

    B) does not always change behavior, but it always produces changes in mental activity.

    C) does not always change thinking, but it always produces changes in behaviors.

    D) produces changes in mental activity that cannot be objectively examined.

    E) always involves either reward or punishment.

Answer: B
Diff: 1   *Page Ref: 219*
Topic: How Does Cognitive Psychology Explain Learning?
Skill: Conceptual

83) Insight learning involves

    A) the perception of familiar objects in new forms or relationships.

    B) the integration of unfamiliar objects into familiar patterns.

    C) a strategy of vicarious trial–and–error.

    D) the development of abstract concepts.

    E) the process of assimilation.

Answer: A
Diff: 3   *Page Ref: 220*
Topic: How Does Cognitive Psychology Explain Learning?
Skill: Conceptual

84) The findings of Wolfgang Kohler oppose the statements of behaviorists, because

    A) the rats behaviors were influenced by their environment.

    B) the rats received food as a reinforcer.

    C) animals are going beyond simple reward/ punishment behaviors.

    D) the rats were demonstrating reflexive responses.

    E) All of the above are correct

Answer: C
Diff: 3   *Page Ref: 219–220*
Topic: How Does Cognitive Psychology Explain Learning?
Skill: Analysis

85) Wolfgang Kohler suggested that chimps

    A) can use a primitive form of language.

    B) would seek affection directly from Kohler.

    C) avoid other chimps.

    D) can come up with novel solutions to new problems using information they have used before.

    E) administer punishment to other chimps.

Answer: D

Diff: 2   Page Ref: 220

Topic: How Does Cognitive Psychology Explain Learning?

Skill: Factual

86) Toleman found that the rats he ran through mazes had created _____ to help them find where the food was placed.

    A) insight learning

    B) cognitive maps

    C) classical conditioning

    D) observational learning

    E) operant conditioning

Answer: B

Diff: 2   Page Ref: 220

Topic: How Does Cognitive Psychology Explain Learning?

Skill: Factual

87) The capacity of an organism to form a "cognitive map" of their environment

    A) was first demonstrated by B.F. Skinner using rats seeking food.

    B) does not require active exploration of the environment.

    C) is maladaptive in that such activity may not result in food reinforcement.

    D) involves the hippocampus.

    E) involves trial-and-error learning in a Thorndike box.

Answer: D

Diff: 3   Page Ref: 221

Topic: How Does Cognitive Psychology Explain Learning?

Skill: Factual

88) Studies of observational learning demonstrate that

    A) nonhuman species cannot learn by imitation.

    B) learning can occur in the absence of personal experience.

    C) television viewing has more influence on behavior than direct observation of live events.

    D) people learn antisocial behaviors (but not prosocial behaviors) through observation.

    E) reward has a greater influence on our behavior than does punishment.

Answer: B
Diff: 2   Page Ref: 222
Topic: How Does Cognitive Psychology Explain Learning?
Skill: Conceptual

89) You see your brother come home after curfew and get grounded by your parents, in the future you come home on time. This type of learning is best explained by

    A) social learning.

    B) insight learning.

    C) classical conditioning.

    D) operant conditioning.

    E) vicarious trial–and–error.

Answer: A
Diff: 2   Page Ref: 222
Topic: How Does Cognitive Psychology Explain Learning?
Skill: Applied

90) In Bandura's classic BoBo doll experiment, those children that saw aggressive models

    A) were more likely to behave violently towards the bobo doll.

    B) were more likely to tell others to respond violently towards the bobo doll.

    C) did not respond any differently than a control group that saw no violent behavior.

    D) were less likely to behave violently towards the bobo doll.

    E) None of the above are correct

Answer: A
Diff: 2   Page Ref: 222
Topic: How Does Cognitive Psychology Explain Learning?
Skill: Recall

91) _____ reported that watching violent behaviors makes children more likely to behave violently?

    A) Watson   B) Thorndike   C) Tolman   D) Bandura   E) Garcia

Answer: D
Diff: 2   Page Ref: 222
Topic: How Does Cognitive Psychology Explain Learning?
Skill: Factual

92) Robert Rescorla believes that the feature of the conditioned stimulus that most facilitates classical conditioning is its

   A) frequency.

   B) informativeness.

   C) intensity.

   D) size.

   E) consistency.

   Answer: B
   Diff: 3   Page Ref: 223
   Topic: How Does Cognitive Psychology Explain Learning?
   Skill: Conceptual

93) In deciding whether there is a fire in your classroom building, which of the following provides the best early information as to whether there is a fire?

   A) the sound of an alarm bell

   B) the appearance of greenish flames

   C) the smell of smoke

   D) the flicker of flames

   E) the appearance of a fireman in your classroom

   Answer: C
   Diff: 3   Page Ref: 223
   Topic: How Does Cognitive Psychology Explain Learning?
   Skill: Conceptual

94) According the Rescorla, we are most likely to pay attention to information that precedes the UCS only if

   A) it also follows the UCS.

   B) one has noticed others who know what the UCS will predict.

   C) it provides information about the UCR.

   D) it provides unique information about the UCS.

   E) it becomes a CR.

   Answer: D
   Diff: 3   Page Ref: 223
   Topic: How Does Cognitive Psychology Explain Learning?
   Skill: Conceptual

95) The notion that learning produces physical changes in the synapses of the brain is consistent with

    A) hemispheric lateralization.

    B) brain imaging.

    C) spatial mapping.

    D) long-term potentiation.

    E) myelinization of neurons.

Answer: D

Diff: 2   Page Ref: 223–224

Topic: How Does Cognitive Psychology Explain Learning?

Skill: Factual

96) Damage to neurons within the _____ that use the the transmitter _____ would be expected to diminish the experience of reward.

    A) limbic system; dopamine

    B) cerebellum; GABA

    C) parietal cortex; epinephrine

    D) medulla; serotonin

    E) cerebrum; acetylcholine

Answer: A

Diff: 3   Page Ref: 224

Topic: How Does Cognitive Psychology Explain Learning?

Skill: Factual

97) Kandel and Hawkins argue that complex organisms have two types of learning "circuits"— one involving simple motor responses and the other involving

    A) "mindless" learning.

    B) observational learning.

    C) operant conditioning.

    D) conscious processing.

    E) A and C are correct

Answer: D

Diff: 3   Page Ref: 224

Topic: How Does Cognitive Psychology Explain Learning?

Skill: Factual

98) Research regarding the learning styles have found that
   A) most people are visual learners.
   B) most people cannot be easily categorized into a single category.
   C) most people are spatial learners.
   D) the research has incredibly high scientific validity.
   E) most people are kinesthetic learners.

Answer: B
Diff: 2   Page Ref: 225
Topic: A Critical Look at "Learning Styles"
Skill: Conceptual

Check Your Understanding Questions

1) Classical conditioning is especially useful for understanding which one of the following examples of learning?
   A) A dog has learned to "sit up" for a food reward.
   B) A psychology student who is learning how memory works.
   C) A child who, after a painful dental visit, has learned to fear the dentist.
   D) An executive who us afraid that she will lose her job.
   E) A rat that has learned to run a maze.

Answer: C
Diff: 2   Page Ref: 205
Topic: Check Your Understanding
Skill: Recall

2) The responses in classical conditioning before any conditioning took place were
   A) innate reflexes.
   B) new behaviors.
   C) premeditated behaviors.
   D) random acts.
   E) trained reflexes.

Answer: A
Diff: 2   Page Ref: 205
Topic: Check Your Understanding
Skill: Recall

3) If you learned to fear electrical outlets after getting a painful shock, what would be the CS?

    A) the electrical outlet

    B) the painful shock

    C) the fear response

    D) the time period between seeing the outlet and getting the shock

    E) the light

Answer: A
Diff: 2   *Page Ref: 205*
Topic: Check Your Understanding
Skill: Applied

4) Which of the following would be most likely to be the unconditioned stimulus (UCS) involved in classical conditioning?

    A) food

    B) a flashing light

    C) music

    D) money

    E) praise

Answer: A
Diff: 2   *Page Ref: 205*
Topic: Check Your Understanding
Skill: Understanding the Core Concept

5) Thorndike's law of effect said that an organism will learn to perform responses that are

    A) rewarded.

    B) reflexive.

    C) prompted.

    D) preceded by a neutral stimulus.

    E) preceded by a conditioned stimulus

Answer: A
Diff: 2   *Page Ref: 218*
Topic: Check Your Understanding
Skill: Recall

6) Suppose that you taught your dog to roll over for the reward of a dog biscuit. Then, one day you run out of dog biscuits. Which schedule of reinforcement would keep your dog responding longer without a biscuit?

A) continuous reinforcement

B) intermittent reinforcement

C) negative reinforcement

D) noncontingent reinforcement

E) positive reinforcement

Answer: B

Diff: 2   Page Ref: 218

Topic: Check Your Understanding

Skill: Applied

7) Which one of the following is an example of negative reinforcement?

A) going to the dentist to have a toothache relieved

B) spanking a child for swearing

C) taking away a child's favorite top when the child misbehaves

D) making a child watch as another child is punished

E) giving a child a toy for misbehaving

Answer: A

Diff: 2   Page Ref: 218

Topic: Check Your Understanding

Skill: Applied

8) Which one of the following is a conditioned reinforcer for most people?

A) money

B) food

C) sex

D) a sharp pain in the back

E) water

Answer: A

Diff: 2   Page Ref: 248

Topic: Check Your Understanding

Skill: Recall

9) Operant conditioning, in contrast with classical conditioning, emphasizes events (such as rewards and punishments) that occur

    A) before the behavior.

    B) after the behavior.

    C) during the behavior.

    D) at the same time as another stimulus.

    E) the timing is not important in operant conditioning.

Answer: B

Diff: 2   Page Ref: 218

Topic: Check Your Understanding

Skill: Understanding the Core Concept

10) When their goal path was blocked, Tolman's rats would take the shortest route around the barrier. This, said Tolman, showed that they had developed

    A) trial-and-error learning.

    B) operant behavior.

    C) cognitive maps.

    D) observational learning.

    E) classical responses.

Answer: C

Diff: 2   Page Ref: 226

Topic: Check Your Understanding

Skill: Recall

11) Cognitive psychologist Robert Rescorla has reinterpreted the process of classical conditioning. In his view, the conditioned stimulus serves as a

    A) cue that signals the onset of the UCS.

    B) stimulus that follows the UCS.

    C) negative reinforcement.

    D) cognitive map.

    E) punisher.

Answer: A

Diff: 2   Page Ref: 226

Topic: Check Your Understanding

Skill: Recall

12) If you were going to use Bandura's findings in developing a program to prevent violence among middle school children, you might
   A) have children watch videos of aggressive children who are not being reinforced for their aggressive behavior.
   B) have children role–play aggressive solutions to interpersonal problems.
   C) have children punch a "bobo" doll to get the aggression out of their system.
   D) punish children for aggressive acts performed at school.
   E) reward children for non–aggressive acts.

Answer: A
Diff: 3   Page Ref: 226
Topic: Check Your Understanding
Skill: Applied

13) Which of the following proved to be difficult to explain in purely behavioral terms?
   A) a trained seal doing a trick for a fish
   B) a dog salivating at the sound of a bell
   C) a chimpanzee using a pile of boxes and a stick to obtain food hung high in its cage
   D) a pigeon learning to press a lever in a Skinner box for a food reward
   E) a child learning to read by receiving a piece of candy for every word he pronounces correctly

Answer: C
Diff: 2   Page Ref: 226
Topic: Check Your Understanding
Skill: Understanding the Core Concept

True/False Questions

1) Under most conditions, the CS and the UCS must be paired at least several times before the CS reliably elicits a CR.

Answer: TRUE
Diff: 2   Page Ref: 199
Topic: What Sort of Learning Does Classical Conditioning Explain?
Skill: Conceptual

2) The process by which we learn not to respond the the repeated presentation of a stimulus is called stimulus generalization.

Answer: FALSE
Diff: 2   Page Ref: 197
Topic: What Sort of Learning Does Classical Conditioning Explain?
Skill: Factual

3) In Pavlov's original experiment, the meat was the conditioned stimulus.

Answer: FALSE
Diff: 2   Page Ref: 199
Topic: What Sort of Learning Does Classical Conditioning Explain?
Skill: Conceptual

4) For a CR to be learned, the CS and the UCS should be close together in time.

Answer: TRUE
Diff: 2   Page Ref: 200
Topic: What Sort of Learning Does Classical Conditioning Explain?
Skill: Conceptual

5) In the process of "extinction," the CS is repeatedly presented without being followed by the UCS.

Answer: TRUE
Diff: 2   Page Ref: 201
Topic: What Sort of Learning Does Classical Conditioning Explain?
Skill: Conceptual

6) In discrimination conditioning, Little Albert came only to fear the white laboratory rat, but nothing else that looked similar to the rat.

Answer: TRUE
Diff: 2   Page Ref: 232
Topic: What Sort of Learning Does Classical Conditioning Explain?
Skill: Factual

7) In counter–conditioning, the subject gradually learns to relax in the presence of the conditioned stimulus.

Answer: TRUE
Diff: 2   Page Ref: 203
Topic: What Sort of Learning Does Classical Conditioning Explain?
Skill: Factual

8) Nutritionists recommend eating a favorite meal right before a cancer patient is to undergo a round of chemotherapy.

Answer: FALSE
Diff: 2   Page Ref: 205
Topic: What Sort of Learning Does Classical Conditioning Explain?
Skill: Conceptual

9) Operant behavior is based on automatic reflex actions.

Answer: FALSE
Diff: 2   Page Ref: 206
Topic: How Do We Learn New Behaviors by Operant Conditioning?
Skill: Conceptual

10) Operant Conditioning typically precedes a behavior.

Answer: FALSE
Diff: 2   Page Ref: 206
Topic: How Do We Learn New Behaviors by Operant Conditioning?
Skill: Factual

11) Reinforcers always follow and strengthen a response.

Answer: TRUE
Diff: 2   Page Ref: 207
Topic: How Do We Learn New Behaviors by Operant Conditioning?
Skill: Conceptual

12) The original operant chamber was designed by B.F. Skinner for his daughter.

Answer: FALSE
Diff: 2   Page Ref: 207
Topic: How Do We Learn New Behaviors by Operant Conditioning?
Skill: Factual

13) Continuous reinforcement should be used when first teaching an organism a new behavior.

Answer: TRUE
Diff: 2   Page Ref: 208
Topic: How Do We Learn New Behaviors by Operant Conditioning?
Skill: Conceptual

14) Fishing is based on a Fixed Ratio schedule.

Answer: FALSE
Diff: 2   Page Ref: 240
Topic: How Do We Learn New Behaviors by Operant Conditioning?
Skill: Applied

15) If Carrie receives $20 every time she has finished stuffing 500 envelopes, she is on a fixed interval schedule of reinforcement.

Answer: FALSE
Diff: 3   Page Ref: 209
Topic: How Do We Learn New Behaviors by Operant Conditioning?
Skill: Applied

16) In a fixed ratio schedule or reinforcement, the organism will work faster than in any of the other intermittent schedules.

Answer: TRUE
Diff: 3   Page Ref: 209
Topic: How Do We Learn New Behaviors by Operant Conditioning?
Skill: Factual

17) If your boss checks up on you on occasion to insure that you are doing your work, he is using a variable interval schedule.

Answer: TRUE
Diff: 3   Page Ref: 210
Topic: How Do We Learn New Behaviors by Operant Conditioning?
Skill: Applied

18) The Premack principle states that a more preferred activity can be used to reinforce a less preferred activity.

Answer: TRUE
Diff: 2   Page Ref: 210–211
Topic: How Do We Learn New Behaviors by Operant Conditioning?
Skill: Conceptual

19) Positive reinforcement increases the probability of a response, and negative reinforcement decreases the probability of a response.

Answer: FALSE
Diff: 3   Page Ref: 212
Topic: How Do We Learn New Behaviors by Operant Conditioning?
Skill: Conceptual

20) Negative reinforcement is a synonym for punishment.

Answer: FALSE
Diff: 2   Page Ref: 212
Topic: How Do We Learn New Behaviors by Operant Conditioning?
Skill: Conceptual

21) According to Operant Conditioning, positive means to add something, while negative means to take something away.

Answer: TRUE
Diff: 2   Page Ref: 212
Topic: How Do We Learn New Behaviors by Operant Conditioning?
Skill: Factual

22) Punishment is more effective than positive reinforcement.

Answer: FALSE
Diff: 2   Page Ref: 213
Topic: How Do We Learn New Behaviors by Operant Conditioning?
Skill: Conceptual

23) Punishment need be immediate to be effective.

Answer: FALSE
Diff: 2   Page Ref: 214
Topic: How Do We Learn New Behaviors by Operant Conditioning?
Skill: Factual

24) Only classical conditioning can account for learning new behaviors.

Answer: FALSE
Diff: 2   Page Ref: 215
Topic: How Do We Learn New Behaviors by Operant Conditioning?
Skill: Conceptual

25) When given complex problems to solve, chimps are unable to incorporate information learned in previous tasks.

Answer: FALSE
Diff: 2   Page Ref: 219
Topic: How Does Cognitive Psychology Explain Learning?
Skill: Factual

26) After being in school for a year, you now have a good sense of the layout of the campus. This is because you have developed a cognitive map of your environment.

Answer: TRUE
Diff: 2   Page Ref: 220
Topic: How Does Cognitive Psychology Explain Learning?
Skill: Applied

27) Tolman conducted studies researching insight learning.

Answer: FALSE
Diff: 2   *Page Ref: 220*
Topic: How Does Cognitive Psychology Explain Learning?
Skill: Factual

28) Tolman's work with cognitive maps' challenged the belief of behavioral psychologists.

Answer: TRUE
Diff: 2   *Page Ref: 221*
Topic: How Does Cognitive Psychology Explain Learning?
Skill: Conceptual

29) Elliot Aronson attributes violent tragedies such as the Columbine massacre to the extensive presence of violence in our media.

Answer: TRUE
Diff: 2   *Page Ref: 222-223*
Topic: How Does Cognitive Psychology Explain Learning?
Skill: Factual

30) Observational learning enables us to acquire behaviors without going through trial-and-error learning.

Answer: TRUE
Diff: 2   *Page Ref: 222*
Topic: How Does Cognitive Psychology Explain Learning?
Skill: Conceptual

31) In Bandura's bobo doll experiment, the participants exposed to a violent model showed no difference in their relations with the bobo doll when compared to a control group.

Answer: FALSE
Diff: 2   *Page Ref: 222*
Topic: How Does Cognitive Psychology Explain Learning?
Skill: Recall

32) Classical conditioning and complex forms of learning, like concept formation, are now thought to occur via two types of nerve circuits.

Answer: TRUE
Diff: 3   *Page Ref: 223*
Topic: How Does Cognitive Psychology Explain Learning?
Skill: Conceptual

33) Most studies to show an important difference in learning when instructors match educational content to different learning styles.

Answer: FALSE
Diff: 2   *Page Ref: 225*
Topic: A Critical Look at "Learning Styles"
Skill: Factual

Short Answer Questions

1) _____ refers to a simple form of learning that involves learning NOT to respond to stimulation.

Answer: Habituation
Diff: 3   *Page Ref: 197*
Topic: Introduction
Skill: Factual

2) In Ivan Pavlov's original experiment, identify the following components, UCS,UCR,CS,CR.

Answer: UCS: food (meat)
              UCR: salivation
              CS: footsteps (tone)
              CR: salivation
Diff: 2   *Page Ref: 199*
Topic: What Sort of Learning Does Classical Conditioning Explain?
Skill: Conceptual

3) The situation in which a CS no longer causes a CR is called _____. If suddenly the CS begins once again to cause a CR this is called _____.

Answer: extinction; spontaneous recovery
Diff: 2   *Page Ref: 201*
Topic: What Sort of Learning Does Classical Conditioning Explain?
Skill: Conceptual

4) List the UCS, UCR, CS and CR in the "Little Albert" experiment.

Answer: UCS: Load noise
              UCR: Fear
              CS: White rat
              CR: Fear
Diff: 2   *Page Ref: 202–203*
Topic: What Sort of Learning Does Classical Conditioning Explain?
Skill: Factual

5) The fact that Little Albert became afraid of anything even remotely similar to the white rat explains _____. If Albert only learned to fear the white rat but no a white rabbit or Santa Claus, he would be demonstrating _____.

Answer: stimulus generalization; stimulus discrimination
Diff: 2   Page Ref: 203
Topic: What Sort of Learning Does Classical Conditioning Explain?
Skill: Conceptual

6) What is food–aversion learning?

Answer: The tendency of organisms to connect illness with certain foods and is a process that seems to have a genetic basis.
Diff: 3   Page Ref: 203–204
Topic: What Sort of Learning Does Classical Conditioning Explain?
Skill: Factual

7) How did Garcia convince wolves to dislike lamb?

Answer: The process of taste aversion learning was applied such that lamb meat containing a mild poison was left in pastures. A wolf that ate this meat became sick and subsequently avoided sheep.
Diff: 3   Page Ref: 204
Topic: What Sort of Learning Does Classical Conditioning Explain?
Skill: Conceptual

8) If Julie receives her allowance every Sunday, assuming she has completed all of her chores, she is on which intermittent schedule of reinforcement?

Answer: fixed interval
Diff: 2   Page Ref: 209
Topic: How Do We Learn New Behaviors by Operant Conditioning?
Skill: Applied

9) Explain the difference between an primary and a secondary reinforcer.

Answer: A primary reinforcer fulfill a basic biological need while a secondary reinforcer has gained it's reinforcing power through association with primary reinforcers.
Diff: 2   Page Ref: 210
Topic: How Do We Learn New Behaviors by Operant Conditioning?
Skill: Conceptual

10) Briefly explain the difference between positive and negative punishment

Answer: Positive punishment adds an averse stimulus while negative punishment takes away something that is desired.
Diff: 2   Page Ref: 211
Topic: How Do We Learn New Behaviors by Operant Conditioning?
Skill: Conceptual

11) How are negative and positive reinforcement different and how are they the same?

Answer: In negative reinforcement a negative stimulus is removed in order to increase the desired behavior. In positive reinforcement a positive addition follows a desired behavior in order to increase that behavior.

Diff: 2   Page Ref: 212

Topic: How Do We Learn New Behaviors by Operant Conditioning?

Skill: Conceptual

12) Under what conditions is punishment effective in the control of behavior?

Answer: must be consistent and in an environment of control

Diff: 3   Page Ref: 214

Topic: How Do We Learn New Behaviors by Operant Conditioning?

Skill: Conceptual

13) What is insight learning?

Answer: This involves a reorganization of a persons perception of a problem.

Diff: 2   Page Ref: 220

Topic: How Does Cognitive Psychology Explain Learning?

Skill: Factual

14) When Tolman was working with rats an running them through mazes, he found that they could often find their way to the reinforcer, even under different conditions. This seems to suggest that the rats had developed a _____.

Answer: cognitive map

Diff: 2   Page Ref: 220

Topic: How Does Cognitive Psychology Explain Learning?

Skill: Factual

15) Explain how Tolman's findings of cognitive maps in rats has implications that threaten the ideas of classical and operant conditioning.

Answer: The rats are demonstrating at least some cognition which necessitates studying what is happening internally in an organism. Not all information that effects behavior is observable.

Diff: 2   Page Ref: 221

Topic: How Does Cognitive Psychology Explain Learning?

Skill: Conceptual

16) According to Albert Bandura, explain the potential implications for children who watch many violent cartoons.

Answer: according the bandura, much of what we learn comes fro watching others. If we observe others acting violent towards one another we are likely to exhibit more violent behavior. Because many violent cartoons suggest that there is no long-term implications following a violent act, children may learn to behave in similar ways.

Diff: 2   Page Ref: 222

Topic: How Does Cognitive Psychology Explain Learning?

Skill: Applied

17) What does Rescorla suggest is the critical factor for a CS in classical conditioning?

Answer: It must be informative (predicts the UCS).

Diff: 2   Page Ref: 223

Topic: How Does Cognitive Psychology Explain Learning?

Skill: Applied

Essay Questions

1) Describe the process of classical conditioning. Define and provide an original example of the following components of classical conditioning. Identify and Explain the NS, CS, CR, UCS and UCR in the example.

Answer: Students should note that CC involves a type of learning in which a stimulus that produces a reflex response becomes associated with a neutral stimulus, which eventually elicits a similar reflex response. The student must provide an example in which she labels and describes the neutral, unconditioned, and conditioned stimuli, as well as the unconditioned and conditioned responses. The example must involve the individual eventually demonstrating a reflex response to something which initially produced no relevant response.

Diff: 3   Page Ref: 198–199

Topic: What Sort of Learning Does Classical Conditioning Explain?

Skill: Applied

2) Contrast the four schedules of reinforcement in operant conditioning and give an example of each.

Answer: Ratio schedules provide a reinforcer for every nth response: Fixed ratio: N is the same from trial to trial; variable ratio: N averages across trials. Interval based schedules: first response after some time interval has elapsed is reinforced. Fixed interval has a constant time period whereas variable interval schedules have a an average time period across trials.

Diff: 3   Page Ref: 208–210

Topic: How Do We Learn New Behaviors by Operant Conditioning?

Skill: Factual

3) If you want to train your puppy to sit down and "play dead", explain how each of the following could be employed to teach your dog this "trick". Be sure to relate all of the examples back to the prompt.
Continuous schedule of reinforcement
Intermittent schedule of reinforcement
shaping
positive reinforcement
negative reinforcement
punishment

Answer: A continuous schedule of reinforcement should be employed when initially teaching the dog to sit, during the acquisition stage dogs will learn much more quickly if they are reinforced every time they perform a given behavior. the dog should eventually be moved to a variable ratio schedule in which they are only reinforced occasionally, this will prevent extinction since they will not know when they are going to get reinforced and should continue the desired behavior. Shaping will be employed by reinforcing successive approximations too the desired behavior. Once the dog moves towards the ground they will get reinforced and then when they go further down and so on until they are exhibiting the desired behavior. Positive reinforcement could be employed by giving the dog a bone each time the desired behavior occurs. Negative reinforcement can be employed by playing an annoying buzzing sound until the dog sits. Punishment could be employed by taking away the dog's favorite toy if they do not sit.

Diff: 3   Page Ref: 208–210

Topic: How Do We Learn New Behaviors by Operant Conditioning?

Skill: Applied

4) Discuss five ways in which classical conditioning is different from operant conditioning.

Answer: 1. In C.C. stimuli precede the response, in O.C. rewards or punishments follow the behavior.
2. C.C. does not involve rewards or reinforcers, O.C. does
3. C.C. works on a new stimulus creating an old reflexive behavior. O.C. creates new behaviors.
4. In C.C. extinction occurs by withholding the UCS. In O.C. extinction is produced by withholding reinforcement
5. in C.C. the learner is passive. In O.C. the learner is active

Diff: 3   Page Ref: 215–216

Topic: Operant and Classical Conditioning Compared

Skill: Conceptual

5) Name and discuss the four major kinds of consequences that function in the process of operant conditioning.

Answer: The student should name positive and negative reinforcement and positive and negative punishment. The student should mention that reinforcement follows and strengthens a response, whereas punishment follows and weakens a response. The student should note that 'positive' involves adding something (in the case of reinforcement it is usually something desired, whereas in punishment it is usually something aversive), whereas 'negative' involves removing something (in the case of reinforcement it is usually something aversive, whereas in punishment it is usually something desired).

Diff: 2   Page Ref: 243

Topic: How Do We Learn New Behaviors by Operant Conditioning?

Skill: Factual

6) Describe the three forms of cognitive learning. Explain the differences between each of these forms and tell which scientist is credited with their Discovery.'

Answer: Kohler's insight learning involves a sudden reorganization of perception. Tolman's cognitive maps involve mental representations of an environment. Bandura's social (or observational) learning involves learning by watching another individual.

Diff: 2   Page Ref: 219–223

Topic: How Does Cognitive Psychology Explain Learning?

Skill: Conceptual

7) Chose one activity that you believe is learned through the behaviorist perspective and one that you believe is learned through the cognitive perspective. How can these two schools of thought coincide with one another?

Answer: We learn to have adverse feelings towards food that at one time has made us ill. This happens naturally and automatically and is a reflexive feeling when we initially eat and again see that particular food. We learn how to get from our house to school each day by using a cognitive map that we have created in our mind. We do not rely only on rewards and punishments for this task. New research regarding simple and complex neural networks may explain the difference between these two types of learning while at the same tie linking the together. Simple connections may represent reflexive behaviors, while complex networks may be more reflective of cognitive or higher order learning.

Diff: 3   Page Ref: 223–244

Topic: How Does Cognitive Psychology Explain Learning?

Skill: Applied

Chapter 7 Cognition

Multiple Choice Questions

1) Between _____ and _____ of children have suffered at least one incident of sexual abuse.

    A) 1%; 3%   B) 4%; 20%   C) 5%; 35%   D) 10%; 15%   E) 20%; 25%

Answer: B
Diff: 2   Page Ref: 234
Topic: What Is Memory?
Skill: Factual

2) _____ refers to the term for any system that encodes, stores, and retrieves information.

    A) Perception

    B) Processing

    C) Learning

    D) Memory

    E) Sensation

Answer: D
Diff: 2   Page Ref: 235
Topic: What Is Memory?
Skill: Factual

3) The reason it may be difficult to remember how many rows of stars appear on the United States flag is most likely due to

    A) the limits of our visual system.

    B) sensory adaptation.

    C) the fact that we pay little attention to such details.

    D) habituation.

    E) sensory interference.

Answer: C
Diff: 2   Page Ref: 235
Topic: What Is Memory?
Skill: Applied

4) The key tasks of a memory system is to
    A) encode, store, and retrieve.
    B) perceive, chunk, and recall.
    C) sense, understand, and rehearse.
    D) process, rearrange, and simplify.
    E) be exposed to, combine, and consider.

Answer: A
Diff: 2   Page Ref: 236
Topic: What Is Memory?
Skill: Conceptual

5) Which of the following is NOT true of the memory process of encoding?
    A) A stimulus is identified during encoding.
    B) Encoding requires conscious attention.
    C) Emotionally charged experiences are easily encoded.
    D) Encoding involves linking a new concept with one already in memory.
    E) B and D are correct

Answer: B
Diff: 3   Page Ref: 236
Topic: What Is Memory?
Skill: Factual

6) A Cognitive understanding of memory, emphasizing how information is changed when it is encoded, stored and retrieved is known as
    A) chunking.
    B) the elaboration method.
    C) the forgetting curve.
    D) the information–processing model.
    E) eidectic imagery.

Answer: D
Diff: 2   Page Ref: 236
Topic: What Is Memory?
Skill: Factual

7) During the memory process of _____, we select, identify the correct format for the memory system.
   A) retrieval
   B) storage
   C) access
   D) processing
   E) encoding

Answer: E
Diff: 2   Page Ref: 236
Topic: What Is Memory?
Skill: Conceptual

8) New information is related to older memory information during the memory process of
   A) retrieval.
   B) encoding.
   C) storage.
   D) elaboration.
   E) rehearsing.

Answer: D
Diff: 2   Page Ref: 236
Topic: What Is Memory?
Skill: Conceptual

9) Our ability to retain encoded material over time is known as
   A) storage.
   B) recognition.
   C) recall.
   D) declarative memory.
   E) chunking.

Answer: A
Diff: 2   Page Ref: 237
Topic: What Is Memory?
Skill: Factual

10) If George was trying to remember information for his Biology exam and he has encoded the information correctly but cannot remember it after two days, there may be a problem with _____.

    A) retrieval.

    B) elaboration.

    C) storage.

    D) rehearsal.

    E) sensory memory.

Answer: C
Diff: 2   Page Ref: 237
Topic: What Is Memory?
Skill: Applied

11) The memory process of elaboration resembles the Piagetian concept of

    A) storage.

    B) recognition.

    C) recall.

    D) assimilation.

    E) egocentrism.

Answer: D
Diff: 2   Page Ref: 237
Topic: What Is Memory?
Skill: Factual

12) Getting information out of memory is known as

    A) encoding.

    B) storage.

    C) elaboration.

    D) retrieval.

    E) chunking.

Answer: D
Diff: 2   Page Ref: 237
Topic: What Is Memory?
Skill: Recall

13) Another term for eidectic imagery is
   A) photographic memory.
   B) recognition.
   C) episodic memory.
   D) engram.
   E) implicit memory.

Answer: A
Diff: 2   Page Ref: 238
Topic: What Is Memory?
Skill: Factual

14) An eidectic image will fade from memory if you .
   A) describe it.
   B) think about it.
   C) are aware of it.
   D) view it for too long.
   E) rehearse it.

Answer: A
Diff: 3   Page Ref: 238
Topic: What Is Memory?
Skill: Conceptual

15) Eidectic memory is most often found in
   A) the elderly.
   B) those with an incredibly high I.Q.
   C) idiot savants.
   D) children.
   E) All of the above

Answer: D
Diff: 1   Page Ref: 238
Topic: What Is Memory?
Skill: Factual

16) Which of the following is NOT a difference between eidectic imagery and other memories?

   A) Eidectic images are more vivid.

   B) Eidectic images are more abstract.

   C) Eidectic images last longer.

   D) Eidectic images are more common for children.

   E) Eidectic images are more like afterimages.

Answer: B
Diff: 3   Page Ref: 238
Topic: What Is Memory?
Skill: Conceptual

17) The three memory stages, in order of processing, are

   A) sensory; cognitive; short term.

   B) sensory; working; short term.

   C) sensory; working; long term.

   D) working; long term; short term.

   E) recall; recognition; rehearsal.

Answer: C
Diff: 1   Page Ref: 239–240
Topic: How Do We Form Memories?
Skill: Factual

18) The awareness of what your friend wore to school last April 21st must first pass through

   A) working.

   B) declarative.

   C) procedural.

   D) sensory.

   E) photographic.

Answer: D
Diff: 2   Page Ref: 239
Topic: How Do We Form Memories?
Skill: Applied

19) When you hear a phone number and are able to recall it for a brief period, the phone number is thought to reside within _____ memory.

    A) sensory

    B) working

    C) gustatory

    D) procedural

    E) long–term

Answer: B
Diff: 2   *Page Ref: 240*
Topic: How Do We Form Memories?
Skill: Applied

20) This type of memory is primarily what contributes to our sense of self.

    A) sensory memory

    B) short-term memory

    C) eidectic memory

    D) long–term memory

    E) procedural memory

Answer: D
Diff: 2   *Page Ref: 240*
Topic: How Do We Form Memories?
Skill: Conceptual

21) How long does sensory memory generally last?

    A) 1 minute

    B) fraction of a second

    C) 1 second

    D) 10 seconds

    E) no limit to how long sensory memory will last

Answer: B
Diff: 1   *Page Ref: 241*
Topic: How Do We Form Memories?
Skill: Recall

22) Sperling's study involving recall of an array of 12 letters suggested that the actual capacity of sensory memory is

    A) two or three items.

    B) seven (plus or minus two) items.

    C) limitless.

    D) nine or more items.

    E) about seven chunks.

Answer: D
Diff: 2   Page Ref: 241
Topic: How Do We Form Memories?
Skill: Factual

23) The sensory register for vision is called _____ memory, whereas the sensory register for hearing is called _____ memory.

    A) declarative; procedural

    B) olfactory; auditory

    C) implicit; explicit

    D) explicit; implicit

    E) iconic; echoic

Answer: E
Diff: 2   Page Ref: 242
Topic: How Do We Form Memories?
Skill: Factual

24) When Suzy scans the store window she decides that there is nothing that she is interested in. She is using her _____ memory and when she is not interested in any of the objects, the information is _____.

    A) echoic; held for one minute

    B) iconic; held for one minute

    C) iconic; immediately disregarded

    D) echoic; immediately disregarded

    E) tactile; hed for one minute

Answer: C
Diff: 2   Page Ref: 242
Topic: How Do We Form Memories?
Skill: Applied

25) Were sensory memories to last longer than normal,

    A) we would need more working memory.

    B) our senses would not work together.

    C) old information would interfere with incoming information.

    D) it would ultimately destroy cortical neurons.

    E) sensory memory would be able to hold more information.

Answer: C
Diff: 2   Page Ref: 242
Topic: How Do We Form Memories?
Skill: Conceptual

26) The capacity of working memory is about _____ items and this theory was developed by

    A) three; Schacter.

    B) seven, Miller.

    C) eleven; Miller.

    D) twenty; Aronson.

    E) thirty; Craik.

Answer: B
Diff: 2   Page Ref: 243
Topic: How Do We Form Memories?
Skill: Factual

27) Because of the limited capacity of _____, it is unsafe to talk on a cell phone while driving on a freeway during rush-hour.

    A) sensory memory

    B) procedural memory

    C) episodic memory

    D) working memory

    E) echoic memory

Answer: D
Diff: 2   Page Ref: 243
Topic: How Do We Form Memories?
Skill: Applied

28) The storage capacity of working memory

    A) is smaller than both sensory and long-term memory.

    B) is larger than both sensory and long-term memory.

    C) varies more than both sensory and long-term memory.

    D) is larger than sensory memory, but smaller than long-term memory.

    E) is larger than long-term memory, but smaller than sensory memory.

Answer: A

Diff: 2   *Page Ref: 243*

Topic: How Do We Form Memories?

Skill: Conceptual

29) Jamal needs to remember his social security number but there are too many numbers for him to hold it in his working memory. What technique would best help Jamal to remember his social security number.

    A) mnemonic device

    B) method of Loci

    C) employ sensory memory

    D) chunking

    E) iconic memory

Answer: D

Diff: 2   *Page Ref: 244*

Topic: How Do We Form Memories?

Skill: Applied

30) Bonnie is trying to remember what grocery items she needs from the stores. She repeats the words, "Eggs, cookies, bread, tortillas, and pretzels" over and over again in her mind. Bonnie is utilizing which memory technique?

    A) elaborative rehearsal

    B) transduction

    C) maintenance rehearsal

    D) chunking

    E) retroactive interference

Answer: C

Diff: 2   *Page Ref: 244*

Topic: How Do We Form Memories?

Skill: Applied

31) Many individuals can remember an entire sentence that is read to them even though it exceeds the amount of information we can generally hold in short-term memory. They do this by

   A) using their sketch pad.

   B) employing the method of Loci.

   C) using the phonological loop.

   D) using sensory memory.

   E) using long-term memory.

Answer: C

Diff: 2   *Page Ref: 244*

Topic: How Do We Form Memories?

Skill: Conceptual

32) When you try to relate psychological terms you are learning in class to personal examples from your life. You are using

   A) the phonological loop.

   B) the method of Loci.

   C) chunking.

   D) elaborative rehearsal.

   E) maintenance rehearsal.

Answer: D

Diff: 2   *Page Ref: 245*

Topic: How Do We Form Memories?

Skill: Applied

33) The best strategy by which to transfer information from working memory to long-term memory is to engage in

   A) eidectic imagery.

   B) maintenance rehearsal.

   C) long-term potentiation.

   D) elaborative rehearsal.

   E) repression.

Answer: D

Diff: 2   *Page Ref: 245*

Topic: How Do We Form Memories?

Skill: Conceptual

34) The _____ theory claims that establishing more connections with long-term memories makes information more meaningful and memorable and thus easier to recall.

    A) levels-of-processing

    B) engram

    C) spatial analyses

    D) distributed learning

    E) mood-congruent

Answer: A

Diff: 3   Page Ref: 245

Topic: How Do We Form Memories?

Skill: Conceptual

35) Working memory involves activity in circuits located with the _____ of the brain.

    A) occipital lobe

    B) parietal lobe

    C) cerebellum

    D) corpus callosum

    E) prefrontal cortex

Answer: E

Diff: 3   Page Ref: 246

Topic: How Do We Form Memories?

Skill: Factual

36) Long-term memory is thought to have

    A) a limited capacity of approximately 1000 items.

    B) an unlimited capacity.

    C) a large chunking capacity.

    D) a repressed capacity.

    E) a seven-item capacity.

Answer: B

Diff: 1   Page Ref: 246

Topic: How Do We Form Memories?

Skill: Factual

37) Knowing how to board a train is considered a _____ memory, while knowing that Abraham Lincoln was the sixteenth president of t he United States is a _____ memory.

   A) recognition; recall

   B) encoding; rehearsal

   C) procedural; declarative memory

   D) semantic; episodic memory

   E) immediate; eventual memory

Answer: C
Diff: 2   Page Ref: 247
Topic: How Do We Form Memories?
Skill: Factual

38) _____ memory is the LTM subsystem that stores memory for how things are done.

   A) Episodic

   B) Semantic

   C) Eventual

   D) Procedural

   E) Declarative

Answer: D
Diff: 2   Page Ref: 247
Topic: How Do We Form Memories?
Skill: Conceptual

39) A guitarist uses _____ to recall how to play the notes of a specific song.

   A) episodic memory

   B) procedural memory

   C) semantic memory

   D) a flashbulb memory

   E) mnemonics

Answer: B
Diff: 2   Page Ref: 247
Topic: How Do We Form Memories?
Skill: Applied

40) Your memory of how much fun you had last Spring break is an example of

A) semantic memory.

B) chunking.

C) procedural memory.

D) episodic memory.

E) sensory memory.

Answer: D

Diff: 2   Page Ref: 247

Topic: How Do We Form Memories?

Skill: Applied

41) Remembering the explanation that your psychology professor gave when she described neural networks is likely held in your

A) procedural memory.

B) priming.

C) implicit memory.

D) distributed learning.

E) semantic memory.

Answer: E

Diff: 2   Page Ref: 248

Topic: How Do We Form Memories?

Skill: Conceptual

42) The physical changes that are associated with memory are known as a(n)

A) phoneme.

B) schema.

C) long-term potentiation.

D) engram.

E) phosgene.

Answer: D

Diff: 2   Page Ref: 248

Topic: How Do We Form Memories?

Skill: Factual

43) Patient H.M. is unable to form _____ memories as a result of the removal of his _____ on both sides of his brain in order to stop epileptic seizures.

    A) episodic; hippocampus and amygdala

    B) semantic; medulla

    C) procedural; thalamus

    D) declarative; frontal cortex

    E) implicit; cerebellum

Answer: A

Diff: 3   Page Ref: 248

Topic: How Do We Form Memories?

Skill: Factual

44) H.M. lost the ability to create new memories after his surgery, he is suffering from

    A) retrograde amnesia.

    B) anterograde amnesia.

    C) retroactive interference.

    D) proactive interference.

    E) repression.

Answer: B

Diff: 2   Page Ref: 248

Topic: How Do We Form Memories?

Skill: Applied

45) many Alzheimer's patients have a memory the initially gives up newer thoughts and memories. They may mistake their grandson for their own son. In many ways this resembles

    A) anterograde amnesia.

    B) retrograde amnesia.

    C) short-term memory.

    D) semantic memories.

    E) long-term memories.

Answer: A

Diff: 2   Page Ref: 248

Topic: How Do We Form Memories?

Skill: Applied

46) Highly emotional memories such as those which many prisoner's of war have experienced may cause post-traumatic stress disorder. Recent research has found which brain structure to play a significant role in these emotional memories?

   A) reticular activating system

   B) pituitary

   C) hypothalamus

   D) amygdala

   E) pons

Answer: D
Diff: 2   Page Ref: 249
Topic: How Do We Form Memories?
Skill: Conceptual

47) The ability of the hippocampus to transfer intermediate memories into long-term memory is known as

   A) transduction.

   B) networking.

   C) consolidation.

   D) engram.

   E) plasticity.

Answer: C
Diff: 3   Page Ref: 249
Topic: How Do We Form Memories?
Skill: Factual

48) Retrograde amnesia involves _____ and is induced by _____.

   A) memory distortion; meditation

   B) the loss of prior memory traces; head trauma

   C) the inability to transfer into LTM; head trauma

   D) the failure of semantic memory; abuse of alcohol

   E) the inability to transfer into LTM; cortical damage

Answer: B
Diff: 2   Page Ref: 250
Topic: How Do We Form Memories?
Skill: Conceptual

49) Long-term potentiation suggests that

    A) sensory memory has the ability to store memories indefinitely.

    B) all incoming messages will be sent to permanent storage in long-term memory.

    C) millions of neurons can be involved in storing a single memory.

    D) a neuron can hold information for more than a minute.

    E) None of the above explain long-term potentiation.

Answer: C
Diff: 2   *Page Ref: 250*
Topic: How Do We Form Memories?
Skill: Factual

50) Your ability to remember where you were the morning of September 11, 2001 is an example of a(n)

    A) flashbulb memory.

    B) semantic memory.

    C) procedural memory.

    D) implicit memory.

    E) sensory memory.

Answer: A
Diff: 2   *Page Ref: 250*
Topic: "Flashbulb" Memories
Skill: Applied

51) Your parents remember details regarding when John F. Kennedy was shot, and you remember details about a mugging you saw last month. Your parents memory is more likely to be _____ and your is likely to be _____.

    A) distorted; distorted

    B) totally wrong; distorted

    C) accurate; accurate

    D) distorted; accurate

    E) accurate; distorted

Answer: D
Diff: 2   *Page Ref: 251*
Topic: How Do We Form Memories?
Skill: Applied

52) We are always aware of _____ memory whereas _____ memory may be incidentally learned.

    A) semantic; episodic

    B) implicit; explicit

    C) episodic; semantic

    D) explicit; implicit

    E) semantic; procedural

Answer: D

Diff: 2   Page Ref: 252

Topic: How Do We Retrieve Memories?

Skill: Conceptual

53) _____ memory could explain how you know a certain person's name even if you cannot explain how you know it.

    A) Semantic

    B) Implicit

    C) Episodic

    D) Explicit

    E) Procedural

Answer: B

Diff: 2   Page Ref: 252

Topic: How Do We Retrieve Memories?

Skill: Conceptual

54) If you look at the particular area on the chalkboard where a certain concept was written to help you remember the term, you are using

    A) a mnemonic device.

    B) a retrieval cue.

    C) implicit memory.

    D) chunking.

    E) eidectic memory.

Answer: B

Diff: 2   Page Ref: 252

Topic: How Do We Retrieve Memories?

Skill: Applied

55) Ted asks Krystal to say the words 'hop,' 'pop,' and 'mop.' Then, Ted asks Krystal, "What do you do at a green light?" Krystal quickly replies, "Stop," (instead of the right answer: "Go") because of

    A) recognition.

    B) encoding specificity.

    C) TOT phenomenon.

    D) priming.

    E) misattribution.

Answer: D

Diff: 3   Page Ref: 253

Topic: How Do We Retrieve Memories?

Skill: Applied

56) if your psychology instructor asks you to provide a definition of assimilation, she is asking you to answer a _____ question.

    A) implicit memory

    B) recognition

    C) recall

    D) memory trace

    E) procedural memory

Answer: C

Diff: 2   Page Ref: 254

Topic: How Do We Retrieve Memories?

Skill: Applied

57) To answer this multiple choice question, you must use

    A) implicit memory.

    B) recognition.

    C) recall.

    D) procedural memory.

    E) the method of loci.

Answer: B

Diff: 2   Page Ref: 254

Topic: How Do We Retrieve Memories?

Skill: Applied

58) Because ideas in LTM are stored in terms of meaning, a practical way to improve memory is to
   A) cut down on alcohol intake on study days.
   B) use only maintenance rehearsal when studying.
   C) study in a noisy crowded environment.
   D) wait until the last moment to learn new material.
   E) make the material meaningful when it is in working memory.

Answer: E
Diff: 2   Page Ref: 254
Topic: How Do We Retrieve Memories?
Skill: Conceptual

59) If you learn material for your political science course in a classroom, as then are asked to take an exam for that course if a large lecture hall on the other side of campus, your scores may not be as high as you would like. What may explain this phenomena?
   A) mood–congruent learning
   B) encoding specificity
   C) recognition
   D) recall
   E) mnemonic devices

Answer: B
Diff: 2   Page Ref: 254
Topic: How Do We Retrieve Memories?
Skill: Applied

60) The observation that depressed people tend to favor recall of depressing memories is known as _____ memory.
   A) sociopathic
   B) anterograde
   C) mood–congruent
   D) retrograde
   E) A and B are correct

Answer: C
Diff: 2   Page Ref: 255
Topic: How Do We Retrieve Memories?
Skill: Factual

61) The TOT phenomenon occurs when

    A) a flood of memories enter consciousness.

    B) memories interfere with one another.

    C) the order of presentation impacts recall.

    D) you know a word but cannot name it.

    E) a person strongly believes that incorrect memories are accurate.

Answer: D
Diff: 2   *Page Ref: 256*
Topic: On the Tip of Your Tongue
Skill: Conceptual

62) The TOT phenomenon is explained as due to a poor match between

    A) retrieval cues and encoding in LTM.

    B) mnemonics and engrams.

    C) semantic memory and recall.

    D) implicit and explicit memory.

    E) episodic memory and recognition.

Answer: A
Diff: 3   *Page Ref: 256*
Topic: On the Tip of Your Tongue
Skill: Conceptual

63) Brian cannot remember the name of the flower he just planted even though he knows he is familiar with it's name, his lack of remembering demonstrates the _____.

    A) mnemonic devices

    B) tip of the tongue phenomena

    C) method of loci

    D) recognition

    E) chunking

Answer: B
Diff: 2   *Page Ref: 256*
Topic: How Do We Retrieve Memories?
Skill: Conceptual

64) Which of the following is NOT one of Daniel Schacter's "seven sins" of memory?

A) bias

B) absent-mindedness

C) suggestibility

D) encoding failure

E) transience

Answer: D

Diff: 3   Page Ref: 257–265

Topic: Why Does Memory Sometimes Fail Us?

Skill: Factual

65) If you are unable to remember the name of your second grade teacher because you haven't thought of her in awhile, you are demonstrating

A) the serial position effect.

B) transience.

C) misattribution.

D) absent-mindedness.

E) encoding specificity.

Answer: B

Diff: 2   Page Ref: 257

Topic: Why Does Memory Sometimes Fail Us?

Skill: Applied

66) The concept of Transience suggests that long-term memory

A) fade in strength over time.

B) remain the same regardless of how much time passes.

C) become distorted by our expectations.

D) increases as time passes.

E) had unlimited capacity.

Answer: A

Diff: 2   Page Ref: 257

Topic: Why Does Memory Sometimes Fail Us?

Skill: Factual

67) A temporary failure to recall where you left your keys is most likely due to

    A) transience.

    B) proactive interference.

    C) misattribution.

    D) absent–mindedness.

    E) the TOT phenomenon.

Answer: D
Diff: 1   Page Ref: 257
Topic: Why Does Memory Sometimes Fail Us?
Skill: Applied

68) Hermann Ebbinghaus' forgetting curve revealed that we forget

    A) immediately after being exposed to new information.

    B) all information that is not personally relevant to us.

    C) nothing, everything is held in long–term memory.

    D) for meaningless information, quickly at first and then forgetting tapers off.

    E) None of the above are correct

Answer: D
Diff: 2   Page Ref: 257
Topic: Why Does Memory Sometimes Fail Us?
Skill: Recall

69) Ebbinghaus found that when he returned to a list of words that he had previously memorized week before, it took him _____.

    A) longer to remember the list again

    B) the same amount of time to remember the list again

    C) less time to remember the list again.

    D) longer to remember the first half of the list

    E) longer to remember insignificant words on the list

Answer: C
Diff: 2   Page Ref: 257
Topic: Why Does Memory Sometimes Fail Us?
Skill: Conceptual

70) Absent-mindedness in a college student would typically involve

    A) trying to study while watching television.

    B) a failure to encode a stimulus event.

    C) a failure to connect new input to previously stored information.

    D) a failure of iconic memory.

    E) an old memory making it difficult to recall a newer one.

Answer: A
Diff: 3   Page Ref: 258
Topic: Why Does Memory Sometimes Fail Us?
Skill: Conceptual

71) Blocking refers to the situation in which competing memories produce _____ leading to forgetting.

    A) transduction

    B) transference

    C) an engram

    D) interference

    E) misattribution

Answer: D
Diff: 2   Page Ref: 258
Topic: Why Does Memory Sometimes Fail Us?
Skill: Conceptual

72) If your mom reminds you to pick up your little brother from soccer practice, and then you friend calls causing to you forget to pick up your brother, you would be said to be experiencing

    A) absent-mindedness.

    B) blocking.

    C) transience.

    D) misattribution.

    E) bias.

Answer: C
Diff: 2   Page Ref: 258
Topic: Why Does Memory Sometimes Fail Us?
Skill: Applied

73) You are at a party, first you are introduced to Tina and immediately following that introduction you meet Gina, they both look similar and you have not met them before, which of the following may be prohibiting you from correctly remembering their names even moments later?

    A) retroactive interference

    B) serial position effect

    C) interference

    D) transience

    E) bias

Answer: C
Diff: 2   Page Ref: 259
Topic: Why Does Memory Sometimes Fail Us?
Skill: Applied

74) If you keep accidentally calling your new girlfriend your old girlfriends name, you are experiencing

    A) misattribution.

    B) encoding specificity.

    C) proactive interference.

    D) repression.

    E) transience.

Answer: C
Diff: 2   Page Ref: 259
Topic: Why Does Memory Sometimes Fail Us?
Skill: Applied

75) In pro active interference, old memories act to

    A) cause us to forget other old memories.

    B) distort our sensory memory.

    C) add additional information to permanent external memory.

    D) reverse the order of items in LTM.

    E) block our ability to learn new information.

Answer: E
Diff: 2   Page Ref: 259
Topic: Why Does Memory Sometimes Fail Us?
Skill: Conceptual

76) _____ occurs when newly learned information prevents the retrieval of previously stored, similar information.

    A) Implicit amnesia

    B) Retroactive interference

    C) Proactive interference

    D) Suppression

    E) Explicit amnesia

Answer: B

Diff: 3   Page Ref: 259

Topic: Why Does Memory Sometimes Fail Us?

Skill: Conceptual

77) If you are trying to remember the names of all the U.S. presidents, the serial position effect would predict that you will have difficulty

    A) remembering more than about seven (plus or minus two) of them.

    B) recognizing the names of the presidents on a list.

    C) recalling the earliest presidents.

    D) recalling the most recent presidents.

    E) recalling the presidents in the middle of the list.

Answer: E

Diff: 2   Page Ref: 259

Topic: Why Does Memory Sometimes Fail Us?

Skill: Applied

78) When you learn the tango, you forget the mambo that you learned last year, this is an example of

    A) proactive interference.

    B) serial position effect.

    C) transience.

    D) persistence.

    E) retroactive interference.

Answer: E

Diff: 2   Page Ref: 259

Topic: Why Does Memory Sometimes Fail Us?

Skill: Conceptual

79) _____ occurs when memories are retrievable, but they are associated with the wrong time, place, or person.

   A) Misattribution

   B) Interference.

   C) Bias

   D) Priming

   E) Repression

Answer: A
Diff: 2   *Page Ref: 260*
Topic: Why Does Memory Sometimes Fail Us?
Skill: Factual

80) Simon read the words 'bed,' 'night,' 'snore,' 'dream,' 'comfort,' and 'pillow' to Jennifer. As a result of misattribution, we could expect Jennifer to

   A) remember the word *sleep*.

   B) experience some sleepiness.

   C) only remember three or four of the words.

   D) remember the first and last words, but not the middle words.

   E) confuse the order of the words.

Answer: A
Diff: 3   *Page Ref: 260*
Topic: Why Does Memory Sometimes Fail Us?
Skill: Applied

81) Suggestibility can cause us to

   A) lose old memories in our LTM.

   B) distort memories and create false ones.

   C) block painful or upsetting memories.

   D) be unable to forget painful memories.

   E) rehearse important material repeatedly.

Answer: B
Diff: 2   *Page Ref: 261*
Topic: Why Does Memory Sometimes Fail Us?
Skill: Conceptual

82) If you witness a mugging and the police ask, :"did you see the scar on the assailants face?" Eve if there was no scar, you might reply that you did indeed see the scar. What fault of memory best explains this honest mistake?

   A) bias

   B) persistence

   C) transience

   D) misinformation effect

   E) interference

Answer: D

Diff: 2   Page Ref: 261

Topic: Why Does Memory Sometimes Fail Us?

Skill: Applied

83) The following eyewitnesses are being asked to recall what they say at an accident site. Who is most likely to report a distorted memory?

   A) Eddie who has told his story already to five different interrogators each of whom asked different questions

   B) George who is 35 and a lawyer

   C) Mandy who knows that the recollection of memories can cause errors to occur

   D) Ellyn, who has told her story to only one interrogator

   E) All of the above are likely to have faulty memories.

Answer: A

Diff: 2   Page Ref: 262

Topic: Why Does Memory Sometimes Fail Us?

Skill: Applied

84) According to Freud, the only way to be free of repressed memories is to

   A) go back to the place where they occurred.

   B) uncover them in therapy.

   C) eliminate interfering information.

   D) acknowledge your bias.

   E) push them deep into the unconscious mind.

Answer: B

Diff: 3   Page Ref: 262

Topic: Why Does Memory Sometimes Fail Us?

Skill: Factual

85) According to Freud, those individuals who had been held in concentration camps during word war II would _____ these memories because they are too painful to remember.

A) project   B) displace   C) repress   D) ignore   E) remember

Answer: C

Diff: 3   Page Ref: 262

Topic: Why Does Memory Sometimes Fail Us?

Skill: Conceptual

86) Modern cognitive research suggests that memory for emotionally arousing events

A) is remembered vividly.

B) cannot be uncovered.

C) is stored deep within the unconscious mind.

D) is distorted.

E) is difficult to retrieve.

Answer: A

Diff: 2   Page Ref: 263

Topic: Why Does Memory Sometimes Fail Us?

Skill: Factual

87) Because _____ memories of events before the age of three are extremely rare, early memories of abuse are likely to be _____.

A) semantic; biased

B) procedural; distorted

C) episodic; misattribution

D) explicit; repressed

E) declarative; forgotten

Answer: C

Diff: 3   Page Ref: 263

Topic: Why Does Memory Sometimes Fail Us?

Skill: Conceptual

88) _____ refers to a situation in which personal beliefs, attitudes and experiences impact memory

   A) Misattribution

   B) Suggestibility

   C) Interference

   D) Transference

   E) Bias

Answer: E

Diff: 3   Page Ref: 263

Topic: Why Does Memory Sometimes Fail Us?

Skill: Factual

89) Because of self-consistency bias,

   A) Don may have trouble remembering how he initially felt about Vicki.

   B) Pete's feelings about Anne may be stronger than they once were.

   C) Sam may not love Florence any more.

   D) Shawna believes that she always felt passionately about Matthew.

   E) Tom believes that he loves Coral more than Mike does.

Answer: D

Diff: 1   Page Ref: 264

Topic: Why Does Memory Sometimes Fail Us?

Skill: Applied

90) When memories for unpleasant events are intrusive, what has occurred?

   A) suggestibility

   B) persistence

   C) mnemonics

   D) bias

   E) transience

Answer: B

Diff: 1   Page Ref: 264

Topic: Why Does Memory Sometimes Fail Us?

Skill: Factual

91) The memory failure caused by transience is adaptive in that it

    A) prevents memory from becoming overwhelmed.

    B) retains the most important information.

    C) eliminates memories that conflict with our beliefs.

    D) makes it difficult to encode sensory memories.

    E) ensures memories are stored by both sight and sound.

Answer: A
Diff: 2   Page Ref: 265
Topic: Why Does Memory Sometimes Fail Us?
Skill: Conceptual

92) Mnemonics are methods for

    A) repressing memories that are too painful to remember.

    B) encoding information by associating it with information already in LTM.

    C) retrieving information that has already been stored in LTM.

    D) reducing the bias we sometimes experience when storing memories.

    E) enhancing our ability to detect sensory information.

Answer: B
Diff: 2   Page Ref: 265
Topic: Improving Your Memory with Mnemonics
Skill: Conceptual

93) You are an actor worried about remembering your lines. In order to help you a friend suggests that you remember each portion of the script by linking it to different places in your home. What memory technique has your friend suggested?

    A) persistence

    B) rote memorization

    C) method of loci

    D) maintenance elaboration

    E) None of the above

Answer: C
Diff: 2   Page Ref: 265
Topic: Improving Your Memory with Mnemonics
Skill: Applied

94) To remember the five Great Lakes, you might remember the word HOMES, because each of the five letters in HOMES is the first letter of one of the Great Lakes. This strategy is known as

A) the method of loci.

B) the tip-of-the-tongue phenomenon.

C) a natural language mediator.

D) a recognition task.

E) maintenance rehearsal.

Answer: C

Diff: 2   *Page Ref: 265*

Topic: Improving Your Memory with Mnemonics

Skill: Applied

95) The idea proposed by Noam Chomsky that suggests that all individuals are born with an innate ability to learn language.

A) linguistic relativity theory

B) grammar

C) language acquisition device

D) overregularization

E) morpheme

Answer: C

Diff: 2   *Page Ref: 267*

Topic: How Do Children acquire Language?

Skill: Conceptual

96) Noam Chomsky believed that language was

A) attributable primarily to nature.

B) attributable primarily to nurture.

C) an equal mix of nature and nurture.

D) only learned after age 2.

E) a result exclusively learned from watching one's parents.

Answer: A

Diff: 2   *Page Ref: 267*

Topic: How Do Children acquire Language?

Skill: Factual

97) Noam Chomsky believes that all children are born

    A) inherently know grammar.

    B) learn only their native language.

    C) knowing only the morphemes within their own language.

    D) knowing syntax.

    E) with the ability to learn all languages.

Answer: E
Diff: 2   Page Ref: 267
Topic: How Do Children acquire Language?
Skill: Factual

98) Which of the following brain areas is primarily concerned with speech production?

    A) hippocampus

    B) Broca's area

    C) hypothalamus

    D) Wernicke's area

    E) parietal lobe

Answer: B
Diff: 2   Page Ref: 267
Topic: How Do Children acquire Language?
Skill: Conceptual

99) Chomsky believed that the Language Acquisition Device (LAD) was

    A) a result our interactions with our environment.

    B) essential if a newborn was to survive.

    C) a combination of speech centers located in the brain.

    D) located in the parietal lobe of the brain.

    E) found in only some cultures.

Answer: C
Diff: 2   Page Ref: 267
Topic: How Do Children acquire Language?
Skill: Conceptual

100) Which of the following provides evidence to support the idea of a Language Acquisition Device (LAD)?

   A) People around the world inherently know the same language.

   B) Parents who talk to their children while in the womb have children who talk much earlier.

   C) All languages share all of the same sounds.

   D) Children worldwide proceed through the steps of language in much the same way.

   E) We learn much of the language we know from our peers and our parents.

   Answer: D
   Diff: 3   Page Ref: 267
   Topic: How Do Children acquire Language?
   Skill: Conceptual

101) As language develops, people

   A) begin to learn rules of grammar.

   B) move from the babbling to the one-word stage.

   C) lose the ability to makes sounds that are heard in other languages.

   D) begin to combine morphemes into meaningful units.

   E) All l of the above are trues about the development of language.

   Answer: E
   Diff: 3   Page Ref: 268
   Topic: How Do Children acquire Language?
   Skill: Conceptual

102) The typical vocabulary of a six-year old is

   A) 1,000 words.

   B) 5,000 words.

   C) 7,000 words.

   D) 10,000 words.

   E) 60,000 words.

   Answer: D
   Diff: 2   Page Ref: 268
   Topic: How Do Children acquire Language?
   Skill: Recall

103) The "naming explosion" begins at about age
   A) 18 months.
   B) 3 years.
   C) 6 years.
   D) 9 months.
   E) All language development occurs evenly throughout the life span.
   Answer: A
   Diff: 2   *Page Ref: 268*
   Topic: How Do Children acquire Language?
   Skill: Factual

104) Children regardless of where they are brought up, speak primarily about which of the following categories of ideas?
   A) parents, moveable objects and themselves
   B) themselves, parents and needs
   C) moveable objects, themselves and locations
   D) locations, movable objects and movers
   E) needs, themselves and movers
   Answer: D
   Diff: 3   *Page Ref: 268*
   Topic: How Do Children acquire Language?
   Skill: Recall

105) Once children understand that there are rules regarding language, they have
   A) reached the two-word stage.
   B) reached the telegraphic stage.
   C) acquired grammar.
   D) acquired syntax.
   E) reached the babbling stage.
   Answer: B
   Diff: 2   *Page Ref: 268*
   Topic: How Do Children acquire Language?
   Skill: Conceptual

106) Place the following stages regarding language development in the correct order.

A) babbling, one–word, telegraphic, two–word

B) one–word, babbling, two–word, telegraphic

C) babbling, one–word, two–word, telegraphic

D) babbling, two–word, one–word, telegraphic

E) one–word, two–word, babbling, telegraphic

Answer: C

Diff: 2   *Page Ref: 268*

Topic: How Do Children acquire Language?

Skill: Analysis

107) A language's set of rules about combining and ordering words.

A) morphemes

B) grammar

C) syntax

D) overregularization

E) accommodation

Answer: B

Diff: 1   *Page Ref: 269*

Topic: How Do Children acquire Language?

Skill: Factual

108) If Ellie who is 21/2 years old says, "Cookie me now", she is demonstrating

A) telegraphic speech.

B) one-word speech.

C) two-word speech.

D) babbling.

E) overregularization.

Answer: A

Diff: 1   *Page Ref: 269*

Topic: How Do Children acquire Language?

Skill: Applied

109) A, an, ill, are all examples of

    A) syntax.

    B) grammar.

    C) phonemes.

    D) morphemes.

    E) overregularization.

Answer: D

Diff: 1   *Page Ref: 269*

Topic: How Do Children acquire Language?

Skill: Applied

110) Sally said, "I goed to the store", she is demonstrating an example of

    A) morphemes.

    B) overregularization.

    C) phonemes.

    D) telegraphic speech.

    E) two-word speech.

Answer: B

Diff: 2   *Page Ref: 269*

Topic: How Do Children acquire Language?

Skill: Applied

111) Social cues that help to express meaning in communication include

    A) body language.

    B) intonation.

    C) facial expressions.

    D) feedback from those they are talking to.

    E) All of the above

Answer: E

Diff: 1   *Page Ref: 269*

Topic: How Do Children acquire Language?

Skill: Conceptual

112) What is the problem with many foreign language programs currently offered in U.S. schools?

    A) They offer children to many different foreign language options.

    B) They begin their foreign language training too early.

    C) They begin their foreign language training too late.

    D) The do not have enough selection in the choices of langauge.

    E) They are not rigorous enough.

Answer: C
Diff: 1   Page Ref: 270
Topic: How Do Children acquire Language?
Skill: Conceptual

113) The odd feeling of recognition you get when visit a new place is known as

    A) a prototype.

    B) a concept hierarchy.

    C) deja vu.

    D) a mental set.

    E) an algorithm.

Answer: C
Diff: 1   Page Ref: 271
Topic: What Are the Components of Thought?
Skill: Applied

114) When you create in your mind a "typical day at school", you are experiencing

    A) deja vu.

    B) an artificial concept.

    C) a prototype.

    D) functional fixedness.

    E) concept formation.

Answer: E
Diff: 2   Page Ref: 271
Topic: What Are the Components of Thought?
Skill: Applied

115) Concepts

    A) can represent objects but not activities.

    B) cannot be directly observed by researchers.

    C) are basically the same from one person to the next.

    D) interfere with our ability to organize new information.

    E) come in exactly two types, visual and auditory.

Answer: B
Diff: 2   *Page Ref: 271*
Topic: What Are the Components of Thought?
Skill: Conceptual

116) You have seen many dogs in your life. Because of this, you have no problem picturing the new lab that your friend is describing to you. This idea of what a dog looks like based on your prior experience is called a

    A) familiar concept.

    B) normative schema.

    C) mental prototype.

    D) natural concept.

    E) deja vu experience.

Answer: D
Diff: 2   *Page Ref: 272*
Topic: What Are the Components of Thought?
Skill: Conceptual

117) The most representative example of a category is called a(n)

    A) prototype.

    B) schema.

    C) availability heuristic.

    D) algorithm.

    E) mental set.

Answer: A
Diff: 2   *Page Ref: 272*
Topic: What Are the Components of Thought?
Skill: Conceptual

118) What is the prototypical example of a vehicle?

    A) boat   B) bus   C) train   D) car   E) bike

Answer: D
Diff: 2   *Page Ref: 272*
Topic: What Are the Components of Thought?
Skill: Applied

119) A "feathered biped" is the artificial concept of a(n)

    A) human.   B) bird.   C) penguin.   D) sea horse.   E) animal.

Answer: B
Diff: 2   *Page Ref: 272*
Topic: What Are the Components of Thought?
Skill: Conceptual

120) Which of the following is true of prototypes?

    A) They are slowly accessed and recalled.

    B) They are never used when the critical features approach applies.

    C) They are formed on the basis of commonly experienced features.

    D) The more often they are perceived, the weaker their overall memory strength.

    E) They are often based on dictionary definitions.

Answer: C
Diff: 3   *Page Ref: 272*
Topic: What Are the Components of Thought?
Skill: Conceptual

121) Which one of the following is NOT an artificial concept?

    A) the dictionary definition of the word 'truth'

    B) Einstein's theory of relativity

    C) your mental image of the statue of Liberty

    D) the lyrics to "New York, New York"

    E) how to determine the radius of a circle

Answer: C
Diff: 3   *Page Ref: 272*
Topic: What Are the Components of Thought?
Skill: Applied

122) In Biology you are learning that a class of animals falls under the broader scope of a kingdom of animals and a family falls under class. You are learning a

    A) script.

    B) syllogism.

    C) hierarchy.

    D) mental set.

    E) cognitive map.

Answer: C
Diff: 2   *Page Ref: 272*
Topic: What Are the Components of Thought?
Skill: Applied

123) Consider the following concept hierarchy—food, desserts, chocolates, _____. The last term should be

 A) brownies.

 B) vanilla ice cream.

 C) main courses.

 D) side dishes.

 E) edible food.

Answer: A

Diff: 2   *Page Ref: 272*

Topic: What Are the Components of Thought?

Skill: Applied

124) A(n) _____ is a cognitive representation of a physical space.

 A) chunk

 B) spatial heuristic

 C) algorithm

 D) cognitive map

 E) confirmation bias

Answer: D

Diff: 2   *Page Ref: 274*

Topic: What Are the Components of Thought?

Skill: Conceptual

125) Your friend Edward is lost and needs your help finding the mall, you find out where he is and then guide him verbally to his destination. Your ability to give Edward good directions to the mall is based on a

 A) prototype.

 B) mental set.

 C) cognitive map.

 D) hierarchy.

 E) hindsight bias.

Answer: C

Diff: 2   *Page Ref: 274*

Topic: What Are the Components of Thought?

Skill: Conceptual

126) _____ was the first to hypothesize that people form cognitive maps of their environment to help guide their actions toward certain goals.

    A) Edward Tolman

    B) John Von Neumann

    C) Noam Chomsky

    D) George Sperling

    E) Bob Greene

Answer: A

Diff: 2   *Page Ref: 274*

Topic: What Are the Components of Thought?

Skill: Factual

127) In studies that were completed regarding students' cognitive maps of the world, researchers found that

    A) all students regardless of where they lived chared a cognitive map that was very similar.

    B) most students placed the United States at the center of the world.

    C) the majority of students held placed Europe at the center of the world.

    D) most students made Australia much smaller than it actually is.

    E) there were no conclusive findings from the study.

Answer: C

Diff: 3   *Page Ref: 274*

Topic: What Are the Components of Thought?

Skill: Recall

128) _____ are unique brain wave patterns that are associated with particular stimuli.

    A) Background "noise"

    B) Artificial concepts

    C) Quantitative trait loci

    D) Event-related potentials

    E) Long-term potentiations

Answer: D

Diff: 2   *Page Ref: 276*

Topic: What Are the Components of Thought?

Skill: Factual

129) Results from PET scan studies suggest that
   A) a single "thinking center" mediates thought.
   B) thought occurs in widely distributed areas of the brain, and that a range of highly specialized modules deal with different kinds of thought.
   C) a single brain region mediates thought.
   D) the cerebellum is loosely divided into subsections which deal with different kinds of thought.
   E) most types of mental processing occur throughout the brainstem.

   Answer: B
   Diff: 2   Page Ref: 276
   Topic: What Are the Components of Thought?
   Skill: Factual

130) I think that all librarians are middle aged women with cardigan sweaters, glasses and a bun. If I meet a librarian who fulfills these expectations, it would reinforce my
   A) schema.
   B) heuristic.
   C) script.
   D) artificial concept.
   E) All of the above

   Answer: A
   Diff: 2   Page Ref: 277
   Topic: Schemas and Scripts Help You Know What to Expect
   Skill: Applied

131) _____ are clusters of knowledge that provide general conceptual frameworks regarding certain topics, events, and situations.
   A) Prototypes
   B) Schemas
   C) Hierarchies
   D) Algorithms
   E) Cognitive maps

   Answer: B
   Diff: 2   Page Ref: 277
   Topic: Schemas and Scripts Help You Know What to Expect
   Skill: Conceptual

132) You go to a new fancy restaurant, and you are nervous because you are on a first date. However, since you have been to other nice restaurants before, you know that you will first be seated, then someone will take your drink order,s then you will have an appetizer, followed by dinner. If all goes well of the date, you may even stay for dessert! What is this an example of?

A) algorithm

B) mental set

C) script

D) episodic memory

E) heuristic

Answer: C

Diff: 2   Page Ref: 277

Topic: Schemas and Scripts Help You Know What to Expect

Skill: Applied

133) Which of the following is a culturally defined script that would violate most Americans ideas of acceptable behavior.

A) The expectation that people stop at red lights.

B) The idea that people who know one another should say 'hello'.

C) The idea that we should listen to our teachers.

D) The idea that women should not reveal their face or arms in public.

E) The expectation that children should share with one another.

Answer: D

Diff: 2   Page Ref: 278

Topic: Schemas and Scripts Help You Know What to Expect

Skill: Applied

134) A "good thinker" possesses which of the following attributes?

A) They are capable of careful reasoning.

B) They make use of effective thinking strategies.

C) They avoid jumping to rash conclusions.

D) They avoid misleading thinking strategies.

E) All of the above are correct

Answer: E

Diff: 2   Page Ref: 311

Topic: What Abilities Do Good Thinkers Possess?

Skill: Conceptual

135) Brad is home when all of his lights suddenly go out. His thought that "this is what happens when a fuse is blown" would be said to

   A) demonstrating functional fixedness.

   B) identifying the problem.

   C) using an algorithm.

   D) utilizing a heuristic.

   E) evaluating a solution.

Answer: B
Diff: 1   Page Ref: 279
Topic: What Abilities Do Good Thinkers Possess?
Skill: Applied

136) A(n) _____ is a step–by–step solution to a problem that is likely to be successful.

   A) rule of thumb

   B) schema

   C) mental operant

   D) algorithm

   E) categorization process

Answer: D
Diff: 2   Page Ref: 280
Topic: What Abilities Do Good Thinkers Possess?
Skill: Conceptual

137) One of the reasons that people use algorithms is that these

   A) are intuitive and obvious.

   B) are flexible, because they are not too precise.

   C) can solve almost any problem.

   D) change over time as we become wiser.

   E) will always work if used properly.

Answer: E
Diff: 2   Page Ref: 280
Topic: What Abilities Do Good Thinkers Possess?
Skill: Conceptual

138) A heuristic is BEST described as a

    A) rule of thumb.

    B) step-by-step procedure.

    C) time-consuming process that guarantees success.

    D) schema.

    E) categorization process from general to specific.

Answer: A
Diff: 2   Page Ref: 280
Topic: What Abilities Do Good Thinkers Possess?
Skill: Conceptual

139) An algorithm would not be the best strategy when trying to

    A) use a mathematical formula to figure out the answer.

    B) follow a specific procedure during a science lab.

    C) calculate your grade point average.

    D) choose whether you would like to have roses or lilacs in your garden.

    E) follow the directions on a box of legos in order to build the fort pictured on the cover.

Answer: D
Diff: 2   Page Ref: 280
Topic: What Abilities Do Good Thinkers Possess?
Skill: Conceptual

140) In problem-solving, a(n)_____ will nearly always to produce the correct answer. We often however use _____ because they are much more efficient and are often still correct.

    A) a mental set; schemas

    B) algorithm; heuristics

    C) mnemonic device; scripts

    D) retrieval cue; cognitive maps

    E) prototype; anchoring bias'

Answer: B
Diff: 2   Page Ref: 280
Topic: What Abilities Do Good Thinkers Possess?
Skill: Conceptual

141) When trying to find the solution to a complicated math problem, some people will begin with the answer and then try and find out how this cam to be, tis process is called

    A) inversion.

    B) working backward.

    C) reversibility.

    D) means–ends analysis.

    E) anchoring bias.

Answer: B
Diff: 1   *Page Ref: 281*
Topic: What Abilities Do Good Thinkers Possess?
Skill: Applied

142) When you begin working n your psychology research project you at first feel overwhelmed. eventually however you begin to take each step at a time until you come to the end of the project. By the end of the school year you have a wonderful research project that was made less overwhelming by

    A) using an algorithm.

    B) working backwards.

    C) formal logic.

    D) breaking the problem into it's subgoals.

    E) using functional fixedness.

Answer: D
Diff: 2   *Page Ref: 281*
Topic: What Abilities Do Good Thinkers Possess?
Skill: Conceptual

143) Leon is an architect, he has been plotting out restaurants. For all of the restaurants in in the past, Leon has worked the traffic flow in a clockwise manner. For the current restaurant this will not work, but Leon cannot think of another way to route the traffic. leon is experiencing

    A) a mental set.

    B) working backward.

    C) an anchoring bias.

    D) incorrectly identifying the problem.

    E) divergent thinking.

Answer: A
Diff: 2   *Page Ref: 282*
Topic: What Abilities Do Good Thinkers Possess?
Skill: Applied

144) Jenny is locked out of her car, it is cold and she is upset. Jenny forgets that she has a purse filled with objects that might be of use in getting her into the car (bobby pins, eyeglass screwdriver, etc.). Jenny is demonstrating

   A) the anchoring bias.

   B) the availability heuristic.

   C) an algorithm.

   D) functional fixedness.

   E) representative heuristic.

Answer: D
Diff: 2   Page Ref: 282
Topic: What Abilities Do Good Thinkers Possess?
Skill: Applied

145) A person who uses a drop of super glue to seal a paper cut on their finger has overcome the obstacle to effective problem solving related to

   A) working backward.

   B) regression to the average.

   C) functional fixedness.

   D) the anchoring bias.

   E) the representativeness heuristic.

Answer: C
Diff: 2   Page Ref: 281
Topic: What Abilities Do Good Thinkers Possess?
Skill: Applied

146) Wendell is a great surfer but he never considers surfing as a career, instead he goes into accounting which he has no real passion for, Wendell is exhibiting

   A) functional fixedness.

   B) self-imposed limitations.

   C) an error identifying the problem.

   D) a algorithm.

   E) a heuristic.

Answer: B
Diff: 2   Page Ref: 283
Topic: What Abilities Do Good Thinkers Possess?
Skill: Applied

147) _____ bias refers to a situation in which people ignore or overlook information that disagrees with their beliefs.

   A) Hindsight

   B) Knowledge

   C) Confirmation

   D) Representativeness

   E) Availability

Answer: C

Diff: 2   Page Ref: 284

Topic: What Abilities Do Good Thinkers Possess?

Skill: Conceptual

148) Sheila is collecting information for a survey. She believes that individual on public aid have a tendency to take advantage of the money they receive from the government. As sheila collects her data, she dismisses the information regarding hard working individuals on public aid and focuses on the information that suggests that people are taking advantage. sheila is demonstrating the _____.

   A) hindsight bias

   B) anchoring bias

   C) type four error

   D) confirmation bias

   E) double-blind research

Answer: D

Diff: 2   Page Ref: 284

Topic: What Abilities Do Good Thinkers Possess?

Skill: Applied

149) After the outcome is known, people often have distorted thinking about their original expectations due to

   A) confirmation bias.

   B) hindsight bias.

   C) representativeness heuristic.

   D) availability heuristic.

   E) their prototypes.

Answer: B

Diff: 2   Page Ref: 285

Topic: What Abilities Do Good Thinkers Possess?

Skill: Conceptual

150) Some people believe that psychology is all "common sense" and that we already knew most of what research tells us about human nature. In reality we cannot make assumptions about human nature without doing research and collecting good data. The false belief that we already knew what psychology tells us is known as _____.

    A) hindsight bias

    B) the anchoring bias

    C) ignoring base rates

    D) the availability bias

    E) convergent thinking

Answer: A
Diff: 2   Page Ref: 285
Topic: What Abilities Do Good Thinkers Possess?
Skill: Applied

151) Usually about 500 people attend the annual exquisite Irish food festival. This year however about 5000 people have attended because the word has spread that the boiled cabbage last year was "out of this world". Kelly who is organizing the event knows that there is usually 500 people there, while she knows more people are in attendance she estimates the crowd to be about 1000 people. She is probably underestimating the crowd due to

    A) the representativeness heuristic.

    B) mental set.

    C) the anchoring bias.

    D) self–imposed limitations.

    E) cognitive maps.

Answer: C
Diff: 3   Page Ref: 285
Topic: What Abilities Do Good Thinkers Possess?
Skill: Applied

152) Meghan is a cheerleader at your high school, she is always happy and outgoing and you assume that the rest of the cheerleaders act much the same way, this potentially false belief is an example of _____.

    A) the confirmation bias

    B) the hindsight bias

    C) the representative bias

    D) an algorithm

    E) backward thinking

Answer: C
Diff: 3   Page Ref: 285
Topic: What Abilities Do Good Thinkers Possess?
Skill: Applied

153) You are baby sitting one Friday evening and after the children are in bed you decide to watch the movie 'Scream'. After watching the movie you are sure that you hear sounds coming from the basement and are frightened that there may be a killer in the house. In reality the chances that someone has broken into the house are no better than they were before you watched the film, however your are still scared. This is an example of which of the following

    A) confirmation bias.

    B) the availability heuristic.

    C) an anchoring bias.

    D) divergent thinking.

    E) hindsight bias.

Answer: B

Diff: 3   *Page Ref: 286*

Topic: What Abilities Do Good Thinkers Possess?

Skill: Applied

154) Many psychologists view creativity as a form of

    A) divergent thinking.

    B) convergent thinking.

    C) intuition.

    D) artificial concepts.

    E) intelligence.

Answer: A

Diff: 2   *Page Ref: 286*

Topic: On Becoming a Creative Genius

Skill: Factual

155) Which of the following is true of creativity?

    A) Creative people have unique personality flaws.

    B) Creativity first involves becoming an expert in a specific field.

    C) Low motivation can facilitate creativity.

    D) A person can become an expert after a year of study.

    E) Creative achievement requires great leap of imagination.

Answer: B

Diff: 2   *Page Ref: 287*

Topic: On Becoming a Creative Genius

Skill: Factual

156) A person who is a fine guitar player would be said to have a(n) _____ for it.

   A) schema

   B) prototype

   C) aptitude

   D) algorithm

   E) divergence

Answer: C

Diff: 2   Page Ref: 287

Topic: On Becoming a Creative Genius

Skill: Applied

157) Which of the following is NOT true of highly creative people?

   A) They are very interested in the problem.

   B) They prefer to work in large groups.

   C) They prefer more complex problems.

   D) They enjoy interacting with other creative thinkers.

   E) They question how problems are presented.

Answer: B

Diff: 2   Page Ref: 287

Topic: On Becoming a Creative Genius

Skill: Conceptual

158) Individuals who have amazingly developed skill despite their mental handicap are referred to as

   A) mentally challenged.

   B) savants.

   C) geniuses.

   D) thriving in emotional intelligence.

   E) None of the above

Answer: B

Diff: 1   Page Ref: 288

Topic: On Becoming a Creative Genius

Skill: Factual

Check Your Understanding Questions

1) Which of the following is a major objection to the "video recorder" theory of memory?

    A) Like perception, memory is an interpretation of experience.

    B) Memories are never accurate.

    C) Unlike a video recorder, memory takes in and stores an enormous quantity of information, not just vision.

    D) Unlike a tape-recorded video memory, human memory cannot be edited and changed at a later time.

    E) Memories do not degrade over time.

    Answer: A
    Diff: 3   Page Ref: 239
    Topic: Check Your Understanding
    Skill: Analysis

2) Which of the following are the three essential tasks of memory?

    A) Encoding, storage, and retrieval

    B) Sensory, working, and long-term

    C) Remembering, forgetting, and repressing

    D) Recall, recognition, and relearning

    E) eidectic memory, short-term memory, and recall

    Answer: A
    Diff: 3   Page Ref: 239
    Topic: Check Your Understanding
    Skill: Recall

3) When you get a new cat, you will note her unique markings, so that you can form a memory of what she looks like in comparison with other cats in the neighborhood. What would a cognitive psychologist call this process of identifying the distinctive features of your cat?

    A) eidectic imagery

    B) encoding

    C) recollection

    D) retrieval

    E) storage

    Answer: B
    Diff: 2   Page Ref: 239
    Topic: Check Your Understanding
    Skill: Analysis

4) Which one of the following systems reconstructs material during retrieval?

    A) computer memory

    B) human memory

    C) video recorder memory

    D) information recorded in a book

    E) eidectic memory

Answer: B
Diff: 2   Page Ref: 239
Topic: Check Your Understanding
Skill: Understanding the Core Concept

5) Which part of memory has the smallest capacity? (That is, which part of memory is considered the "bottleneck" in the memory system).

    A) sensory memory

    B) working memory

    C) long-term memory

    D) implicit memory

    E) explicit memory

Answer: B
Diff: 2   Page Ref: 251
Topic: Check Your Understanding
Skill: Recall

6) Which part of long-term memory stores autobiographical memory?

    A) semantic memory

    B) procedural memory

    C) recognition memory

    D) episodic memory

    E) eidectic memory

Answer: D
Diff: 2   Page Ref: 251
Topic: Check Your Understanding
Skill: Recall

7) In order to get material into permanent storage, it must be made meaningful while it is in
   A) sensory memory.
   B) working memory.
   C) long-term memory.
   D) recall memory.
   E) eidectic memory.

Answer: B
Diff: 2   Page Ref: 251
Topic: Check Your Understanding
Skill: Recall

8) As you study the vocabulary in this book, which method would result in the deepest level of processing?
   A) learning the definition given in the marginal glossary
   B) marking each term with a high lighter each time it occurs in a sentence in the text
   C) thinking of an example of each term
   D) having a friend read a definition, with you having to identify the term in question in question form, as on the TV show *Jeopardy!*
   E) looking over the information, knowing that you will see it later

Answer: C
Diff: 2   Page Ref: 251
Topic: Check Your Understanding
Skill: Applied

9) As the information in this book passes from one stage of your memory to the next, the information becomes more
   A) important.
   B) meaningful.
   C) interesting.
   D) accurate.
   E) astute.

Answer: B
Diff: 2   Page Ref: 251
Topic: Check Your Understanding
Skill: Understanding the Core Concept

10) Remembering names is usually harder than remembering faces because names require
_____, while faces require _____.

A) short-term memory; long-term memory

B) declarative memory; procedural memory

C) encoding; retrieval

D) recall; recognition

E) storage;recall

Answer: D

Diff: 2   Page Ref: 256

Topic: Check Your Understanding

Skill: Applied

11) At a high-school class reunion you are likely to experience a flood of memories that would be
unlikely to come to mind under other circumstances. What memory process explains this?

A) implicit memory

B) anterograde amnesia

C) encoding specificity

D) the TOT phenomenon

E) retrograde amnesia

Answer: C

Diff: 2   Page Ref: 256

Topic: Check Your Understanding

Skill: Conceptual

12) A person experiencing the TOT phenomenon is unable to _____ a specific word.

A) recognize   B) recall   C) encode   D) learn   E) store

Answer: B

Diff: 1   Page Ref: 256

Topic: Check Your Understanding

Skill: Recall

13) An implicit memory may be activated by priming, and an explicit memory may be activated by
a recognizable stimulus. In either case, a psychologist would say that these memories are
being

A) cued.   B) recalled.   C) stored.   D) chunked.   E) learned.

Answer: A

Diff: 2   Page Ref: 256

Topic: Check Your Understanding

Skill: Understanding the Core Concept

14) Which of the following statements best describes forgetting, as characterized by Ebbinghaus's forgetting curve?

    A) We forget at a constant rate.

    B) We forget slowly at first and more rapidly as time goes on.

    C) We forget rapidly at first and then more slowly as time goes on.

    D) Ebbinghaus's method of relearning showed that we never really forget.

    E) We never forget.

Answer: C
Diff: 2   *Page Ref: 266*
Topic: Check Your Understanding
Skill: Recall

15) Which kind of forgetting is involved when the sociology I studied yesterday makes it more difficult to learn and remember the psychology I am studying today?

    A) proactive interference

    B) retroactive interference

    C) decay

    D) retrieval failure

    E) heuristics

Answer: A
Diff: 2   *Page Ref: 266*
Topic: Check Your Understanding
Skill: Applied

16) What is the term for the controversial notion that memories can be blocked off in the unconscious, where they can cause physical and mental problems?

    A) interference

    B) repression

    C) persistence

    D) absent-mindedness

    E) transience

Answer: B
Diff: 2   *Page Ref: 266*
Topic: Check Your Understanding
Skill: Recall

17) Which one of the seven "sins" of memory is disputed by those who believe that memories of childhood abuse can, in many cases, be recovered during adulthood?

  A) transience

  B) persistence

  C) absent-mindedness

  D) suggestibility

  E) decay

Answer: D

Diff: 2   Page Ref: 266

Topic: Check Your Understanding

Skill: Recall

18) Which one of the seven "sins" of memory probably helps us avoid dangerous situations we have encountered before?

  A) suggestibility

  B) bias

  C) persistence

  D) misattribution

  E) absent-mindedness

Answer: C

Diff: 2   Page Ref: 266

Topic: Check Your Understanding

Skill: Understanding the Core Concept

19) Noam Chomsky has presented evidence supporting his theory that

  A) children learn language by imitating their parents.

  B) children are born with some rules of grammar programmed into their brains.

  C) vocabulary is innate, but grammar is learned.

  D) different languages may have entirely different rules of grammar.

  E) grammar interferes with a child's ability to learn languages.

Answer: B

Diff: 2   Page Ref: 270

Topic: Check Your Understanding

Skill: Recall

20) A child's acquisition of grammar first becomes apparent at
   A) the babbling stage.
   B) the one-word stage.
   C) the two-word stage.
   D) the concrete operational stage.
   E) adolescence.

Answer: C
Diff: 2   Page Ref: 270
Topic: Check Your Understanding
Skill: Recall

21) Which psychologist believes that all people are born with a Language acquisition Device?
   A) Skinner
   B) chomsky
   C) Whorf
   D) Lennenburg
   E) Freud

Answer: B
Diff: 2   Page Ref: 270
Topic: Check Your Understanding
Skill: Factual

22) A dictionary definition would be an example of
   A) an artificial concept.
   B) a natural concept.
   C) a core concept.
   D) an abstract concept.
   E) a concrete concept.

Answer: A
Diff: 2   Page Ref: 278
Topic: Check Your Understanding
Skill: Applied

23) Which one of the following would represent a concept hierarchy?

    A) cat, dog, giraffe, elephant

    B) animal, mammal, dog, cocker spaniel

    C) woman, girl, man, boy

    D) lemur, monkey, chimpanzee, human

    E) beaver, fox, cat, cougar

Answer: B
Diff: 2   Page Ref: 278
Topic: Check Your Understanding
Skill: Applied

24) Knowing how to check out a book at the library is an example of

    A) a natural concept.

    B) an event–related potential.

    C) a cognitive map.

    D) a script.

    E) an artificial concept.

Answer: D
Diff: 2   Page Ref: 278
Topic: Check Your Understanding
Skill: Applied

25) All of the following are components of thought except

    A) concepts.   B) images.   C) schemas.   D) stimuli.   E) scripts.

Answer: D
Diff: 2   Page Ref: 278
Topic: Check Your Understanding
Skill: Understanding the Core Concept

26) What is the first step in problem solving?

    A) selecting a strategy

    B) avoiding pitfalls

    C) searching for analogies

    D) identifying the problem

    E) developing algorithms

Answer: D
Diff: 2   Page Ref: 289
Topic: Check Your Understanding
Skill: Recall

27) A math problem calls for finding the area of a triangle. You know the formula, so you multiply 1/2 the base times the height. You have used

A) an algorithm.

B) a heuristic.

C) functional fixedness.

D) intuition.

E) an analogy.

Answer: A
Diff: 2   Page Ref: 289
Topic: Check Your Understanding
Skill: Applied

28) Good problem solvers often use "tricks of the trade" or "rules of thumb" known as

A) algorithms.

B) heuristics.

C) trial and error.

D) deductive reasoning.

E) scripts.

Answer: B
Diff: 2   Page Ref: 289
Topic: Check Your Understanding
Skill: Recall

29) Which one of the following would be an example of the confirmation bias at work?

A) Mary ignores negative information about her favorite political candidate.

B) Aaron agrees with Joel's taste in music.

C) Natasha refuses to eat a dish she dislikes.

D) Bill buts a new RV, even though his wife was opposed to the purchase.

E) Frank buys a lottery ticket because he read abut a lotto winner.

Answer: A
Diff: 2   Page Ref: 289
Topic: Check Your Understanding
Skill: Applied

30) Which of the following is NOT a characteristic that is consistently found among highly creative people.

   A) independence

   B) a high level of motivation

   C) willingness to restructure the problem

   D) extremely high intelligence

   E) open–mindedness

   Answer: D
   Diff: 2   Page Ref: 289
   Topic: Check Your Understanding
   Skill: Recall

31) Heuristic strategies show that our thinking is often based on

   A) logic rather than emotion.

   B) experience rather than logic.

   C) trial and error learning rather than algorithms.

   D) common sense rather than learning.

   E) logic rather than creativity.

   Answer: B
   Diff: 2   Page Ref: 289
   Topic: Check Your Understanding
   Skill: Understanding the Core Concept

True/False Questions

1) More than 20% of all U.S. children experience some form of sexual abuse.

   Answer: FALSE
   Diff: 2   Page Ref: 234
   Topic: What Is Memory?
   Skill: Factual

2) Human memory is always completely accurate.

   Answer: FALSE
   Diff: 2   Page Ref: 235
   Topic: What Is Memory?
   Skill: Factual

3) The three main components of memory in the order they occur are storage, encoding, retrieval.

   Answer: FALSE
   Diff: 2   Page Ref: 236–237
   Topic: What Is Memory?
   Skill: Recall

4) Eidectic imagery tends to increase as language skills increase.

Answer: FALSE
Diff: 2   Page Ref: 237–238
Topic: Would You Want a "Photographic" Memory?
Skill: Factual

5) Working memory is sometimes called short-term memory.

Answer: TRUE
Diff: 2   Page Ref: 239
Topic: How Do We Form Memories?
Skill: Factual

6) Working memory has an unlimited capacity.

Answer: FALSE
Diff: 2   Page Ref: 239
Topic: How Do We Form Memories?
Skill: Conceptual

7) Sensory memories last for about 20 seconds.

Answer: FALSE
Diff: 2   Page Ref: 239
Topic: How Do We Form Memories?
Skill: Factual

8) One's sense of self in held in their long–term memory.

Answer: TRUE
Diff: 2   Page Ref: 240
Topic: How Do We Form Memories?
Skill: Conceptual

9) If our sensory memories were not constantly updated, our minds would become cluttered.

Answer: TRUE
Diff: 2   Page Ref: 241
Topic: How Do We Form Memories?
Skill: Factual

10) The sensory register for hearing is called iconic memory.

Answer: FALSE
Diff: 3   Page Ref: 242
Topic: How Do We Form Memories?
Skill: Conceptual

11) Memories seem to get "bottlenecked' during sensory memory.

Answer: FALSE
Diff: 2   Page Ref: 243
Topic: How Do We Form Memories?
Skill: Conceptual

12) Nick wants to remember Jessica's phone number unfortunately she does not live near him so he also needs to remember her area code. If he breaks this 10-digit number into three chunks, it should be easier to remember.

Answer: TRUE
Diff: 2   Page Ref: 244
Topic: How Do We Form Memories?
Skill: Applied

13) An example of elaborative rehearsal is when you keep repeating a new phone number over and over.

Answer: FALSE
Diff: 2   Page Ref: 245
Topic: How Do We Form Memories?
Skill: Applied

14) Brain imaging studies indicate that frontal cortex is activated during a working memory task.

Answer: TRUE
Diff: 2   Page Ref: 246
Topic: How Do We Form Memories?
Skill: Factual

15) Procedural and declarative memories are the two major forms of long-term memory.

Answer: TRUE
Diff: 2   Page Ref: 247
Topic: How Do We Form Memories?
Skill: Factual

16) An example of a procedural memory would be remembering how to ride a bike.

Answer: TRUE
Diff: 2   Page Ref: 247
Topic: How Do We Form Memories?
Skill: Applied

17) The definition of the word helix would be held in semantic memory.

Answer: TRUE
Diff: 2   Page Ref: 248
Topic: How Do We Form Memories?
Skill: Applied

18) Patient H.M. suffered from retrograde amnesia.

Answer: FALSE
Diff: 2   Page Ref: 248
Topic: How Do We Form Memories?
Skill: Factual

19) A "flashbulb" memory is a an exceptionally vivid episodic memory.

Answer: TRUE
Diff: 2   Page Ref: 250
Topic: How Do We Form Memories?
Skill: Factual

20) Implicit memory affects your behavior, but you have no conscious awareness of learning it.

Answer: TRUE
Diff: 2   Page Ref: 252
Topic: How Do We Form Memories?
Skill: Conceptual

21) Studying for an exam is a good example of explicit memory.

Answer: FALSE
Diff: 2   Page Ref: 252
Topic: How Do We Retrieve Memories?
Skill: Applied

22) Singing a song to the alphabet often works as a primer to help children remember the alphabet.

Answer: TRUE
Diff: 2   Page Ref: 253
Topic: How Do We Retrieve Memories?
Skill: Applied

23) Being asked to describe the definition of a word is an example of recall.

Answer: TRUE
Diff: 1   Page Ref: 254
Topic: How Do We Retrieve Memories?
Skill: Factual

24) Mood has no influence on memory.

Answer: TRUE
Diff: 2   Page Ref: 255
Topic: How Do We Retrieve Memories?
Skill: Factual

25) Transience refers to the fact that memories can fade with time.

Answer: TRUE
Diff: 2   Page Ref: 257
Topic: Why Does Memory Sometimes Fail Us?
Skill: Conceptual

26) Absent-mindedness deals with the gradual loss of long-term memories.

Answer: FALSE
Diff: 2   Page Ref: 258
Topic: Why Does Memory Sometimes Fail Us?
Skill: Factual

27) When you call your old telephone number because you cannot remember you new number you are demonstrating retroactive interference.

Answer: FALSE
Diff: 2   Page Ref: 259
Topic: Why Does Memory Sometimes Fail Us?
Skill: Conceptual

28) It is possible to cause people to remember events that never happened.

Answer: TRUE
Diff: 2   Page Ref: 260
Topic: Why Does Memory Sometimes Fail Us?
Skill: Factual

29) Eyewitness testimony is always accurate.

Answer: FALSE
Diff: 2   Page Ref: 262
Topic: Why Does Memory Sometimes Fail Us?
Skill: Conceptual

30) If we expect that someone is not honest, we may remember them as doing something bad, even if they didn't.

Answer: TRUE
Diff: 2   Page Ref: 264
Topic: Why Does Memory Sometimes Fail Us?
Skill: Conceptual

31) The memory issue of persistence may contribute to the fear state experienced by a person with a phobia.

Answer: TRUE
Diff: 2   Page Ref: 264
Topic: Why Does Memory Sometimes Fail Us?
Skill: Conceptual

32) The method of loci allows you to remember lists based on walking through a familiar place.

Answer: FALSE
Diff: 2   Page Ref: 265
Topic: Improving Your Memory with Mnemonics
Skill: Factual

33) Chomsky proposed that the Language acquisition Device was primarily influenced by one's environment.

Answer: FALSE
Diff: 2   Page Ref: 267
Topic: How Do Children acquire Language?
Skill: Factual

34) Regardless of one's surroundings, children world wide proceed through very similar stages of learning their native language.

Answer: TRUE
Diff: 2   Page Ref: 267
Topic: How Do Children acquire Language?
Skill: Factual

35) Children begin to understand rules of grammar at about 2 years of age.

Answer: TRUE
Diff: 2   Page Ref: 268
Topic: How Do Children acquire Language?
Skill: Factual

36) The "naming explosion" occurs in children beginning at 9 months old.

Answer: FALSE
Diff: 2   Page Ref: 268
Topic: How Do Children acquire Language?
Skill: Conceptual

37) After children can describe their physical world in words, they begin to talk about their psychological world.

Answer: TRUE
Diff: 2   Page Ref: 269
Topic: How Do Children acquire Language?
Skill: Factual

38) Our concepts of items need to be tangible.

Answer: FALSE
Diff: 2   Page Ref: 271
Topic: What Are the Components of Thought?
Skill: Conceptual

39) Artificial concepts have specific rules such as mathematical formulas.

Answer: TRUE
Diff: 2   Page Ref: 272
Topic: What Are the Components of Thought?
Skill: Factual

40) A prototype of a pet may be a dog.

Answer: TRUE
Diff: 3   Page Ref: 272
Topic: What Are the Components of Thought?
Skill: Factual

41) When you give your boyfriend directions to your house, you are using a cognitive map.

Answer: TRUE
Diff: 2   *Page Ref: 274*
Topic: What Are the Components of Thought?
Skill: Conceptual

42) Those with damaged parietal lobes may experience problems with 'common sense'.

Answer: FALSE
Diff: 2   *Page Ref: 276*
Topic: What Are the Components of Thought?
Skill: Factual

43) Event schemas are also called scripts.

Answer: TRUE
Diff: 2   *Page Ref: 277*
Topic: Schemas and Scripts Help You Know What to Expect
Skill: Conceptual

44) Bill is asked to unscramble the letters 'M,' 'I,' 'L,' and 'F' to form a common word. If Bill writes down each of the 16 possible letter combinations, he has used trial-and-error to solve the problem.

Answer: FALSE
Diff: 2   *Page Ref: 282*
Topic: What Abilities Do Good Thinkers Possess?
Skill: Applied

45) The use of a heuristic will guarantee a successful solution to a problem.

Answer: FALSE
Diff: 2   *Page Ref: 282*
Topic: What Abilities Do Good Thinkers Possess?
Skill: Conceptual

46) Fred cannot figure out how to keep his door open in the summer to let the breeze in. Even though he has many heavy objects around the house that would serve the purpose just fine. Fred is demonstrating functional fixedness.

Answer: TRUE
Diff: 2   *Page Ref: 282*
Topic: What Abilities Do Good Thinkers Possess?
Skill: Applied

47) Confirmation bias is sometimes called the "I-knew-it-all-along" effect.

Answer: FALSE
Diff: 2   Page Ref: 284–285
Topic: What Abilities Do Good Thinkers Possess?
Skill: Conceptual

48) After hurricane Katrina, many more people all over the country bought flood insurance even though they were no more likely to get flooded than they were before the storm. This is an example of the availability heuristic.

Answer: TRUE
Diff: 3   Page Ref: 286
Topic: What Abilities Do Good Thinkers Possess?
Skill: Applied

49) Most studies have found that it takes about two or three years of work to be fully competent in any field.

Answer: FALSE
Diff: 2   Page Ref: 287
Topic: On Becoming a Creative Genius
Skill: Factual

50) If someone has a high I.Q., it is likely that they will be a genius.

Answer: FALSE
Diff: 2   Page Ref: 288
Topic: On Becoming a Creative Genius
Skill: Conceptual

Short Answer Questions

1) List the three basic tasks of memory.

Answer: Encoding, storage, and retrieval
Diff: 2   Page Ref: 236–237
Topic: What Is Memory?
Skill: Factual

2) What is the term for a cognitive understanding of memory, which emphasize how information is changed when it is encoded, stored and retrieved?

Answer: Information-processing model of memory
Diff: 3   Page Ref: 236
Topic: What Is Memory?
Skill: Factual

3) Briefly provide the Best; example of one who we would expect to have a photographic memory, how does this skill seem to decline and what is it's scientific name?

Answer: A child, as language skills increase photographic memory seems to decrease, eidectic memory

Diff: 3   Page Ref: 238

Topic: What Is Memory?

Skill: Conceptual

4) Explain the difference between the two forms of rehearsal.

Answer: Maintenance rehearsal may involve simply repeating out loud the material to be learned. Elaborative rehearsal involves repetition as well as trying the connect the new information to existing knowledge.

Diff: 2   Page Ref: 244–245

Topic: How Do We Form Memories?

Skill: Conceptual

5) Briefly describe and give an example of the two types of declarative memory.

Answer: Semantic memory: An example would be learning the meaning of a fugue in music class
Episodic memory: An example would be getting married and remembering details about your wedding day

Diff: 2   Page Ref: 247–248

Topic: How Do We Form Memories?

Skill: Applied

6) Describe the difference between retrograde and anterograde amnesia.

Answer: anterograde amnesia occurs when an individual cannot encode new memories as in the case of H.M. retrograde amnesia occurs when older details are lost but newer ones are remembered.

Diff: 3   Page Ref: 248–250

Topic: How Do We Form Memories?

Skill: Factual

7) Explain what a 'flashbulb' memory is, give and example and briefly explain the validity of this type of memory.

Answer: A vivid detail about a meaningful and emotional event. An example would be where you were when you heard about the tragic events of 9-11. The validity of these memories initially seems quite good, but is subject to distortion as time passes.

Diff: 3   Page Ref: 251

Topic: How Do We Form Memories?

Skill: Conceptual

8) What is the capacity of short-term memory? Give an example of a real-life example that is consistent with this theory.

Answer: About seven chunks of information. Telephone numbers.

Diff: 2   Page Ref: 239

Topic: How Do We Form Memories?

Skill: Factual

9) Name the three memory systems that contribute to getting information into our memory.

Answer: sensory memory, working (short-term) memory, long-term memory

Diff: 2   Page Ref: 239

Topic: How Do We Form Memories?

Skill: Conceptual

10) How do implicit and explicit memory differ?

Answer: Implicit memories are memories that we do not know how we know. Explicit memories are those that we make a conscious effort to learn.

Diff: 2   Page Ref: 252

Topic: How Do We Retrieve Memories?

Skill: Recall

11) Give an example of recognition and recall as it relates to school exams.

Answer: Recall is used to give specific details of information and is used on free response exams, recognition is used on multiple choice exams where the individual simply needs to choose the correct answer from a number of choices presented.

Diff: 2   Page Ref: 254

Topic: How Do We Retrieve Memories?

Skill: Conceptual

12) Explain how mood congruent memories occur.

Answer: When we are in a bad mood, we have a tendencies to remember only bad things, when we are in a good mood, we are much more optimistic about the world.

Diff: 2   Page Ref: 255

Topic: How Do We Retrieve Memories?

Skill: Factual

13) Briefly explain the difference between retroactive and proactive interference.

Answer: Proactive interference deals with the inability to remember new information because old information gets in the way. Retroactive interference deals with the inability to remember old information, because new information has taken its place.

Diff: 3   Page Ref: 259

Topic: Why Does Memory Sometimes Fail Us?

Skill: Conceptual

14) Provide three reasons why investigators should be hesitant to depend solely on eyewitness testimony in court cases.

Answer: 1. the passage of time allows the original memory to fade and individuals may be more susceptible to misinformation.
2. Each time a person is asked to recall a memory it is more likely to be modified.
3. People's memories may be influenced by leading questions.

Diff: 2   Page Ref: 262

Topic: Why Does Memory Sometimes Fail Us?

Skill: Applied

15) How would you use the method of Loci if you wanted to remember a speech for class?

Answer: You could walk around your house and remember a portion of the speech in each room. You can connect certain concepts in the speech to certain pieces f furniture in each room.

Diff: 2   Page Ref: 265

Topic: Improving Your Memory with Mnemonics

Skill: Applied

16) The name for Noam Chomsky's Theory that language is innate.

Answer: Language acquisition Device

Diff: 2   Page Ref: 267

Topic: How Do Children acquire Language?

Skill: Conceptual

17) List the correct order of the four major stages that children pass through as they learn language.

Answer: babbling stage, one-word stage, two-word stage, telegraphic

Diff: 2   Page Ref: 268

Topic: How Do Children acquire Language?

Skill: Factual

18) The smallest unit of meaning in language.

Answer: morpheme

Diff: 2   Page Ref: 269

Topic: How Do Children acquire Language?

Skill: Factual

19) Define what is involved in cognition.

Answer: Cognition refers to the mental processes involved in thinking and intelligence.

Diff: 1   Page Ref: 303

Topic: What Are the Components of Thought?

Skill: Factual

20) Briefly explain the difference between natural and artificial concepts. Define each and provide an example.

Answer: Natural concepts are mental representations of objects drawn from our direct experience. The idea that all dogs are furry and have four legs is a natural concept. An artificial concept is based on specific rules, the quadratic formula is an example of an artificial concept.

Diff: 2   Page Ref: 272

Topic: What Are the Components of Thought?

Skill: Applied

21) Explain and give an example of a concept hierarchy.

Answer: A concept hierarchy is composed on the most general to the most specific categories. a example would be Athletics-track and field-long jump.

Diff: 2   Page Ref: 272

Topic: What Are the Components of Thought?

Skill: Conceptual

22) Briefly explain a script for going to a professional basketball game.

Answer: (Answers may vary) Buy tickets ahead of time-wear gear that supports your team of choice-find your appropriate seats-stand for the national anthem-5 players from each team will attempt to shoot a ball into a basket.

Diff: 2   Page Ref: 277

Topic: Schemas and Scripts Help You Know What to Expect

Skill: Applied

23) Name two general approaches to problem-solving.

Answer: A algorithm is a step-by-step procedure that will allow an individual to get the correct answer by using all possibilities. A heuristic is a 'rule-of-thumb' tactic that is more efficient and saves on time. This is not always assured to give the correct answer.

Diff: 2   Page Ref: 282-282

Topic: What Abilities Do Good Thinkers Possess?

Skill: Applied

24) Ronald just moved into a new apartment and has no holiday ornaments, and little money to buy them so he leaves his holiday tree empty. He does not see that he can decorate his christmas tree with some paper ornaments that he makes himself or with trinkets from around the house, Ronald is demonstrating

Answer: functional fixedness.

Diff: 2   Page Ref: 282

Topic: What Abilities Do Good Thinkers Possess?

Skill: Applied

25) What are the terms to explain researchers who only look for information that will support their hypothesis and those individuals who after data had been analyzed have a tendency to say, "I knew that".

Answer: confirmation bias; hindsight bias
Diff: 2   *Page Ref: 285*
Topic: What Abilities Do Good Thinkers Possess?
Skill: Conceptual

26) What is the term used to describe an innate potential ability that we have within a specific domain?

Answer: aptitude
Diff: 1   *Page Ref: 287*
Topic: On Becoming a Creative Genius
Skill: Conceptual

Essay Questions

1) Explain how those with eidectic memory report their experiences and how the talent may begin to decline. What is one downfall of eidectic memory.

Answer: Most individuals with eidectic memory claim to describe their memory images as having the vividness of the original experience. they visualize their images as being outside of their head. These memories can last for several minutes, but when individuals try to describe their experiences they tend to decline. The development of language skills also seem to cause the skill to decline. one downfall of eidectic memory is that individuals with the skill claim that the images can clutter other things they want to think about.
Diff: 2   *Page Ref: 238*
Topic: What Is Memory?
Skill: Conceptual

2) Name the three memory stages and discuss the duration and capacity of each stage, and biologically how each one operates.

Answer: Sensory memory may hold nine or more items. Visual images last about 1/4 of a second, whereas sounds last up to four seconds, and is carried by sensory pathways. Working (or, short-term memory) holds between 5 and 9 items, and information stays there for, at most, 20 seconds., this involves the hippocampus and frontal lobes. Information in long-term memory may remain permanently, and its capacity is unlimited, it is held in the cerebral cortex.
Diff: 2   *Page Ref: 239–244*
Topic: How Do We Form Memories?
Skill: Factual

3) Name and discuss the two types of long-term memories and their subcategories.

Answer: The two main forms are procedural memory (which involve remembering how to do things) and declarative memory (which involves more specific information). The two main types of declarative memories are episodic memory (which involves memory for specific events) and semantic memory (which stores facts and the meanings of words and concepts).A "flashbulb memory" (which is a clear memory for an important event) is one type of episodic memory.

Diff: 3   *Page Ref: 275–277*

Topic: How Do We Form Memories?

Skill: Factual

4) Explain how retrieval cues such as priming, elaborative rehearsal and recall and recognition can help us to recall information. about Abraham Lincoln.

Answer: If you are trying to remember information about Abraham Lincoln, you could prime your memory by talking about events in the Civil War. Using elaborative rehearsal you could remember that he was born in Illinois, had four sons, was married to Mary Todd Lincoln, etc. In Recall you would be asked specific information about Abraham Lincoln and in recognition, you would simply select the correct answer from a number presented.

Diff: 3   *Page Ref: 252–254*

Topic: How Do We Retrieve Memories?

Skill: Applied

5) Briefly describe and give one example of each of Schacter's seven sins of memory.

Answer: transience: impermanence of long-term memory. Hermann Ebbinghaus's forgetting curve for nonsense syllables shows that we forget much meaningless information quickly and then forgetting gradually levels off.
Absent-Mindedness: Forgetting due to lapses in attention. When you are cooking dinner and the phone rings you accidentally burn what you are cooking.
Misattribution: Memory faults that occur when memories occur in the wrong context. You think that your 5th birthday party was actually your 7th birthday party.
suggestibility: Memory distortion as the result of deliberate or accidental suggestion. When people witnesses the same car accident and are asked if they saw the cars bump or crash into one another each group will say yes, but provide different estimates of the speed of the cars.
Bias: People's beliefs, attitudes and experiences influence memory. if a person believes that all tall people are criminals and then witness a crime they are more likely to believe that a tall person committed the crime even if they are innocent.
Self-Consistency: Our memories reduce a sense of cognitive dissonance in our beliefs about ourselves. if we are currently a Democrat we will overestimate the number of democratic candidates we have voted foor over the years and "forget" about the times that they voted for Republicans.
persistence: A memory problem in which unwanted memories can be put out of the mind. We want to forget memories that are painful to us.

Diff: 3   *Page Ref: 257–265*

Topic: Why Does Memory Sometimes Fail Us?

Skill: Conceptual

6) Explain the nature nurture debate in the acquisition of language.

 Answer: Chomsky believes that all children are born with a Language acquisition Device, which is centered in the speech centers of children's brains and allows allow children to learn any language. This is still influenced by our environment as the sounds that we hear are those that we will imitate and we will eventually lose the ability to make sounds heard in other languages.

 Diff: 2   Page Ref: 269

 Topic: How Do Children acquire Language?

 Skill: Analysis

7) Describe the roles played by schemas and scripts in rational thought.

 Answer: A schemas is a cluster of related concepts that form a framework for thinking about a topic or event. Schemas provide expectations that allow us to use a term in different contexts. Schemas can accumulate new information or can be altered to accommodate new facts. A schema for an event (going to the restaurant) is known as a script. These help us decide how to act in a specific situation.

 Diff: 2   Page Ref: 277

 Topic: Schemas and Scripts Help You Know What to Expect

 Skill: Factual

8) Describe by giving a specific example about politics of how the following concepts might interfere with one's thinking or research.
 Confirmation Bias
 Hindsight Bias
 Representative Bias
 availability Bias

 Answer: Confirmation Bias: if the researcher was a democrat and they were pro-choice, they might look only for information that suggested that most other felt they same way as they felt about the issue.
 Hindsight Bias: The results of the political study suggest that there are more declared Republicans than democrats in the country today. People look at the data and say, "I could have told you that".
 Representative Bias: A conservative Republican senator believes that all liberal Democrats are 'tree hugging' environmentalists.
 availability Bias: after hearing that one politician is corrupt, you believe that your local congress person may also be corrupt.

 Diff: 3   Page Ref: 284-287

 Topic: What Abilities Do Good Thinkers Possess?

 Skill: Applied

Chapter 8 Emotion and Motivation

Multiple Choice Questions

1) The key components of _____ are feelings, behavioral expression, and physiological arousal.
   A) motivation
   B) sensation
   C) instinct
   D) behavioral control
   E) emotion

   Answer: E
   Diff: 1   Page Ref: 299
   Topic: What Do Our Emotions Do for Us?
   Skill: Conceptual

2) _____ is an arousal state that is adaptive for coping with important emergency situations.
   A) Motivation
   B) Emotion
   C) Instinct
   D) Perception
   E) Homeostasis

   Answer: B
   Diff: 2   Page Ref: 299
   Topic: What Do Our Emotions Do for Us?
   Skill: Factual

3) According to _____, people around the world share and recognize at least seven basic emotions.
   A) Robert Plutchik
   B) Abraham Maslow
   C) Walter Cannon
   D) Paul Ekman
   E) Hans Eysenck

   Answer: D
   Diff: 2   Page Ref: 300
   Topic: What Do Our Emotions Do for Us?
   Skill: Factual

4) Which of the following is NOT one of the emotions which Pal Ekman believes are universally recognized?

   A) sadness   B) fear   C) contempt   D) jealousy   E) disgust

   Answer: D
   Diff: 2   *Page Ref: 300*
   Topic: What Do Our Emotions Do for Us?
   Skill: Factual

5) Ekman found that fear, sadness, joy, anger, disgust, contempt and happiness were

   A) recognized only by individuals in the U.S. and European nations.

   B) recognized universally.

   C) culturally created.

   D) not easily recognized in Asian cultures.

   E) the only emotions that people feel.

   Answer: B
   Diff: 2   *Page Ref: 300*
   Topic: What Do Our Emotions Do for Us?
   Skill: Factual

6) Darwin argued that

   A) emotional reactions are unrelated to states of arousal.

   B) people are unable to cognitively label the source of their arousal.

   C) some simple emotional expressions cross species boundaries.

   D) understanding an emotional experience must occur before arousal can occur.

   E) there is an infinite number of emotions for people throughout the world.

   Answer: C
   Diff: 3   *Page Ref: 300*
   Topic: What Do Our Emotions Do for Us?
   Skill: Conceptual

7) The fact that widely different cultures use the same facial expression to express an emotion would lead researchers to believe that expressions are _____.

   A) situational   B) cognitive   C) unreliable   D) innate   E) physical

   Answer: D
   Diff: 2   *Page Ref: 300–301*
   Topic: What Do Our Emotions Do for Us?
   Skill: Conceptual

8) Robert Plutchik believes that

    A) there are 8 universal facial expressions that combine to form many other emotional responses.

    B) facial expressions are learned primarily as a result of modeling our parents facial expressions.

    C) Ekman is correct when proposing the idea of seven universal facial expressions.

    D) there are no universally recognized facial expressions.

    E) only individuals with a similar cultural background can recognize one another's facial expressions.

Answer: A
Diff: 3   Page Ref: 301
Topic: What Do Our Emotions Do for Us?
Skill: Conceptual

9) According to Robert Plutchik, the experience of the emotion of "love" is a complex blend of

    A) friendship and romance.

    B) togetherness and care.

    C) belonging and happiness.

    D) joy and acceptance.

    E) sincerity and commitment.

Answer: D
Diff: 3   Page Ref: 301
Topic: What Do Our Emotions Do for Us?
Skill: Conceptual

10) Robert Plutchik's "emotion wheel" proposes that

    A) four pairs of opposite emotions are the basis for all other emotions.

    B) ten emotions are the basis of all other emotions.

    C) humans have an infinite number of emotions which cannot be separated from each other.

    D) infants can feel only three different kinds of emotions.

    E) humans cannot experience two or more emotions simultaneously.

Answer: A
Diff: 2   Page Ref: 301
Topic: What Do Our Emotions Do for Us?
Skill: Conceptual

11) Women are more likely than men to show emotional disturbances in _____ and _____.
   A) emotional arousal; anger
   B) panic disorder; depression
   C) fear; loathing
   D) self–discipline; happiness
   E) alcohol addiction; intense shyness

Answer: B
Diff: 1   Page Ref: 302
Topic: Emotional Differences between Men & Women Depend on Culture
Skill: Factual

12) In almost all cultures, women tend to _____ than men.
   A) hide more emotions
   B) show more anger during conflicts
   C) use different emotional display rules
   D) show more sadness
   E) be more emotional

Answer: C
Diff: 2   Page Ref: 303
Topic: Emotional Differences between Men & Women Depend on Culture
Skill: Factual

13) Roger is sad, but he does not want to cry in front of his friends because of the _____ he has been taught.
   A) emotions
   B) display rules
   C) cognitions
   D) emotional intelligence
   E) locus of control

Answer: B
Diff: 2   Page Ref: 300
Topic: Emotional Differences between Men & Women Depend on Culture
Skill: Applied

14) The _____ memory system is linked to an emotion processing system that functions at an unconscious level.

    A) long–term

    B) procedural

    C) working

    D) retroactive

    E) implicit

Answer: E

Diff: 2   Page Ref: 304

Topic: Where do Our Emotions Come From?

Skill: Factual

15) The _____ memory system is linked to an emotion processing system that functions at an conscious level.

    A) long–term

    B) explicit

    C) working

    D) retroactive

    E) implicit

Answer: B

Diff: 2   Page Ref: 305

Topic: Where do Our Emotions Come From?

Skill: Factual

16) The role of the limbic system in emotion is to

    A) trigger the internal and external behaviors involved in emotions.

    B) arouse the whole brain simultaneously when we are aroused.

    C) makes a person's heart race when aroused.

    D) dampen emotional arousal.

    E) integrates the hormonal and neural emotional aspects.

Answer: E

Diff: 2   Page Ref: 306

Topic: Where do Our Emotions Come From?

Skill: Conceptual

17) Damage to the _____ would be expected to render a wild animal tame and placid.
   A) cerebellum
   B) limbic system
   C) blood–brain barrier
   D) parasympathetic system
   E) temporal lobe

Answer: B
Diff: 2   Page Ref: 306–307
Topic: Where do Our Emotions Come From?
Skill: Applied

18) The _____ is important for arousing the brain during a crisis.
   A) reticular activating system
   B) limbic system
   C) thalamus
   D) hypothalamus
   E) endocrine gland

Answer: A
Diff: 3   Page Ref: 306
Topic: Where do Our Emotions Come From?
Skill: Applied

19) In animal experiments. those who received lesions to the amygdala were found to
   A) have a decreased level of fear.
   B) have induced anxiety and fear.
   C) have decreased capacity for language.
   D) have an increased appetite.
   E) suffer from impaired spatial ability.

Answer: A
Diff: 2   Page Ref: 306
Topic: Where do Our Emotions Come From?
Skill: Applied

20) The right hemisphere of the cerebral cortex is most likely to be involved when a person is

    A) scared by the appearance of a spider above their head.

    B) elated at their wedding reception.

    C) surprised after winning $10,000 in a lottery.

    D) under pressure to complete a term paper by tomorrow.

    E) depressed after the loss of the favorite pet.

Answer: E
Diff: 2   *Page Ref: 306*
Topic: Where do Our Emotions Come From?
Skill: Applied

21) The left hemisphere of the cerebral cortex is likely to

    A) brood after failing an important exam.

    B) focus on someone smiling at you.

    C) be angry at someone cutting you off while you ride your bike.

    D) activate the sympathetic nervous system.

    E) None of the above

Answer: B
Diff: 2   *Page Ref: 306*
Topic: Where do Our Emotions Come From?
Skill: Applied

22) The sympathetic nervous system

    A) keeps rage and death instincts under control.

    B) only operates during times of low stress.

    C) permits people to react with empathy to tragic situations.

    D) prepares the body to cope with a dangerous situation.

    E) inhibits the release of hormones.

Answer: D
Diff: 2   *Page Ref: 306*
Topic: Where do Our Emotions Come From?
Skill: Factual

23) When we experience unpleasant stimulation, the _____ is more active; with a pleasant emotion, the _____ is more active.

A) reticular activating system; hypothalamus

B) limbic system; endocrine system

C) left hemisphere; right hemisphere

D) sympathetic division; parasympathetic division

E) hypothalamus; thalamus

Answer: D

Diff: 2   Page Ref: 306

Topic: Where do Our Emotions Come From?

Skill: Factual

24) A person whose job is dirty, exhausting, and dangerous may be under severe stress because their _____ is constantly being activated.

A) emotional intelligence

B) emergency response

C) parasympathetic nervous system

D) display rule

E) reticular activating system

Answer: B

Diff: 2   Page Ref: 359

Topic: Where do Our Emotions Come From?

Skill: Applied

25) In terms of positive and negative emotions, the sympathetic nervous systems in much like _____, while the parasympathetic nervous system is more like _____.

A) hippocampus; amygdala

B) hypothalamus; amygdala

C) parietal lobe; occipital lobe

D) the cerebral cortex; hypothalamus

E) right hemisphere; left hemisphere

Answer: E

Diff: 3   Page Ref: 306

Topic: Where do Our Emotions Come From?

Skill: Analysis

26) Which of the following hormones is often associated with depression?

    A) steroids

    B) serotonin

    C) acetylcholine

    D) norepinephrine

    E) epinephrine

Answer: B
Diff: 2   Page Ref: 307
Topic: Where do Our Emotions Come From?
Skill: Recall

27) _____ proposed that emotions are the result of a physical state.

    A) James and Lange

    B) Lazarus and Schachter

    C) Masters and Johnson

    D) Plutchik and Rotter

    E) Maslow and Kinsey

Answer: A
Diff: 2   Page Ref: 307
Topic: Where do Our Emotions Come From?
Skill: Factual

28) According to the James–Lange theory of emotion, if we are driving to school and a school bus slams on his brakes in front of the car we

    A) feel afraid and then brake.

    B) feel afraid and brake at the same time.

    C) determine if the situation warrants fast action, if so we brake.

    D) brake and then feel afraid.

    E) feel sad and shortly thereafter happy.

Answer: D
Diff: 3   Page Ref: 307
Topic: Where do Our Emotions Come From?
Skill: Applied

29) Stanley Schacter's theory of emotion proposes that emotion results when
    A) you cognitively label the arousal and give it emotional meaning.
    B) you simultaneously experience arousal and an emotional experience.
    C) you look back over your experiences to try and identify the arousal you just experienced.
    D) your sensory experiences fail to have any personal significance.
    E) you are unable to control any of your personal circumstances.

Answer: A
Diff: 2   Page Ref: 308
Topic: Where do Our Emotions Come From?
Skill: Conceptual

30) Which two components are part of Schacter and Singer's theory of emotion?
    A) our physical state and the situation we are in
    B) our physical and and psychological state
    C) the situations we are currently in, and the environment in which we were raised
    D) our emotional and physical state
    E) our physical state and the last time we felt a given emotion

Answer: A
Diff: 2   Page Ref: 308
Topic: Where do Our Emotions Come From?
Skill: Conceptual

31) You go to a party and everyone is chatting and happy. Eventually you start to feel yourself get a bit more energy and join the the conversation. You feel that your neutral mood from earlier is changing in a more positive way. Which of the following emotional theories would best explain you current emotional state?
    A) James–Lange
    B) Two–Factor
    C) Opponent–Process
    D) Trichromatic
    E) Cannon–Bard

Answer: B
Diff: 2   Page Ref: 308
Topic: Where do Our Emotions Come From?
Skill: Applied

32) Annika and philip survive a plane crash. Before the flight, they were strangers; shortly afterward, they marry. Stanley Schacter might call their marriage an example of

    A) misattribution of emotion.

    B) cognition of true love.

    C) redistribution of affection.

    D) moment of order among disorder.

    E) emotional intelligence.

Answer: A
Diff: 3   Page Ref: 309
Topic: Where do Our Emotions Come From?
Skill: Applied

33) This theory is based on the idea that emotions have pairs that play off on one another, when one is triggered, the other is suppressed.

    A) James–Lange theory

    B) Trichromatic Theory

    C) Opponent–Process

    D) Cannon–Bard Theory

    E) Two–Factor Theory

Answer: C
Diff: 1   Page Ref: 309
Topic: Where do Our Emotions Come From?
Skill: Factual

34) _____ proposed that emotion and cognition are intertwined and that changing our cognitions can help us reduce emotions that are self–defeating.

    A) Richard Lazarus

    B) Julian Rotter

    C) Caroll Izard

    D) Robert Zajonc

    E) Abraham Maslow

Answer: A
Diff: 3   Page Ref: 310
Topic: Where do Our Emotions Come From?
Skill: Factual

35) The notion that some arousal can facilitate performance but that too much arousal inhibits behavior is known as the

    A) notion of homeostasis.

    B) inverted "U" function.

    C) James–Lange theory of emotion.

    D) two–factor theory.

    E) display rules theory.

Answer: B

Diff: 2   *Page Ref: 310*

Topic: Arousal, Performance, and the Inverted 'U'

Skill: Applied

36) Phil makes widgets at the local factory, he has been working here for 14 years and while he is not challenged at all he needs the job According to the Inverted U theory regarding levels of arousal, what would the optimal level of arousal be for Phil when he is at work?

    A) relatively low

    B) very low

    C) relatively high

    D) moderate

    E) very high

Answer: C

Diff: 2   *Page Ref: 310*

Topic: Arousal, Performance, and the Inverted 'U'

Skill: Applied

37) A person who is a sensation seeker

    A) has acute sensory ability.

    B) experience mainly positive emotions.

    C) is highly driven to succeed.

    D) may try to minimize stimulation.

    E) has a high desire for excitement.

Answer: E

Diff: 2   *Page Ref: 310*

Topic: Arousal, Performance, and the Inverted 'U'

Skill: Conceptual

38) The ability to understand and control emotional responses is known as

    A) anger management.

    B) emotional intelligence.

    C) empathy.

    D) savant syndrome.

    E) motivation.

Answer: B
Diff: 2   Page Ref: 312
Topic: How Much Control do We Have Over Our Emotions?
Skill: Recall

39) A person who has a high level of _____ can easily hide their emotions.

    A) self-denial

    B) emotional intelligence

    C) intelligence

    D) overjustification

    E) external locus of control

Answer: B
Diff: 2   Page Ref: 312
Topic: How Much Control do We Have Over Our Emotions?
Skill: Applied

40) According to Daniel Goleman, the ability of a four-year-old child to delay _____ predicts their level of success in later life.

    A) intelligence

    B) cognition

    C) gratification

    D) toilet training

    E) embarrassment

Answer: C
Diff: 2   Page Ref: 312
Topic: How Much Control do We Have Over Our Emotions?
Skill: Factual

41) Goleman reports that the children in the emotional intelligence experiment who were tempted by a marshmallow but did not eat it immediately were late in life

   A) in more trouble with the law.

   B) could not control their tempers.

   C) were more self-reliant.

   D) had more trouble getting along with their r peers.

   E) have more negative feelings.

   Answer: C
   Diff: 2   Page Ref: 312-313
   Topic: How Much Control do We Have Over Our Emotions?
   Skill: Factual

42) Which of the following techniques is accepted as a reliable means of detecting deception?

   A) an interview

   B) a polygraph examination

   C) a paper-and-pencil "integrity" test

   D) a PET scan

   E) None of the above are correct.

   Answer: E
   Diff: 2   Page Ref: 313
   Topic: How Much Control do We Have Over Our Emotions?
   Skill: Conceptual

43) A person who is trying to hide their true feelings will

   A) show a forced smile.

   B) become more aroused.

   C) show dilation of the pupils.

   D) end to speak more rapidly.

   E) tend to blink more frequently.

   Answer: B
   Diff: 2   Page Ref: 313
   Topic: How Much Control do We Have Over Our Emotions?
   Skill: Conceptual

44) A person who is attempting to deceive others would do well to remember that the _____ is/are easier to control than are _____.

A) body; facial expressions

B) facial expressions; bodily actions

C) idiosyncratic actions; facial expressions

D) tone of voice; facial expressions

E) bodily actions; words

Answer: B

Diff: 2   Page Ref: 314

Topic: How Much Control do We Have Over Our Emotions?

Skill: Factual

45) A polygraph test assesses all of the following except

A) heart rate.

B) breathing rate.

C) perspiration.

D) eye movements.

E) blood pressure.

Answer: D

Diff: 2   Page Ref: 314

Topic: How Much Control do We Have Over Our Emotions?

Skill: Recall

46) Polygraph tests are often not used in court cases because

A) they information they receive is often gained under coercive situations.

B) they are only used if there are no eyewitnesses to a crime.

C) most people refuse to take a polygraph test.

D) they can only be admitted as evidence if all of the other information has already been discussed in the court case.

E) they will give roughly 5% false positives, making innocent people appear guilty.

Answer: E

Diff: 2   Page Ref: 315

Topic: How Much Control do We Have Over Our Emotions?

Skill: Analysis

47) New brain scanning techniques have replace the polygraph test in many areas. What type of brain waves are often linked with attention-getting cues?

   A) beta   B) delta   C) alpha   D) theta   E) P300

Answer: E
Diff: 2   Page Ref: 316
Topic: How Much Control do We Have Over Our Emotions?
Skill: Factual

48) Which of the following is true of the emotion of anger?

   A) Only 10% of angry people show aggression.

   B) There is no clinical category for a person who has high levels of anger.

   C) Anger can be associated with violence.

   D) Anger can have a positive effect.

   E) All of the above are correct.

Answer: E
Diff: 2   Page Ref: 316
Topic: Controlling Anger
Skill: Conceptual

49) A key step in the Integrated Anger Management program is to

   A) learn to express safely anger.

   B) eliminate most sources of anger.

   C) understand the purpose of anger.

   D) rid oneself of unrealistic goals.

   E) use anger in a healthy way.

Answer: A
Diff: 2   Page Ref: 317
Topic: Controlling Anger
Skill: Factual

50) The process of _____ involves starting, directing, and maintaining physical and psychological activities.

   A) arousal

   B) emotion

   C) drive

   D) motivation

   E) self-actualization

Answer: D
Diff: 1   Page Ref: 318
Topic: Motivation: What Makes Us Act as We Do?
Skill: Conceptual

51) Motivation does which of the following?

    A) assures that we will meet all of our goals

    B) connects observable behavior to internal states

    C) creates a state of physical arousal

    D) influenced solely by our environment

    E) influenced solely by our genes

Answer: B

Diff: 2   *Page Ref: 318*

Topic: Motivation: What Makes Us Act as We Do?

Skill: Conceptual

52) _____ is a form of motivation that plays an important role in survival and reproduction.

    A) Drive

    B) Emotion

    C) Homeostasis

    D) Negative feedback

    E) Cognition

Answer: A

Diff: 1   *Page Ref: 319*

Topic: Motivation: What Makes Us Act as We Do?

Skill: Factual

53) Which of the following is the best example of a drive?

    A) your political views

    B) the need for achievement

    C) hunger

    D) earning money by working at a job

    E) volunteering time to feed the hungry

Answer: C

Diff: 1   *Page Ref: 319*

Topic: Motivation: What Makes Us Act as We Do?

Skill: Applied

54) Our desire to play a competitive game of golf is primarily driven by

   A) drives.

   B) extrinsic motivation.

   C) motives.

   D) unconscious motivation.

   E) fixed–action patterns.

Answer: C
Diff: 2   Page Ref: 319
Topic: Motivation: What Makes Us Act as We Do?
Skill: Applied

55) Your parents give you $20 every time you get an A on your report card, this is an example of

   A) a drive but not a motive.

   B) an intrinsic motivation.

   C) an extrinsic motivation.

   D) an unconscious motivation.

   E) an external locus of control.

Answer: C
Diff: 2   Page Ref: 319
Topic: Motivation: What Makes Us Act as We Do?
Skill: Applied

56) Susan volunteers at the local grade school to tutor students who need extra help in reading. She is not paid, but she loves to go each week, her behavior is an example of

   A) intrinsic motivation.

   B) extrinsic motivation.

   C) high "n Ach".

   D) low "n Ach".

   E) locus of control.

Answer: A
Diff: 2   Page Ref: 319
Topic: Motivation: What Makes Us Act as We Do?
Skill: Applied

57) A person who visits a cafeteria to be with his friends would be said to show _____ motivation whereas another person might show _____ motivation because they are only there to get some free pizza.

   A) extrinsic; intrinsic

   B) intrinsic; extrinsic

   C) deferred; peripheral

   D) peripheral; deferred

   E) conscious; unconscious

Answer: B

Diff: 2   Page Ref: 319

Topic: Motivation: What Makes Us Act as We Do?

Skill: Applied

58) _____ theory can account for regular cycles of animal activity.

   A) Drive

   B) Psychoanalytic

   C) Instinct

   D) Homeostatic

   E) The James–Lange

Answer: C

Diff: 2   Page Ref: 320

Topic: Motivation: What Makes Us Act as We Do?

Skill: Conceptual

59) According to drive-reduction theory, _____ refers to the balance among the body's systems and processes.

   A) optimal arousal

   B) psychic energy

   C) a fixed–action pattern

   D) homeostasis

   E) external motivation

Answer: D

Diff: 2   Page Ref: 320

Topic: Motivation: What Makes Us Act as We Do?

Skill: Conceptual

60) The currently-preferred term for instinct is

    A) negative incentive.

    B) homeostatic function.

    C) fixed-action pattern.

    D) internal cognition.

    E) external motivation.

Answer: C

Diff: 1   Page Ref: 320

Topic: Motivation: What Makes Us Act as We Do?

Skill: Factual

61) The fact that when we are hungry we seek to satisfy that need is explained best by the
_____ theory of motivation.

    A) instinct

    B) Freud's

    C) locus of control

    D) drive-reduction

    E) homeostasis

Answer: D

Diff: 2   Page Ref: 320

Topic: Motivation: What Makes Us Act as We Do?

Skill: Applied

62) Drive-reduction theory does not explain why

    A) we look for something to eat when we are hungry.

    B) we drink wanter when we are thirsty.

    C) we go to bed when we are tired.

    D) we try to seek shelter when it is cold outside.

    E) we want to do well on semester exams.

Answer: E

Diff: 3   Page Ref: 320

Topic: Motivation: What Makes Us Act as We Do?

Skill: Conceptual

63) Julian Rotter is known in psychology for endorsing which motivation theory?

A) drive theory

B) instinct theory

C) incentive theory

D) humanistic theory

E) social–learning theory

Answer: E

Diff: 3   Page Ref: 321

Topic: Motivation: What Makes Us Act as We Do?

Skill: Factual

64) Locus of control refers to a person's

A) inner desire to succeed.

B) belief about whether he or she can control outcomes.

C) ability to control or motivate others.

D) overall level of stress.

E) belief about whether he or she can cope with stress successfully.

Answer: B

Diff: 2   Page Ref: 321

Topic: Motivation: What Makes Us Act as We Do?

Skill: Conceptual

65) The two factors that determine the likelihood of engaging in behavior, according to Rotter's social–learning theory, are _____.

A) want and need

B) desire and love

C) time and money

D) nature and nurture

E) expectation and value

Answer: E

Diff: 2   Page Ref: 321

Topic: Motivation: What Makes Us Act as We Do?

Skill: Conceptual

66) If you attribute your success on an an exam to your study habits, you are using _____ to explain your performance.

    A) internal locus of control

    B) intrinsic motivation

    C) external locus of control

    D) preconscious motivation

    E) unconscious motivation

Answer: A

Diff: 2   Page Ref: 321

Topic: Motivation: What Makes Us Act as We Do?

Skill: Applied

67) During hurricane Katrina, many victims never tried to apply for federal aid because they believed that the decision to receive aid was in the hands of the government and there was nothing they as individuals could do about it. These individual have

    A) negative incentive motivation.

    B) an internal locus of control.

    C) an external locus of control.

    D) impaired motivation.

    E) extrinsic motivation.

Answer: C

Diff: 2   Page Ref: 321

Topic: Motivation: What Makes Us Act as We Do?

Skill: Applied

68) According to Freud, aggression is to thanatos as sex drive is to _____.

    A) creativity

    B) libido

    C) charity

    D) perception

    E) drive theory

Answer: B

Diff: 3   Page Ref: 321

Topic: Motivation: What Makes Us Act as We Do?

Skill: Conceptual

69) The only theory of Motivation to take a developmental approach is
    A) Freud's.
    B) Maslow's.
    C) locus of control.
    D) drive reduction theory.
    E) instinct theory.

Answer: A
Diff: 3   Page Ref: 321
Topic: Motivation: What Makes Us Act as We Do?
Skill: Conceptual

70) Identify the case below in which the more basic need is listed before the "higher" need, according to Maslow's theory of motivation.
    A) esteem before safety
    B) attachment before biology
    C) self-actualization before affiliation
    D) affiliation before biology
    E) attachment before esteem

Answer: E
Diff: 2   Page Ref: 322–323
Topic: Motivation: What Makes Us Act as We Do?
Skill: Conceptual

71) Maslow's humanistic theory of motivation has difficulty in explaining why
    A) a person would ask for dessert after eating a delicious meal.
    B) two people would fall in love.
    C) you study hard to do well on your exams.
    D) Ghandi would starve for political freedom.
    E) you go to sleep earlier than usual when you are feeling tired.

Answer: D
Diff: 3   Page Ref: 322–323
Topic: Motivation: What Makes Us Act as We Do?
Skill: Conceptual

72) Maslow defined _____ as the state in which a person seeks to move beyond basic human needs in the quest for the fullest development of their potential

A) locus of control

B) optimal arousal

C) self-actualization

D) psychoanalysis

E) drive

Answer: C

Diff: 2   Page Ref: 323

Topic: Motivation: What Makes Us Act as We Do?

Skill: Conceptual

73) Maslow's hierarchy of needs has been criticized because

A) it is primarily applicable in individualistic cultures.

B) an individual may be in two levels at the same time.

C) instead of a pyramid is should be a slope as individuals gradually move fro one stage to another rather than "jumping from one level to the next.

D) does not explain risky behaviors.

E) All of the above are criticisms of the hierarchy of needs.

Answer: E

Diff: 2   Page Ref: 323

Topic: Motivation: What Makes Us Act as We Do?

Skill: Analysis

74) Providing an external reward for a behavior that is already intrinsically motivated may result in a

A) sense of irritation.

B) refusal to accept rewards of any kind.

C) slower rate of learning.

D) reduction in the rewarded behavior.

E) new locus of control.

Answer: D

Diff: 2   Page Ref: 324

Topic: Rewards Can (Sometimes) Squelch Motivation

Skill: Conceptual

75) Overjustification is most likely to occur when

    A) Cindy is given a trophy for riding her bicycle.

    B) Jan is punished for refusing to set the dinner table.

    C) Marcia is asked out to her senior prom.

    D) Bobby walks his dog, Tiger.

    E) Peter receives a trip to Hawaii for being named Salesman Of The Year.

Answer: A
Diff: 3   Page Ref: 324
Topic: Rewards Can (Sometimes) Squelch Motivation
Skill: Applied

76) The task of a person taking a projective test such as the Thematic Apperception Test (TAT) is to

    A) describe a vague picture.

    B) have their brain scanned while reading.

    C) take a paper-and-pencil inventory.

    D) talk about their future plans.

    E) play a role from a script.

Answer: A
Diff: 2   Page Ref: 326
Topic: How Are Achievement, Hunger, and Sex Alike? Different?
Skill: Factual

77) The Thematic Apperception Test (TAT) is a type of _____ test.

    A) personality

    B) intelligence

    C) achievement

    D) projection

    E) aptitude

Answer: D
Diff: 2   Page Ref: 326
Topic: How Are Achievement, Hunger, and Sex Alike? Different?
Skill: Factual

78) Those who score high in nAch display which of the following when comparing them to those who score low in nAch?

   A) higher IQ scores

   B) take more competitive jobs

   C) assume more leadership roles

   D) ear more rapid promotions.

   E) All of the above

Answer: E

Diff: 2   Page Ref: 326

Topic: How Are Achievement, Hunger, and Sex Alike? Different?

Skill: Recall

79) _____ in the cultures of Latin America and the Middle East may act to discourage individual achievement.

   A) Extrinsic motivations

   B) Euphemism

   C) Collectivism

   D) Structuralism

   E) Self–actualization

Answer: C

Diff: 2   Page Ref: 326

Topic: How Are Achievement, Hunger, and Sex Alike? Different?

Skill: Conceptual

80) The _____ would explain that Charissa's decision to munch on popcorn depends on whether she enjoys popcorn, how long it has been since she last ate, and what time of day it is.

   A) "stop" center concept

   B) set point theory

   C) multiple–system approach

   D) needs hierarchy view

   E) theory of drive

Answer: C

Diff: 2   Page Ref: 327

Topic: How Are Achievement, Hunger, and Sex Alike? Different?

Skill: Applied

81) Mice that lack the hormone _____ will continue to eat even when they are full of food.

    A) leptin   B) ghrelin   C) insulin   D) estrogen   E) thyroxin

Answer: A
Diff: 2   *Page Ref: 327*
Topic: How Are Achievement, Hunger, and Sex Alike? Different?
Skill: Factual

82) The sensation of hunger in response to low blood sugar is due to activation of the _____.

    A) amygdala

    B) lateral hypothalamus

    C) adrenal gland

    D) ventromedial hypothalamus

    E) hippocampus

Answer: B
Diff: 2   *Page Ref: 327*
Topic: How Are Achievement, Hunger, and Sex Alike? Different?
Skill: Factual

83) Which of the following is true with regard to weight control?

    A) Only about 10% of all Americans are overweight.

    B) Most diets have been found to be effective in helping people lose weight and keep it off.

    C) No diet has ever produced long-term weight loss for the majority of people who have tried it.

    D) Humans evolved the ability to handle a calorie-rich diet..

    E) Surgeries and drugs work in helping most people lose weight, but diets do not.

Answer: C
Diff: 2   *Page Ref: 328*
Topic: How Are Achievement, Hunger, and Sex Alike? Different?
Skill: Factual

84) _____ refers to the tendency of the body to maintain a certain level of body fat and body weight.

    A) Metabolism

    B) Blood sugar level

    C) Hunger drive

    D) The set point

    E) Cataplexy

Answer: D
Diff: 2   *Page Ref: 327*
Topic: How Are Achievement, Hunger, and Sex Alike? Different?
Skill: Factual

85) Annie has gone in a diet, initially she lost much weight, but now her weight seems to have stabilized, this is probably because

    A) her lateral hypothalamus is damaged.

    B) her ventromedial hypothalamus is damaged.

    C) she has reached the lower end of her set point.

    D) she is producing the hormone ghrelin.

    E) she has used up all of her bodies fat reserves.

Answer: C
Diff: 2   Page Ref: 327
Topic: How Are Achievement, Hunger, and Sex Alike? Different?
Skill: Applied

86) The Centers for Disease control reports that _____ of the U.S. population os overweight and about _____ are clinically obese

    A) 50%; 25%   B) 75%; 50%   C) 50%; 10%   D) 75%; 25%   E) 25%; 10%

Answer: A
Diff: 2   Page Ref: 328
Topic: How Are Achievement, Hunger, and Sex Alike? Different?
Skill: Factual

87) By definition, anorexia nervosa involves a person who weighs less than _____ of their ideal body weight and still is concerned about being fat.

    A) 95%   B) 90%   C) 85%   D) 75%   E) 60%

Answer: C
Diff: 2   Page Ref: 329
Topic: How Are Achievement, Hunger, and Sex Alike? Different?
Skill: Factual

88) Which of the following factors may contribute to eating disorders in young people?

    A) seeing models who are extremely thin

    B) being told they look good when they are thin

    C) the ability to have some control over their lives

    D) trying to reach an unrealistic goal of thinness

    E) All of the above

Answer: E
Diff: 2   Page Ref: 329
Topic: How Are Achievement, Hunger, and Sex Alike? Different?
Skill: Conceptual

89) Which of the following has the highest mortality rate of any mental disorder?

  A) depression

  B) schizophrenia

  C) anorexia

  D) bipolar

  E) alcoholism

Answer: C

Diff: 2   Page Ref: 329

Topic: How Are Achievement, Hunger, and Sex Alike? Different?

Skill: Factual

90) From an evolutionary perspective, people may be overeat because

  A) they have no willpower.

  B) they enjoy food.

  C) being overweight was a sign of status.

  D) they are reserving fat stores in case of famine.

  E) they did not exercise.

Answer: D

Diff: 2   Page Ref: 329

Topic: How Are Achievement, Hunger, and Sex Alike? Different?

Skill: Conceptual

91) _____ is caused by a drop in blood plasma levels, while _____ results from water moving through the cell walls of your body and escaping in the form of sweat, urine, feces and moisture in your breath.

  A) Hunger; thirst

  B) Volumetric thirst; hunger

  C) Hunger; osmotic thirst

  D) Volumetric thirst; osmotic thirst

  E) Thirst; hunger

Answer: D

Diff: 2   Page Ref: 330

Topic: How Are Achievement, Hunger, and Sex Alike? Different?

Skill: Factual

92) Sexual motivation resembles hunger in that

    A) each produces an arousal that is pleasurable.

    B) deprivation of each behavior can be life–threatening.

    C) each is accounted for by drive theory.

    D) each plays a role in survival of the species.

    E) both are homeostatic drives.

Answer: D
Diff: 2   Page Ref: 330
Topic: How Are Achievement, Hunger, and Sex Alike? Different?
Skill: Conceptual

93) Who did the first widely published study n sexual behavior?

    A) Freud

    B) Kinsey

    C) Masters and Johnson

    D) Ford and Beach

    E) Maslow

Answer: B
Diff: 2   Page Ref: 331
Topic: How Are Achievement, Hunger, and Sex Alike? Different?
Skill: Factual

94) Masters and Johnson contributed to the study of human sexuality by

    A) interviewing 17,000 Americans about their sexual behavior.

    B) directly observing and recording physiological patterns in sexual performance.

    C) developing sexual scripts for sexual responsiveness.

    D) looked for brain abnormalities as the cause of male homosexuality.

    E) setting up video cameras in people's homes to measure their sexual behaviors.

Answer: B
Diff: 3   Page Ref: 331
Topic: How Are Achievement, Hunger, and Sex Alike? Different?
Skill: Factual

95) The _____ phase of the sexual response cycle involves the swelling of blood vessels in the pelvic region.

    A) excitement

    B) plateau

    C) orgasm

    D) resolution

    E) intercourse

Answer: A
Diff: 1   *Page Ref: 332*
Topic: How Are Achievement, Hunger, and Sex Alike? Different?
Skill: Factual

96) A maximum level of sexual arousal is reached during the _____ phase of the human sexual response cycle.

    A) orgasm

    B) resolution

    C) excitement

    D) plateau

    E) climax

Answer: D
Diff: 2   *Page Ref: 332*
Topic: How Are Achievement, Hunger, and Sex Alike? Different?
Skill: Factual

97) The correct order of the stages of human sexual response as reported by Masters and Johnson are

    A) plateau, orgasm, resolution, excitement.

    B) excitement, plateau, orgasm, resolution.

    C) excitement, orgasm, plateau, resolution.

    D) resolution, excitement, plateau, orgasm.

    E) excitement, plateau, resolution, orgasm.

Answer: B
Diff: 2   *Page Ref: 332*
Topic: How Are Achievement, Hunger, and Sex Alike? Different?
Skill: Conceptual

98) Women are different in men in their sexual responses in that they

    A) they remain aroused longer than men.

    B) go through different stages than men during the sexual response cycle.

    C) they do not go through the orgasm stage.

    D) they more more quickly through the stages than men.

    E) the stay aroused for a shorter time than men.

Answer: A
Diff: 2   *Page Ref: 332*
Topic: How Are Achievement, Hunger, and Sex Alike? Different?
Skill: Conceptual

99) The _____ is considered to be the most important human sex organ.

    A) penis   B) clitoris   C) vagina   D) brain   E) pelvis

Answer: D
Diff: 1   *Page Ref: 333*
Topic: How Are Achievement, Hunger, and Sex Alike? Different?
Skill: Conceptual

100) Which of the following was NOT a conclusion reached by Masters and Johnson?

    A) Men and women have similar patterns of sexual responses, regardless of the source of arousal.

    B) The psychological aspects of sexuality are as important as the physiological aspects.

    C) Penis size is generally unrelated to any aspect of sexual performance (except in terms of attitude).

    D) The sequence of phases of the sexual response cycle is similar in the two sexes; however, men tend to respond more quickly than women.

    E) Many women can have multiple orgasms, whereas few men have this ability.

Answer: B
Diff: 3   *Page Ref: 333*
Topic: How Are Achievement, Hunger, and Sex Alike? Different?
Skill: Factual

101) A(n) _____ is a socially-learned program of sexual responsiveness.

   A) schema

   B) instinct

   C) orientation

   D) sexual script

   E) plateau

Answer: D

Diff: 2   Page Ref: 333

Topic: How Are Achievement, Hunger, and Sex Alike? Different?

Skill: Conceptual

102) Wilma touches her friend, Fred, to offer him support. However, Fred interprets this as a sign that Wilma would like to kiss him. Fred and Wilma have different

   A) sexual values.

   B) sexual response cycles.

   C) levels of sensitivity.

   D) sexual orientations.

   E) sexual scripts.

Answer: E

Diff: 2   Page Ref: 333

Topic: How Are Achievement, Hunger, and Sex Alike? Different?

Skill: Conceptual

103) According to the evolutionary theory, the goal of both sexes is to

   A) achieve orgasm.

   B) create as many offspring as possible.

   C) eat until full.

   D) get a consistent amount of nightly sleep.

   E) reduce anger and stress.

Answer: B

Diff: 2   Page Ref: 334

Topic: How Are Achievement, Hunger, and Sex Alike? Different?

Skill: Factual

104) Evolutionary psychologists suggest that men may have more extramarital affairs than women because

    A) men are less satisfied in their marriages.

    B) women feel more of a responsibility to their family.

    C) Women can only produce a limited number of children in their lifetime, but men attempt to produce as many as possible.

    D) Women look for men with more resources.

    E) men are more concerned with personality than women.

Answer: C

Diff: 2   Page Ref: 334

Topic: How Are Achievement, Hunger, and Sex Alike? Different?

Skill: Conceptual

105) Susan is at the mall she has $30 to buy a new shirt. She sees two that she likes equally as well as one another, but she only has enough money to buy one. This scenario demonstrates which of the following types of conflict?

    A) approach–avoidance

    B) approach–approach

    C) avoidance–avoidance

    D) multiple approach–avoidance

    E) none of the above

Answer: B

Diff: 2   Page Ref: 334

Topic: How Are Achievement, Hunger, and Sex Alike? Different?

Skill: Applied

106) Ned is excited about going off to college, but he knows he will miss his mothers cooking. He is excited to meet new people, but he will miss his fiends from high school. He looks forward to having more freedom to do as he would like, but knows he will miss the safe environment of his old neighborhood. Ned is experiencing which of the following types of conflicts.

    A) multiple approach–avoidance

    B) avoidance–avoidance

    C) approach–approach

    D) approach–avoidance

    E) None of the above

Answer: A

Diff: 2   Page Ref: 334

Topic: How Are Achievement, Hunger, and Sex Alike? Different?

Skill: Applied

107) Jenny does not want to exercise, but she also does not want to be out of shape for the upcoming tennis season. She is struggling through _____ conflict.

    A) approach–approach

    B) approach–avoidance

    C) avoidance–avoidance

    D) multiple approach–avoidance

    E) None of the above

Answer: C

Diff: 2   *Page Ref: 334*

Topic: How Are Achievement, Hunger, and Sex Alike? Different?

Skill: Applied

108) Pillard and Bailey's studies on sexual orientation in twins showed that

    A) there is little relationship between the sexual orientations of twins.

    B) there is an almost perfect relationship between the sexual orientations of twins.

    C) the rate of homosexuality among identical twins is ten times higher than in the general population.

    D) when one identical twin is a homosexual, the chance of the other being homosexual is about 50 percent.

    E) most people do have some homosexual interests.

Answer: D

Diff: 2   *Page Ref: 335*

Topic: The Origins of Sexual Orientation

Skill: Conceptual

109) Simon LeVay found that a part of the _____ in homosexual men was significantly _____ than that structure in the brains of heterosexual men.

    A) RAS; larger

    B) testicle; smaller

    C) hypothalamus; smaller

    D) thalamus; larger

    E) DNA structure; smoother

Answer: C

Diff: 3   *Page Ref: 336*

Topic: The Origins of Sexual Orientation

Skill: Factual

Check Your Understanding Questions

1) From the evolutionary perspective, we can understand emotions as helping organisms identify
   A) others of their own gender.
   B) important and recurring situations.
   C) beauty and wonder in the world around them.
   D) locations in which to find food and mates.
   E) sources of danger.

   Answer: B
   Diff: 2   Page Ref: 303
   Topic: Check Your Understanding
   Skill: Recall

2) Which one of the following is NOT one of the culturally universal emotions identified by Ekman's research?
   A) anger   B) surprise   C) contempt   D) regret   E) fear

   Answer: D
   Diff: 2   Page Ref: 303
   Topic: Check Your Understanding
   Skill: Recall

3) Plutchik would say that regret is
   A) one of the thousand distinct emotions of which people are capable.
   B) one of the basic emotions.
   C) a combination of more basic emotions.
   D) not really an emotions, because it does not appear on the emotion wheel.
   E) a universally recognized emotion.

   Answer: C
   Diff: 2   Page Ref: 303
   Topic: Check Your Understanding
   Skill: Recall

4) In which respect do men and women differ in their emotional expressions?
   A) Women are, overall, more emotionally expressive than men.
   B) Certain emotional disorders, such as depression, occur more often in women.
   C) In Asian countries, men are more open about their feelings than are women.
   D) Men are more rational in their emotional responses than women.
   E) Women are more rational in their emotional responses than men.

   Answer: B
   Diff: 2   Page Ref: 303
   Topic: Check Your Understanding
   Skill: Recall

5) According to this section of the chapter, what is the adaptive value of communicating our emotional states?

    A) It helps us to understand our own needs better.

    B) It allows us to deceive others about our emotional states and get what we want.

    C) It allows us to anticipate each other's responses and so to live more easily in groups.

    D) Communicating our emotional state helps us get rid of strong negative emotions, such as fear and anger.

    E) It helps us to achieve self-awareness.

Answer: C
Diff: 2   Page Ref: 303
Topic: Check Your Understanding
Skill: Understanding the Core Concept

6) During emotional arousal, the _____ nervous system sends messages to internal organs.

    A) somatic

    B) parasympathetic

    C) autonomic

    D) motor

    E) afferent

Answer: C
Diff: 2   Page Ref: 311
Topic: Check Your Understanding
Skill: Recall

7) We would be most likely to misattribute the source of our arousal when

    A) taking a drug such as a diet pill, that has the unexpected effect of physical arousal.

    B) taking a drug such as caffeine, that we know causes arousal.

    C) winning a race.

    D) feeling depressed after the death of a loved one.

    E) losing a race.

Answer: A
Diff: 2   Page Ref: 311
Topic: Check Your Understanding
Skill: Applied

8) In the field of emotion, theorists have long debated whether
    A) feelings are associated with emotional responses.
    B) we are aware of our emotions.
    C) cognition and emotion are independent of each other.
    D) men are sensitive to women's emotions.
    E) emotions are valid.

Answer: C
Diff: 2   Page Ref: 311
Topic: Check Your Understanding
Skill: Recall

9) Which two factors are emphasized by the two-factor theory of emotion?
    A) subjective feelings and behavioral expression
    B) cognitive interpretation and behavioral expression
    C) biological arousal and cognitive interpretation
    D) biological arousal and subjective feelings
    E) subjective feelings and cognitive interpretation

Answer: C
Diff: 2   Page Ref: 311
Topic: Check Your Understanding
Skill: Understanding the Core Concept

10) People with emotional intelligence
    A) feel no emotions.
    B) are extremely emotionally responsive
    C) know how to control their emotional responses.
    D) can always deceive a polygrapher.
    E) are extremely intelligent.

Answer: C
Diff: 2   Page Ref: 317
Topic: Check Your Understanding
Skill: Recall

11) When lying by giving false information, you are likely to

    A) become more animated in your gesturing.

    B) become more constrained in your gesturing.

    C) control your body more easily than you control your face.

    D) look someone "straight in the eye."

    E) shift your eyes to the left.

Answer: B
Diff: 2   Page Ref: 317
Topic: Check Your Understanding
Skill: Recall

12) "Lie detectors" detect

    A) feelings.

    B) physical arousal.

    C) motivation.

    D) untruthfulness.

    E) emotions.

Answer: B
Diff: 2   Page Ref: 317
Topic: Check Your Understanding
Skill: Recall

13) Many psychologists have become concerned about the widespread use of polygraphy because

    A) polygraph testing is not done under the supervision of qualified psychologists.

    B) hypnosis is more accurate than polygraphy in the detection of lying.

    C) innocent people can be incorrectly identified as lying.

    D) people who are lying can be incorrectly identified as innocent.

    E) they may decrease the need for detectives, because they are so accurate.

Answer: C
Diff: 2   Page Ref: 317
Topic: Check Your Understanding
Skill: Recall

14) Psychological research suggests that it might be best to handle your feelings of anger toward a friend by

    A) hitting a punching bag.

    B) venting your anger by yelling at your friend.

    C) calmly telling your friend that you feel angry.

    D) doing nothing except "stewing" in your angry feelings.

    E) engaging in other, unrelated activities.

Answer: C
Diff: 2   Page Ref: 317
Topic: Check Your Understanding
Skill: Applied

15) Research suggests that the ability to control one's emotional responses is

    A) a personality trait that cannot be changed.

    B) largely a matter of hormones.

    C) closely connected to IQ.

    D) a skill that can be learned.

    E) a genetic predisposition.

Answer: D
Diff: 2   Page Ref: 317
Topic: Check Your Understanding
Skill: Understanding the Core Concept

16) Psychologists use the concept of motivation in several important ways. Which of the following is NOT among them?

    A) to connect observable behavior to internal states

    B) to account for variability in behavior

    C) to explain perseverance despite adversity

    D) to explain reflexive responses

    E) to relate behavior to internal feelings

Answer: D
Diff: 2   Page Ref: 324
Topic: Check Your Understanding
Skill: Recall

17) One reason that the term instinct has dropped out of favor with psychologists is that

    A) human behavior has no genetic basis.

    B) all behavior is learned.

    C) the term has become a label for behavior, rather than an explanation for behavior.

    D) instinct applies to animal behavior, not to human behavior.

    E) instincts are the root of all behavior.

Answer: C
Diff: 2   *Page Ref: 324*
Topic: Check Your Understanding
Skill: Recall

18) Maslow's theory of motivation has been criticized as a theory of motivation because

    A) it does not take into account emotion.

    B) an individual can forgo a need in a lower level and still fulfill a need higher along the hierarchy.

    C) it places physiological needs as the most important.

    D) it does not explain highly motivated individuals.

    E) it does not address relationships.

Answer: B
Diff: 2   *Page Ref: 325*
Topic: Check Your Understanding
Skill: Analysis

19) Motivation takes many forms, but all involve inferred mental processes that select and direct our behavior. Thus, the psychology of motivation attempts to explain why a certain _____ is selected.

    A) emotion

    B) action

    C) sensation

    D) reward

    E) perception

Answer: B
Diff: 1   *Page Ref: 325*
Topic: Check Your Understanding
Skill: Understanding the Core Concept

20) Which one of the following is often considered to be a biological drive?

   A) hunger   B) safety   C) *nAch*   D) fear   E) esteem

Answer: A
Diff: 2   Page Ref: 336
Topic: Check Your Understanding
Skill: Recall

21) How did Murray and McClelland measure *nAch*?

   A) with a polygraph

   B) with the Thematic Apperception Test

   C) by measuring achievement–related hormones in the blood

   D) by using grade point averages (GPAs)

   E) by using Advanced Placement exams

Answer: B
Diff: 2   Page Ref: 336
Topic: Check Your Understanding
Skill: Recall

22) According to Masters and Johnson's research, the sexual response cycles of men and women are essentially the same, except for

   A) women's ability for multiple orgasm.

   B) men's sexual receptivity at any time of the month.

   C) men's responsiveness to many different kinds of stimulation.

   D) women's need for commitment in a sexual relationship.

   E) the cycles through which they pass in the sexual response cycle.

Answer: A
Diff: 2   Page Ref: 336
Topic: Check Your Understanding
Skill: Recall

23) Which motive seems to regulate behavior in order to maintain a certain physical condition in the body, known as a *set point*?

   A) achievement

   B) hunger

   C) sex

   D) homeostasis

   E) drive reduction

Answer: A
Diff: 2   Page Ref: 336
Topic: Check Your Understanding
Skill: Recall

24) In which of the following would biological factors be *least important* in accounting for the motivational differences between individuals?

    A) hunger   B) thirst   C) *nAch*   D) sex   E) motives

Answer: C
Diff: 1   *Page Ref: 336*
Topic: Check Your Understanding
Skill: Understanding the Core Concept

True/False Questions

1) Emotions can produce behaviors.

Answer: TRUE
Diff: 1   *Page Ref: 298*
Topic: Introduction
Skill: Conceptual

2) Emotions are entirely programmed by genetics.

Answer: FALSE
Diff: 1   *Page Ref: 301*
Topic: What Do Our Emotions Do for Us?
Skill: Conceptual

3) Babies typically begin to produce facial expressions to reflect their feelings at about two weeks of age.

Answer: FALSE
Diff: 1   *Page Ref: 300*
Topic: What Do Our Emotions Do for Us?
Skill: Factual

4) Paul Ekman believed that the universally recognized facial expressions included, fear, surprise, jealousy, contempt, happiness and anger.

Answer: FALSE
Diff: 1   *Page Ref: 300*
Topic: What Do Our Emotions Do for Us?
Skill: Factual

5) Robert Plutchik believed that we form secondary emotions by combining our basic emotions.

Answer: TRUE
Diff: 3   *Page Ref: 301*
Topic: What Do Our Emotions Do for Us?
Skill: Conceptual

6) Panic disorders and depression occur more commonly in women than men.

Answer: TRUE
Diff: 2   Page Ref: 303
Topic: Emotional Differences between Men & Women Depend on Culture
Skill: Factual

7) When afraid because of a loud noise, Simon's amygdala is likely to be activated.

Answer: TRUE
Diff: 2   Page Ref: 306
Topic: Where do Our Emotions Come From?
Skill: Applied

8) If the amygdala of a rabbit was lesioned, it is likely that the rabbit would become fearful.

Answer: TRUE
Diff: 2   Page Ref: 306
Topic: Where do Our Emotions Come From?
Skill: Conceptual

9) Some emotional reactions begin with the reticular activating system arousing the whole brain.

Answer: TRUE
Diff: 2   Page Ref: 306
Topic: Where do Our Emotions Come From?
Skill: Factual

10) The right hemisphere seems to respond the positive emotions while the left side seems more wired for negative emotions.

Answer: FALSE
Diff: 2   Page Ref: 306
Topic: Where do Our Emotions Come From?
Skill: Conceptual

11) Serotonin has been link with depression.

Answer: TRUE
Diff: 2   Page Ref: 307
Topic: Where do Our Emotions Come From?
Skill: Factual

12) The view that physical responses underlie our emotions is known as the James–Lange theory of emotion.

Answer: TRUE
Diff: 3   Page Ref: 307
Topic: Where do Our Emotions Come From?
Skill: Factual

13) The two-factor theory proposes that we feel physical and emotional responses at the same time.

Answer: FALSE
Diff: 3   Page Ref: 308
Topic: Where do Our Emotions Come From?
Skill: Conceptual

14) For the best performance on a difficult task, we should have a relatively low level of arousal, according to the inverted u theory.

Answer: TRUE
Diff: 2   Page Ref: 310
Topic: Arousal, Performance, and the Inverted 'U'
Skill: Conceptual

15) Emotional intelligence involves knowing how to control our own emotions.

Answer: TRUE
Diff: 2   Page Ref: 312
Topic: How Much Control do We Have Over Our Emotions?
Skill: Conceptual

16) Impulse control plays an important role in Emotional Intelligence.

Answer: TRUE
Diff: 2   Page Ref: 312
Topic: How Much Control do We Have Over Our Emotions?
Skill: Conceptual

17) Generally speaking, a person who is lying will have longer pauses in their speech than when they are telling the truth.

Answer: TRUE
Diff: 2   Page Ref: 313
Topic: How Much Control do We Have Over Our Emotions?
Skill: Factual

18) It is highly unlikely that a polygraph machine would be wrong.

Answer: FALSE
Diff: 2   Page Ref: 314
Topic: How Much Control do We Have Over Our Emotions?
Skill: Conceptual

19) A polygraph test measures one's perspiration.

Answer: TRUE
Diff: 2   Page Ref: 314
Topic: How Much Control do We Have Over Our Emotions?
Skill: Factual

20) Newly developed test for detecting lies such as 'integrity tests' have been highly successful in determining who is lying.

Answer: FALSE
Diff: 2   Page Ref: 315
Topic: How Much Control do We Have Over Our Emotions?
Skill: Conceptual

21) Retaliation usually leads to intense satisfaction and a reduction in anger.

Answer: FALSE
Diff: 2   Page Ref: 316-317
Topic: Controlling Anger
Skill: Conceptual

22) Working for a paycheck is an example of extrinsic motivation.

Answer: TRUE
Diff: 2   Page Ref: 319
Topic: Motivation: What Makes Us Act as We Do?
Skill: Applied

23) Individuals who work only for some kind of reward are said to have intrinsic motivation.

Answer: FALSE
Diff: 2   Page Ref: 319
Topic: Motivation: What Makes Us Act as We Do?
Skill: Conceptual

24) The instincts of an animal are called "fixed action patterns" by ethologists.

Answer: TRUE
Diff: 2   Page Ref: 320
Topic: Motivation: What Makes Us Act as We Do?
Skill: Factual

25) When we are cold we shiver. This is an example of how our body attempts to remain homeostatic.

Answer: TRUE
Diff: 2   Page Ref: 320
Topic: Motivation: What Makes Us Act as We Do?
Skill: Conceptual

26) We have an internal locus of control orientation if we think that the outcomes of our actions are contingent on events outside of our personal control.

Answer: FALSE
Diff: 1   Page Ref: 321
Topic: Motivation: What Makes Us Act as We Do?
Skill: Conceptual

27) Freud would suggest that a creative artist paints in order to find an acceptable outlet for their sexual energy.

Answer: FALSE
Diff: 2   Page Ref: 321
Topic: Motivation: What Makes Us Act as We Do?
Skill: Conceptual

28) According to Maslow's hierarchy of needs, our highest need is to find love.

Answer: FALSE
Diff: 2   Page Ref: 323
Topic: Motivation: What Makes Us Act as We Do?
Skill: Factual

29) Maslow believed that lower needs must be met before one could seek to reach those in higher levels.

Answer: TRUE
Diff: 2   Page Ref: 323
Topic: Motivation: What Makes Us Act as We Do?
Skill: Factual

30) Overjustification explains how rewarding people for certain behaviors can make them less motivated.

Answer: TRUE
Diff: 2   Page Ref: 324
Topic: Motivation: What Makes Us Act as We Do?
Skill: Factual

31) People who are high in nACH tend to get promoted more rapidly than those who score low in nACH.

Answer: TRUE
Diff: 2   Page Ref: 326
Topic: How Are Achievement, Hunger, and Sex Alike? Different?
Skill: Conceptual

32) Feeding is started when the amygdala is activated by a high level of blood sugar.

Answer: FALSE
Diff: 3   Page Ref: 380
Topic: How Are Achievement, Hunger, and Sex Alike? Different?
Skill: Factual

33) Collectivist cultures tend to value personal achievement over group loyalty.

Answer: FALSE
Diff: 2   Page Ref: 326
Topic: How Are Achievement, Hunger, and Sex Alike? Different?
Skill: Conceptual

34) The lateral hypothalamus allows you to gauge when you are full.

Answer: FALSE
Diff: 2   Page Ref: 327
Topic: How Are Achievement, Hunger, and Sex Alike? Different?
Skill: Factual

35) It is difficult to lose weight once you go under your set point.

Answer: TRUE
Diff: 2   Page Ref: 327
Topic: How Are Achievement, Hunger, and Sex Alike? Different?
Skill: Factual

36) Obesity is not currently a problem in the United States.

Answer: FALSE
Diff: 1   Page Ref: 329
Topic: How Are Achievement, Hunger, and Sex Alike? Different?
Skill: Factual

37) Sexual scripts are innate programs that animals know from birth that determine how to act in sexual situations.

Answer: FALSE
Diff: 2   Page Ref: 333
Topic: How Are Achievement, Hunger, and Sex Alike? Different?
Skill: Conceptual

38) Whether to buy a new BMW or a new Lexus would be an example of an Approach–Avoidance conflict.

Answer: FALSE
Diff: 2   Page Ref: 335
Topic: How Are Achievement, Hunger, and Sex Alike? Different?
Skill: Applied

39) Whether a person is homosexual or heterosexual depends on early childhood experiences.

Answer: FALSE
Diff: 2   Page Ref: 335
Topic: The Origins of Sexual Orientation
Skill: Conceptual

Short Answer Questions

1) Name the seven emotions that Paul Ekman believes can be recognized universally.

Answer: happiness, fear, contempt, disgust, anger, sadness and surprise
Diff: 3   Page Ref: 300
Topic: What Do Our Emotions Do for Us?
Skill: Conceptual

2) Briefly explain the differences often found in the U.S. between men and women in terms of how they display emotions.

Answer: Men are taught to show more anger while women more often express sadness.
Diff: 2   Page Ref: 303
Topic: What Do Our Emotions Do for Us?
Skill: Factual

3) The discovery of the _____ between arousal and performance implies that there is an optimal arousal level for one's best performance.

Answer: inverted–U function

Diff: 2   Page Ref: 362–263

Topic: Arousal, Performance, and the Inverted 'U'

Skill: Conceptual

4) Explain the key idea behind the James–Lange theory of emotion.

Answer: The theory states that the primary source of our emotions stems from physical responses (we run, therefore we are afraid).

Diff: 2   Page Ref: 307

Topic: Where do Our Emotions Come From?

Skill: Factual

5) Name the two factors in Stanley Schacter's theory of emotion.

Answer: physical arousal; cognitive interpretation of the physical arousal

Diff: 2   Page Ref: 308

Topic: Where do Our Emotions Come From?

Skill: Conceptual

6) Name the four theories that propose to explain emotions.

Answer: James–Lange, Canon–Bard, Opponent–Process and Two–Factor

Diff: 3   Page Ref: 307–309

Topic: Where do Our Emotions Come From?

Skill: Recall

7) What is emotional intelligence?

Answer: According to Daniel Goleman, people who effectively use and understand their emotions exhibit a high level of emotional intelligence

Diff: 2   Page Ref: 312–313

Topic: How Much Control do We Have Over Our Emotions?

Skill: Conceptual

8) Briefly explain how a lie detector works and address it's accuracy.

Answer: It measures perspiration, blood pressure, breathing rate, and heat rate and compares these to a base line lie and a base line truth. they are not very accurate and can produce a 5% false positive, thereby accusing innocent people of lying.

Diff: 2   Page Ref: 314

Topic: How Much Control do We Have Over Our Emotions?

Skill: Analysis

9) Provide an example of something you do primarily because of intrinsic motivation and something because of extrinsic motivation.

Answer: Answers will vary, but correct answers must refer to something that the student finds pleasurable for its own sake, not because of (the possibility of) receiving some reward. For extrinsic motivation the explanation must address somehow that they are receiving some sort of reward or reinforcement for their behavior.

Diff: 2   *Page Ref: 319*

Topic: Motivation: What Makes Us Act as We Do?

Skill: Conceptual

10) What is the difference between drive and motive?

Answer: Drive reefers to motivation that is assumed to be primarily biological, and motive refers to psychological and social needs that are assumed to be learned through personal experience.

Diff: 3   *Page Ref: 319–320*

Topic: Motivation: What Makes Us Act as We Do?

Skill: Conceptual

11) List the levels of Maslow's hierarchy in the correct order.

Answer: physiological, safety belonging, esteem and self-actualization

Diff: 2   *Page Ref: 322–323*

Topic: Motivation: What Makes Us Act as We Do?

Skill: Recall

12) We seek to eat when we are hungry and drink when we are thirsty primarily because our body tries to maintain a constant balance, this balance is called

Answer: homeostasis.

Diff: 2   *Page Ref: 320*

Topic: Motivation: What Makes Us Act as We Do?

Skill: Factual

13) Ernie does not study fo his final exams because he does not think that studying will do any good. He believes that the professor just selects his five favorite students and hey will receive A's, since Ernie is not in this category he thinks it is worthless, because Ernie believes that he had no control over his environment he is said to have an

Answer: external locus of control.

Diff: 2   *Page Ref: 321*

Topic: Motivation: What Makes Us Act as We Do?

Skill: Applied

14) Students with a high _____ are likely to strive harder to achieve good grades when the class is especially difficult.

Answer: *n Ach* (need for achievement)
Diff: 2   *Page Ref: 352*
Topic: How Are Achievement, Hunger, and Sex Alike? Different?
Skill: Factual

15) Whenever fats stored in specialized fat cells fall below a specific level, called the _____, signals are sent to the body to being eating once again.

Answer: set point
Diff: 2   *Page Ref: 327*
Topic: How Are Achievement, Hunger, and Sex Alike? Different?
Skill: Factual

16) What are some of the factors that are responsible for the growing degree of obesity in the U.S. population?

Answer: too little exercise; too much high-calorie food
Diff: 2   *Page Ref: 329*
Topic: How Are Achievement, Hunger, and Sex Alike? Different?
Skill: Factual

17) In the 1940s and 1950s, whose research involved interviewing 17,000 Americans regarding their sexual behavior?

Answer: Alfred Kinsey
Diff: 2   *Page Ref: 331*
Topic: How Are Achievement, Hunger, and Sex Alike? Different?
Skill: Factual

18) In the sexual response cycle, the _____ phase is when the maximum level of arousal is reached.

Answer: plateau
Diff: 2   *Page Ref: 332*
Topic: How Are Achievement, Hunger, and Sex Alike? Different?
Skill: Factual

19) In order, name the four phases that Masters and Johnson found in the human sexual response cycle.

Answer: excitement phase, plateau phase, orgasm phase, and resolution phase
Diff: 3   *Page Ref: 332*
Topic: How Are Achievement, Hunger, and Sex Alike? Different?
Skill: Factual

20) Explain and give an example of a multiple approach–avoidance conflict.

Answer: A multiple approach avoidance conflict involves a necessary choice between options that both have many negative and many positive aspects. An example is when a family may have to move. They may look forward to a new job opportunity and meeting new people, but they know they will miss their old friends and they might have to leave great schools.

Diff: 2   Page Ref: 334

Topic: How Are Achievement, Hunger, and Sex Alike? Different?

Skill: Applied

Essay Questions

1) Discuss the biological components of emotional arousal of the following theories of Emotion. Provide a specific example of how all of the following would explain a physical response to the same situation.
James–Lange Theory
Cannon Bard
Two–Factor theory
Opponent Process

Answer: The James-Lange theory of emotion claims that actions occur before (and underlie) emotional responses. You are walking through the woods and see a bear, your heart races and then are afraid.
The Cannon-Bard theory suggests that the emotional feeling and the internal physical response occur simultaneously. You see a bear in the woods, your heart races and get scared at the same time.
The two–factor theory claims that emotions occur due to our appraisal of both our physical state and our current situation. you see a bear and think that you should be scared and you also feel nervous, therefore you determine that you are scared.
Opponent-Process: This theory claims that when you feel a given emotion, that it's opposite is suppressed and will eventually display itself. you see a bear in the woods and you are frightened, late you may feel more courageous than usual.

Diff: 3   Page Ref: 307–309

Topic: Where do Our Emotions Come From?

Skill: Conceptual

2) Explain the theory behind lie detection and explain why evidence from such tests are not admissible in court.

Answer: Theory is that a lie is accompanied by subtle (but measurable) changes in autonomic physiology (e.g. heart rate). The key problem is that such tests have an unacceptably high "false–positive" rate (too many innocent people are declared guilty).

Diff: 2   Page Ref: 313–315

Topic: How Much Control do We Have Over Our Emotions?

Skill: Factual

3) Describe and critique Abraham Maslow's theory of motivation.

Answer: His humanistic theory proposed a needs hierarchy which said that people must first fulfill 'lower' needs before 'higher' ones can be attended to. The needs (from lowest to highest) are: biological (such as hunger and thirst), safety (such as avoiding danger), attachment/affiliation (such as finding love and being with others), esteem (such as liking oneself and feeling competent), and self-actualization (which involves seeking our fullest potential). Some claimed that it is possible to fulfill higher needs while lower ones go unmet (for example, pursuing our career while depriving ourself of sleep). However, Maslow did believe that social motivation was a factor in decisions, too. The theory is difficult to test.

Diff: 1   Page Ref: 322-323

Topic: Motivation: What Makes Us Act as We Do?

Skill: Conceptual

4) Contrast the research methods and findings of Alfred Kinsey with those of Masters and Johnson.

Answer: Both studied sexuality, however Kinsey pioneered the usage of interviews in the 1940s and 1950s whereas Masters and Johnson (M&J) measured physiological response in their laboratories. Kinsey found that many behaviors considered rare or abnormal (such as oral sex) were actually reported to be quite widespread. M&J found that there were four phases (excitement, plateau, orgasm, and resolution) involved in the sexual response cycle. Better students may describe what occurs in each phase.} They also found that women's and men's sexual response cycles were quite similar, regardless of the type of sexual behavior. They also found that women tend to respond more slowly, but they stay aroused longer. They also found that physical sex characteristics (such as penis or breast size) was unrelated to sexual performance, and women are far more capable of multiple orgasms within a short period of time than are men.

Diff: 3   Page Ref: 331-333

Topic: How Are Achievement, Hunger, and Sex Alike? Different?

Skill: Factual

5) Explain and provide an example of the four different types of Conflict.

Answer: Approach-Approach: A conflict between two equally attractive options. You cannot decide between two flavors of ice cream that you really like.

Approach-Avoidance: a conflict in which there are both appealing and negative aspects to the decision being made. You do not know if you should lie to your parents about where you are going on Friday night. You really want to go, but you know that you should not lie, but your parents would not approve of your plans.

Avoidance-Avoidance: A conflict in which one has to decide between two equally unattractive options. You do not want to go to the dentist, but you do not want you teeth to fall out.

Multiple approach-Avoidance: A conflict in which one must choose between options that have many positive and negative aspects. You are upset with your significant other and do not want to break-up but you do not like how they have been behaving lately and there are many things that upset you in terms of your relationship, you are unsure what to do.

Diff: 1   *Page Ref: 334*

Topic: How Are Achievement, Hunger, and Sex Alike? Different?

Skill: Applied

Chapter 9 Psychological Development

Multiple Choice Questions

1) The case of the "Jim Twins"
    A) provides incontrovertible evidence of the power of environment over heredity.
    B) provides incontrovertible evidence of the power of heredity over environment.
    C) proves that heredity and environment have equal influence.
    D) could have more to do with coincidence than heredity.
    E) alerts us to the dangers of assuming that development is continuous.

   Answer: D
   Diff: 2   Page Ref: 359–360
   Topic: Introduction
   Skill: Conceptual

2) A key research interest in developmental psychology is to
    A) trace the evolution of the human race.
    B) identify the biochemical processes involved in thought.
    C) determine how organisms change over time.
    D) predict adult behavior.
    E) study the effects of genetic mutations on behavior.

   Answer: C
   Diff: 1   Page Ref: 362
   Topic: How Do Psychologists Explain Development?
   Skill: Conceptual

3) The nature–nurture controversy is primarily concerned with
    A) the use of a chronological versus a longitudinal approach.
    B) the difference between developmental and chronological age.
    C) the relative importance of heredity and environment.
    D) the extent to which development is continuous or discontinuous.
    E) whether to study similarities or differences between people.

   Answer: C
   Diff: 1   Page Ref: 362–363
   Topic: How Do Psychologists Explain Development?
   Skill: Conceptual

4) In regard to the nature–nurture controversy, most researchers

    A) feel that nature is clearly more important.

    B) feel that nurture is clearly more important.

    C) are more interested in the interaction of nature and nurture.

    D) believe that changes are gradual over time.

    E) accept that development occurs in stages.

Answer: C

Diff: 2   Page Ref: 363

Topic: How Do Psychologists Explain Development?

Skill: Conceptual

5) Down Syndrome

    A) cannot be helped by learning and environmental factors.

    B) can be completely alleviated by factors such as environment and learning.

    C) can be measurably improved by learning-based treatments.

    D) demonstrate the total dominance of heredity over environment.

    E) can be cured by utilizing genetic-based treatments.

Answer: C

Diff: 2   Page Ref: 363

Topic: How Do Psychologists Explain Development?

Skill: Conceptual

6) Adoption studies have often found that

    A) adopted children are much like their birth parents.

    B) adopted children have a mix of characteristics from their adoptive and birth families.

    C) adopted children are much like the siblings in their adoptive family.

    D) adopted children are much like their adoptive parents.

    E) adopted children are much like their birth siblings.

Answer: B

Diff: 2   Page Ref: 363

Topic: How Do Psychologists Explain Development?

Skill: Conceptual

7) Distinct changes in behavior that occur at defined points of life are
    A) always controlled by the environment.
    B) typically studied in the elderly.
    C) part of the continuity view.
    D) consistent with the trial-and-error view of development.
    E) known as developmental stages.

Answer: E
Diff: 2   Page Ref: 364
Topic: How Do Psychologists Explain Development?
Skill: Factual

8) The notion that development occurs in stages
    A) assumes a learning perspective.
    B) is supports by interactionist theory.
    C) is consistent with the process of cumulative action.
    D) assumes that behavior is mainly determined by nature.
    E) endorses the discontinuity view.

Answer: E
Diff: 2   Page Ref: 364
Topic: How Do Psychologists Explain Development?
Skill: Applied

9) Which of the following has been found to be influenced by your genes?
    A) depression
    B) huntington's disease
    C) schizophrenia
    D) extroversion
    E) All of the above

Answer: E
Diff: 1   Page Ref: 365
Topic: Psychological Traits in Your Genes
Skill: Conceptual

10) Which of the following situations involves a self-fulfilling prophecy?

    A) Andy is hungry, so he makes himself a tuna fish sandwich.

    B) Cheryl thinks she'll fail her history test, and she does.

    C) Danielle is very smart, so her parents enroll her in a program for gifted students.

    D) Kyle believes that Sue will not want to go on a date with him, but she does.

    E) June is a great tennis player because she had an excellent coach.

Answer: B
Diff: 3   Page Ref: 365–366
Topic: Psychological Traits in Your Genes
Skill: Applied

11) The zygotic period ends after

    A) 10 days after conception.

    B) at birth.

    C) when the child can walk.

    D) 12 weeks after conception.

    E) 8 weeks after conception.

Answer: A
Diff: 1   Page Ref: 367
Topic: What Capabilities Does the Child Possess?
Skill: Applied

12) The correct order of the three stages of a human prenatal development are

    A) differentiation, implantation, and strengthening.

    B) embryo, zygote, and fetus.

    C) placental, umbilical, and embryonic.

    D) embryonic, placental, and umbilical.

    E) zygote, embryo, and fetus.

Answer: E
Diff: 2   Page Ref: 367
Topic: What Capabilities Does the Child Possess?
Skill: Factual

13) The cells that eventually form the organ systems of the infant start development during the
_____ phase.

    A) zygotic   B) menarche   C) infancy   D) fetal   E) embryonic

Answer: E
Diff: 2   Page Ref: 367
Topic: What Capabilities Does the Child Possess?
Skill: Factual

14) The embryo develops in three layers, the outermost layer will eventually be the _____, the middle layer will become the _____, and the inner layer will become the _____.

   A) muscles, bones and internal organs
      nervous system and skin
      digestive system, lungs and glands

   B) digestive system, lungs and glands
      nervous system and skin
      muscles, bones and internal organs

   C) nervous system and skin
      digestive system, lungs and glands
      muscles, bones and internal organs

   D) nervous system and skin
      muscles, bones and internal organs
      digestive system, lungs and glands

   E) digestive system, lungs and glands
      muscles, bones and internal organs
      nervous system and skin

Answer: D
Diff: 3   Page Ref: 367
Topic: What Capabilities Does the Child Possess?
Skill: Recall

15) A heartbeat generally appears at about _____.

   A) 6 months   B) 3 weeks   C) 9 weeks   D) 12 weeks   E) 16 weeks

Answer: B
Diff: 2   Page Ref: 367
Topic: What Capabilities Does the Child Possess?
Skill: Recall

16) Among the most common teratogens are

   A) clay and pebbles.
   B) morphemes and phonemes.
   C) caffeine and glucose.
   D) LSD and thalidomide.
   E) nicotine and alcohol.

Answer: E
Diff: 2   Page Ref: 367
Topic: What Capabilities Does the Child Possess?
Skill: Factual

17) Substances from the environment including viruses, drugs and other chemicals that can damage the developing organism during the prenatal period.

    A) placenta

    B) morphemes

    C) teratogens

    D) irreversibility

    E) accommodation

Answer: C

Diff: 1   Page Ref: 367

Topic: What Capabilities Does the Child Possess?

Skill: Factual

18) Which of the following is TRUE about sensory development in infants?

    A) Infants do not respond to the smell of rotten eggs.

    B) Infants show signs of pleasure at the taste of sugar water.

    C) Infants prefer unsalted to salted cereal.

    D) Infants cannot move their eyes for several days after birth.

    E) Infants are more strongly attracted to male than female faces.

Answer: B

Diff: 2   Page Ref: 367–368

Topic: What Capabilities Does the Child Possess?

Skill: Conceptual

19) Which of the following is TRUE of infant vision?

    A) Infants can see at 20 feet what most people can see at 50 feet.

    B) At one week, a child can detect the contours of a head at a close distance.

    C) Infants prefer human faces to most other stimuli.

    D) Babies typically can distinguish color at about three weeks.

    E) At birth, a baby can scan the features of a caregiver's face.

Answer: C

Diff: 2   Page Ref: 368

Topic: What Capabilities Does the Child Possess?

Skill: Conceptual

20) Which of the following is NOT a reflexive or sensory capacity that would be present in a newborn?

   A) choosing between different colors

   B) clinging to a caregiver

   C) responding to stimulation

   D) discriminating between "good" and "bad" odors

   E) distinguishing between tastes with differing amounts of sweetness

Answer: A
Diff: 2   Page Ref: 369
Topic: What Capabilities Does the Child Possess?
Skill: Applied

21) Synaptic pruning refers to

   A) the axons of a neural network shortening up in order for the communication to take place more quickly.

   B) uncommitted neurons are returned to an uncommitted state awaiting a role in future development.

   C) destroying some neural networks to ensure that those that are working are as efficient as possible.

   D) neural tissue expanding rapidly.

   E) neural networks building themselves rapidly in infancy.

Answer: B
Diff: 3   Page Ref: 369
Topic: What Capabilities Does the Child Possess?
Skill: Conceptual

22) Britney is a young infant who takes part in a conditioning study. Dr. Gibbs plays music by the Beatles and then provides Britney with brief access to sugar water (from a nipple). Eventually we could expect that

   A) Britney will stop drinking the sugar water.

   B) drinking the sugar water will cause Britney to desire more music by the Beatles.

   C) the music of the Beatles will cause Britney to get excited.

   D) Britney will only enjoy the sugar water when the Beatles music is playing.

   E) Britney would turn her head in the direction the sugar water came from when she hears the Beatles music.

Answer: E
Diff: 3   Page Ref: 370
Topic: What Capabilities Does the Child Possess?
Skill: Applied

23) The intense, enduring, social–emotional relationship that develops between a child and a caretaker is termed

    A) imprinting.

    B) intimacy.

    C) attachment.

    D) menarche.

    E) temperament.

Answer: C

Diff: 1   Page Ref: 370

Topic: What Capabilities Does the Child Possess?

Skill: Factual

24) The innate predisposition of some species to form attachment to a figure observed at birth is termed

    A) menarche.

    B) imprinting.

    C) assimilation.

    D) centration.

    E) discontinuity.

Answer: B

Diff: 2   Page Ref: 370

Topic: What Capabilities Does the Child Possess?

Skill: Factual

25) In the Looney Toons cartoon, when the little Chick follows Fog Horn Leg Horn around and believes that he is the chicks mother, _____ could be said to have taken place.

    A) assimilation

    B) accommodation

    C) imprinting

    D) attachment

    E) centration

Answer: C

Diff: 2   Page Ref: 370–371

Topic: What Capabilities Does the Child Possess?

Skill: Applied

26) Three-month-old Brianna would be expected to have the lowest skin temperature when she is
   A) left in a room with her mother.
   B) left alone with a stranger.
   C) completely alone.
   D) in a room with her mother and a stranger.
   E) None of the above are correct

Answer: B
Diff: 3   *Page Ref: 371*
Topic: What Capabilities Does the Child Possess?
Skill: Applied

27) According to Ainsworth, an anxious-ambivalent child would be expected to
   A) have difficulties with mastering languages.
   B) lack confidence about his/her athletic ability.
   C) make wise moral decisions.
   D) be confident that s/he can cry out for help if needed.
   E) cry with fear and anger when his/her mother leaves.

Answer: E
Diff: 2   *Page Ref: 371*
Topic: What Capabilities Does the Child Possess?
Skill: Applied

28) Which of the following explains why avoidant children act unconcerned when separated from their mother in a strange situation?
   A) They no longer seek attachment because their efforts have met with rejection in the past.
   B) They are so securely attached that they feel confident in strange situations.
   C) They are so smothered by maternal attention that they are grateful for a break.
   D) They are of a personality type that does not crave attachment.
   E) They really want their mothers to be there, but they cannot communicate this.

Answer: A
Diff: 3   *Page Ref: 371*
Topic: What Capabilities Does the Child Possess?
Skill: Conceptual

29) As adults, 'secure' individuals tend to

    A) be able to form strong relationships with other individuals.

    B) value relationships as much as they value work.

    C) admit that they are jealous of others.

    D) expect that relationships will fail.

    E) claim that the end of a relationship does not bother them.

Answer: A

Diff: 2   *Page Ref: 371*

Topic: What Capabilities Does the Child Possess?

Skill: Conceptual

30) _____ is the idea that we form attachments to those who provide reassurance through physical touch, as opposed to feeding us.

    A) Proximity

    B) Generativity

    C) Contact comfort

    D) Imprinting

    E) Identity

Answer: C

Diff: 2   *Page Ref: 372*

Topic: What Capabilities Does the Child Possess?

Skill: Factual

31) The Harlow's challenged the idea that infants form a strong bond with their mother because

    A) she provides as sense of security.

    B) she provides physical comfort for the child.

    C) she provides needed nourishment in the form on breast milk.

    D) her voice is generally higher and more appealing than the voice of males.

    E) they generally have children who have a secure attachment.

Answer: C

Diff: 2   *Page Ref: 372*

Topic: What Capabilities Does the Child Possess?

Skill: Conceptual

32) Physical neglect in young children has been shown to cause

    A) psychosocial dwarfism.

    B) failure to thrive.

    C) emotional detachment.

    D) slow growth and bone development.

    E) All of the above

Answer: E

Diff: 2   *Page Ref: 373*

Topic: What Capabilities Does the Child Possess?

Skill: Recall

33) _____ is the term for the predictable process of growth that is typical of all species members reared in adequate environments.

    A) Maturation

    B) Habituation

    C) Dishabituation

    D) Temperament

    E) Differentiation

Answer: A

Diff: 2   *Page Ref: 373*

Topic: What Capabilities Does the Child Possess?

Skill: Factual

34) If Kaia is a normal six-month-old, we would expect her to be able to

    A) smile at a mirror image.

    B) ring a bell purposively.

    C) show some early stepping motions.

    D) sit alone steadily.

    E) vocalize at least ten different syllables.

Answer: A

Diff: 3   *Page Ref: 374*

Topic: What Capabilities Does the Child Possess?

Skill: Applied

35) _____ is the increase in the length of an infants' body, which occurs in discontinuous bursts.

A) Dishabituation

B) Habituation

C) Maturation

D) Saltation

E) Menarche

Answer: D

Diff: 3   Page Ref: 143

Topic: What Capabilities Does the Child Possess?

Skill: Factual

36) Children typically begin to walk alone at about

A) 6 months.

B) 9 months.

C) 12 months.

D) 18 months.

E) 24 months.

Answer: C

Diff: 2   Page Ref: 374

Topic: What Capabilities Does the Child Possess?

Skill: Factual

37) The survival functions that are evident in a neonate are

A) synchronicity and homeostasis.

B) saltation and dishabituation.

C) maturation and habituation.

D) finding sustenance and maintaining contact.

E) A and C are correct.

Answer: D

Diff: 2   Page Ref: 375

Topic: What Capabilities Does the Child Possess?

Skill: Factual

38) Often developmental psychologists believe that children display saltation as the grow, this means

    A) they grow in "leaps".

    B) they grow continuously.

    C) they grow discontinuously.

    D) they grow steadily at first and then plateau off after about two–years.

    E) None of the above

Answer: A
Diff: 2   Page Ref: 375
Topic: What Capabilities Does the Child Possess?
Skill: Factual

39) A two month old infant would be able to

    A) recognize its mother.

    B) smile socially.

    C) turn from back to side.

    D) lift its head and hold it erect and steady.

    E) become quiet when picked up by the caretaker.

Answer: C
Diff: 2   Page Ref: 375
Topic: Does Your Child Measure Up?
Skill: Factual

40) Cognitive development refers to the study of the changing processes

    A) for thinking, perceiving, and remembering.

    B) of the human body.

    C) of a person's behaviors.

    D) of the family unit.

    E) of our culture.

Answer: A
Diff: 1   Page Ref: 376
Topic: What are the Developmental Tasks of Infancy and Childhood?
Skill: Conceptual

41) _____ was a cognitive theorist who began his investigations by carefully observing his own three children.

A) Skinner

B) Piaget

C) Kübler–Ross

D) Bowlby

E) Freud

Answer: B

Diff: 2   Page Ref: 376

Topic: What are the Developmental Tasks of Infancy and Childhood?

Skill: Factual

42) Piaget used the term _____ to refer to the mental structures that guide thoughts.

A) operations   B) phonemes   C) strategies   D) schemas   E) imprints

Answer: D

Diff: 2   Page Ref: 377

Topic: What are the Developmental Tasks of Infancy and Childhood?

Skill: Factual

43) Because Michelle has an idea that when she sees a dog it will eventually bark and perhaps chase a cat, Piaget would say that Michelle has

A) imprinted the idea of a dog.

B) learned to assimilate a dog to a cat.

C) learned dogs operations.

D) failed to develop overregularization.

E) a schema for dogs.

Answer: E

Diff: 2   Page Ref: 377

Topic: What are the Developmental Tasks of Infancy and Childhood?

Skill: Applied

44) Assimilation is said to occur when a child

A) believes that object exists even if it can't be seen at that moment.

B) add increasingly more symbolic representations of outer reality.

C) update or change existing schemes as a result of new information.

D) modify new information to fit into what is already known.

E) forget information that has not been accessed recently.

Answer: D

Diff: 2   Page Ref: 377

Topic: What are the Developmental Tasks of Infancy and Childhood?

Skill: Conceptual

45) Joey is watching a horse race, he knows that his dog at home has four legs, a tail and fur. When he sees the horses in the race, they also have four legs, fur and a tail so e shouts out, 'Doggies'. Joey is demonstrating

   A) accommodation.

   B) assimilation.

   C) conservation.

   D) irreversibility.

   E) an algorithm.

Answer: B
Diff: 2   Page Ref: 377
Topic: What are the Developmental Tasks of Infancy and Childhood?
Skill: Applied

46) Accommodation is said to occur when a child

   A) believes that object exists even if it can't be seen at that moment.

   B) add increasingly more symbolic representations of outer reality.

   C) update or change existing schemes as a result of new information.

   D) modify new information to fit into what is already known.

   E) forget information that has not been accessed recently.

Answer: C
Diff: 2   Page Ref: 367
Topic: What are the Developmental Tasks of Infancy and Childhood?
Skill: Conceptual

47) Susan has been taken to the ocean for the first time. initially upon seeing to ocean, she declares 'pool', eventually she is able to understand that these are not the same, and she can distinguish between a pool and the ocean. After this insight occurs, Susan could be said to have demonstrated

   A) assimilation.

   B) reversibility.

   C) centration.

   D) accommodation.

   E) conservation.

Answer: D
Diff: 2   Page Ref: 367
Topic: What are the Developmental Tasks of Infancy and Childhood?
Skill: Applied

48) In the process of _____ new information fits our earlier scheme whereas in _____, our scheme changes to fit new information.

   A) assimilation; accommodation

   B) assimilation; homeostasis

   C) centration; differentiation

   D) reversibility; centration

   E) differentiation; centration

   Answer: A
   Diff: 2   Page Ref: 367
   Topic: What are the Developmental Tasks of Infancy and Childhood?
   Skill: Applied

49) The correct sequence of Piaget's stages of cognitive development are

   A) preoperational; sensorimotor; concrete operational; formal operational.

   B) preoperational; concrete operational; sensorimotor; formal operational.

   C) sensorimotor; preoperational; concrete operational; formal operational.

   D) sensorimotor; preoperational; concrete operational; postoperational.

   E) sensorimotor; preconventional; conventional; postconventional.

   Answer: C
   Diff: 2   Page Ref: 378-379
   Topic: What are the Developmental Tasks of Infancy and Childhood?
   Skill: Conceptual

50) Which of the following is an example of sensorimotor intelligence?

   A) the ability to think abstractly

   B) the inability to take another's perspective

   C) clinging, crying, and smiling

   D) the ability to represent objects mentally that are not physically present

   E) abstract problem-solving and logical decision-making

   Answer: C
   Diff: 2   Page Ref: 378
   Topic: What are the Developmental Tasks of Infancy and Childhood?
   Skill: Conceptual

51) Johnny is playing in his crib, his beloved teddy bear, Mr. Peeps falls under the crib and Johnny cries knowing that Mr. Peeps exists somewhere. Johnny is demonstrating

   A) centration.

   B) object permanence.

   C) reversibility.

   D) conservation.

   E) egocentrism.

   Answer: B
   Diff: 2   Page Ref: 378
   Topic: What are the Developmental Tasks of Infancy and Childhood?
   Skill: Applied

52) _____ is a term used by Piaget to refer to a child who is unable to take another's perspective and who sees the world only in terms of themselves.

   A) Egocentrism

   B) Conservation

   C) Abstract thinking

   D) Centration

   E) Imprinting

   Answer: A
   Diff: 2   Page Ref: 378
   Topic: What are the Developmental Tasks of Infancy and Childhood?
   Skill: Applied

53) Piaget would use the concept of _____ to explain why a child would state that "my G.I. Joe is hungry."

   A) centration

   B) animistic thinking

   C) assimilation

   D) accommodation

   E) egocentrism

   Answer: B
   Diff: 3   Page Ref: 379
   Topic: What are the Developmental Tasks of Infancy and Childhood?
   Skill: Applied

54) Donna is so focused on the idea of having a "big bowl" of ice cream, that she refuses to eat ice cream off a plate, even though the plate has more ice cream. Her refusal is an example of

    A) egocentrism.

    B) conservation.

    C) animistic thinking.

    D) centration.

    E) object permanence.

Answer: D

Diff: 3   Page Ref: 379

Topic: What are the Developmental Tasks of Infancy and Childhood?

Skill: Applied

55) Three year old Teddy understands that he has an aunt and a grandmother. he cannot understand however that his cousins share the same grandmother. His inability to see things from another person's perspective demonstrates

    A) reversibility.

    B) irreversibility.

    C) that he does not yet have conservation.

    D) that he does not yet have object permanence.

    E) centration.

Answer: B

Diff: 2   Page Ref: 379

Topic: What are the Developmental Tasks of Infancy and Childhood?

Skill: Applied

56) John is babysitting for the twins Chandler and Joey (they are 4 years old). When John makes them a sandwich he cuts Joey's in half and leaves Chandlers whole. Chandler becomes upset because he only has one and Joey has two, he does not realize that the total size of the sandwich is the same. Chandler has not yet demonstrated the concept of

    A) conservation.

    B) egocentrism.

    C) object permanence.

    D) animism.

    E) reversibility.

Answer: A

Diff: 3   Page Ref: 379

Topic: What are the Developmental Tasks of Infancy and Childhood?

Skill: Applied

57) Which of the following is an example of animistic thought?

   A) An object ceases to exist when hidden from sight.

   B) A child is unwilling to share their toys.

   C) A child sucks on an nipple.

   D) A child chooses a tall thin glass of milk over a short squat glass of milk.

   E) After witnessing a traffic accident, a child refers to a damaged fender as an "Owie".

Answer: E
Diff: 2   Page Ref: 379
Topic: What are the Developmental Tasks of Infancy and Childhood?
Skill: Applied

58) During Piaget's formal operational stage, thinking becomes

   A) egocentric.

   B) animistic.

   C) abstract.

   D) habituated.

   E) impulsive.

Answer: C
Diff: 1   Page Ref: 380
Topic: What are the Developmental Tasks of Infancy and Childhood?
Skill: Conceptual

59) Which of Piaget's stages is associated with adolescence?

   A) fensorimotor stage

   B) formal operational stage

   C) preoperational stage

   D) concrete operational stage

   E) postconventional stage

Answer: B
Diff: 1   Page Ref: 380
Topic: What are the Developmental Tasks of Infancy and Childhood?
Skill: Factual

60) An individual who is able to understand the concepts of philosophy and calculus would be found in which of Piaget's stages of Cognitive Development?

    A) Concrete Operational

    B) Formal Operational

    C) Sensorimotor

    D) Post-Conventional

    E) Conventional

Answer: B

Diff: 2   Page Ref: 380

Topic: What are the Developmental Tasks of Infancy and Childhood?

Skill: Conceptual

61) All of the following are critiques regarding Piaget's theory except

    A) children are often found to move through the stages more rapidly than Piaget proposed.

    B) it is flexible enough to adapt to new research.

    C) researchers believe that children do not develop in discontinuous stages.

    D) children often can understand concepts before they can express those same concepts.

    E) children can understand emotional responses that are not always consistent with their outside expressions.

Answer: B

Diff: 3   Page Ref: 380

Topic: What are the Developmental Tasks of Infancy and Childhood?

Skill: Conceptual

62) The gradual "wave metaphor" for psychological development was proposed by

    A) Siegler.   B) Piaget.   C) Kohlberg.   D) Kagan.   E) Erikson.

Answer: A

Diff: 3   Page Ref: 381

Topic: What are the Developmental Tasks of Infancy and Childhood?

Skill: Factual

63) In order to establish successful social interactions and relationships it is important that a child

    A) master conservation.

    B) develop postconventional morality.

    C) master centration.

    D) develop a theory of mind.

    E) A and C are correct.

Answer: D

Diff: 2   Page Ref: 381

Topic: What are the Developmental Tasks of Infancy and Childhood?

Skill: Conceptual

64) _____ is defined as a person's usual way of responding to the world.

    A) Attachment

    B) Integrity

    C) Contact comfort

    D) Generativity

    E) Temperament

Answer: E
Diff: 2   *Page Ref: 382*
Topic: What are the Developmental Tasks of Infancy and Childhood?
Skill: Conceptual

65) The zone of proximal development explains

    A) the personal space zone that children quickly develop.

    B) the difference between what a child can do with help and what the child can do without help or guidance.

    C) the gaining of centration in cognitive development.

    D) the different types of parenting styles.

    E) why children develop different temperaments.

Answer: B
Diff: 2   *Page Ref: 382*
Topic: What are the Developmental Tasks of Infancy and Childhood?
Skill: Conceptual

66) Research on parenting styles suggest that authoritative parents produce children that are

    A) confident and self-reliant.

    B) prone to become delinquents.

    C) less mature.

    D) more impulsive.

    E) more dependent and needy.

Answer: A
Diff: 2   *Page Ref: 382*
Topic: What are the Developmental Tasks of Infancy and Childhood?
Skill: Factual

67) Authoritative parents tend to be

    A) easy going and allows the child to make make decisions before the child is ready.

    B) make reasonable demands of their children ad include them in decision making tasks.

    C) highly demanding of their children and often criticize them.

    D) indifferent to the child's point of view.

    E) completely uninvolved in their children's lives.

Answer: C
Diff: 2   *Page Ref: 383*
Topic: What are the Developmental Tasks of Infancy and Childhood?
Skill: Factual

68) Eddies parents often include him in decisions such as when to set his curfew and what types of chores he will do around the house. Once a decision is collectively made the rules are enforced and he is expected to carry through o the agreement. It seems as if Eddie's parents are using a _____ parenting style.

    A) authoritative

    B) permissive

    C) uninvolved

    D) rejecting–neglecting

    E) authoritarian

Answer: E
Diff: 2   *Page Ref: 383*
Topic: What are the Developmental Tasks of Infancy and Childhood?
Skill: Applied

69) Research suggests that daycare is

    A) is always good for children.

    B) if the children are well cared for, it is developmentally enriching.

    C) always bad for children.

    D) more often bad than good.

    E) None of the above

Answer: B
Diff: 2   *Page Ref: 383*
Topic: What are the Developmental Tasks of Infancy and Childhood?
Skill: Analysis

70) Boys when playing together tend to

    A) work cooperatively with one another.

    B) create a "pecking" order.

    C) tend to share more than girls.

    D) play more aggressively than girls.

    E) B and D are correct.

Answer: E
Diff: 2   Page Ref: 385
Topic: What are the Developmental Tasks of Infancy and Childhood?
Skill: Conceptual

71) The first stage of Erikson's psychosocial theory involves an infant's need to

    A) develop a basic sense of trust in the environment.

    B) explore and manipulate objects.

    C) initiate intellectual and motor tasks.

    D) experience a comfortable sense of autonomy.

    E) receive enough food necessary for survival.

Answer: A
Diff: 2   Page Ref: 385
Topic: Childhood Influences on Your Personality
Skill: Conceptual

72) When baby Stephanie starts crying, her mother or father hurries to see if she needs and anything and they comfort her when she is upset. According to Erik Erikson Stephanie is likely to develop

    A) competence.

    B) trust.

    C) inferiority.

    D) mistrust.

    E) autonomy.

Answer: B
Diff: 2   Page Ref: 386
Topic: What are the Developmental Tasks of Infancy and Childhood?
Skill: Applied

73) A four-year-old child who insists on choosing and putting on her clothes without any assistance from her mother would be classified by Erikson as being in the _____ stage.

   A) concrete operational

   B) trust vs. mistrust

   C) initiative vs. guilt

   D) intimacy vs. isolation

   E) competence vs. inferiority

   Answer: C
   Diff: 2   Page Ref: 386
   Topic: Childhood Influences on Your Personality
   Skill: Applied

74) Inadequate resolution of the _____ stage would results in a lack of self-confidence and a feeling of failure.

   A) competence vs. inferiority

   B) autonomy vs. self-doubt

   C) trust vs. mistrust

   D) identity vs. role confusion

   E) generativity vs. stagnation

   Answer: A
   Diff: 2   Page Ref: 387
   Topic: Childhood Influences on Your Personality
   Skill: Factual

75) Erikson would explain a child's interest in achieving goals on the sporting field or in the classroom as being due to

   A) a reinforcement of stereotypes.

   B) a way to channel nervous energy.

   C) the need to feel a sense of competence.

   D) a rebellion against authority figures.

   E) a way to establish trust with teammates.

   Answer: C
   Diff: 2   Page Ref: 387
   Topic: Childhood Influences on Your Personality
   Skill: Applied

76) An important criticism of Erikson's developmental theory involves
    A) focusing on one narrow aspect of the life cycle.
    B) failing to capture female development as well as it does male development.
    C) having an overly rigid scientific basis.
    D) ignoring findings derived from clinical observation.
    E) failing to give children enough credit for all the things they could do.

Answer: B
Diff: 3   Page Ref: 387
Topic: Childhood Influences on Your Personality
Skill: Conceptual

77) Psychologists argue that _____ is the first concrete indicator of the end of childhood.
    A) the development of an integrated identity
    B) attachment
    C) puberty
    D) the pubescent growth spurt
    E) graduating from elementary school

Answer: C
Diff: 1   Page Ref: 388
Topic: What Changes Mark the Transition to Adolescence?
Skill: Factual

78) Which of the following is true of adolescence?
    A) Adolescents are preoccupied with body image.
    B) Friendships among girls are based on emotional closeness.
    C) Adolescents spend more time with peers than with adults.
    D) Surges in testosterone contribute to sexual awakening in boys.
    E) All of the above are correct.

Answer: E
Diff: 2   Page Ref: 388–390
Topic: What Changes Mark the Transition to Adolescence?
Skill: Factual

79) During Piaget's Formal operational Stage, which of the following is likely to develop?

   A) reversibility

   B) centration

   C) abstract thought

   D) conservation

   E) object permanence

   Answer: C
   Diff: 2   Page Ref: 389
   Topic: What Changes Mark the Transition to Adolescence?
   Skill: Conceptual

80) During adolescence, girls often get together 'just to talk" while boys get together and focus on

   A) supporting each other emotionally.

   B) emphasizing activities such as sports.

   C) engaging in cooperative activities.

   D) building emotional closeness with one another.

   E) getting together to study.

   Answer: B
   Diff: 2   Page Ref: 390
   Topic: What Changes Mark the Transition to Adolescence?
   Skill: Recall

81) Most adolescents feel

   A) close to their parents.

   B) at odds with their parents.

   C) ambivalent about their parents.

   D) estranged from their parents.

   E) afraid of their parents.

   Answer: A
   Diff: 2   Page Ref: 391
   Topic: What Changes Mark the Transition to Adolescence?
   Skill: Factual

82) Homosexual feelings are difficult to resolve during adolescence because
    A) adolescence is a time when individuals are especially concerned with social norms.
    B) only half of all young people have engaged in sexual intercourse by the age of 17.
    C) the challenges presented by the physical changes of puberty obscure the question of sexual identity.
    D) society offers little support for a homosexual orientation.
    E) A and D are correct.

Answer: E
Diff: 3   Page Ref: 392
Topic: What Changes Mark the Transition to Adolescence?
Skill: Conceptual

83) Recent research regarding sexual behavior in adolescence reveals that
    A) more teenagers are having sex now than ever before.
    B) about 75% of teenagers have engaged in intercourse by the time they are 17.
    C) about 25% of teenagers have engaged in intercourse by the time they are 17.
    D) during the 1990s there was about a 10% drop in teenagers reporting being sexually active.
    E) about 95% of all teenagers have engaged in intercourse by the tie they are 20 years old.

Answer: D
Diff: 2   Page Ref: 392
Topic: What Changes Mark the Transition to Adolescence?
Skill: Factual

84) A child who refuses to steal candy because of a fear of being caught is most likely demonstrating
    A) postconventional morality.
    B) centration.
    C) formal operational thought.
    D) animistic thinking.
    E) preconventional morality.

Answer: E
Diff: 3   Page Ref: 393–394
Topic: The Development of Moral Thinking
Skill: Applied

85) Kohlberg suggests that the highest stage of moral reasoning is evident when an individual acts in order to

    A) gain acceptance and avoid disapproval from others.

    B) follow rules and avoid penalties.

    C) support universal principles of conscience.

    D) promote the welfare of her society.

    E) achieve rewards and avoid punishments.

Answer: C
Diff: 3   Page Ref: 393–394
Topic: The Development of Moral Thinking
Skill: Conceptual

86) _____ argued that individuals of all cultures go through the same stages of moral development in the same order.

    A) Harlow

    B) Piaget

    C) Erikson

    D) Kohlberg

    E) Kubler-Ross

Answer: D
Diff: 2   Page Ref: 393
Topic: The Development of Moral Thinking
Skill: Factual

87) Which of the following is a serious flaw in Kohlberg's theory of moral development?

    A) The lower stages have not been found in all cultures.

    B) Moral reasoning does not predict actual behavior.

    C) The higher stages are not associated with education.

    D) The stages as a whole do not parallel Piaget's stages.

    E) All cultures attain the stages in the same order.

Answer: B
Diff: 3   Page Ref: 394
Topic: The Development of Moral Thinking
Skill: Conceptual

88) _____ argued that women base moral decisions on social relationships and personal caring.

    A) Gilligan   B) Chomsky   C) Piaget   D) Erikson   E) Harlow

Answer: A
Diff: 2   Page Ref: 395
Topic: The Development of Moral Thinking
Skill: Factual

89) Gilligan is critical od Kohlberg's theory of moral development because

    A) it does not address morality from cultures other than the U.S.

    B) it does not take into account individual differences in moral decision making.

    C) it does not consider how women have been socialized to make moral decisions differently than men.

    D) it does not account for the differences in our decision making ability and what we will actually DO in a similar situation.

    E) All of the above

Answer: C
Diff: 3   *Page Ref: 395*
Topic: What Changes Mark the Transition to Adolescence?
Skill: Conceptual

90) Freud believed that adult development is driven primarily by

    A) love and belonging.

    B) intimacy and generativity.

    C) generativity and stagnation.

    D) love and work.

    E) unconscious and sex.

Answer: D
Diff: 3   *Page Ref: 396*
Topic: What Developmental Challenges do Adults Face?
Skill: Conceptual

91) Intimacy was defined as Kohlberg as the

    A) exploration of one's integrated identity.

    B) prerequisite to attaining an identity.

    C) ability to reproduce.

    D) capacity to make a full commitment to another person.

    E) desire to be sexually active.

Answer: D
Diff: 2   *Page Ref: 396*
Topic: What Developmental Challenges do Adults Face?
Skill: Factual

92) For Erikson, _____ is the final stage to resolve in life.

    A) ego integrity vs. despair

    B) generativity vs. stagnation

    C) intimacy vs. isolation

    D) trust vs. mistrust

    E) living vs. dying

Answer: A

Diff: 2   *Page Ref: 397*

Topic: What Developmental Challenges do Adults Face?

Skill: Factual

93) Modern marriages have changed in that the

    A) the women has primary responsibility for child care.

    B) the women takes care of the majority of household chores.

    C) man is the primary bread winner.

    D) there is more of a partnership in terms of sharing responsibilities.

    E) there are fewer double-income families.

Answer: D

Diff: 2   *Page Ref: 397*

Topic: The Last Developmental Challenges You Will Face

Skill: Conceptual

94) Erikson believed that you cannot move into the period of generativity until you have

    A) a stable marriage.

    B) reached the age of 50.

    C) achieved worldly-wise, adult cognitive style.

    D) faced and accepted your own mortality.

    E) successfully met the challenges of identity and intimacy.

Answer: E

Diff: 2   *Page Ref: 397*

Topic: What Developmental Challenges do Adults Face?

Skill: Conceptual

95) How is the population of the United States changing?

A) The population as a whole is growing older.

B) There are more families deciding to have children.

C) There is a higher percentage of people under the age of 17 than ever before.

D) new illnesses such as AIDS and viruses are killing off more of the population each year.

E) Families are having more children than ever before.

Answer: A

Diff: 2   Page Ref: 398

Topic: The Last Developmental Challenges You Will Face

Skill: Factual

96) The despair of a person who is in Erikson's final psychosocial crisis is most likely caused by

A) their fear of dying.

B) their decrease in mental ability and physical stamina.

C) their incomplete resolution of earlier developmental crises.

D) societal discrimination against the elderly.

E) lack of social support from friends and family members.

Answer: C

Diff: 3   Page Ref: 399

Topic: The Last Developmental Challenges You Will Face

Skill: Conceptual

97) As we age, we tend to

A) show gains in wisdom.

B) have difficulty with conserving energy.

C) acquire new information more quickly.

D) lose our expert skills.

E) have difficulty with controlling our emotions.

Answer: A

Diff: 2   Page Ref: 400

Topic: What Developmental Challenges do Adults Face?

Skill: Factual

98) Some of the physical signs of growing old are

    A) reduced thinking and problem solving ability.

    B) reduced memory.

    C) reduced hearing and vision.

    D) increased knowledge for facts.

    E) likelihood of developing Alzheimer's disease.

Answer: C
Diff: 2   Page Ref: 400
Topic: The Last Developmental Challenges You Will Face
Skill: Conceptual

99) Older adults seem to engage in selective social interaction which means.

    A) they are likely to become more dependent on a large group of friends.

    B) they will remain in contact with individuals they have known their entire life.

    C) they will actively try and find more friends with whom to spend their spare time.

    D) they will maintain only the most rewarding of social contacts.

    E) they will have very little social interaction with anyone.

Answer: D
Diff: 1   Page Ref: 401
Topic: The Last Developmental Challenges You Will Face
Skill: Factual

100) The individual who created the five stages all terminally ill patients go through is

    A) Freud.

    B) Piaget.

    C) Kubler–Ross.

    D) Gilligan.

    E) Kohlberg.

Answer: C
Diff: 3   Page Ref: 402
Topic: The Last Developmental Challenges You Will Face
Skill: Factual

101) According to Elizabeth Kubler-Ross, what is the stage in which you try to get more time to live. Bob wants to live at least long enough to attend his daughter's wedding.

A) bargaining

B) acceptance

C) denial

D) depression

E) anger

Answer: A

Diff: 3   Page Ref: 402

Topic: The Last Developmental Challenges You Will Face

Skill: Conceptual

Check Your Understanding Questions

1) Psychologists have resolved the nature–nurture controversy by saying that we are the products of

A) heredity.

B) environment.

C) both heredity and environment.

D) neither heredity nor environment.

E) all of our experiences.

Answer: C

Diff: 3   Page Ref: 366

Topic: Check Your Understanding

Skill: Recall

2) Which of the following statements is most accurate with regard to the "Jim twins"?

A) We cannot say for certain that their similarities are mainly genetic.

B) It is reasonably certain that their similarities come from shared early experiences.

C) It has been proven that their similarities are due to chance.

D) They are similar because they were raised in the same family environment.

E) They are no more similar than other siblings.

Answer: A

Diff: 2   Page Ref: 366

Topic: Check Your Understanding

Skill: Applied

3) Which perspective says that developmental change is a gradual process?

  A) the continuity view

  B) the discontinuity view

  C) the hereditarian view

  D) the environmental view

  E) the longitudinal view

Answer: A
Diff: 2   Page Ref: 366
Topic: Check Your Understanding
Skill: Recall

4) Which one of the following best exemplifies a developmental stage that results from an interaction of heredity and environment?

  A) the appearance of facial hair in a teenaged boy

  B) eye color

  C) a child learning to talk

  D) meeting the person of your dreams in adolescence

  E) hair color

Answer: C
Diff: 2   Page Ref: 366
Topic: Check Your Understanding
Skill: Understanding the Core Concept

5) Which of the following does not appear before birth?

  A) the heartbeat

  B) movement of limbs

  C) growth and migration of neurons

  D) vocalization

  E) all appear before birth

Answer: D
Diff: 2   Page Ref: 375
Topic: Check Your Understanding
Skill: Recall

6) After birth, brain development emphasizes the

   A) migration of neurons.

   B) development of connections among neurons.

   C) development of the brain stem.

   D) multiplication of neurons.

   E) function of individuals neurons.

Answer: B
Diff: 2   Page Ref: 375
Topic: Check Your Understanding
Skill: Recall

7) You are a psychologist working in a pediatric hospital. What would you recommend as one of the most important things that the staff could do for newborn babies to promote their healthy development?

   A) talk to them

   B) touch them

   C) make eye contact with them

   D) feed them on demand

   E) introduce them to children of their own age

Answer: B
Diff: 2   Page Ref: 376
Topic: Check Your Understanding
Skill: Applied

8) You would expect your newborn baby to

   A) quickly learn to recognize the sound of his or her name.

   B) react negatively to the taste of lemon.

   C) prefer the father's deeper voice to the mother's higher voice.

   D) smile when eating.

   E) mimic facial expressions.

Answer: B
Diff: 2   Page Ref: 376
Topic: Check Your Understanding
Skill: Applied

9) Mary Ainsworth's found two main types of attachment,

    A) shy and bold.

    B) introverted and extroverted.

    C) secure and insecure.

    D) strong and weak.

    E) nature and nurture.

Answer: C
Diff: 2   Page Ref: 376
Topic: Check Your Understanding
Skill: Recall

10) Which one of the following is an innate ability that promotes survival?

    A) the grasping reflex

    B) recognition of the mother's face

    C) toilet training

    D) sharp vision

    E) the stepping reflex

Answer: A
Diff: 2   Page Ref: 376
Topic: Check Your Understanding
Skill: Understanding the Core Concept

11) Ivan is now able to recognize that his brothers also have a brother and it is Ivan. he is demonstrating what Piagetian concept?

    A) centration

    B) reversibility

    C) conservation

    D) object permanence

    E) abstract thinking

Answer: B
Diff: 2   Page Ref: 387
Topic: Check Your Understanding
Skill: Applied

12) Imagine that you are a family counselor. Which parenting style would you encourage parents to adopt in order to encourage their children to become self-confident and reliable?

   A) authoritarian

   B) authoritative

   C) permissive

   D) uninvolved

   E) rejecting–neglecting

Answer: B

Diff: 2   Page Ref: 387

Topic: Check Your Understanding

Skill: Applied

13) A child who likes to explore on their own and begin drawing tasks without the hep of their parents would be said to be in the

   A) trust–vs mistrust stage.

   B) autonomy vs. shame and doubt stage.

   C) competence vs inferiority stage.

   D) identity vs. role confusion.

   E) generativity vs. stagnation.

Answer: C

Diff: 2   Page Ref: 387

Topic: Check Your Understanding

Skill: Conceptual

14) Piaget's formal operational stage is marked by

   A) the ability to think in two dimensions.

   B) the ability to think abstractly.

   C) the ability to accommodate new information into old schemas.

   D) object permanence.

   E) reversibility.

Answer: B

Diff: 2   Page Ref: 387

Topic: Check Your Understanding

Skill: Factual

15) Which one of the following would be considered a secondary sex characteristic?

    A) deepening of the voice in males

    B) production of semen

    C) menarche

    D) maturation of the genitals

    E) ovulation

Answer: A
Diff: 2   *Page Ref: 395*
Topic: Check Your Understanding
Skill: Recall

16) Which one is a stage of life that is not recognized by some cultures?

    A) childhood

    B) adolescence

    C) adulthood

    D) old age

    E) infancy

Answer: B
Diff: 2   *Page Ref: 395*
Topic: Check Your Understanding
Skill: Recall

17) Which one is associated with major challenge of adolescence, according to Erikson?

    A) ego integrity

    B) intimacy

    C) generativity

    D) identity

    E) stagnation

Answer: D
Diff: 2   *Page Ref: 395*
Topic: Check Your Understanding
Skill: Recall

18) Which one of the following groups becomes most influential in the lives of adolescents?

    A) parents   B) teachers   C) peers   D) celebrities   E) children

Answer: C
Diff: 2   *Page Ref: 395*
Topic: Check Your Understanding
Skill: Recall

19) According to Kohlberg, as moral reasoning advances, individuals become less
    A) emotional.
    B) self-centered.
    C) ruled by instinct.
    D) attached to their parents.
    E) questioning.
    Answer: B
    Diff: 2   Page Ref: 395
    Topic: Check Your Understanding
    Skill: Recall

20) Which one of the following is a cognitive change appearing in adolescence that affects one's ability to think more deeply and abstractly about the social pressures of adolescence?
    A) depression
    B) formal operational thought
    C) conservation
    D) assimilation and accommodation
    E) Nature vs. Nurture
    Answer: B
    Diff: 2   Page Ref: 395
    Topic: Check Your Understanding
    Skill: Understanding the Core Concept

21) According to Erikson, a person who successfully faces the issue of intimacy versus isolation will have
    A) a meaningful career.
    B) children.
    C) a thirst for knowledge.
    D) social support.
    E) people to attend to their basic needs.
    Answer: D
    Diff: 2   Page Ref: 402
    Topic: Check Your Understanding
    Skill: Recall

22) According to Erikson, people at mid life most want to

    A) have the freedom and independence to pursue their leisure interests.

    B) spend time with their friends.

    C) develop independence.

    D) maintain or improve their physical appearance.

    E) make a contribution to their career, society, or future generations.

Answer: E
Diff: 2   Page Ref: 402
Topic: Check Your Understanding
Skill: Recall

23) A major demographic shift is now in progress. This change involves

    A) a culture that is increasingly focusing on youth.

    B) an increase in the average age of the population.

    C) the roles of worker and parent becoming more rigidly defined.

    D) fewer women assuming professional roles.

    E) adolescence is occurring later.

Answer: B
Diff: 3   Page Ref: 403
Topic: Check Your Understanding
Skill: Applied

24) Old age eventually means that the person will experience decline in which of the following?

    A) thinking and problem abilities

    B) social support from family

    C) vision and hearing

    D) emotional well being

    E) all cognition.

Answer: C
Diff: 2   Page Ref: 403
Topic: Check Your Understanding
Skill: Understanding the Core Concept

25) Elizabeth Kubler–Ross believed that _____ was the final stage in death and dying.

   A) bargaining

   B) acceptance

   C) denial

   D) depression

   E) anger

   Answer: B
   Diff: 2   Page Ref: 403
   Topic: Check Your Understanding
   Skill: Factual

True/False Questions

   1) The similarities of the "Jim twins" are due solely to their genetic code.

   Answer: FALSE
   Diff: 1   Page Ref: 361
   Topic: Introduction
   Skill: Conceptual

   2) Any individual's personality is made up of 50% nature and 50% nurture.

   Answer: FALSE
   Diff: 1   Page Ref: 362
   Topic: How Do Psychologists Explain Development?
   Skill: Conceptual

   3) Heredity and environment interact to determine behavior.

   Answer: TRUE
   Diff: 1   Page Ref: 363
   Topic: How Do Psychologists Explain Development?
   Skill: Factual

   4) Developmental stages are periods of life initiated by significant transitions or changes in physical or psychological functioning.

   Answer: TRUE
   Diff: 1   Page Ref: 365
   Topic: Psychological Traits in Your Genes
   Skill: Factual

5) According to the discontinuity view, change occurs in bursts.

Answer: TRUE
Diff: 2   Page Ref: 364
Topic: How Do Psychologists Explain Development?
Skill: Factual

6) The order of the stages of prenatal development is zygote, embryo and fetus.

Answer: TRUE
Diff: 2   Page Ref: 367
Topic: What Capabilities Does the Child Possess?
Skill: Factual

7) An expectant mother can usually feel the first movements of her fetus at about 8 weeks after conception.

Answer: FALSE
Diff: 3   Page Ref: 367
Topic: What Capabilities Does the Child Possess?
Skill: Factual

8) Children shortly after birth have 20/20 vision.

Answer: FALSE
Diff: 2   Page Ref: 368
Topic: What Capabilities Does the Child Possess?
Skill: Factual

9) Our brain attains its ultimate mass when we are about 11 years of age.

Answer: TRUE
Diff: 2   Page Ref: 369
Topic: What Capabilities Does the Child Possess?
Skill: Factual

10) The grasping reflex meets a survival need by allowing the infant to cling to the care giver.

Answer: TRUE
Diff: 2   Page Ref: 369
Topic: What Capabilities Does the Child Possess?
Skill: Factual

11) In Harlow's research with isolated monkeys, it was found that contact was less important than food in determining attachment.

Answer: FALSE
Diff: 2   Page Ref: 370-371
Topic: What Capabilities Does the Child Possess?
Skill: Factual

12) Children with a insecure attachment in mary Ainsworth's strange situation experiment responded to their mother's with anxiety or avoidance.

Answer: TRUE
Diff: 2   Page Ref: 371
Topic: What Capabilities Does the Child Possess?
Skill: Conceptual

13) Lack of human contact can affect the time at which a child becomes capable of walking.

Answer: TRUE
Diff: 2   Page Ref: 373
Topic: What Capabilities Does the Child Possess?
Skill: Factual

14) Maturation is the process by which the genetic program manifests itself over time.

Answer: TRUE
Diff: 2   Page Ref: 373
Topic: What Capabilities Does the Child Possess?
Skill: Factual

15) Most children begin to walk at about 6 months old.

Answer: FALSE
Diff: 2   Page Ref: 374
Topic: What Capabilities Does the Child Possess?
Skill: Factual

16) Piaget devised a stage theory of moral development.

Answer: FALSE
Diff: 2   Page Ref: 376-379
Topic: What are the Developmental Tasks of Infancy and Childhood?
Skill: Factual

17) A child who knows that the family dog still exists, even when it leaves the room, has acquired object permanence.

Answer: TRUE
Diff: 2   Page Ref: 376
Topic: What are the Developmental Tasks of Infancy and Childhood?
Skill: Applied

18) Assimilation results from genetic changes, whereas accommodation occurs due to environmental events.

Answer: FALSE
Diff: 2   Page Ref: 377
Topic: What are the Developmental Tasks of Infancy and Childhood?
Skill: Conceptual

19) A child in the sensorimotor stage typically demonstrates egocentrism and animistic thinking.

Answer: FALSE
Diff: 2   Page Ref: 377
Topic: What are the Developmental Tasks of Infancy and Childhood?
Skill: Conceptual

20) A child in the concrete operational stage should be aware that if you change the shape of a given object you have not necessarily changed the mass.

Answer: TRUE
Diff: 2   Page Ref: 378
Topic: What are the Developmental Tasks of Infancy and Childhood?
Skill: Conceptual

21) Temperament is considered to be an innate personality disposition.

Answer: TRUE
Diff: 1   Page Ref: 381
Topic: What are the Developmental Tasks of Infancy and Childhood?
Skill: Conceptual

22) Authoritative parents often have children that are well adjusted and responsible.

Answer: TRUE
Diff: 2   Page Ref: 382
Topic: What are the Developmental Tasks of Infancy and Childhood?
Skill: Factual

23) Boys engage in more aggressive play than do girls.

Answer: FALSE
Diff: 2   Page Ref: 385
Topic: What are the Developmental Tasks of Infancy and Childhood?
Skill: Conceptual

24) Children in the stage of initiative vs. guilt learn to feel comfortable with themselves as a person.

Answer: FALSE
Diff: 2   Page Ref: 386
Topic: What are the Developmental Tasks of Infancy and Childhood?
Skill: Conceptual

25) Those children who develop a sense of competence often engage in activities with their peers and pursue academic abilities on their own.

Answer: TRUE
Diff: 2   Page Ref: 386
Topic: What are the Developmental Tasks of Infancy and Childhood?
Skill: Conceptual

26) The onset of puberty marks the start of childhood.

Answer: FALSE
Diff: 2   Page Ref: 388
Topic: What Changes Mark the Transition to Adolescence?
Skill: Factual

27) Secondary y sex characteristics involve the enlargement of breasts and the development of body hair.

Answer: TRUE
Diff: 1   Page Ref: 388-389
Topic: What Changes Mark the Transition to Adolescence?
Skill: Factual

28) Most teenagers report adolescence to be a time of emotional turmoil and conflict with their parents.

Answer: FALSE
Diff: 2   Page Ref: 390
Topic: What Changes Mark the Transition to Adolescence?
Skill: Conceptual

29) Females report that emotional involvement is an important aspect of sexual attraction.

Answer: TRUE
Diff: 2   Page Ref: 391–391
Topic: What Changes Mark the Transition to Adolescence?
Skill: Factual

30) Lawrence kohlberg's theory of moral development concentrates on whether you decide to do the right thing or the wrong thing, but is not concerned with why you make those decisions.

Answer: FALSE
Diff: 2   Page Ref: 394
Topic: What Changes Mark the Transition to Adolescence?
Skill: Conceptual

31) Lawrence Kohlberg's theory of moral development has been criticized for not addressing the moral development of women or individuals from cultures other than the United States as well as it explains the moral development common in American men.

Answer: TRUE
Diff: 2   Page Ref: 394
Topic: What Changes Mark the Transition to Adolescence?
Skill: Factual

32) Failure to resolve Erikson's intimacy vs. isolation stage leads to the inability to connect to others in meaningful ways.

Answer: TRUE
Diff: 2   Page Ref: 396–397
Topic: What Developmental Challenges do Adults Face?
Skill: Conceptual

33) In Erikson's stage of generativity versus stagnation an individual becomes more concerned with their contributions to the community.

Answer: TRUE
Diff: 2   Page Ref: 397
Topic: What Developmental Challenges do Adults Face?
Skill: Factual

34) The demographics of the US will shift such that by the year 2030, there will be more people who are 60 and older than there are people who are younger than 20.

Answer: TRUE
Diff: 2   Page Ref: 398
Topic: The Last Developmental Challenges You Will Face
Skill: Factual

35) According to Erikson, if individuals in their old age believe that they have led a good worthwhile life, they tend to experience Ego–integrity.

Answer: TRUE
Diff: 3   *Page Ref: 399*
Topic: The Last Developmental Challenges You Will Face
Skill: Factual

36) Older adults will typically see a decline in their vocabulary.

Answer: FALSE
Diff: 2   *Page Ref: 400*
Topic: The Last Developmental Challenges You Will Face
Skill: Factual

37) If one suffers from a terminal illness, and they are trying to live just to have one more christmas with their family they are in the anger stage.

Answer: FALSE
Diff: 2   *Page Ref: 402*
Topic: The Last Developmental Challenges You Will Face
Skill: Applied

Short Answer Questions

1) According to the _____ view, development occurs in abrupt stages.

Answer: discontinuity
Diff: 2   *Page Ref: 132*
Topic: How Do Psychologists Explain Development?
Skill: Conceptual

2) Briefly explain the nature versus nurture debate.

Answer: Nature believes that we are who we are because of our genetic make-up, while nurture proposes that it is because f our environment.
Diff: 2   *Page Ref: 362*
Topic: How Do Psychologists Explain Development?
Skill: Conceptual

3) What are three three stages of prenatal development, and when does each begin and end?

Answer: The zygote from conception to 10 days old, the embryonic stage lasts until 8 weeks old and finally the fetus stage that lasts until birth.
Diff: 2   *Page Ref: 367*
Topic: What Capabilities Does the Child Possess?
Skill: Factual

4) Toxic substances that can harm or damage the fetus are labelled as what?

Answer: teratogens
Diff: 2   *Page Ref: 367*
Topic: What Capabilities Does the Child Possess?
Skill: Factual

5) Briefly explain synaptic pruning.

Answer: Synaptic pruning involves unused neural connections being stored for later use rather than being destroyed.
Diff: 3   *Page Ref: 369*
Topic: What Capabilities Does the Child Possess?
Skill: Factual

6) Explain How imprinting occurs in chicks.

Answer: Imprinting occurs when the child forms a strong attachment to the first moving figure it sees.
Diff: 2   *Page Ref: 370*
Topic: What Capabilities Does the Child Possess?
Skill: Conceptual

7) Mary Ainsworth describes three different types of attachment that infants have with their mothers, name them.

Answer: secure attachment, insecure attachment and anxious ambivalent attachment
Diff: 2   *Page Ref: 371*
Topic: What Capabilities Does the Child Possess?
Skill: Conceptual

8) Explain what Harlow finds regarding contact comfort in monkeys.

Answer: He believed that infants form a strong bond with their mothers not because they provided them milk (cupboard theory), but rather because they provide them with a sense of soft security and physical comfort.
Diff: 2   *Page Ref: 372*
Topic: What Capabilities Does the Child Possess?
Skill: Conceptual

9) Briefly explain Piaget's concepts of assimilation and accommodation.

Answer: Assimilation occurs when the child attempts to place new information into previously learned categories, while accommodation occurs when the child learns a new category.
Diff: 2   *Page Ref: 376*
Topic: What are the Developmental Tasks of Infancy and Childhood?
Skill: Conceptual

10) What are the characteristics of a preoperational child?

Answer: Children are self-centered and egocentric; animism is present.
Diff: 2   Page Ref: 378
Topic: What are the Developmental Tasks of Infancy and Childhood?
Skill: Conceptual

11) Billy looks at two identical strings of beads, one stretched out in a line and the other heaped in a small pile. His ability to recognize that although the beads look different they are not different in number is called _____.

Answer: conservation
Diff: 2   Page Ref: 379
Topic: What are the Developmental Tasks of Infancy and Childhood?
Skill: Conceptual

12) Explain temperament.

Answer: An individual's characteristic manner of behavior or reaction, which is assumed to have a strong genetic basis.
Diff: 2   Page Ref: 381
Topic: What are the Developmental Tasks of Infancy and Childhood?
Skill: Recall

13) Explain how authoritative and authoritarian parents differ in their dealings with their children.

Answer: Authoritative parents tend to seek their children's input and stick to reasonably made rules. Authoritarian parents believe that it is "my way or the highway", they make all of the decisions for their children and set fir unchangeable rules that will not be amended regardless of the situation.
Diff: 2   Page Ref: 382
Topic: What are the Developmental Tasks of Infancy and Childhood?
Skill: Conceptual

14) Explain the happenings in Erik Erikson's stage of trust vs. mistrust.

Answer: The child develops a basic sense of safety and security and the ability to rely on others, if not they learn not to rely on other people for their needs.
Diff: 2   Page Ref: 385
Topic: What are the Developmental Tasks of Infancy and Childhood?
Skill: Conceptual

15) Define and give an example of a rite of passage in the united States.

Answer: A rite of passage is a social ritual that marks the transition between childhood and adulthood. In the U.S. a rit of passage would be getting a driver's licence around the age of 16, or being able to drink at age 21.

Diff: 2   *Page Ref: 388*

Topic: What Changes Mark the Transition to Adolescence?

Skill: Conceptual

16) Explain what occurs in Piaget's formal operational stage.

Answer: One gains the ability to think abstractly and can deal with intangible issues such as justice, love and truth.

Diff: 2   *Page Ref: 389*

Topic: What Changes Mark the Transition to Adolescence?

Skill: Conceptual

17) What is a key criticism of Kohlberg's morality theory?

Answer: Moral thought does not predict moral behavior, he also does not address the moral decision making proposed by other cultures and does not address the potentially different reasoning techniques that men and women may use.

Diff: 3   *Page Ref: 393–394*

Topic: The Development of Moral Thinking

Skill: Conceptual

18) Briefly explain Erikson's stage of Generativity vs. Stagnation.

Answer: At this stage, an adult looks beyond one's self to see what contributions they have made to society, their family and to future generations. If they feel they have done this well, they experience generativity. If they feel they have not accomplished these goals, they will experience Stagnation.

Diff: 3   *Page Ref: 397*

Topic: What Developmental Challenges do Adults Face?

Skill: Conceptual

19) Explain how cognition may change in older adults.

Answer: They will see and increase in vocabulary but a decrease in fluid intelligence or the ability to think abstractly. Overall however intellectual ability remains much the same throughout later adulthood.

Diff: 2   *Page Ref: 400*

Topic: The Last Developmental Challenges You Will Face

Skill: Analysis

20) Briefly explain the stage of bargaining in Elizabeth Kubler-Ross stages of death and dying.

Answer: At this stage, the individual attempts to "get more time", they negotiate if they cn only be cured of their illness.

Diff: 2   Page Ref: 402

Topic: The Last Developmental Challenges You Will Face

Skill: Conceptual

Essay Questions

1) Explain how twin and adoption studies have contributed to our understanding of the Nature vs. Nurture debate.

Answer: Twins separated at birth have been studies by researchers in Minnesota. They often have seemingly unusual similarities but they may be no better than chance that they share some similar characteristics in common with one another. The similarities shown in twin studies tend to be mostly regarding characteristics such as temperament, intelligence, gestures and posture. While identical twins share 1005 of their genes they are not the same if they are raised together or apart indicating that there must be some environmental factors that play a role in who we become although our genetic makeup may to a certain degree influence how we interact with our environment. Adoption studies have also showed that children share some characteristics with their birth parents and some with their adoptive parents, once again supporting the interaction model.

Diff: 2   Page Ref: 361–363

Topic: Introduction

Skill: Analysis

2) Describe the sensory and reflexive abilities and preferences of an infant.

Answer: Newborn have certain sensory preferences (for example: smell of banana, salted to unsalted cereal, female voice, familiar sound patterns, etc.). All senses are in place at birth, but that vision (20/500) is relatively weak. Infants are capable of certain sucking, postural, and grasping reflexes.

Diff: 2   Page Ref: 368–369

Topic: What Capabilities Does the Child Possess?

Skill: Applied

3) Describe the four stages in Piaget's theory of cognitive development. Be sure to address the abilities and limits of each stage.

Answer: The stages—in order—are sensorimotor (ages 0-2) preoperational (2-6 or 7), concrete operational (7-11), and formal operational (12 and on). The student should address concepts such as object permanence, egocentrism, animistic thinking, centration, conservation, and mental operations. Mental representations, logic, and abstract thinking should be addressed as well.

Diff: 2   Page Ref: 376–379

Topic: What are the Developmental Tasks of Infancy and Childhood?

Skill: Conceptual

4) Your are driving through some rather bad weather. It is snowing and you are having trouble controlling your car. unfortunately you lose control and drive into a parked car. You do not know if you should leave a note or not. explain why you would or would not a leave a note according to each of lawrence Kohlberg's stages of Moral Development.

Answer: Punishment vs. obedience Stage: You would leave a note because if you did not and the police found out you would get in trouble.
Cost–Benefit orientation: You do not leave a note, because you think, " If this person his me, they probably would not leave a note"
approval–Seeking: You do leave a note because a pedestrian saw you hit the car and you do not want them to think you are a bad person.
Law and Order: You do leave a note because it is against the law to "hit and run".
Social Contract Theory: You leave a note, if you are to be a good person you should follow the general guidelines that you would expect everyone else to follow.
Universal Ethics: You leave a note, you think that it is more important to be honest than be worried about whether you will be in trouble with the law.

Diff: 3   Page Ref: 392–394

Topic: What Changes Mark the Transition to Adolescence?

Skill: Applied

5) Name and provide an example of an individual moving through elizabeth Kubler–Ross' stages of death and dying.

Answer: Denial: refusing to believe that one is ill. Ed Thinks that his doctor has misdiagnosed his illness, and he is going to go to another doctor for a second opinion.
Anger: person displays anger that hey are sick. Ed does why he has been hit with Cancer, after all he has been a good person.
bargaining: Trying to make a deal in truth for a cure. Ed says, " If I am cured of my cancer I promise I will spend more time with my family".
Depression: general loss of sleep, interest and appetite. Ed does not get out of bed some days because he figures, "Why Bother".
Acceptance: Patients recognizes that death is imminent and embraces it. Ed says, " I have lived a good life e and I am ready to go".

Diff: 2   Page Ref: 401–402

Topic: What Developmental Challenges do Adults Face?

Skill: Applied

Chapter 10 Personality

Multiple Choice Questions

1) Margaret Sanger is best known for her attempts to develop
   A) effective personality tests.
   B) successful therapy to treat depression.
   C) valid psychological personality theories.
   D) humane in-patient clinics.
   E) oral birth control pills.

   Answer: E
   Diff: 2   Page Ref: 409–410
   Topic: Introduction
   Skill: Factual

2) According to the text, a key aspect of personality is it's _____ quality.
   A) unique
   B) ever-changing
   C) situationally-determined
   D) continuous
   E) invariant

   Answer: D
   Diff: 2   Page Ref: 410
   Topic: Introduction
   Skill: Factual

3) _____ is defined as the unique qualities and distinctive behavior patterns of an individual across time and situations.
   A) Genetic makeup
   B) Psychopathology
   C) Personality
   D) Social history
   E) Psychic determinism

   Answer: C
   Diff: 1   Page Ref: 410
   Topic: Introduction
   Skill: Conceptual

4) Psychoanalytic psychologists ten d for focus on

   A) the good in all people.

   B) the future.

   C) learning through rewards and punishments.

   D) unconscious motives.

   E) our thought processes.

Answer: D
Diff: 1   Page Ref: 411
Topic: What Forces Shape Our Personalities?
Skill: Recall

5) Physicians in the late 1800s were puzzled by hysteria, a condition in which

   A) moods fluctuated wildly throughout the course of the day.

   B) physical symptoms had no apparent physical cause.

   C) physical pain was worsened due to poor coping.

   D) people had multiple personalities.

   E) people experienced severe injuries without experiencing pain.

Answer: B
Diff: 2   Page Ref: 412
Topic: What Forces Shape Our Personalities?
Skill: Factual

6) _____ was one of the first individuals to place patients in a hypnotic trance to relieve their hysterical symptoms.

   A) Sigmund Freud

   B) Karen Horney

   C) Jean Charcot

   D) Erik Erikson

   E) Jean Piaget

Answer: C
Diff: 2   Page Ref: 412
Topic: What Forces Shape Our Personalities?
Skill: Factual

7) Freud first used _____ to help his patients and later developed _____ as a therapy.

   A) hypnotism; behaviorism

   B) hypnotism; the psychoanalytic approach

   C) dream interpretation; religion

   D) psychic determinism; humanism

   E) medication; hypnotism

Answer: B

Diff: 3   *Page Ref: 412*

Topic: What Forces Shape Our Personalities?

Skill: Factual

8) What is the central assumption of all psychodynamic theories?

   A) The hierarchy of the id, ego, and superego is destructive.

   B) There is no interplay between Thanatos and Eros.

   C) Most of an individual's personality is governed by unconscious forces.

   D) Early experiences have little impact on the adult personality.

   E) Perception and social experience greatly influence our personalities.

Answer: C

Diff: 2   *Page Ref: 412*

Topic: What Forces Shape Our Personalities?

Skill: Conceptual

9) According to Freud, our unconscious held mostly

   A) images and thoughts from the previous day.

   B) threatening and anxiety-provoking contents.

   C) ideas about what we would do in the future.

   D) information regarding rewards we have received in the past.

   E) information about our culture and religion.

Answer: B

Diff: 2   *Page Ref: 412*

Topic: What Forces Shape Our Personalities?

Skill: Factual

10) Freud believed that Thanatos was the driving force behind

    A) sex and loving behaviors.

    B) altruistic and pro social behaviors.

    C) destructive and aggressive behaviors.

    D) self-preservation.

    E) hunger and thirst drives.

Answer: C
Diff: 3   *Page Ref: 413*
Topic: What Forces Shape Our Personalities?
Skill: Factual

11) Freud's 'libido', comes from the Latin word meaning

    A) life force.   B) love.   C) sex.   D) death.   E) lust.

Answer: E
Diff: 2   *Page Ref: 413*
Topic: What Forces Shape Our Personalities?
Skill: Recall

12) A Freudian psychoanalyst would interpret a client's impulsive need for immediate gratification as due to an overactive

    A) id.

    B) ego.

    C) superego.

    D) defense mechanism.

    E) instinct.

Answer: A
Diff: 2   *Page Ref: 413*
Topic: What Forces Shape Our Personalities?
Skill: Applied

13) The _____ is the unconscious part of a personality versus the _____ that is primarily in our conscious mind.

    A) ego; superego

    B) superego; ego

    C) id; superego

    D) ego; id

    E) defense mechanism; ego

Answer: C
Diff: 2   *Page Ref: 413*
Topic: What Forces Shape Our Personalities?
Skill: Factual

14) The key function of the ego is to resolves conflicts between the _____ and the _____.
   A) id; superego
   B) id; anima
   C) superego; animus
   D) defense mechanisms; superego
   E) collective unconscious; superego defense mechanisms

   Answer: A
   Diff: 2   Page Ref: 413
   Topic: What Forces Shape Our Personalities?
   Skill: Conceptual

15) A Freudian analyst would interpret a church-going person who views premarital sex as a sin as being ruled by their
   A) id.   B) ego.   C) superego.   D) libido.   E) Thanatos.

   Answer: C
   Diff: 2   Page Ref: 413
   Topic: What Forces Shape Our Personalities?
   Skill: Applied

16) Alice is on a diet, she is at an ice cream shop with some of her friends and is conflicted about what she should order. Her _____ tells her to get a banana split, her _____ tells her to get a glass of water, and her _____ tells her to order a low fat yogurt.
   A) superego; id; ego
   B) id; ego; superego
   C) id; superego; ego
   D) ego; superego; id
   E) superego; ego; id

   Answer: C
   Diff: 2   Page Ref: 413
   Topic: What Forces Shape Our Personalities?
   Skill: Applied

17) In the different _____ stages, children are thought to associate pleasure with different bodily regions.

    A) psychosexual

    B) psychogenic

    C) psychic

    D) psychotic

    E) psycho physiological

Answer: A
Diff: 1   Page Ref: 414
Topic: What Forces Shape Our Personalities?
Skill: Factual

18) Fixations that may occur because of being weened improperly include

    A) being messy.

    B) having problems with one's parents.

    C) smoking.

    D) being excessively clean.

    E) becoming unnecessarily modest.

Answer: C
Diff: 2   Page Ref: 414
Topic: What Forces Shape Our Personalities?
Skill: Conceptual

19) The Anal Stage is primarily concerned with

    A) weening.

    B) toilet training.

    C) the Oedipus complex.

    D) mature sexual relationships.

    E) hostility towards same sex parent.

Answer: B
Diff: 2   Page Ref: 414
Topic: What Forces Shape Our Personalities?
Skill: Recall

20) The personality of a child who is fixated in the anal stage tends to be excessively

    A) clean.   B) jealous.   C) modest.   D) honest.   E) neurotic.

Answer: A
Diff: 3   Page Ref: 414
Topic: What Forces Shape Our Personalities?
Skill: Applied

21) According to Freud, a male child who is experiencing the Oedipus complex is most likely to
   A) try to bond with his brother.
   B) identify with his father.
   C) enjoy spending time with his grandmother.
   D) feel a rivalry with other boys.
   E) dislike his mother.

Answer: B
Diff: 2   Page Ref: 414
Topic: What Forces Shape Our Personalities?
Skill: Applied

22) Freud believed that women are attracted to men as a result of _____.
   A) fixation
   B) the Oedipus complex
   C) Thanatos
   D) their superego
   E) penis envy

Answer: E
Diff: 2   Page Ref: 415
Topic: What Forces Shape Our Personalities?
Skill: Conceptual

23) _____ are used to help protect ourselves from our own unwanted sexual and aggressive desires.
   A) Self-actualizing strategies
   B) Schemas
   C) Ego defense mechanisms
   D) Archetypes
   E) The anima and the animus

Answer: C
Diff: 2   Page Ref: 415
Topic: What Forces Shape Our Personalities?
Skill: Conceptual

24) _____ is the ego defense mechanisms that functions to exclude unacceptable feelings from consciousness.

   A) Sublimation

   B) Repression

   C) Denial

   D) Projection

   E) Accommodation

Answer: B

Diff: 2   Page Ref: 415

Topic: What Forces Shape Our Personalities?

Skill: Conceptual

25) After a lecture that did not go well, Dr. Hoemann thinks, "I bet the students hated class today." He tells himself this, rather than thinking, "I hated my lecture today," due to

   A) repression.

   B) his superego.

   C) his id.

   D) animus.

   E) projection.

Answer: E

Diff: 3   Page Ref: 416

Topic: What Forces Shape Our Personalities?

Skill: Applied

26) Jeremy is upset and angry that he did not pass his physics test. He is very angry at his instructor, but he cannot yell at him or else he will be in trouble. Instead Jeremy releases some of his aggressive energy on the football field. What defense mechanism is Jeremy using?

   A) sublimation

   B) projection

   C) reaction formation

   D) regression

   E) repression

Answer: A

Diff: 3   Page Ref: 416

Topic: What Forces Shape Our Personalities?

Skill: Applied

27) Which defense mechanism involves acting the opposite of how one really feels?

   A) denial

   B) regression

   C) reaction formation

   D) projection

   E) sublimation

Answer: C
Diff: 2   Page Ref: 416
Topic: What Forces Shape Our Personalities?
Skill: Factual

28) after missing a put on the final hole of a competitive golf tournament, Greg yells and throws his club. He is demonstrating

   A) repression.

   B) reaction formation.

   C) projection.

   D) regression.

   E) rationalization.

Answer: D
Diff: 2   Page Ref: 416
Topic: What Forces Shape Our Personalities?
Skill: Applied

29) Erin is supposed to be saving money from her job to contribute to her college fund. She is at the mall and sees a shirt that she loves, but she will have to dip into her fund alloted for college in order to buy it. She justifies her behavior by saying, " I have worked really hard this week and I deserve it". Erin is using what Freudian defense mechanism?

   A) sublimation

   B) rationalization

   C) displacement

   D) denial

   E) regression

Answer: B
Diff: 2   Page Ref: 416
Topic: What Forces Shape Our Personalities?
Skill: Applied

30) _____ occurs when you yell at your dog after receiving an 'F' on a term paper.

A) Repression

B) Depression

C) Sublimation

D) Reaction formation

E) Displacement

Answer: E

Diff: 2   Page Ref: 416

Topic: What Forces Shape Our Personalities?

Skill: Conceptual

31) Assessment instruments in which individuals are asked to describe ambiguous stimuli are called _____ tests.

A) objective

B) projective

C) retrospective

D) subjective

E) multiphasic

Answer: B

Diff: 1   Page Ref: 416

Topic: What Forces Shape Our Personalities?

Skill: Conceptual

32) The Rorschach inkblot test is said to

A) be highly valid.

B) have questionable accuracy.

C) be very objective.

D) used frequently today in clinical settings.

E) None of the above

Answer: B

Diff: 2   Page Ref: 416

Topic: What Forces Shape Our Personalities?

Skill: Conceptual

33) a personality test that involves looking at ambiguous pictures and describing what is happening, what happened before and how the situation will end is likely taking a

    A) TAT test.

    B) Rorschach inkblot.

    C) MMPI.

    D) NEO–PI.

    E) MBTI.

Answer: A
Diff: 2   Page Ref: 417
Topic: What Forces Shape Our Personalities?
Skill: Factual

34) Freudian slips are believed to reveal

    A) brain dysfunctions.

    B) speech problems.

    C) a mild form of mental retardation.

    D) unconscious conflicts or desires.

    E) physical hunger.

Answer: D
Diff: 2   Page Ref: 418
Topic: What Forces Shape Our Personalities?
Skill: Conceptual

35) While at a Mexican restaurant, an attractive waitress asks Raul what kind of beer he would like. Instead of saying, "Dos Equis," he says, "Dos sexy." This accidental slip of the tongue could best be explained as

    A) Thanatos.

    B) the Oedipus complex.

    C) a Freudian slip.

    D) repression.

    E) the superego.

Answer: C
Diff: 1   Page Ref: 418
Topic: What Forces Shape Our Personalities?
Skill: Applied

36) The concept of psychic determinism suggests that

   A) situational variables dictated how people respond in a given circumstance.

   B) all acts are determined by motives, not by chance.

   C) people are reinforced by significant others and tend to repeat behaviors that are reinforced.

   D) people learn behaviors and ways of interacting by watching others.

   E) much of what we do is random or accidental.

Answer: B
Diff: 2   Page Ref: 418
Topic: What Forces Shape Our Personalities?
Skill: Conceptual

37) Many female psychologists who have studies Freudian theory, take issue with his idea of

   A) id, ego, superego.

   B) all women experiencing penis envy.

   C) psychosexual stages.

   D) that we are guided by unconscious forces.

   E) Freudian slips.

Answer: B
Diff: 2   Page Ref: 418
Topic: What Forces Shape Our Personalities?
Skill: Conceptual

38) All of the following are criticisms of Freud's psychoanalytic theory except

   A) it lacks objectivity.

   B) it treats men as superiors.

   C) it overemphasizes the influence of the unconscious.

   D) we use defense mechanisms to protect ourselves from things we do not want to know.

   E) it focuses too intently on past events.

Answer: D
Diff: 2   Page Ref: 418
Topic: What Forces Shape Our Personalities?
Skill: Conceptual

39) Freud is to sexuality as Jung is to _____.

   A) the ego
   B) the id
   C) spirituality
   D) the unconscious
   E) A and B are correct

   Answer: C
   Diff: 3   Page Ref: 420
   Topic: What Forces Shape Our Personalities?
   Skill: Conceptual

40) _____ proposed the concept of the collective unconscious.

   A) Jung   B) Freud   C) Bandura   D) Adler   E) Rotter

   Answer: A
   Diff: 2   Page Ref: 420
   Topic: What Forces Shape Our Personalities?
   Skill: Applied

41) The concept of _____ includes "instinctive" memories that are shared by all people of all cultures.

   A) working memory
   B) the preconscious
   C) undeclarative memory
   D) collective unconscious
   E) wish fulfillment

   Answer: D
   Diff: 2   Page Ref: 420
   Topic: What Forces Shape Our Personalities?
   Skill: Applied

42) According to Jung's principle of opposites, each personality is balanced between _____ and _____.

   A) shadow; light
   B) introversion; extroversion
   C) aggression; passivity
   D) joy; despair
   E) animus; anima

   Answer: B
   Diff: 2   Page Ref: 420
   Topic: What Forces Shape Our Personalities?
   Skill: Conceptual

43) The "warrior," the "hero," and the "earth mother" are examples of the Jungian concept of

A) ego defenses.

B) archetypes.

C) cardinal traits.

D) extroversion.

E) humors.

Answer: B
Diff: 2   Page Ref: 420
Topic: What Forces Shape Our Personalities?
Skill: Conceptual

44) Jung explains that our idea f masculinity and femininity are often created by our parents. Jung terms for the masculine and feminine sides of our personality are coined.

A) anima and animus

B) thanatos and eros

C) libido and animus

D) thanatos and anima

E) eros and anima

Answer: A
Diff: 2   Page Ref: 420
Topic: What Forces Shape Our Personalities?
Skill: Factual

45) In the film 'Star Wars", Darth Vader plays the evil leader, Luke plays the hero, Yoda plays the wise one. All of these characters according to Carl Jung represent

A) our shadow personality.

B) the personal unconscious.

C) archetypes.

D) the principle of opposites.

E) defense mechanisms.

Answer: C
Diff: 2   Page Ref: 420
Topic: What Forces Shape Our Personalities?
Skill: Conceptual

46) Karen Horney believed that _____ may block the normal development of a personality.
    A) fear of death
    B) castration anxiety
    C) the Electra complex
    D) basic anxiety
    E) the 'shadow'

Answer: D
Diff: 2   Page Ref: 421
Topic: What Forces Shape Our Personalities?
Skill: Conceptual

47) Karen Horney believed that normal desires taken to extremes were called
    A) defense mechanisms.
    B) inferiority complex.
    C) neurotic needs.
    D) archetypes.
    E) collective unconscious.

Answer: C
Diff: 2   Page Ref: 421
Topic: What Forces Shape Our Personalities?
Skill: Factual

48) The main concept that Erik Erikson believed most children developed in childhood is
    A) the Oedipus complex.
    B) an inferiority complex.
    C) fixations.
    D) neurotic needs.
    E) a personal unconscious.

Answer: B
Diff: 2   Page Ref: 422
Topic: What Forces Shape Our Personalities?
Skill: Factual

49) In order to overcome feelings of inferiority, Adler believed that individuals will

    A) use projection.

    B) model an archetype.

    C) create neurotic needs.

    D) create fixations.

    E) compensate.

Answer: E
Diff: 3   Page Ref: 422
Topic: What Forces Shape Our Personalities?
Skill: Factual

50) Post–Freudian theorists changed psychodynamic personality theory through their

    A) extension of personality development beyond childhood.

    B) emphasis of urges over social variables.

    C) expansion of the role of libidinal energy.

    D) de–emphasis of ego defenses.

    E) creation of the Thanatos concept.

Answer: A
Diff: 3   Page Ref: 422
Topic: What Forces Shape Our Personalities?
Skill: Conceptual

51) Humanistic theories are _____ about the nature of human personality.

    A) skeptical

    B) optimistic

    C) deterministic

    D) pessimistic

    E) unconcerned

Answer: B
Diff: 2   Page Ref: 422
Topic: What Forces Shape Our Personalities?
Skill: Conceptual

52) _____ proposed the first trait theory, involving Cardinal, central and secondary traits.

    A) Allport

    B) Maslow

    C) Costa and McCrae

    D) Bandura

    E) Rogers

Answer: A

Diff: 2   Page Ref: 423

Topic: What Forces Shape Our Personalities?

Skill: Recall

53) Maslow identified _____ as the "third force" of psychology.

    A) behavioral theories

    B) positive psychology

    C) the neo–Freudian movement

    D) nurture

    E) the humanistic view

Answer: E

Diff: 2   Page Ref: 423

Topic: What Forces Shape Our Personalities?

Skill: Factual

54) Maslow identified _____ as an example of a self–actualized personality.

    A) Walt Disney

    B) Abraham Lincoln

    C) Albert Neuman

    D) Teddy Roosevelt

    E) Thomas Edison

Answer: B

Diff: 2   Page Ref: 423

Topic: What Forces Shape Our Personalities?

Skill: Factual

55) A psychologist who gives their clients a brochure entitled "Personal Growth And Making Life Improvements" is likely to have a(n) _____ orientation.

A) humanistic

B) Freudian

C) neo-Freudian

D) cognitive-behavioral

E) eclectic

Answer: A

Diff: 2   Page Ref: 423

Topic: What Forces Shape Our Personalities?

Skill: Applied

56) Which is TRUE of self-actualization?

A) It is at the core of Adler's system of psychology.

B) It is completely a biological drive.

C) It is different for every individual.

D) It is easily achieved by most people.

E) It arises from a restriction of basic biological needs.

Answer: C

Diff: 2   Page Ref: 423

Topic: What Forces Shape Our Personalities?

Skill: Applied

57) _____ refer to the lifelong process of striving to realize one's full potential.

A) The self-fulfilling prophecy

B) Wish fulfillment

C) Sublimation

D) Self-actualization

E) Projection

Answer: D

Diff: 1   Page Ref: 423

Topic: What Forces Shape Our Personalities?

Skill: Conceptual

58) Carl Rogers would say that a student _____ when they view themselves as brilliant, but earn Cs in all their classes.

    A) is self-actualized

    B) has a dark shadow

    C) has a strong superego

    D) has low need for achievement

    E) is experiencing incongruence

Answer: E

Diff: 2   Page Ref: 424

Topic: What Forces Shape Our Personalities?

Skill: Applied

59) Carl Rogers defined the _____ as our tendency to respond to reality as we perceive it.

    A) ego

    B) phenomenal field

    C) locus of control

    D) unconditional positive regard

    E) temperament

Answer: B

Diff: 2   Page Ref: 424

Topic: What Forces Shape Our Personalities?

Skill: Conceptual

60) A child who has done something wrong and whose parents communicate love while letting the child know they are unhappy with their action, but that they still love the child are practicing what Carl Rogers would refer to as _____.

    A) anger displacement

    B) conflicted feelings

    C) unconditional positive regard

    D) a repressed expression of aggression

    E) a positive phenomenal field

Answer: C

Diff: 2   Page Ref: 424

Topic: What Forces Shape Our Personalities?

Skill: Applied

61) Which of the following is NOT associated with Carl Rogers?

    A) unconditional positive regard

    B) person-centered therapy

    C) dream analysis

    D) the humanistic approach

    E) congruence

Answer: C
Diff: 2   Page Ref: 424
Topic: What Forces Shape Our Personalities?
Skill: Factual

62) Motivation is viewed as _____ by humanist theorists such as Rogers and Maslow.

    A) negative and potentially destructive

    B) a test of an individual's self-knowledge

    C) fundamentally positive and striving for positive growth

    D) a measure of normal and abnormal functioning

    E) determined by deep-seated unconscious issues

Answer: C
Diff: 2   Page Ref: 425
Topic: What Forces Shape Our Personalities?
Skill: Conceptual

63) A key criticism of the humanistic approach is that it

    A) was too specific to apply to all people.

    B) overemphasized society's influence on a person.

    C) relied too much on theories of the unconscious.

    D) could reflect an Eastern bias by being too "group-focused."

    E) was quite difficult to test objectively.

Answer: E
Diff: 2   Page Ref: 425
Topic: What Forces Shape Our Personalities?
Skill: Conceptual

64) _____ refers to a recently developed psychological movement that emphasizes the study of desirable aspects of human functioning.

    A) Psychoanalysis

    B) Cognitive psychology

    C) Self–esteem theory

    D) Biobehaviorism

    E) Positive psychology

Answer: E
Diff: 1   Page Ref: 425
Topic: What Forces Shape Our Personalities?
Skill: Factual

65) Cross–Cultural psychologist take issue with humanistic psychology because

    A) there is too much focus on the unconscious.

    B) there is to much focus on the self.

    C) the theories are not always objective.

    D) they base all learning off of rewards and punishments.

    E) they disregard the environment.

Answer: B
Diff: 2   Page Ref: 425
Topic: What Forces Shape Our Personalities?
Skill: Conceptual

66) Cognitive personality theories are based on

    A) case studies.

    B) experimental research.

    C) subjective concepts.

    D) unconscious motives.

    E) untestable hypothesis.

Answer: B
Diff: 1   Page Ref: 425
Topic: What Forces Shape Our Personalities?
Skill: Conceptual

67) Social–Cognitive Psychologists are different from humanists or psychoanalytic psychologists in that they emphasize

    A) the unconscious.

    B) rewards and punishments.

    C) expectations.

    D) to good in all people.

    E) neurotic needs.

Answer: C

Diff: 1   *Page Ref: 425*

Topic: What Forces Shape Our Personalities?

Skill: Conceptual

68) A key concept of Bandura's personality theory is his belief that

    A) social learning has no impact on our personalities.

    B) people can learn new behaviors through observation of others.

    C) people cannot learn by observation.

    D) the unconscious mind largely determines our behavior.

    E) self–actualization is a more important goal than is food.

Answer: B

Diff: 2   *Page Ref: 426*

Topic: What Forces Shape Our Personalities?

Skill: Factual

69) Observational learning is the focus of the personality theory devised by

    A) Carl Jung.

    B) Karen Horney.

    C) Carl Rogers.

    D) Albert Bandura.

    E) Julian Rotter.

Answer: D

Diff: 1   *Page Ref: 426*

Topic: What Forces Shape Our Personalities?

Skill: Applied

70) _____ refers to the concept of the mutual influence of person, behavior, and environment.

A) Sublimation

B) Reciprocal determinism

C) Environmental psychology

D) Field theory

E) Psychoanalysis

Answer: B

Diff: 3   Page Ref: 426

Topic: What Forces Shape Our Personalities?

Skill: Factual

71) The _____ was created by Julian Rotter to measure our sense of personal power.

A) Internal–External Locus of Control Scale.

B) Minnesota Multiphasic Personality Inventory.

C) Thematic Apperception Test.

D) Rorschach Test.

E) Stanford–Binet scale.

Answer: A

Diff: 2   Page Ref: 426

Topic: What Forces Shape Our Personalities?

Skill: Factual

72) Jesse has an internal locus of control if after being involved in a car accident, he believes the accident was due to

A) his sister playing the radio too loud.

B) the street sign being poorly marked.

C) his old car's faulty brakes.

D) the other driver's negligence.

E) his lack of concentration.

Answer: E

Diff: 2   Page Ref: 426–427

Topic: What Forces Shape Our Personalities?

Skill: Applied

73) A critique often waged against the Social-Cognitive Theory of personality is

    A) it does not take into account the role of the environment.

    B) it does not take into account the role of thought processes.

    C) it overemphasizes the role of rational information processing.

    D) it overemphasizes the unconscious.

    E) it does not address our ability to control our own environment.

Answer: C

Diff: 2   Page Ref: 427

Topic: What Forces Shape Our Personalities?

Skill: Conceptual

74) A strength of the Social-Cognitive theory that it not true of either the humanistic or psychoanalytic approach to personality is

    A) it's focus on the individual.

    B) it's focus on the unconscious.

    C) it's focus on the growth potential in individuals.

    D) it's focus on one's ability to be all that they can be.

    E) it's focus on solid psychological research.

Answer: E

Diff: 2   Page Ref: 427

Topic: What Forces Shape Our Personalities?

Skill: Conceptual

75) The unit of analysis in _____ systems theory is the _____ rather than an individual.

    A) social; society

    B) racial; racial unit

    C) family; family unit

    D) aging; elderly

    E) cultural; culture

Answer: C

Diff: 2   Page Ref: 428

Topic: What Forces Shape Our Personalities?

Skill: Factual

76) The emphasis of modern personality theories is on

    A) individuals with psychological problems.

    B) commonalities between the unconscious and conscious self.

    C) case studies.

    D) individualistic societies.

    E) diversity and group processes.

Answer: E
Diff: 2   Page Ref: 428
Topic: What Forces Shape Our Personalities?
Skill: Conceptual

77) _____ proposed the idea that bodily fluids, or humors, were associated with different temperaments.

    A) Freud

    B) Hippocrates

    C) Bandura

    D) Kagan

    E) Socrates

Answer: B
Diff: 2   Page Ref: 430-431
Topic: What Persistent Patterns Are Found in Personality?
Skill: Factual

78) A choleric temperament was associated with

    A) blood.

    B) phlegm.

    C) black bile.

    D) yellow bile.

    E) saliva.

Answer: D
Diff: 2   Page Ref: 430
Topic: What Persistent Patterns Are Found in Personality?
Skill: Factual

79) Match up the correct humor with its corresponding temperament.
   A) sanguine; warm blood
   B) melancholy; yellow bile
   C) sanguine; yellow bile
   D) unemotional; black bile
   E) pessimistic; phlegm

Answer: A
Diff: 2   Page Ref: 430–431
Topic: What Persistent Patterns Are Found in Personality?
Skill: Factual

80) The key function of type and trait theories of personality is to
   A) explain how personality develops.
   B) allow us to categorize people into a manageable number of categories.
   C) emphasize the ever-changing personality.
   D) believe personality is determined by unconscious forces.
   E) focus on how the environment impacts personality.

Answer: B
Diff: 2   Page Ref: 431
Topic: What Persistent Patterns Are Found in Personality?
Skill: Conceptual

81) Distinct clusters of personality traits are called
   A) personality types.
   B) psychic determinism.
   C) psychodynamic mechanisms.
   D) ego defenses.
   E) humors.

Answer: A
Diff: 1   Page Ref: 431
Topic: What Persistent Patterns Are Found in Personality?
Skill: Factual

82) The modern view of temperament proposed by Jerome Kagan claim that it

    A) is inherited.

    B) first emerges during adolescence.

    C) has no bearing on behavior.

    D) is a mixture of the four humors.

    E) changes radically at adolescence.

Answer: A
Diff: 1   Page Ref: 432
Topic: What Persistent Patterns Are Found in Personality?
Skill: Conceptual

83) Jerome Kagan's recent studies of shyness found that

    A) most children are born as more bold than shy.

    B) 10-15% of all children are born shy.

    C) most people outgrow shyness by the time of college.

    D) life experiences have little effect on shyness.

    E) shyness is seldom consistent over time.

Answer: B
Diff: 2   Page Ref: 432
Topic: What Persistent Patterns Are Found in Personality?
Skill: Factual

84) A _____ is a relatively stable personality tendency.

    A) trait

    B) dimension

    C) type

    D) behavioral constant

    E) cluster

Answer: A
Diff: 2   Page Ref: 432
Topic: What Persistent Patterns Are Found in Personality?
Skill: Factual

85) _____ theorists have determined five major characteristics of personality.

  A) Cognitive

  B) Learning

  C) Psychodynamic

  D) Trait

  E) Humanistic

Answer: D

Diff: 2   Page Ref: 432

Topic: What Persistent Patterns Are Found in Personality?

Skill: Conceptual

86) The factor of _____ is NOT one of the "Big Five" dimensions underlying personality.

  A) agreeableness

  B) conscientiousness

  C) openness to experience

  D) extroversion

  E) persistence

Answer: E

Diff: 2   Page Ref: 432–433

Topic: What Persistent Patterns Are Found in Personality?

Skill: Factual

87) Jeanne enjoys making other people happy, she gets along well with her family peers and boyfriend. She could be said to be high in which of the big-Five personality characteristics?

  A) extroversion

  B) openness to experience

  C) neuroticism

  D) agreeableness

  E) conscientiousness

Answer: D

Diff: 3   Page Ref: 433

Topic: What Persistent Patterns Are Found in Personality?

Skill: Applied

88) Which of the following Big–Five personality characteristics are often associated with negative emotions?

    A) conscientiousness

    B) extroversion

    C) openness to Experience

    D) neuroticism

    E) agreeableness

Answer: D
Diff: 3   Page Ref: 433
Topic: What Persistent Patterns Are Found in Personality?
Skill: Conceptual

89) Jim loves being around people, he has many friends and loves to be social regardless of his situation. Jim probably would score high on which of the big–five personality characteristics?

    A) extroversion

    B) openness to experience

    C) agreeableness

    D) neuroticism

    E) conscientiousness

Answer: A
Diff: 2   Page Ref: 433
Topic: What Persistent Patterns Are Found in Personality?
Skill: Applied

90) Which of the following is the correct acronym for the "Big–5" personality factors?

    A) L–A–K–E–S

    B) O–C–E–A–N

    C) P–O–N–D–S

    D) T–R–A–I–T–S

    E) T–Y–P–E–S

Answer: B
Diff: 2   Page Ref: 433
Topic: What Persistent Patterns Are Found in Personality?
Skill: Factual

91) The _____ is designed to assess the "Big Five" factors of personality.

    A) Rorschach

    B) MMPI

    C) NEO-PI

    D) TAT

    E) Internal–External Locus of Control Scale

Answer: C
Diff: 1   *Page Ref: 433*
Topic: What Persistent Patterns Are Found in Personality?
Skill: Factual

92) The _____ is a test used to measure serious mental problems, such as schizophrenia and depression.

    A) CPI   B) MMPI-2   C) Rorschach   D) TAT   E) NEO-PI

Answer: B
Diff: 2   *Page Ref: 434*
Topic: What Persistent Patterns Are Found in Personality?
Skill: Factual

93) Which of the following is true of the MMPI-2?

    A) It cannot detect lying.

    B) It is based on norms from Eastern cultures.

    C) It was originally designed to diagnose minority group members.

    D) It measures 'normal' personality.

    E) It contains ten clinical scales.

Answer: E
Diff: 3   *Page Ref: 434*
Topic: What Persistent Patterns Are Found in Personality?
Skill: Factual

94) A serious criticism of trait theories is that these

    A) ignore inherited aspects of personality.

    B) do not allow for predictions of behavior.

    C) are too complex to explain simple behaviors.

    D) explain the development of personality but do not explain specific behaviors.

    E) believe personality is fixed and static.

Answer: E
Diff: 3   *Page Ref: 435*
Topic: What Persistent Patterns Are Found in Personality?
Skill: Conceptual

95) Mischel argues that personality variables have the greatest effect on behavior when
    A) your personality is strong.
    B) the person is in love.
    C) situational cues are weak or ambiguous.
    D) situations are strong and clear.
    E) the individual is emotionally aroused.

Answer: C
Diff: 3   Page Ref: 435
Topic: What Persistent Patterns Are Found in Personality?
Skill: Factual

96) The Myers–Briggs Type Indicator (MBTI) is
    A) given to nearly 100,000 people each year.
    B) based on the work of Alfred Adler.
    C) able to assign people to one of ten personality types.
    D) a widely used projective test.
    E) often used for career counseling.

Answer: E
Diff: 2   Page Ref: 436
Topic: Finding Your Type
Skill: Factual

97) The Myers–Brigg Type Indicator test does not measure
    A) dominance and subordination.
    B) sensing and intuiting.
    C) introversion and extroversion.
    D) thinking and feeling.
    E) judgement and perception.

Answer: A
Diff: 2   Page Ref: 437
Topic: Finding Your Type
Skill: Factual

98) A serious criticism of the Myers-Briggs Type Indicator test is that

    A) it does measure intuition.

    B) scores on the test are inconsistent when taken by the same person on two occasions.

    C) there is little evidence that the test predicts occupational success.

    D) it has strong validity.

    E) B and C are correct.

Answer: E
Diff: 2   Page Ref: 437
Topic: Finding Your Type
Skill: Factual

99) Your first impression of a new professor is

    A) inherently inaccurate.

    B) an example of an implicit personality theory.

    C) a naive behavioral explanation.

    D) unprofessional and misleading.

    E) an example of a explicit belief.

Answer: B
Diff: 2   Page Ref: 439
Topic: What "Theories" Do People Use to Understand Each Other?
Skill: Conceptual

100) Susie's naive belief that all artists are emotionally sensitive is an example of

    A) poor self-efficacy.

    B) using an implicit personality theory.

    C) psychic determinism.

    D) a projective personality profile.

    E) basic attribution error.

Answer: B
Diff: 2   Page Ref: 439
Topic: What "Theories" Do People Use to Understand Each Other?
Skill: Applied

101) Buck watches as Janet trips. Buck assumes this occurred because Janet is a clutz (rather than thinking it was because the sidewalk was filled with gravel). Buck has committed the _____ error?

    A) stereotyping

    B) fundamental attribution

    C) labeling

    D) validity

    E) reliability

Answer: B
Diff: 2   Page Ref: 439
Topic: What "Theories" Do People Use to Understand Each Other?
Skill: Applied

102) The fundamental attribution error is less likely to occur in _____ cultures.

    A) individualistic

    B) pluralistic

    C) lonely

    D) happy

    E) collectivist

Answer: E
Diff: 2   Page Ref: 439
Topic: What "Theories" Do People Use to Understand Each Other?
Skill: Conceptual

103) In Individualistic societies the focus is on the

    A) community.

    B) family.

    C) person.

    D) religious group.

    E) school groups.

Answer: C
Diff: 2   Page Ref: 439
Topic: What "Theories" Do People Use to Understand Each Other?
Skill: Conceptual

104) Which of the following is not a measure on which Individualistic and Collectivist societies differ?

A) stoicism

B) concern for loved ones

C) status of different age groups

D) locus of control

E) thinking vs. feeling

Answer: B
Diff: 2   Page Ref: 440
Topic: What "Theories" Do People Use to Understand Each Other?
Skill: Factual

Check Your Understanding Questions

1) The psychodynamic theories emphasize

A) motivation.

B) learning.

C) consciousness.

D) the logical basis of behavior.

E) behavior.

Answer: A
Diff: 2   Page Ref: 430
Topic: Check Your Understanding
Skill: Recall

2) Freud believed that mental disorders stem from conflicts and drives that are repressed by the

A) ego.   B) superego.   C) id.   D) Eros.   E) Thanatos.

Answer: C
Diff: 2   Page Ref: 430
Topic: Check Your Understanding
Skill: Recall

3) Which of the following behaviors would Freud say is driven by Thanatos?

A) sexual intercourse

B) a violent assault

C) dreaming

D) flying on an airplane

E) eating

Answer: B
Diff: 2   Page Ref: 430
Topic: Check Your Understanding
Skill: Applied

4) What is the ego defense mechanism on which the Rorschach and TAT are based?
    A) displacement
    B) fantasy
    C) regression
    D) projection
    E) reaction formation
Answer: D
Diff: 2   *Page Ref: 430*
Topic: Check Your Understanding
Skill: Recall

5) If you react strongly to to angry outbursts in others, you may be struggling with which Jungian archetype?
    A) the anima
    B) the shadow
    C) introversion
    D) the hero
    E) the animus
Answer: B
Diff: 2   *Page Ref: 430*
Topic: Check Your Understanding
Skill: Applied

6) Karen Horney believed that the main forces behind our behaviors are
    A) social.
    B) sexual.
    C) aggressive and destructive.
    D) the result of the Oedipus complex.
    E) unconscious.
Answer: A
Diff: 2   *Page Ref: 430*
Topic: Check Your Understanding
Skill: Recall

7) The humanistic theorists were very different from the psychodynamic theorists because of their emphasis on

    A) the cognitive forces behind behavior.

    B) the healthy personality.

    C) mental disorder.

    D) emotional intelligence.

    E) the role of the unconscious.

Answer: B
Diff: 1   Page Ref: 430
Topic: Check Your Understanding
Skill: Recall

8) This theory of personality theory has it's roots in sound scientific research.

    A) the psychodynamic theories.

    B) the humanistic theories.

    C) the cognitive theories.

    D) the sociocultural theory.

    E) the behaviorist theory.

Answer: C
Diff: 2   Page Ref: 430
Topic: Check Your Understanding
Skill: Recall

9) What do the psychodynamic, humanistic, and cognitive theories of personality have in common?

    A) They all view personality as largely unconscious.

    B) They all acknowledge the internal mental processes underlying our personality characteristics.

    C) They all say that men and women have entirely different motives underlying their behaviors.

    D) They all have a strong basis in psychological research.

    E) They all focus on different aspects of personality.

Answer: B
Diff: 2   Page Ref: 430
Topic: Check Your Understanding
Skill: Understanding the Core Concept

10) Temperament refers to personality characteristics that

    A) cause people to be "nervous" or unreliable.

    B) are learned, especially from one's parents and peers.

    C) have a substantial biological basis.

    D) cause mental disorders.

    E) have their roots in the unconscious.

Answer: C
Diff: 2   *Page Ref: 438*
Topic: Check Your Understanding
Skill: Recall

11) A friend of yours always seems agitated and anxious, even when nothing in the circumstances would provoke such a response. Which one of the five traits applies to this characteristic of your friend?

    A) introversion

    B) agreeableness

    C) neuroticism

    D) conscientiousness

    E) extroversion

Answer: C
Diff: 2   *Page Ref: 438*
Topic: Check Your Understanding
Skill: Applied

12) Walter Mischel argued that _____ is(are) less important than _____.

    A) traits; the situation

    B) traits; temperament

    C) the conscious mind; the unconscious

    D) emotions; reason

    E) the situation; emotions

Answer: A
Diff: 2   *Page Ref: 438*
Topic: Check Your Understanding
Skill: Recall

13) What is found in most psychodynamic, humanistic, and cognitive theories, but is not found in most temperament, trait, and type theories?

    A) a description of the components of personality

    B) labels for common mental disorders

    C) concepts that are useful for individuals involved in personnel selection

    D) a description of the processes of development and change underlying personality

    E) nothing, because these theories all share the same components

Answer: D
Diff: 2   Page Ref: 438
Topic: Check Your Understanding
Skill: Understanding the Core Concept

14) You would expect to find the concept of self emphasized in

    A) the culture of an industrialized country.

    B) a wealthy culture.

    C) an individualistic culture.

    D) a collectivist culture.

    E) the social–cognitive theory.

Answer: C
Diff: 2   Page Ref: 442
Topic: Check Your Understanding
Skill: Applied

15) Cross–cultural psychologists say that a basic distinction among cultures is their emphasis on

    A) capitalism or socialism.

    B) external or internal locus of control.

    C) thoughts or feelings.

    D) individualism or collectivism.

    E) nature or nurture.

Answer: D
Diff: 2   Page Ref: 442
Topic: Check Your Understanding
Skill: Recall

16) You are making the *fundamental attribution error* when

    A) you decide to dislike someone who speaks angrily to you.

    B) you see someone who is nice looking and assume she is self-centered and arrogant.

    C) you go to a foreign country and assume that everyone thinks the way that you do.

    D) you think someone is clumsy when he trips and drops his books.

    E) you swap one emotion for one that is less threatening.

Answer: D
Diff: 2   Page Ref: 442
Topic: Check Your Understanding
Skill: Applied

17) Implicit personality theories involve

    A) the assumptions that people make about each other's motives, intentions, and behaviors.

    B) assumptions about themselves that people want to hide from others.

    C) unconscious instincts, memories, and conflicts.

    D) opinions that people privately hold about others, but will not say openly.

    E) conclusions that are obvious.

Answer: A
Diff: 2   Page Ref: 442
Topic: Check Your Understanding
Skill: Understanding the Core Concept

True/False Questions

1) Personality is basically the psychological qualities that make an individual's thoughts and actions continuous at different times or in different situations.

Answer: TRUE
Diff: 1   Page Ref: 410
Topic: Introduction
Skill: Conceptual

2) According to Freud, Eros is the driving force related to sexual urges, and Thanatos is a force that urges people toward aggressive and destructive behaviors.

Answer: TRUE
Diff: 2   Page Ref: 413
Topic: What Forces Shape Our Personalities?
Skill: Factual

3) The superego stores repressed and primitive impulses.

Answer: FALSE
Diff: 2   Page Ref: 413
Topic: What Forces Shape Our Personalities?
Skill: Conceptual

4) The oedipus complex occurs in the anal stage.

Answer: FALSE
Diff: 3   Page Ref: 414
Topic: What Forces Shape Our Personalities?
Skill: Conceptual

5) According to Freud, defense mechanisms operate at an unconscious level.

Answer: TRUE
Diff: 2   Page Ref: 415
Topic: What Forces Shape Our Personalities?
Skill: Conceptual

6) Projection refers to the defense mechanism in which we revert to childlike behaviors.

Answer: FALSE
Diff: 2   Page Ref: 416
Topic: What Forces Shape Our Personalities?
Skill: Factual

7) The TAT is an example of a projective personality test.

Answer: TRUE
Diff: 2   Page Ref: 417
Topic: What Forces Shape Our Personalities?
Skill: Factual

8) Many of freud's ideas lack objectivity.

Answer: TRUE
Diff: 2   Page Ref: 418
Topic: What Forces Shape Our Personalities?
Skill: Conceptual

9) Karen Horney created the concept of 'penis envy'.

Answer: FALSE
Diff: 2   Page Ref: 418
Topic: What Forces Shape Our Personalities?
Skill: Factual

10) Jung thought of spirituality as more important motivating factor than sex.

Answer: TRUE
Diff: 2   Page Ref: 420
Topic: What Forces Shape Our Personalities?
Skill: Factual

11) Jung created the concept the inferiority complex.

Answer: FALSE
Diff: 2   Page Ref: 420
Topic: What Forces Shape Our Personalities?
Skill: Factual

12) Carl Jung adds to Freud's unconscious by adding the concept of the collective unconscious.

Answer: TRUE
Diff: 2   Page Ref: 420
Topic: What Forces Shape Our Personalities?
Skill: Factual

13) Adler created the idea that we all have neurotic needs which are normal desires carried to extremes.

Answer: FALSE
Diff: 2   Page Ref: 421
Topic: What Forces Shape Our Personalities?
Skill: Factual

14) Humanistic personality theories emphasize individuals potential for good.

Answer: TRUE
Diff: 2   Page Ref: 422
Topic: What Forces Shape Our Personalities?
Skill: Conceptual

15) Maslow searched among healthy, productive people for the basis of his theory of personality.

Answer: TRUE
Diff: 2   Page Ref: 423
Topic: What Forces Shape Our Personalities?
Skill: Conceptual

16) Rogers believed that a healthy person demonstrated a large degree of congruence between the person they wanted to be and the person they actually were.

Answer: TRUE
Diff: 2   *Page Ref: 424*
Topic: What Forces Shape Our Personalities?
Skill: Factual

17) Modern day Positive Psychology is much like humanistic psychology.

Answer: TRUE
Diff: 2   *Page Ref: 425*
Topic: What Forces Shape Our Personalities?
Skill: Factual

18) Bandura's theory states that people regulate behavior by monitoring its impact on other people, on the environment, and on themselves.

Answer: TRUE
Diff: 2   *Page Ref: 426*
Topic: What Forces Shape Our Personalities?
Skill: Conceptual

19) Students with an external locus of control tend to earn higher grades.

Answer: FALSE
Diff: 2   *Page Ref: 426–427*
Topic: What Forces Shape Our Personalities?
Skill: Factual

20) An athlete who believes if they train hard they will be successful is likely to have an internal locus of control.

Answer: TRUE
Diff: 2   *Page Ref: 426–427*
Topic: What Forces Shape Our Personalities?
Skill: Applied

21) Family systems theory emphasizes interactions with parents (and peers).

Answer: TRUE
Diff: 1   *Page Ref: 428*
Topic: What Forces Shape Our Personalities?
Skill: Conceptual

22) The four humors refer to saliva, blood, urine, and sweat.

Answer: FALSE
Diff: 2   Page Ref: 430
Topic: What Persistent Patterns Are Found in Personality?
Skill: Conceptual

23) Hippocrates devised the theory that different temperaments reflect the mixture of different fluids in the body.

Answer: TRUE
Diff: 2   Page Ref: 430
Topic: What Persistent Patterns Are Found in Personality?
Skill: Factual

24) Jerome Kagan believes that all people have the same quantities of different types of neurotransmitters.

Answer: FALSE
Diff: 2   Page Ref: 431
Topic: What Persistent Patterns Are Found in Personality?
Skill: Factual

25) Jerome Kagan found that even newborns differ in the degree to which they are shy or bold.

Answer: TRUE
Diff: 2   Page Ref: 432
Topic: What Persistent Patterns Are Found in Personality?
Skill: Factual

26) The acronym for the Big 5 personality factors is: LAKES.

Answer: FALSE
Diff: 2   Page Ref: 432
Topic: What Persistent Patterns Are Found in Personality?
Skill: Factual

27) The MMPI–2 is primarily used to determine to compare individuals who are testing to ten clinical traits.

Answer: TRUE
Diff: 2   Page Ref: 433
Topic: What Persistent Patterns Are Found in Personality?
Skill: Conceptual

28) Raymond Catell measured individuals on the big–five personality characteristics.

Answer: FALSE
Diff: 2   Page Ref: 433
Topic: What Persistent Patterns Are Found in Personality?
Skill: Factual

29) A good test should have the measurement qualities of high reliability and high validity.

Answer: TRUE
Diff: 2   Page Ref: 434
Topic: What Persistent Patterns Are Found in Personality?
Skill: Factual

30) Walter Mischel proposed the idea of the person–situation controversy.

Answer: TRUE
Diff: 2   Page Ref: 435
Topic: What Persistent Patterns Are Found in Personality?
Skill: Factual

31) The Myers–Briggs Type Indicator (MBTI) is based on the ideas of Carl Jung.

Answer: TRUE
Diff: 2   Page Ref: 436
Topic: Finding Your Type
Skill: Factual

32) The MBTI is a highly reliable test.

Answer: FALSE
Diff: 2   Page Ref: 437
Topic: Finding Your Type
Skill: Factual

33) The implicit personality theory makes assumptions about personality that are held by people to simplify the task of understanding others.

Answer: FALSE
Diff: 2   Page Ref: 439
Topic: What "Theories" Do People Use to Understand Each Other?
Skill: Factual

34) The assumption that an error made by someone else is due to some weakness in their personality instead of the circumstances involved is called the fundamental attribution error.

Answer: TRUE
Diff: 2   Page Ref: 439
Topic: What "Theories" Do People Use to Understand Each Other?
Skill: Conceptual

35) Americans tend to prefer competition to cooperation.

Answer: TRUE
Diff: 2   Page Ref: 440
Topic: What "Theories" Do People Use to Understand Each Other?
Skill: Factual

Short Answer Questions

1) Name the source of energy that Freud viewed as driving sensual pleasure.

Answer: libido
Diff: 2   Page Ref: 413
Topic: What Forces Shape Our Personalities?
Skill: Conceptual

2) What are the terms Freud uses to our life and death instincts?

Answer: Eros and Thanatos
Diff: 2   Page Ref: 413
Topic: What Forces Shape Our Personalities?
Skill: Factual

3) Give an example of a conflict that might be faced by the id, ego and superego.

Answer: You want to speed because you like driving fast (id), but you should not break the law (superego), so you go about ten over the speed limit because you think this will allow you to speed a little bit without getting a ticket (ego).
Diff: 2   Page Ref: 413
Topic: What Forces Shape Our Personalities?
Skill: Applied

4) Name the five psychosexual stages identified by Freud.

Answer: oral, anal, phallic, latency, and genital
Diff: 2   Page Ref: 414
Topic: What Forces Shape Our Personalities?
Skill: Factual

5) Briefly explain why we use defense mechanisms.

Answer: We use defense mechanisms to protect our conscious from letting in information that may be threatening to us.

Diff: 2   Page Ref: 415

Topic: What Forces Shape Our Personalities?

Skill: Conceptual

6) Describe the rationale for a projective test and name two test that fall into this category.

Answer: The idea is that a person asked to describe a vague stimulus will "project" parts of their thoughts into their description of the stimulus. Rorschach inkblot test and Thematic Apperception Test (TAT).

Diff: 2   Page Ref: 416–417

Topic: What Forces Shape Our Personalities?

Skill: Factual

7) Carl Jung divided the unconscious into the _____ unconscious and the _____ unconscious.

Answer: personal; collective

Diff: 2   Page Ref: 420

Topic: What Forces Shape Our Personalities?

Skill: Factual

8) Jung's concept of animus explains _____ archetypes, whereas the anima explains _____ archetypes.

Answer: masculine/male; feminine/female

Diff: 2   Page Ref: 420

Topic: What Forces Shape Our Personalities?

Skill: Conceptual

9) Karen Horney discusses three patterns of attitudes and behaviors that people use to deal with basic anxiety, name them.

Answer: moving toward,moving away and moving against others

Diff: 3   Page Ref: 421

Topic: What Forces Shape Our Personalities?

Skill: Factual

10) What types of subjects did Maslow test to form his theory of personality?

Answer: He sought information from historical persons such as Abraham Lincoln and Thomas Jefferson.

Diff: 2   Page Ref: 423

Topic: What Forces Shape Our Personalities?

Skill: Applied

11) Bandura's idea of reciprocal determinism involved what three forces?

Answer: environment, behavior and cognition
Diff: 3   Page Ref: 426
Topic: What Forces Shape Our Personalities?
Skill: Conceptual

12) What are the four humors that Hippocrates believed influenced our personality?

Answer: blood, yellow bile, black bile and mucus
Diff: 2   Page Ref: 430
Topic: What Persistent Patterns Are Found in Personality?
Skill: Factual

13) Some modern psychologists describe people in terms of enduring personality characteristics called _____. Clusters of these are called _____.

Answer: traits; types
Diff: 2   Page Ref: 432–433
Topic: What Persistent Patterns Are Found in Personality?
Skill: Factual

14) Name the "Big Five" personality traits.

Answer: extroversion, agreeableness, conscientiousness, neuroticism, and openness to experience
Diff: 3   Page Ref: 433
Topic: What Persistent Patterns Are Found in Personality?
Skill: Factual

15) What personality test is often given to compare individuals on ten clinical scales.

Answer: MMPI
Diff: 2   Page Ref: 434
Topic: What Persistent Patterns Are Found in Personality?
Skill: Factual

16) According to Mischel, when are personality variables most important in controlling behavior?

Answer: When the situation is ambiguous or weak, personality variables will have their greatest impact on behavior.
Diff: 3   Page Ref: 436
Topic: What Persistent Patterns Are Found in Personality?
Skill: Factual

17) What is the critique often waged against the Myers Briggs Personality Inventory (MBTI)

Answer: It scores low on measures of reliability and validity.
Diff: 2   Page Ref: 437
Topic: What Persistent Patterns Are Found in Personality?
Skill: Factual

18) Your personal explanation for how and why people behave the way they do has been called your _____ personality theory.

Answer: implicit
Diff: 2   Page Ref: 474
Topic: What "Theories" Do People Use to Understand Each Other?
Skill: Conceptual

19) Explain why those in individualistic societies are more likely to make the commit the fundamental attribution error.

Answer: The are mor likely to blame the individual fo their behavior rather than the situation.
Diff: 2   Page Ref: 439
Topic: What "Theories" Do People Use to Understand Each Other?
Skill: Conceptual

Essay Questions

1) Name and describe the three personality parts according to Freud. Be sure to describe how the parts of personality interrelate, and what strategies mediate between motivation and the expression of personality and behavior.

Answer: The student must name and describe the three parts and discuss what happens during times when the id and superego conflict. Present at birth, the id is primitive and unconscious. It acts on impulses and desires immediate gratification. The superego (our conscience) is in charge of values and morals learned from society. The ego is conscious and rational. It tries to satisfy the needs of the id without violating our morals. When there is conflict, mental disorder may occur or the individual may use ego defense mechanisms, which prevent upset feelings temporarily. However, these mechanisms leave the underlying conflict unresolved.
Diff: 2   Page Ref: 413
Topic: What Forces Shape Our Personalities?
Skill: Conceptual

2) Explain the basis by which ego defense mechanisms reduce anxiety. Name, describe and give five practical examples of such mechanisms.

Answer: (Answers will vary based n the defense mechanism that the student chooses to describe) The notion behind these mechanisms is that each serves to limit the access of unconscious motives and impulses into the level of consciousness, thus sparing the person anxiety.

Repression: Pushing painful memories out of our conscious mind. Ernie wants to forget the awful abuse he faced at the hands of his evil friend Burt as a child. He claims that he cannot remember these events happening.

Denial: The person fails to recognize that a problem exists. Harry will not admit that he has a drinking problem, he says he just drink socially even though it is effecting his work and his relationships.

Projection: We attribute our own unconscious desires onto other people or objects. Carry is thinking about cheating on an exam, she believes that everyone else in her class is cheating.

Displacement: Anger or aggression os taken out on someone or something other than the source of one's anger. Peggy was yelled at by her boss at work, later she comes home and hits her little brother.

Reaction Formation: When an individual acts the opposite of how they actually feel. Mary does not like her teacher, but she acts "sweet as pie" whenever towards her teacher.

Diff: 2   Page Ref: 416

Topic: What Forces Shape Our Personalities?

Skill: Conceptual

3) Explain how the Psychoanalytic, Humanistic and Social-Cognitive Theories in terms of their approaches to personality. Be sure to include at least one prominent individual and the basic components and at least one disadvantage of each theory.

Answer: Psychoanalytic: Freud believed that we are motivated by our past and that we are primarily driven be sex and aggression. Because we cannot accept that we hold these unacceptable unconscious wishes we seek to keep them represses. Freud believed that psychoanalytic treatment would eventually uncover one's unconscious wishes and the individual could then bring them to their awareness where they could be dealt with and healed. The Neo-Freudians attempted to place mor focus on the conscious mind and included social values i the shaping of our personalities. they also sought to extend personality theory beyond childhood, extending upon Freud's psychosexual stages which ended at puberty. A disadvantage to the psychoanalytic theory is that it lacks good scientific research to support the ideas of Freud and other Neo-Freudians. Humanistic: This theory focuses on the good in all people and the idea that all people want to achieve as much as they we able. This theory focuses on the future rather than the past and looks to the potential in individuals. Abraham Maslow creates his hierarchy of needs focusing on the potential of each individual to reach self-actualization. Some people believe that by not recognizing the power of the unconscious humanistic psychologists are missing part of the explanation for human behavior.
Social-Cognitive: This theory takes into account our expectations in different situations. How we perceive and interpret a situations is a large determining factor deciding how we will behave. modern day social-cognitive psychologists such as Bandura and Rotter emphasize the interaction of behavior, the environment and our cognition. critics of the Social-Cognitive theory say that it over emphasizes the role of rational information processing and overlooks emotion and unconscious forces.

Diff: 3   *Page Ref: 413-427*

Topic: What Forces Shape Our Personalities?

Skill: Analysis

4) Compare and contrast the personality theory developed by Carl Jung and the Big Five system of traits.

Answer: Jung's theory is psychoanalytic/psychodynamic, whereas the Big Five is part of a trait or type theory. Jung believed that each of us has a personal and collective unconscious. The collective unconscious houses our archetypes (such as anima and animus), whereas the personal unconscious is analogous to Freud's id concept. Jung believed that personality is essentially a balance between opposing unconscious tendencies. Likewise, the Big Five says that we have a series of traits that are each bipolar. The student should name the five traits in the Big Five. These traits are believed to be relatively stable.

Diff: 2   *Page Ref: 420, 432-433*

Topic: What Persistent Patterns Are Found in Personality?

Skill: Conceptual

5) Compare projective test to trait personality tests. Tell what they measure and how they measure it.

   Answer: Projective tests:The Rorschach Inkblot Technique is a projective test for assessing personality by asking participants to describe what a series of inkblots look like. Similarly, the Thematic Apperception Test (TAT) is a projective test to measure personality. However, the TAT asks participants to generate stories about what is happening in a series of pictures.
   Trait Theory: The NEO–PI measures the stability of the Big Five personality traits. The MMPI–2 measures serious mental problems on ten clinical scales by asking participants to respond to 567 statements regarding their beliefs and preferences. The Myers–Briggs Type Indicator (MBTI) is based on Jungian types, and it places people in a four–dimensional personality type based on how individuals perceive the world and relate to others.

   Diff: 2   Page Ref: 416–417; 433–437

   Topic: What Persistent Patterns Are Found in Personality?

   Skill: Factual

6) Explain three main differences between Individualistic and Collectivist societies.

   Answer: In collectivist societies value is given to old age as it is associated with wisdom. Stoicism, many collectivist societies encourage the hiding on emotions while in individualistic societies we show your emotions often. In collectivist societies more people demonstrate an external locus of control in which they think that changes in their environment are out of their control. In Individualistic societies more people demonstrate and internal locus of control.

   Diff: 2   Page Ref: 439

   Topic: What "Theories" Do People Use to Understand Each Other?

   Skill: Analysis

Chapter 11 Testing and Individual Differences

Multiple Choice

1) Insuring that a test measures what it is supposed to measure is _____, while a test that yields consistent results over time is said to be _____.

   A) reliable; valid

   B) have good criterion validity; have good construct validity

   C) validity; reliable

   D) have good split–half reliability; have good content validity

   E) item analysis; factor analysis

   Answer: C
   Diff: 2   Page Ref: 452
   Topic: How Do we Measure Individual Differences?
   Skill: Factual

2) If Steven sits down to take his Chemistry exam and it appears to test the information that he studied and that was discussed in class, the test would be said to have high

   A) content validity.

   B) face validity.

   C) criterion validity.

   D) test–retest reliability.

   E) split–half reliability.

   Answer: B
   Diff: 2   Page Ref: 452
   Topic: How Do we Measure Individual Differences?
   Skill: Applied

3) If a test seems to represent the larger body of knowledge about the subject which the test covers, it would be said to have

   A) content validity.

   B) face validity.

   C) test–retest reliability.

   D) split–half reliability.

   E) criterion validity.

   Answer: A
   Diff: 2   Page Ref: 452
   Topic: How Do we Measure Individual Differences?
   Skill: Factual

4) Item analysis, in which each question is examined to see how it is related to the learning objectives being tested is typically used with _____.

    A) test–retest reliability

    B) content validity

    C) split–half reliability

    D) criterion reliability

    E) face validity

Answer: B

Diff: 3   Page Ref: 452

Topic: How Do we Measure Individual Differences?

Skill: Conceptual

5) Jose takes his ACT in the spring of his junior year of high school and takes the exam again in the fall of his senior year of high school. Jose receives a 28 the first time he takes the exam and a 19 the second time he takes it. With these results we would have the question the _____ of the exam.

    A) split–half reliability

    B) content validity

    C) criterion validity

    D) face validity

    E) test–retest reliability

Answer: E

Diff: 3   Page Ref: 452

Topic: How Do we Measure Individual Differences?

Skill: Applied

6) If you want to see how penny did on the even questions compared to the odd questions for her driver's education exam you would use _____.

    A) criterion validity

    B) content validity

    C) test–retest reliability

    D) split–half reliability

    E) face validity

Answer: D

Diff: 2   Page Ref: 453

Topic: How Do we Measure Individual Differences?

Skill: Applied

7) In a normal distribution, what percentage of he population should fall within the normal range?

    A) 98%   B) 35%   C) 67%   D) 50%   E) 42%

Answer: C
Diff: 2   Page Ref: 453
Topic: How Do we Measure Individual Differences?
Skill: Factual

8) When establishing norms it is important to first _____ before comparing other people to the norm.

    A) be sure to give them a valid test

    B) test a significantly significant sample

    C) be sure to give them a reliable test

    D) test adults rather than children

    E) be sure to test individuals from all different racial and ethnic backgrounds

Answer: B
Diff: 2   Page Ref: 453
Topic: How Do we Measure Individual Differences?
Skill: Conceptual

9) Whe considering IQ scores, what is the normal range?

    A) 80–120   B) 90–110   C) 100   D) 70–130   E) 50–150

Answer: D
Diff: 2   Page Ref: 453
Topic: How Do we Measure Individual Differences?
Skill: Factual

10) If someone has an IQ score above 130, they are defined as being

    A) smart.

    B) gifted.

    C) a genius.

    D) brilliant.

    E) a member of MENSA.

Answer: C
Diff: 2   Page Ref: 453
Topic: How Do we Measure Individual Differences?
Skill: Factual

11) Tests that can be scored easily by a machine, are generally referred to as _____.

    A) intelligence tests

    B) aptitude tests

    C) objective tests

    D) subjective tests

    E) achievement tests

Answer: C

Diff: 2   *Page Ref: 454*

Topic: How Do we Measure Individual Differences?

Skill: Factual

12) Which of the following is an example of a subjective test?

    A) the SAT

    B) the Minnesota Multiphasic Personality Inventory (MMPI)

    C) the Myers Briggs Type Indicator (MBTI)

    D) the Thematic Apperception Test (TAT)

    E) the multiple choice portion of your last psychology unit exam

Answer: D

Diff: 2   *Page Ref: 454*

Topic: How Do we Measure Individual Differences?

Skill: Factual

13) Which of the following exams would need to be concerned with inter-rater reliability effecting the outcome of the scores on the exam?

    A) the SAT (multiple choice)

    B) the drivers education exam

    C) the Rorschach inkblot test

    D) the Myers Briggs Type Indicator (MBTI)

    E) the Minnesota Multiphasic Personality Inventory (MMPI)

Answer: C

Diff: 2   *Page Ref: 454*

Topic: How Do we Measure Individual Differences?

Skill: Conceptual

14) More of an effort has been made recently to place students who were at one time taught in separate classroom s into a regular classroom setting. What is this practice generally called?

A) tracking

B) special education

C) mainstreaming

D) remediation

E) open enrollment

Answer: C

Diff: 1   Page Ref: 455

Topic: How Do we Measure Individual Differences?

Skill: Factual

15) Often times Advanced Placement courses or honors courses are open to only a small percentage of the school population. Students may also be prepared for four-year colleges, two-year colleges or vocational training according to different programs. What is this practice called?

A) mainstreaming

B) routing

C) remediation

D) tracking

E) favoritism

Answer: D

Diff: 1   Page Ref: 455

Topic: How Do we Measure Individual Differences?

Skill: Factual

16) Which of the following is true of intelligence?

A) It can be directly measuring in a test.

B) Intelligence scores do not predict school performance.

C) It can be thought of as the ability to solve problems.

D) Intelligence is an absolute term.

E) B and D are correct.

Answer: C

Diff: 2   Page Ref: 456

Topic: How Is Intelligence Measured?

Skill: Conceptual

17) The purpose of the Binet test was to

    A) determine which children needed remedial help.

    B) weed poor students out of the educational system.

    C) match workers with the appropriate job.

    D) test Galton's theories of intelligence.

    E) improve the educational system of France.

Answer: A
Diff: 2   Page Ref: 456
Topic: How Is Intelligence Measured?
Skill: Factual

18) The Binet–Simon approach to the assessment of school abilities was unique in that

    A) they only measured current performance.

    B) they wanted to be able to label the slow learners.

    C) they believed training would not affect intelligence.

    D) their test was tied to Spearman's intelligence theory.

    E) their test measured innate intelligence.

Answer: A
Diff: 2   Page Ref: 457
Topic: How Is Intelligence Measured?
Skill: Conceptual

19) _____ is defined as the the average age at which normal (average) individuals achieve a particular intelligence score.

    A) IQ

    B) Mental age

    C) Performance IQ

    D) Crystallized intelligence

    E) Chronological age

Answer: B
Diff: 3   Page Ref: 457
Topic: How Is Intelligence Measured?
Skill: Conceptual

20) What is chronological age?

   A) the average age at which normal individuals achieve a particular score on a measure of intelligence

   B) the age at which someone's test score is equal to current age

   C) the number of years since an individual's birth

   D) the mental age multiplied by the IQ

   E) the age determined based on the number of questions correctly answered on an IQ test

Answer: C

Diff: 1   *Page Ref: 457*

Topic: How Is Intelligence Measured?

Skill: Conceptual

21) Which of the following events was a factor that led to mass intelligence testing in the United States?

   A) World War I

   B) Reconstruction following the Civil War

   C) World War II

   D) the Industrial Revolution

   E) the Great Depression

Answer: A

Diff: 2   *Page Ref: 457*

Topic: How Is Intelligence Measured?

Skill: Factual

22) One of the first ways IQ tests were used in the United States was to

   A) determine which students would get into college.

   B) separate those who could benefit from education or military leadership from those who could not.

   C) revamp the educational system in the United States.

   D) allow high scoring individuals to apply for MENSA.

   E) determine the genetic basis for those who scored low.

Answer: B

Diff: 2   *Page Ref: 457*

Topic: How Is Intelligence Measured?

Skill: Factual

23) What group of people were often labeled 'morons' by early intelligence tests because they had limited English skills?

    A) Army recruits

    B) people with schizophrenia

    C) very young children

    D) immigrants to the United States

    E) persons living in the South

Answer: D
Diff: 2   Page Ref: 458
Topic: How Is Intelligence Measured?
Skill: Factual

24) On an IQ test, a six year old child scores a mental age of eight years. What is their IQ score?

    A) 75   B) 80   C) 112   D) 120   E) 133

Answer: E
Diff: 2   Page Ref: 458
Topic: How Is Intelligence Measured?
Skill: Conceptual

25) The Stanford–Binet test was adopted by

    A) Simon.   B) Terman.   C) Cattell.   D) Stern.   E) Wechsler.

Answer: B
Diff: 2   Page Ref: 458
Topic: How Is Intelligence Measured?
Skill: Factual

26) Terman believed that intelligence was largely _____ and that an IQ test could measure it precisely.

    A) learned in school

    B) learned in the home

    C) learned through peers

    D) always changing

    E) innate

Answer: E
Diff: 2   Page Ref: 458
Topic: How Is Intelligence Measured?
Skill: Factual

27) The term _____ refers to the ratio of mental age divided by chronological age multiplied by 100.

    A) intellectual ratio

    B) aptitude

    C) mental ratio

    D) standardized intelligence

    E) intelligence quotient

Answer: E
Diff: 1   Page Ref: 458
Topic: How Is Intelligence Measured?
Skill: Factual

28) In the original Stanford–Binet Intelligence Scale, the intelligence quotient (IQ) was calculated as

    A) $IQ = CA/MA \times 100$.

    B) $IQ = 100/CA \times MA$.

    C) $IQ = MA/100 \times CA$.

    D) $IQ = MA/CA \times 100$.

    E) $IQ = CA/100 \times MA$.

Answer: D
Diff: 2   Page Ref: 458
Topic: How Is Intelligence Measured?
Skill: Factual

29) If Ralph's computed IQ score is 75, then

    A) he might be a twelve-year-old who is as smart as the average nine-year-old.

    B) he correctly answered three-fourths of the questions on the intelligence test.

    C) he is 75 years old.

    D) he might be a six-year-old who is as intelligent as most eight-year-olds.

    E) he is as smart as the average 75-year-old.

Answer: A
Diff: 2   Page Ref: 458
Topic: How Is Intelligence Measured?
Skill: Applied

30) The WAIS, WISC, and WPPSI are tests of _____ that were created by _____.

   A) mental aptitude; the SAT corporation

   B) components of intelligence; David Weschler

   C) creativity; Howard Gardner

   D) independence; Leland Stanford

   E) creativity; David Weschler

Answer: B
Diff: 3   Page Ref: 459
Topic: How Is Intelligence Measured?
Skill: Factual

31) A key problem with Terman's original formula for computing IQs is that it

   A) caused people to believe that IQ is unchangeable.

   B) made it seem as if people grow less intelligent with age.

   C) was never standardized and difficult to compute.

   D) caused mathematical difficulties for people far below the average.

   E) did not correlate with actual intelligence at any point in a person's life.

Answer: B
Diff: 2   Page Ref: 460
Topic: How Is Intelligence Measured?
Skill: Conceptual

32) Which of the following pairs of children features one child who would be classified as mentally retarded and one child who would be classified as gifted?

   A) Tammy's IQ is 88, and Preki's IQ is 188.

   B) Pua's IQ is 99, and Jared's IQ is 1200.

   C) Brock's IQ is 79, and Chandler's IQ is 112.

   D) Bill's IQ is 54, and Missy's IQ is 137.

   E) Ricardo's IQ is 14, and Herve's IQ is 84.

Answer: D
Diff: 2   Page Ref: 460
Topic: What Can You Do for an Exceptional Child?
Skill: Applied

33) A child whose IQ score is _____ would be classified as _____.

A) 60; normal

B) 100; gifted

C) 60; mentally retarded

D) 150; normal

E) 60; gifted

Answer: C

Diff: 2   *Page Ref: 460*

Topic: What Can You Do for an Exceptional Child?

Skill: Applied

34) With optimal educational programs parents of children who have been classified as mentally retarded may see an IQ gain of up to

A) 100 points.

B) 50 points.

C) 15 points.

D) 2 points.

E) 7 points.

Answer: C

Diff: 2   *Page Ref: 461*

Topic: What Can You Do for an Exceptional Child?

Skill: Recall

35) Using most tests of intelligence, the cut-off score at which a person is labeled as "gifted" is

A) above 130.   B) above 150.   C) below 70.   D) above 100.   E) above 50.

Answer: A

Diff: 2   *Page Ref: 461*

Topic: What Can You Do for an Exceptional Child?

Skill: Factual

36) Which of the following can benefit a mentally retarded child?

A) Encourage them to study harder.

B) Provide early interventions.

C) Place them in special group homes.

D) Provide programs that include sensory stimulation and social interaction.

E) B and D are correct.

Answer: E

Diff: 2   *Page Ref: 461*

Topic: What Can You Do for an Exceptional Child?

Skill: Factual

37) Those who are labelled as 'gifted' usually fall in the top _____ of individuals taking IQ tests.

    A) 10%   B) 1–2%   C) 5%   D) 25%   E) 50%

Answer: B

Diff: 2   Page Ref: 461

Topic: What Can You Do for an Exceptional Child?

Skill: Factual

38) In his decades–long study of giftedness, Lewis Terman found

    A) that there were surprisingly few professionals in his sample.

    B) there were a great many professionals and even an "Einstein" or two.

    C) that most gifted children generally grew up to be healthy and happy adults.

    D) academic success was unrelated to IQ.

    E) that high IQ was practically a guarantee of wealth and fame.

Answer: C

Diff: 2   Page Ref: 461

Topic: What Can You Do for an Exceptional Child?

Skill: Factual

39) Savants typically have

    A) high IQ scores.

    B) low IQ scores.

    C) IQ scores in the normal range.

    D) superb educational backgrounds.

    E) superb genetics.

Answer: B

Diff: 2   Page Ref: 463

Topic: What Are The Components of Intelligence?

Skill: Conceptual

40) Which of the following people would be considered a savant?

    A) Carrie, who is mentally retarded

    B) Luka, who is mentally retarded but has superb mathematical skills

    C) Carter, who is gifted and does well at most tasks

    D) Abby, who is gifted but has major difficulties with spelling

    E) Cleo, who is of average intelligence, but is great at math and terrible at spelling

Answer: B

Diff: 2   Page Ref: 463

Topic: What Are The Components of Intelligence?

Skill: Applied

41) The area of psychology that specializes in mental testing is known as

    A) measurement science.

    B) psychometrics.

    C) experimental psychology.

    D) statistics.

    E) intellectualization.

Answer: B
Diff: 2   *Page Ref: 330*
Topic: What Are the Components of Thought?
Skill: Conceptual

42) The concept of _____ was denoted by the symbol"g" by Charles Spearman.

    A) general intelligence

    B) gender

    C) giftedness

    D) genetics

    E) genius

Answer: A
Diff: 2   *Page Ref: 464*
Topic: What Are The Components of Intelligence?
Skill: Factual

43) This individual created the g factor to represent one's general intellectual ability.

    A) Binet   B) Gardner   C) Cattell   D) Spearman   E) Terman

Answer: D
Diff: 2   *Page Ref: 464*
Topic: What Are The Components of Intelligence?
Skill: Factual

44) Charles Spearman argued that individual differences in intelligence

    A) were subject to change from environmental influences.

    B) could be altered by early intervention in childhood educational programs.

    C) were innately determined.

    D) were due to the influence of invisible "flux" fields that affect neurotransmitters.

    E) could not be accurately measured.

Answer: C
Diff: 2   *Page Ref: 464*
Topic: Is Intelligence One or Many Abilities?
Skill: Conceptual

45) Cattell would argue that a person who can name all seven of the dwarfs possesses _____ intelligence.

   A) divergent

   B) crystallized

   C) fluid

   D) practical

   E) experiential

Answer: B
Diff: 2   Page Ref: 464
Topic: Is Intelligence One or Many Abilities?
Skill: Applied

46) If you know all of the answers to the questions on Jeopardy, you would be said to be high in _____ intelligence(s).

   A) crystallized

   B) fluid

   C) general

   D) multiple

   E) emotional

Answer: A
Diff: 2   Page Ref: 464
Topic: What Are The Components of Intelligence?
Skill: Applied

47) Robert Sternberg would say that a person who does not do well in school in spite of having lot of "street smarts"

   A) lacks fluid intelligence.

   B) has a high "g."

   C) lacks divergent intelligence.

   D) has much practical intelligence.

   E) has much crystallized intelligence.

Answer: D
Diff: 2   Page Ref: 464
Topic: Is Intelligence One or Many Abilities?
Skill: Applied

48) According to Sternberg, your college grades would reflect your _____ intelligence.

   A) fluid

   B) analytical

   C) experiential

   D) practical

   E) triarchic

Answer: B
Diff: 2   Page Ref: 465
Topic: Is Intelligence One or Many Abilities?
Skill: Conceptual

49) According to Sternberg, Picasso would score as high in _____ intelligence.

   A) creative

   B) analytical

   C) experiential

   D) practical

   E) triarchic

Answer: A
Diff: 2   Page Ref: 465
Topic: Is Intelligence One or Many Abilities?
Skill: Conceptual

50) Sternberg would say that is is necessary to have _____ intelligence to design the interior of a home, but they would need _____ to do well on their Final exams.

   A) creative; analytical

   B) practical; creative

   C) analytical; creative

   D) practical; analytical

   E) analytical; practical

Answer: A
Diff: 2   Page Ref: 464–465
Topic: What Are The Components of Intelligence?
Skill: Applied

51) Janet cannot get along well with others, but she is the best in her class at reading. According to Howard Gardner, she lacks _____ intelligence but possesses much _____ intelligence.

    A) musical; spatial

    B) rhythmic; logical

    C) bodily-kinesthetic; intrapersonal

    D) interpersonal; linguistic

    E) spatial; linguistic

Answer: D

Diff: 3   *Page Ref: 466*

Topic: Is Intelligence One or Many Abilities?

Skill: Applied

52) Interpersonal intelligence is to intrapersonal intelligence as

    A) others are to self.

    B) self is to others.

    C) positive is to negative.

    D) "street smarts" is to "book smarts."

    E) "book smarts" is to "street smarts."

Answer: A

Diff: 2   *Page Ref: 466*

Topic: Is Intelligence One or Many Abilities?

Skill: Conceptual

53) Which of the mental abilities noted by Gardner could be thought of as relating to emotional intelligence?

    A) musical; spatial

    B) rhythmic; logical

    C) bodily-kinesthetic; intrapersonal

    D) interpersonal; intrapersonal

    E) spatial; linguistic

Answer: D

Diff: 3   *Page Ref: 466*

Topic: Is Intelligence One or Many Abilities?

Skill: Applied

54) Which of the following types of Gardner's intelligence have been cited as needing more empirical evidence to support?

   A) linguistic

   B) bodily-kinesthetic

   C) existential

   D) interpersonal

   E) spatial

   Answer: C
   Diff: 2   Page Ref: 466
   Topic: What Are The Components of Intelligence?
   Skill: Conceptual

55) John Berry's found that the explanation of intelligence by members of the Cree culture focuses on

   A) wealth.

   B) respect.

   C) active thinking.

   D) speed.

   E) innate ability.

   Answer: B
   Diff: 2   Page Ref: 466
   Topic: Is Intelligence One or Many Abilities?
   Skill: Conceptual

56) Let's say that Frida is a substitute teacher who is taking over for Susan. Susan's two classes are equally good, but Susan decides to tell Frida that the afternoon class is smarter. Based on the research of Rosenthal and Jacobson, we could expect

   A) the afternoon class to perform better.

   B) Frida to try to treat the two classes the same.

   C) to defend the morning class by saying they are smarter.

   D) Frida to figure out that Susan was lying.

   E) the morning class to get better treatment from Frida.

   Answer: A
   Diff: 2   Page Ref: 468
   Topic: Test Scores and the Self-Fulfilling Prophecy
   Skill: Applied

57) A self-fulfilling prophecy occurs when people
   A) forget their original expectations once the results are in.
   B) achieve at their expected level.
   C) perform better than expected.
   D) try harder when others have negative expectations.
   E) give up because of low motivation.

Answer: B
Diff: 2   Page Ref: 468
Topic: Test Scores and the Self-Fulfilling Prophecy
Skill: Conceptual

58) An example of _____ is a person who expects to do poorly on a math test and then does poorly.
   A) divergent thinking
   B) lack of interpersonal intelligence
   C) high crystallized intelligence
   D) an accurate "g"
   E) a self-fulfilling prophecy

Answer: E
Diff: 2   Page Ref: 468
Topic: Test Scores and the Self-Fulfilling Prophecy
Skill: Applied

59) The highest correlation among IQ scores is for
   A) identical twins.
   B) parent and child.
   C) non-twin siblings.
   D) foster parent and child.
   E) fraternal twins.

Answer: A
Diff: 2   Page Ref: 470
Topic: How Do Psychologists Explain IQ Differences Among Groups?
Skill: Factual

60) Which of the following has been shown to increase IQ scores

    A) a stimulating environment.

    B) contact early in life.

    C) good nutrition early in life.

    D) problem solving.

    E) All of the above have been shown to improve IQ scores.

Answer: E

Diff: 2   Page Ref: 471

Topic: How Do Psychologists Explain IQ Differences Among Groups?

Skill: Conceptual

61) We can speak of _____ only within a group of individuals who have shared the same environment.

    A) achievement tests

    B) heritable differences

    C) intelligence quotients

    D) interpersonal validity

    E) aptitude reliability

Answer: B

Diff: 1   Page Ref: 471–472

Topic: How Do Psychologists Explain IQ Differences Among Groups?

Skill: Conceptual

62) Heritability refers to

    A) differences between identical twins raised apart.

    B) the amount of variation in a group that can be attributed to genetic differences.

    C) the impact of schooling on IQ scores.

    D) concordance differences between siblings.

    E) the impact of sensory deprivation on cognitive growth.

Answer: B

Diff: 2   Page Ref: 472

Topic: How Do Psychologists Explain IQ Differences Among Groups?

Skill: Conceptual

63) Heritability refers to _____ not _____.

    A) stereotype effect; self-fulfilling prophecies

    B) positive labeling; negative labeling

    C) within-group differences; between group differences

    D) aptitude; achievement

    E) validity; reliability

Answer: C

Diff: 2   Page Ref: 472

Topic: How Do Psychologists Explain IQ Differences Among Groups?

Skill: Conceptual

64) Arthur Jensen proposed that their are limits to increases in the improvement of IQ scores for _____ because of heredity.

    A) different racial groups

    B) different genders

    C) different age groups

    D) children

    E) None of the above

Answer: A

Diff: 2   Page Ref: 472

Topic: How Do Psychologists Explain IQ Differences Among Groups?

Skill: Factual

65) Critics claimed that Jensen minimized or ignored the impact of all of the following in terms of racial differences EXCEPT for

    A) the effects of racism.

    B) different teacher expectations in school.

    C) lack of opportunity.

    D) low self-esteem.

    E) heredity.

Answer: E

Diff: 2   Page Ref: 472

Topic: How Do Psychologists Explain IQ Differences Among Groups?

Skill: Conceptual

66) Based on Scarr and Weinberg's study, you would expect that black and white children who were _____ at birth would exhibit IQ' scores that reflected a strong effect of the environment.

    A) mentally-retarded

    B) from lower social classes

    C) adopted

    D) low in weight at

    E) placed in special facilities

Answer: C

Diff: 2   Page Ref: 473

Topic: How Do Psychologists Explain IQ Differences Among Groups?

Skill: Factual

67) The research of Scarr and Weinberg points to the fact that _____ can have a powerful effect on IQ.

    A) nature

    B) environment

    C) siblings

    D) good genes

    E) having pets

Answer: B

Diff: 2   Page Ref: 473

Topic: How Do Psychologists Explain IQ Differences Among Groups?

Skill: Factual

68) Scarr and Weinberg found that _____ by the time of late adolescence.

    A) there was no difference between Black and White adoptees IQ scores

    B) White adoptees IQ scores were higher than Black children's

    C) Black adoptees IQ scores were higher than White children's

    D) White adoptees IQ scores improved while Black adoptees scores plummeted

    E) Black and White adoptees IQ scores decreased

Answer: A

Diff: 2   Page Ref: 473

Topic: How Do Psychologists Explain IQ Differences Among Groups?

Skill: Factual

69) A problem with the Head Start enrichment program is that it

    A) may not start early enough.

    B) has had no impact on IQ scores.

    C) cannot undo the effects of poverty.

    D) reaches all of the children who need it.

    E) has no long term impact.

Answer: A
Diff: 2   Page Ref: 474
Topic: How Do Psychologists Explain IQ Differences Among Groups?
Skill: Applied

70) A source of bias that may explain racial IQ differences is the fact that most IQ tests rely heavily on

    A) math skills.

    B) vocabulary level.

    C) the ability to pay attention.

    D) individual responsibility.

    E) interpersonal intelligence.

Answer: B
Diff: 2   Page Ref: 474
Topic: How Do Psychologists Explain IQ Differences Among Groups?
Skill: Conceptual

71) A example of a potentially biased question on an IQ exam is which of the following?

    A) What does the word "opulent' mean?

    B) Find the next letter in a pattern.

    C) What do the following numbers have in common?

    D) Place the missing letter in the word BA_K.

    E) Figure out the missing number in a pattern.

Answer: A
Diff: 2   Page Ref: 474
Topic: How Do Psychologists Explain IQ Differences Among Groups?
Skill: Applied

72) What research rule do Murray and Hernstein ignore when they suggest that there are hereditary differences between races?

A) Correlation does not prove causation.

B) They must run a double blind study.

C) They must adhere to APA's ethic guidelines.

D) They do not test a large enough population.

E) All of the above

Answer: A

Diff: 3   Page Ref: 475

Topic: How Do Psychologists Explain IQ Differences Among Groups?

Skill: Conceptual

73) The best predictors of a child's IQ at age four are

A) family's financial status and mother's level of education.

B) race and presence of a father.

C) money and numbers of books in the home.

D) gender and race.

E) whether the mother works out of the home.

Answer: A

Diff: 2   Page Ref: 476

Topic: Helping Others Think Critically about Group Differences

Skill: Factual

74) A philosophy and political movement that encourage biologically superior people to interbreed and sought to discourage biologically inferior people from having offspring.

A) superiority

B) extermination

C) eugenics

D) euthanasia

E) None of the above

Answer: C

Diff: 2   Page Ref: 476

Topic: How Do Psychologists Explain IQ Differences Among Groups?

Skill: Factual

75) To become a world–class chef, you should expect to spend about how many years of intense study and practice?

    A) 2 or 3   B) 5 to 7   C) 13   D) 15 to 20   E) 10

Answer: E
Diff: 2   Page Ref: 478
Topic: Developing Expertise in Psychology
Skill: Applied

Check Your Understanding Questions

1) When we check to see whether a test will yield the same results over time, we are assessing it's
    A) reliability.
    B) validity.
    C) normality.
    D) objectivity.
    E) subjectivity.

Answer: A
Diff: 2   Page Ref: 455
Topic: Check Your Understanding
Skill: Applied

2) The Thematic Apperception Test (TAT) is a(n)_____ test.
    A) fill–in–the–blank
    B) essay
    C) multiple–choice
    D) objective
    E) subjective

Answer: E
Diff: 2   Page Ref: 455
Topic: Check Your Understanding
Skill: Applied

3) What percentage of women should fall between 5'1 and 5'9 if you have taken a statistically significant sample?

    A) 50%   B) 67%   C) 84%   D) 99.7%   E) 46%

Answer: B
Diff: 2   Page Ref: 455
Topic: Check Your Understanding
Skill: Conceptual

4) All of the following are components of ethical testing except

   A) item analysis.

   B) validity.

   C) reliability.

   D) objectivity.

   E) instinct.

Answer: E
Diff: 2   Page Ref: 455
Topic: Check Your Understanding
Skill: Conceptual

5) One of Binet's great ideas, was that of mental age, which was defined as

   A) the average age at which people achieve a particular score on an intelligence test.

   B) an individual's biological age plus the score he or she achieves on a mental test.

   C) and individual's level of emotional maturity, as judged by the examiner.

   D) the variability in scores seen when an individual is tested repeatedly.

   E) a means of measuring performance on a test against a specific learning goal.

Answer: A
Diff: 2   Page Ref: 463
Topic: Check Your Understanding
Skill: Recall

6) You have tested a 12–year–old child and found out that she has a mental age of 15. Using the original IQ formula, what is her IQ?

   A) 50   B) 75   C) 100   D) 115   E) 125

Answer: E
Diff: 2   Page Ref: 463
Topic: Check Your Understanding
Skill: Applied

7) A problem with the original IQ formula is that it gave a distorted picture of the intellectual abilities of

   A) adults.

   B) children.

   C) retarded persons.

   D) gifted students.

   E) the elderly.

Answer: A
Diff: 2   Page Ref: 463
Topic: Check Your Understanding
Skill: Recall

8) If intelligence is a normally distributed characteristic, then you would expect to find it
    A) to be different abilities in different people.
    B) to be spread throughout the population, but with most people clustered near the middle of the range.
    C) to a significant degree only in people whose IQ scores are above 100.
    D) to be determined entirely by hereditary factors.
    E) to be determined entirely be environmental factors.

Answer: A
Diff: 2   Page Ref: 463
Topic: Check Your Understanding
Skill: Understanding the Core Concept

9) From the perspective of Cattell's theory, the ability to use algorithms and heuristics would be an aspect of
    A) convergent thinking.
    B) crystallized intelligence.
    C) logical thinking.
    D) fluid intelligence.
    E) divergent thinking.

Answer: D
Diff: 2   Page Ref: 469
Topic: Check Your Understanding
Skill: Applied

10) A friend tells you that he has found a way to improve his grades by stopping at his psychology professor's office once a week to ask questions about the reading. If this is successful, you could say that your friend has shown
    A) practical intelligence.
    B) logical reasoning.
    C) experiential intelligence.
    D) convergent thinking.
    E) divergent thinking.

Answer: A
Diff: 2   Page Ref: 469
Topic: Check Your Understanding
Skill: Applied

11) Which of Gardner's seven intelligences is most like that measured on standard IQ tests?

A) linguistic ability

B) bodily-kinesthetic ability

C) intrapersonal ability

D) interpersonal ability

E) spatial ability

Answer: A
Diff: 2   Page Ref: 469
Topic: Check Your Understanding
Skill: Recall

12) A self-fulfilling prophecy comes true because of

A) innate factors.

B) a lack of logic-mathematical ability.

C) the lack of precision of IQ tests.

D) people's expectations.

E) cultural norms.

Answer: D
Diff: 2   Page Ref: 469
Topic: Check Your Understanding
Skill: Recall

13) Which of the following most aptly characterizes the current debate about intelligence?

A) mental age versus chronological age

B) single versus multiple

C) practical versus logical

D) cognitive versus behavioral

E) fluid versus crystallized

Answer: B
Diff: 2   Page Ref: 469
Topic: Check Your Understanding
Skill: Understanding the Core Concept

14) In their analysis of racial IQ factors, Herrnstein and Murray confuse _____ with _____.

   A) nature; nurture

   B) reporting; bias

   C) proof; rumor

   D) correlation; causation

   E) stereotyping; discrimination

Answer: D
Diff: 2   Page Ref: 476
Topic: Check Your Understanding
Skill: Conceptual

15) Most early American psychologists working on intelligence believed that the dominant influence on intelligence was

   A) heredity.

   B) experience.

   C) gender.

   D) the size of one's brain.

   E) environment.

Answer: A
Diff: 2   Page Ref: 476
Topic: Check Your Understanding
Skill: Recall

16) It is most accurate to say that

   A) intelligence is more influenced by heredity than environment.

   B) intelligence is more influenced by is more influenced by environment than heredity.

   C) intelligence is the result of interaction of heredity and environment.

   D) the influence of environment on intelligence is most powerful in the children of minority groups.

   E) intelligence is influenced more by family makeup than by any interactions of heredity and environment.

Answer: C
Diff: 2   Page Ref: 476
Topic: Check Your Understanding
Skill: Analysis

17) The concept of heritability refers to genetic variation
    A) within an individual's sperm cells or eggs.
    B) between one group or another.
    C) within an individual's immediate family.
    D) within a group of individuals that have had the same environment.
    E) between family members.

    Answer: D
    Diff: 2   Page Ref: 477
    Topic: Check Your Understanding
    Skill: Recall

18) Although everyone agrees that heredity affects _____ intelligence, there is no evidence that it accounts for differences among _____.
    A) individuals; groups
    B) groups; individuals
    C) social; the mentally retarded
    D) academic; practical
    E) fluid; individuals

    Answer: A
    Diff: 2   Page Ref: 477
    Topic: Check Your Understanding
    Skill: Understanding the Core Concept

True/False Questions

1) Albert Einstein always excelled in academic settings.

   Answer: FALSE
   Diff: 2   Page Ref: 451
   Topic: How Do we Measure Individual Differences?
   Skill: Factual

2) A test that yields consistent results on two (or more) separate occasions is said to be valid.

   Answer: FALSE
   Diff: 2   Page Ref: 452
   Topic: How Do we Measure Individual Differences?
   Skill: Factual

3) Item analysis is most closely associated with content validity.

   Answer: TRUE
   Diff: 3   Page Ref: 452
   Topic: How Do we Measure Individual Differences?
   Skill: Conceptual

4) In order to be identified as a CPA, one has to meets a set requirement on all portions of an exam, this is an example of criterion validity.

Answer: TRUE
Diff: 3   Page Ref: 452
Topic: How Do we Measure Individual Differences?
Skill: Applied

5) About 87% of individuals will fall into the normal range for a given set of scores.

Answer: FALSE
Diff: 2   Page Ref: 453
Topic: How Do we Measure Individual Differences?
Skill: Factual

6) Objective tests are dependent on good inter–rater reliability.

Answer: FALSE
Diff: 2   Page Ref: 454
Topic: How Do we Measure Individual Differences?
Skill: Factual

7) Binet originally created IQ tests to determine if children were ready for school or if they needed special help.

Answer: TRUE
Diff: 2   Page Ref: 457
Topic: What Can You Do for an Exceptional Child?
Skill: Factual

8) IQ tests have had the effect over the years of reinforcing prevailing prejudices about certain racial and ethnic groups.

Answer: FALSE
Diff: 2   Page Ref: 458
Topic: How Is Intelligence Measured?
Skill: Conceptual

9) If a four–year–old child had a mental age of 4, he would have an IQ of 120.

Answer: FALSE
Diff: 2   Page Ref: 458
Topic: How Is Intelligence Measured?
Skill: Applied

10) The intelligence tests created by David Wecshler are frequently used today.

Answer: TRUE
Diff: 2   Page Ref: 459
Topic: How Is Intelligence Measured?
Skill: Factual

11) Fetal alcohol syndrome is an example of an environmental cause of mental retardation.

Answer: TRUE
Diff: 2   Page Ref: 460
Topic: What Can You Do for an Exceptional Child?
Skill: Factual

12) Most of the high IQ children in Terman's studies grew up to be healthy and happy.

Answer: TRUE
Diff: 2   Page Ref: 461
Topic: What Can You Do for an Exceptional Child?
Skill: Factual

13) Robbie scores incredibly low on IQ tests. However, he has the ability to remember what he has eaten every day for the last 18 years. Robbie may be suffering from savant syndrome.

Answer: FALSE
Diff: 2   Page Ref: 463
Topic: What Are The Components of Intelligence?
Skill: Applied

14) Gardner creates the idea of the g factor as representing one's overall intelligence.

Answer: FALSE
Diff: 2   Page Ref: 464
Topic: What Are The Components of Intelligence?
Skill: Factual

15) Practical intelligence, logical reasoning, and experiential intelligence are among the forms of intelligence identified by Sternberg.

Answer: FALSE
Diff: 2   Page Ref: 464–465
Topic: Is Intelligence One or Many Abilities?
Skill: Factual

16) Practical intelligence is one of Gardner's multiple intelligences.

Answer: FALSE
Diff: 2   Page Ref: 466
Topic: Is Intelligence One or Many Abilities?
Skill: Applied

17) The Cree culture values respect over persuasion.

Answer: TRUE
Diff: 2   Page Ref: 467
Topic: What Are The Components of Intelligence?
Skill: Factual

18) Henry Goddard believed that intelligence was a hereditary trait.

Answer: TRUE
Diff: 2   Page Ref: 470
Topic: How Do Psychologists Explain IQ Differences Among Groups?
Skill: Factual

19) An enriching environment seems to aid in increasing IQ scores.

Answer: TRUE
Diff: 3   Page Ref: 471
Topic: What Evidence Shows Heredity Influences Intelligence?
Skill: Factual

20) In adoption studies, children's IQ scores were found to be higher than their biological parents, but not as high as their adoptive parents.

Answer: TRUE
Diff: 2   Page Ref: 473
Topic: How Do Psychologists Explain IQ Differences Among Groups?
Skill: Factual

21) Head Start programs have been found to have no effect on children's school performance.

Answer: FALSE
Diff: 2   Page Ref: 474
Topic: How Do Psychologists Explain IQ Differences Among Groups?
Skill: Factual

22) In their book, The Bell Curve, Murray and Hernstein claim that races are inherently different from one another, and that some may have lower IQ scores because of their genetic make-up.

Answer: TRUE
Diff: 2   Page Ref: 475
Topic: How Do Psychologists Explain IQ Differences Among Groups?
Skill: Factual

23) Socioeconomic status is correlated with IQ scores.

Answer: TRUE
Diff: 2   Page Ref: 473
Topic: How Do Psychologists Explain IQ Differences Among Groups?
Skill: Factual

24) Black children tend to score higher on IQ tests when tested by a black examiner.

Answer: TRUE
Diff: 2   Page Ref: 340
Topic: How Do Psychologists Explain IQ Differences Among Groups?
Skill: Factual

Short Answer Questions

1) Compare test-retest reliability to split-half reliability.

Answer: test retest reliability involves taking an exam on at least two separate occasions and getting almost the same score, while split-half reliability involves comparing two halves of the exam to make sure that he test taker is scoring roughly he same on each half.
Diff: 2   Page Ref: 452
Topic: How Do we Measure Individual Differences?
Skill: Factual

2) How is item analysis related to content validity?

Answer: Item analysis matches each question to a specific learning objective to insure that the test had good content validity.
Diff: 2   Page Ref: 452
Topic: How Do we Measure Individual Differences?
Skill: Conceptual

3) Explain and give an example of an objective test.

Answer: An objective test is one that can easily be scored by a machine and has a correct answer, a unit exam in psychology consisting of multiple choice questions would be an objective test.
Diff: 2   Page Ref: 454
Topic: How Do we Measure Individual Differences?
Skill: Factual

4) Explain why inter–rater reliability is so important when scoring subjective tests.

Answer: Having good inter–rater reliability insures that each grader is going to grade the tests similarly. this insures that all test takers are being treated fairly and accurately.
Diff: 2   *Page Ref: 454*

Topic: How Do we Measure Individual Differences?

Skill: Conceptual

5) What was the formula used to compute IQ?

Answer: IQ = Mental Age (MA) divided Chronological Age (CA) times 100
Diff: 2   *Page Ref: 458*

Topic: How Is Intelligence Measured?

Skill: Factual

6) Who initially brought IQ test to the United States and what university was he affiliated with?

Answer: Lewis Terman; Stanford University
Diff: 2   *Page Ref: 458*

Topic: How Is Intelligence Measured?

Skill: Conceptual

7) How is giftedness defined in terms of IQ scores? What percentage of the population generally fall into this category?

Answer: a test score greater than 130; 1–2%
Diff: 2   *Page Ref: 461*

Topic: How Is Intelligence Measured?

Skill: Factual

8) Cattell used the term _____ intelligence to describe the ability to see complex relationships and solve problems, while those with _____ can come up with answers to crossword puzzles.

Answer: fluid; crystallized
Diff: 2   *Page Ref: 464*

Topic: Is Intelligence One or Many Abilities?

Skill: Conceptual

9) Name Sternberg's three components to the Triarchic theory of Intelligence.

Answer: Practical, Analytical, Creative
Diff: 2   *Page Ref: 465*

Topic: What Are The Components of Intelligence?

Skill: Factual

10) What form of intelligence was defined by Gardner as the ability to understand yourself? The Ability to interact and understand others?

Answer: intrapersonal intelligence; interpersonal intelligence
Diff: 3   Page Ref: 466
Topic: Is Intelligence One or Many Abilities?
Skill: Conceptual

11) The amount of variability within a group that is due to genetics is known as what?

Answer: heritability
Diff: 3   Page Ref: 471–472
Topic: How Do Psychologists Explain IQ Differences Among Groups?
Skill: Conceptual

12) Briefly explain the findings of the Scarr and Weinberg study.

Answer: The children's IQ scores were higher than their biological parents, but not as high as their adoptive parents.
Diff: 3   Page Ref: 473
Topic: How Do Psychologists Explain IQ Differences Among Groups?
Skill: Analysis

13) Explain a potential bias that may occur on an IQ test?

Answer: Words that are not known in all populations such as "opulent".
Diff: 2   Page Ref: 474
Topic: How Do Psychologists Explain IQ Differences Among Groups?
Skill: Applied

Essay Questions

1) Explain how the following types of reliability and validity contribute to good test construction by defining and giving an example of each.
Content Validity
Criterion Validity
Face Validity
Split–Half Reliability
Test–Retest Reliability

   Answer: Content validity involves a test in which each item is representative of the large body of knowledge about the subject that the test covers. A unit exam in Biology has questions that sample the larger body of knowledge in Biology but cannot test everything in the content area.
   Criterion Validity a test that measures performance of the test taker against a specific learning goal. If individuals applying for flight school have to achieve a certain standard on the test in order to get into flight school
   Face Validity: The test looks like it measures what it is supposed to measure. If your next psychology exam has problems from your reading and what you discussed in class it has good face validity.
   Split–Half Reliability: An exam is split into two halves and he scores are compared. If you teacher checks your final exam to see that most people are getting about the same number of odd and even questions correct, she is using split–half reliability.
   Test–Retest Reliability: Individuals taking a test more than once tend to get similar scores. If you took the ACT two times and received a 28 the first time and a 29 the seconde, it would have good test–retest reliability.

   Diff: 3   *Page Ref: 452–453*

   Topic: How Do we Measure Individual Differences?

   Skill: Conceptual

2) Provide a brief history of the IQ tests, including purpose, important individuals and problems

   Answer: Binet and Simon created the first IQ tests in france in 1904 to determine which children needed special help before starting school. The intended to test current performance and tested students empirically.. This test is created for children and cannot be applied to adults. Ten years later terman brings a revised version of the test to the US where it is used to identify those who could be educated or who would benefit from military training although some said is was used to reinforce stereotypes of certain racial and ethnic groups. Terman used the IQ quotient created by Stern and based on a 100 scale. This worked well for children but not for adults. Today we still use 100 as the baseline but no longer use the IQ formula. David Weschler has created a series of tests that assess intelligence on a number of different levels unlike the Stanford–Binet which was largely based on vocabulary. These tests are also created for adults and children.

   Diff: 3   *Page Ref: 456–460*

   Topic: How Is Intelligence Measured?

   Skill: Analysis

3) Compare and contrast Sternberg and Gardner's theory of intelligence.

   Answer: Both Sternberg and Gardner believe that traditional IQ tests which generally gauge linguistic ability are not addressing all of a person's intelligence. Sternberg created his Triarchic theory or intelligence involving practical ("street smarts"), analytical (school smarts) and creative (novel ideas). Gardner believed that intelligence should be broken down even further, his original theory had seven types of intelligence. Gardner's intelligence scales includes the traditional linguistic and logic mathematical intelligence, but also included Spatial, Musical, Bodily-Kinesthetic, Interpersonal, and intrapersonal intelligence. sternberg believed that gardner's theory was too watered down and that some of his said intelligences were really talents.

   Diff: 3   *Page Ref: 464–466*

   Topic: What Are The Components of Intelligence?

   Skill: Analysis

4) Describe some of the factors that may account for differences between the IQ scores between blacks and whites.

   Answer: These differences may be due to genetics (Jensen's view), whereas others claim it has more to do with upbringing and environment. In terms of the environment, poverty, schooling, poor prenatal health, nutrition, access to books and computers, parental time and education, self-fulfilling prophecies, school quality, test bias, training, and who is doing the testing may all impact scores.

   Diff: 2   *Page Ref: 471–475*

   Topic: How Do Psychologists Explain IQ Differences Among Groups?

   Skill: Conceptual

Chapter 12 Psychological Disorders

Multiple Choice Questions

1) Rosenhan's study on mental hospitals alerts us to
   A) the challenge of getting admitted into an overcrowded psychiatric facility.
   B) how difficult it is for patients with psychological problems to spot fakers.
   C) how difficult it is to overcome schizophrenia and depression.
   D) how rapidly mental health professionals can successfully treat psychiatric problems.
   E) how labeling can affect perceptions of normal or abnormal behavior.

   Answer: E
   Diff: 3   Page Ref: 483–484
   Topic: Introduction
   Skill: Conceptual

2) The participants in Rosenhan's study were likely to be released with the diagnosis of
   A) depression.
   B) schizophrenia in remission.
   C) bipolar disorder.
   D) phobia.
   E) seasonal affective disorder.

   Answer: B
   Diff: 2   Page Ref: 484
   Topic: Introduction
   Skill: Factual

3) The National Institutes of Mental Health estimates that approximately _____ percent of the population suffers from diagnoseable mental health problems.
   A) 5   B) 15   C) 25   D) 35   E) 45

   Answer: B
   Diff: 2   Page Ref: 485
   Topic: Introduction
   Skill: Factual

4) Delusions are

    A) emotions that fluctuate wildly.

    B) emotions that are flattened.

    C) false or irrational beliefs.

    D) false or imagined sensory perceptions.

    E) ritualistic behaviors.

Answer: C
Diff: 2   Page Ref: 485
Topic: What is Psychological Disorder?
Skill: Conceptual

5) Eddie believes that he is Abraham Lincoln, she dresses like him, talks like him and if anyone every challenges the idea that he is actually Lincoln he gets quite upset. Eddie may be suffering from a(n)

    A) hallucination.

    B) bipolar disorder.

    C) delusion.

    D) anxiety disorder.

    E) seasonal affective disorder.

Answer: C
Diff: 2   Page Ref: 485
Topic: What is Psychological Disorder?
Skill: Applied

6) The presence of delusions or hallucinations in a person's behavior is a strong indicator of

    A) personal distress.

    B) psychodynamics.

    C) physical illness.

    D) psychopathology.

    E) depression.

Answer: D
Diff: 2   Page Ref: 485
Topic: What is Psychological Disorder?
Skill: Conceptual

7) George feels like their are spiders crawling on his arms (they are not), he is having a
   A) delusion.
   B) anxiety disorder.
   C) panic attack.
   D) hallucination.
   E) mood disorder.

Answer: D
Diff: 2   *Page Ref: 485*
Topic: What is Psychological Disorder?
Skill: Applied

8) A false sensory experience that may suggest mental disorder.
   A) phobia
   B) affect
   C) panic attack
   D) hallucination
   E) delusions

Answer: D
Diff: 2   *Page Ref: 485*
Topic: What is Psychological Disorder?
Skill: Factual

9) Which of the following disorders was taken out of the DSM in 1973?
   A) schizophrenia
   B) depression
   C) phobias
   D) homosexuality
   E) neurosis

Answer: D
Diff: 2   *Page Ref: 486*
Topic: What is Psychological Disorder?
Skill: Factual

10) The view that mental problems are caused by physical illness is known as the

    A) clinical model.

    B) diathesis view.

    C) medical model of mental disorder.

    D) psychodynamic model.

    E) psycho trauma model.

Answer: C
Diff: 2   *Page Ref: 486*
Topic: What is Psychological Disorder?
Skill: Factual

11) The psychological view argues that mental disorders are physical symptoms interacting with

    A) childhood experiences.

    B) factors outside the person.

    C) repressed memories.

    D) diseases of the brain.

    E) genetic factors.

Answer: B
Diff: 2   *Page Ref: 486*
Topic: What is Psychological Disorder?
Skill: Conceptual

12) The Greek physician _____ declared that abnormal behavior was attributable to an imbalance of fluids in the body.

    A) Aristotle

    B) Hippocrates

    C) Plato

    D) Linnaeus

    E) Galen

Answer: B
Diff: 2   *Page Ref: 487*
Topic: What is Psychological Disorder?
Skill: Factual

13) During the Middle Ages, authorities involved in the Inquisition viewed mental illness as due to

   A) genetics.

   B) an imbalance of humors.

   C) brain structure abnormality.

   D) unconscious conflicts.

   E) the Devil.

Answer: E

Diff: 3   Page Ref: 487

Topic: What is Psychological Disorder?

Skill: Factual

14) A physician trained in the medical model of mental disorder is most likely to treat their patients by

   A) teaching about stress reduction.

   B) probing their unconscious.

   C) asking about patients' self esteem.

   D) exploring the patients' childhood.

   E) prescribing medications.

Answer: E

Diff: 1   Page Ref: 488

Topic: What is Psychological Disorder?

Skill: Applied

15) The young girls who accused people in Salem on being witches probably were

   A) schizophrenic.

   B) looking for attention.

   C) suffering from a bile imbalance.

   D) experiencing hallucinations.

   E) abused by their parents.

Answer: D

Diff: 2   Page Ref: 488

Topic: What is Psychological Disorder?

Skill: Factual

16) During the latter part of eighteenth century, the mentally ill were typically treated
   A) in asylums for the insane.
   B) with a fungus that grows on grains of rye.
   C) with primitive medicines related to alcohol.
   D) according to the principles of the psychodynamic approach.
   E) by torture and execution.

Answer: A
Diff: 3   *Page Ref: 488*
Topic: What is Psychological Disorder?
Skill: Factual

17) A serious criticism of the medical model involves the idea that mental illness is
   A) learned.
   B) genetic.
   C) a disease.
   D) an imbalance of fluids in the body.
   E) the fault of those experiencing the illness.

Answer: C
Diff: 1   *Page Ref: 488*
Topic: What is Psychological Disorder?
Skill: Conceptual

18) Psychological models of mental illness emphasize the contribution of
   A) historical, sexual, and physical factors.
   B) fear, anxiety, and stress.
   C) cognitive, environmental, and biological factors.
   D) the family, the individual, and society.
   E) the unconscious, our senses, and our pre-existing beliefs.

Answer: C
Diff: 2   *Page Ref: 488*
Topic: What is Psychological Disorder?
Skill: Conceptual

19) The cognitive perspective views _____ as key factors in mental disorder.

   A) how we perceive and think

   B) our unconscious influences

   C) our search for self-actualization

   D) chemical imbalances

   E) learning

Answer: A

Diff: 2   Page Ref: 489

Topic: What is Psychological Disorder?

Skill: Conceptual

20) Janet believes that all people are out to harm her, she perceives all interactions with others as threatening and has retreated to her own home. Janet's irrational fear of social situations could best be explained by the _____ approach.

   A) behavioral

   B) psychoanalytic

   C) cognitive

   D) humanistic

   E) sociocultural

Answer: C

Diff: 2   Page Ref: 489

Topic: What is Psychological Disorder?

Skill: Applied

21) The _____ approach to psychological disorders focuses on abnormalities in the brain and nervous system

   A) behavioral

   B) biopsychology

   C) psychodynamic

   D) cognitive

   E) bioanalytic

Answer: B

Diff: 1   Page Ref: 489

Topic: What is Psychological Disorder?

Skill: Conceptual

22) If I believe that George is experiencing signs of schizophrenia because it runs in his family, I believe in the _____ model of mental illness.

A) medical

B) behavioral

C) biopsychological

D) cognitive

E) social

Answer: C
Diff: 2   Page Ref: 489
Topic: What is Psychological Disorder?
Skill: Applied

23) The etiology of a mental disorder is another term for its

A) symptoms.

B) prevention.

C) cure.

D) prevalence.

E) cause.

Answer: E
Diff: 3   Page Ref: 489
Topic: What is Psychological Disorder?
Skill: Applied

24) Phoebe thinks that if she goes outside a swarm of bees will kill her. Eve though it is winter and there is little chance of this occurring. Phoebe is exhibiting the _____ indicator of abnormality.

A) hallucinations

B) irrationality

C) maladaptiveness

D) observer discomfort

E) unpredictability

Answer: B
Diff: 2   Page Ref: 490
Topic: What is Psychological Disorder?
Skill: Applied

25) An example of _____ is when an person becomes overwhelmed for no good reason.

    A) unpredictability

    B) maladaptiveness

    C) observer discomfort

    D) irrationality

    E) distress

Answer: E
Diff: 2   *Page Ref: 490*
Topic: What is Psychological Disorder?
Skill: Applied

26) A person who wears a leotard to the office each day is displaying

    A) distress.

    B) irrationality.

    C) unpredictability.

    D) observer discomfort.

    E) unconventionality.

Answer: E
Diff: 2   *Page Ref: 490*
Topic: What is Psychological Disorder?
Skill: Applied

27) A Susan sometimes is happy to see you, but other times believes that you are trying to hurt her, she is demonstrating _____.

    A) unpredictability.

    B) distress.

    C) psychosis.

    D) depression.

    E) maladaptiveness.

Answer: A
Diff: 2   *Page Ref: 490*
Topic: What is Psychological Disorder?
Skill: Applied

28) Which of the following is true of psychopathology?

    A) Once established, psychopathology rarely goes away.

    B) Symptoms of abnormality are usually quite intense.

    C) All psychological disorders involve exaggerations of normal functions.

    D) Symptoms of abnormality are easy to spot.

    E) Medical students rarely think about their own health as they study.

Answer: C
Diff: 2   *Page Ref: 491*
Topic: What is Psychological Disorder?
Skill: Conceptual

29) The Diagnostic and Statistical Manual of Mental Disorders (4th Ed.) is organized by

    A) causes.

    B) situations.

    C) cultural signifiers.

    D) symptoms.

    E) treatments.

Answer: D
Diff: 2   *Page Ref: 492*
Topic: How Are Psychological Disorders Classified?
Skill: Factual

30) Psychologists now use the term _____ when referring to what was formerly called neurosis.

    A) symptom   B) pathology   C) disorder   D) disease   E) insanity

Answer: C
Diff: 2   *Page Ref: 493*
Topic: How Are Psychological Disorders Classified?
Skill: Factual

31) Psychosis involves

    A) profound euphoria.

    B) sadness.

    C) a distortion of perception.

    D) flashes of temper.

    E) a break with reality.

Answer: E
Diff: 2   *Page Ref: 493*
Topic: How Are Psychological Disorders Classified?
Skill: Factual

32) Which of the following is true of the DSM-IV?

    A) It uses the language of medicine.

    B) It contains no diagnosis of "normal".

    C) It provides extensive descriptions of syndromes.

    D) It is a mixture of science and tradition.

    E) All of the above are correct.

Answer: E
Diff: 2   Page Ref: 493
Topic: How Are Psychological Disorders Classified?
Skill: Conceptual

33) _____ is the most common of all major mental disturbances.

    A) Mania

    B) Major depression

    C) Seasonal effective disorder

    D) An eating disorder

    E) Alcohol abuse

Answer: B
Diff: 2   Page Ref: 494
Topic: How Are Psychological Disorders Classified?
Skill: Factual

34) A minor form of depression that is found with some degree of frequency is called

    A) seasonal affective disorder.

    B) dysthymia.

    C) bipolar.

    D) psychosis.

    E) borderline.

Answer: B
Diff: 2   Page Ref: 494
Topic: How Are Psychological Disorders Classified?
Skill: Factual

35) Depression is related to

    A) the brain neurotransmitters dopamine, norepinephrine, and serotonin.

    B) a genetic predisposition.

    C) low brain wave activity of the left frontal cortex.

    D) a viral infection.

    E) All of the above are correct

Answer: E
Diff: 2   *Page Ref: 494*
Topic: How Are Psychological Disorders Classified?
Skill: Factual

36) In cross–cultural studies, it was found that _____ was the most prevalent illness worldwide.

    A) bipolar

    B) anxiety disorders

    C) depression

    D) alcoholism

    E) schizophrenia

Answer: C
Diff: 2   *Page Ref: 494*
Topic: How Are Psychological Disorders Classified?
Skill: Factual

37) Depression is related to reduced brain activity within the

    A) right temporal lobe.

    B) right parietal lobe.

    C) right occipital lobe.

    D) left temporal lobe.

    E) left frontal lobe.

Answer: E
Diff: 3   *Page Ref: 495*
Topic: How Are Psychological Disorders Classified?
Skill: Factual

38) Seasonal affective disorder may be related to levels of _____ produced by the body.

    A) dopamine

    B) acetylcholine

    C) serotonin

    D) melatonin

    E) GABA

Answer: D
Diff: 3   *Page Ref: 495*
Topic: How Are Psychological Disorders Classified?
Skill: Factual

39) A person suffering with seasonal affective disorder would be expected to be most depressed when

    A) it is nighttime.

    B) there is a full moon.

    C) they travel to the South.

    D) their sleep has been interrupted by noise.

    E) it is winter.

Answer: E
Diff: 1   *Page Ref: 496*
Topic: How Are Psychological Disorders Classified?
Skill: Conceptual

40) The tendency for some depressed persons to think that they can not do anything to change their negative fate is termed _____ by Martin Seligman.

    A) observer discomfort

    B) learned helplessness

    C) unconventionality

    D) narcissism

    E) somatoform disorder

Answer: B
Diff: 2   *Page Ref: 496*
Topic: How Are Psychological Disorders Classified?
Skill: Factual

41) Which of the following can contribute to the onset of depression?

    A) stress

    B) prolonged devastation after the loss of a loved one

    C) genetic predisposition

    D) a negative thought cycle

    E) All of the above can contribute to the onset of depression

Answer: E
Diff: 2   Page Ref: 495–496
Topic: How Are Psychological Disorders Classified?
Skill: Recall

42) _____ for the treatment of depression involves teaching a patient to alter their helpless thinking and to cope in unpleasant situations.

    A) Medication and moral support

    B) Bioanalysis

    C) Cognitive-behavioral techniques

    D) Mood therapy

    E) Psychoanalysis

Answer: C
Diff: 2   Page Ref: 496
Topic: How Are Psychological Disorders Classified?
Skill: Conceptual

43) Research has found that stress hormones effect neurons especially those in the _____.

    A) hypothalamus

    B) hippocampus

    C) amygdala

    D) frontal lobe

    E) brain stem

Answer: B
Diff: 3   Page Ref: 496
Topic: How Are Psychological Disorders Classified?
Skill: Factual

44) The tendency for women to _____ accounts for their higher depression rates relative to men.

    A) experience monthly changes in biochemistry

    B) nutritional distress

    C) outlive men

    D) ruminate about their problems

    E) watch too much national media

Answer: D
Diff: 2   Page Ref: 497
Topic: How Are Psychological Disorders Classified?
Skill: Conceptual

45) Which of the following does Martin Seligman attribute to the increasing diagnosis of depression in recent years?

    A) better health-care systems

    B) the self-esteem movement

    C) well trained physicians

    D) a better recognition of the illness among patients

    E) less of a stigma against those who suffer from mental illness

Answer: B
Diff: 2   Page Ref: 497
Topic: How Are Psychological Disorders Classified?
Skill: Recall

46) Bipolar disorder was once known as

    A) manic-depressive disorder.

    B) clinical depression.

    C) catatonic schizophrenia.

    D) a dissociative disorder.

    E) ADHD.

Answer: A
Diff: 1   Page Ref: 497
Topic: How Are Psychological Disorders Classified?
Skill: Factual

47) A person who feels euphoric and hyperactive may be experiencing

    A) a panic attack.

    B) a manic episode.

    C) dementia.

    D) a fugue.

    E) hypochondriasis.

Answer: B

Diff: 2   Page Ref: 497

Topic: How Are Psychological Disorders Classified?

Skill: Applied

48) Which of the following may occur during a manic stage?

    A) deep set depression

    B) extravagant spending sprees

    C) loss of touch with reality

    D) extensive sleepiness

    E) trouble getting along with others

Answer: B

Diff: 2   Page Ref: 497

Topic: How Are Psychological Disorders Classified?

Skill: Conceptual

49) Which of the following factors suggests that there may be a genetic component to obsessive–compulsive disorder?

    A) good response to behavioral therapy

    B) If parents suffer from the disorder, the children also will.

    C) high response rates to medication

    D) highly effective psychoanalytic treatment

    E) highly effective cognitive therapy

Answer: C

Diff: 3   Page Ref: 497

Topic: How Are Psychological Disorders Classified?

Skill: Conceptual

50) The DSM–IV considers _____ to be an anxiety disorder.

    A) schizophrenia

    B) obsessive–compulsive disorder

    C) bipolar disorder

    D) amnesia

    E) dissociative identity disorder

Answer: B
Diff: 2   *Page Ref: 498*
Topic: How Are Psychological Disorders Classified?
Skill: Factual

51) While sitting in class, Sherman suddenly experiences the following: a racing heart, clammy hands, dizziness and shaking. Sherman has many of the symptoms typical of

    A) DID.

    B) a panic attack.

    C) a fugue state.

    D) irrationality.

    E) SAD.

Answer: B
Diff: 1   *Page Ref: 498*
Topic: How Are Psychological Disorders Classified?
Skill: Applied

52) Nancy feels anxious all of the time, but is not afraid of anything in particular, she likely suffers from

    A) panic attacks.

    B) paranoia.

    C) agoraphobia.

    D) generalized anxiety disorder.

    E) anticipatory anxiety.

Answer: D
Diff: 2   *Page Ref: 498*
Topic: How Are Psychological Disorders Classified?
Skill: Applied

53) The dread of the next anxiety attack can leave someone with _____ feeling helpless and out of control.

   A) paranoia

   B) mania

   C) amnesia

   D) panic disorder

   E) bipolar disorder

Answer: D

Diff: 2   Page Ref: 498

Topic: How Are Psychological Disorders Classified?

Skill: Conceptual

54) Agoraphobia is defined as a fear of

   A) blood.

   B) needles.

   C) being in public places or open spaces.

   D) being in closed spaces.

   E) shopping.

Answer: C

Diff: 2   Page Ref: 498

Topic: How Are Psychological Disorders Classified?

Skill: Conceptual

55) The _____ is key brain region responsible for panic attacks.

   A) hypothalamus

   B) amygdala

   C) temporal lobe

   D) cerebellum

   E) corpus callosum

Answer: B

Diff: 3   Page Ref: 498

Topic: How Are Psychological Disorders Classified?

Skill: Factual

56) The fear of being in a public space is known as

    A) social phobia.

    B) acrophobia.

    C) agoraphobia.

    D) claustrophobia.

    E) photophobia.

Answer: C

Diff: 1   Page Ref: 498

Topic: How Are Psychological Disorders Classified?

Skill: Conceptual

57) If Jeremy cannot leave his home because he is afraid he will be caught in a situation from which he cannot escape, he is said to have

    A) arachnophobia.

    B) agoraphobia.

    C) acrophobia.

    D) cynophobia.

    E) claustrophobia.

Answer: B

Diff: 3   Page Ref: 498

Topic: How Are Psychological Disorders Classified?

Skill: Applied

58) _____ involves a persistent and irrational fear of a specific object, activity, or situation that causes disruption to one's life?

    A) Somatoform disorder

    B) Obsessive–compulsive disorder

    C) Phobic disorder

    D) Panic disorder

    E) Mood disorder

Answer: C

Diff: 2   Page Ref: 499

Topic: How Are Psychological Disorders Classified?

Skill: Factual

59) The _____ suggests that we are innately predisposed to fear some stimuli more than others.

  A) learned helplessness theory

  B) self-fulfilling prophecy

  C) preparedness hypothesis

  D) halo effect theory

  E) psychogenic phobia theory

Answer: C

Diff: 2   Page Ref: 499

Topic: How Are Psychological Disorders Classified?

Skill: Conceptual

60) According to the preparedness hypothesis, we would be most likely to develop an intense fear of _____.

  A) clowns

  B) the sight of blood

  C) needles

  D) books

  E) snakes

Answer: E

Diff: 2   Page Ref: 499

Topic: How Are Psychological Disorders Classified?

Skill: Conceptual

61) Obsessive-Compulsive Disorder effects what percentage of the population?

  A) 25%   B) 12%   C) 10%   D) 2.5%   E) 1%

Answer: D

Diff: 2   Page Ref: 499

Topic: How Are Psychological Disorders Classified?

Skill: Recall

62) An obsession is a repetitive _____ whereas a compulsion is a compulsive _____.

  A) thought; behavior

  B) behavior; thought

  C) stressor; action

  D) action; stressor

  E) situation; fear

Answer: A

Diff: 2   Page Ref: 500

Topic: How Are Psychological Disorders Classified?

Skill: Conceptual

63) Cynoophobia involves a fear of _____, whereas thanatophobia involves a fear of _____.

    A) death; public speaking

    B) dogs; death

    C) fire; illness

    D) closed spaces; open spaces

    E) birds; strangers

Answer: B
Diff: 2   Page Ref: 500
Topic: How Are Psychological Disorders Classified?
Skill: Factual

64) Which of the following is TRUE of obsessions?

    A) They persist despite attempts to suppress them.

    B) They are repetitive behaviors.

    C) They can lead to euphoria.

    D) They are obvious to the sufferer's friends.

    E) They are usually pleasant.

Answer: A
Diff: 2   Page Ref: 500
Topic: How Are Psychological Disorders Classified?
Skill: Conceptual

65) If Ned have an uncontrollable urge to check under his car to make sure that he has not harmed anyone every time he passes a parked car on the street, he is suffering from

    A) obsessive–compulsive disorder.

    B) bipolar disorder.

    C) paranoid schizophrenia.

    D) a phobia.

    E) panic attacks.

Answer: A
Diff: 2   Page Ref: 501
Topic: How Are Psychological Disorders Classified?
Skill: Applied

66) A(n) _____ is a repetitive act performed in response to tension.

   A) obsession

   B) compulsion

   C) phobia

   D) manic episode

   E) somatization disorder

   Answer: B

   Diff: 2   Page Ref: 501

   Topic: How Are Psychological Disorders Classified?

   Skill: Conceptual

67) Which of the following is TRUE of compulsions?

   A) They can be resisted easily with will-power.

   B) They are performed randomly and without rules.

   C) They are intended to reduce or prevent discomfort.

   D) They are recurring thoughts and images.

   E) They are viewed as being rational by sufferers.

   Answer: C

   Diff: 2   Page Ref: 501

   Topic: How Are Psychological Disorders Classified?

   Skill: Conceptual

68) Unwanted, involuntary movements known as _____ are common for people with obsessive-compulsive disorder.

   A) neuroses   B) psychosis   C) tics   D) obsessions   E) fugues

   Answer: C

   Diff: 2   Page Ref: 501

   Topic: How Are Psychological Disorders Classified?

   Skill: Factual

69) A key feature of _____ is the appearance of physical symptoms without an apparent biological cause.

   A) affective

   B) dissociative

   C) organic mental

   D) somatoform

   E) hallucinatory

   Answer: D

   Diff: 3   Page Ref: 501

   Topic: How Are Psychological Disorders Classified?

   Skill: Conceptual

70) Jaci has just become blind. The fact that there is no physical reason for this suggests that Jaci may be suffering from

  A) conversion disorder.

  B) observer discomfort.

  C) panic disorder.

  D) generalized anxiety disorder.

  E) physical paranoia.

Answer: A
Diff: 2   *Page Ref: 501*
Topic: How Are Psychological Disorders Classified?
Skill: Applied

71) Freud explained conversion disorder as involving the conversion of

  A) religious energy into psychological symptoms.

  B) unconscious anxiety into physical symptoms.

  C) obsessions into compulsions.

  D) stress into panic.

  E) physical symptoms into psychological problems.

Answer: B
Diff: 3   *Page Ref: 502*
Topic: How Are Psychological Disorders Classified?
Skill: Conceptual

72) Why may somatoform disorders often go undiagnosed?

  A) The DSM–IV does not recognize somatoform disorders as an illness.

  B) Currently, there are no effective treatments for the disorder.

  C) Many doctors attribute the problem to being "all in the patients head".

  D) There are no physical signs that the illness is present.

  E) All of the above are correct.

Answer: C
Diff: 3   *Page Ref: 502*
Topic: How Are Psychological Disorders Classified?
Skill: Conceptual

73) The defining feature of _____ is an exaggerated concern about physical health that leads the person to bounce from doctor to doctor.

   A) conversion disorder

   B) triskaidekaphobia

   C) hypochondriasis

   D) obsessive–compulsive disorder

   E) dissociative fugue

   Answer: C
   Diff: 3   Page Ref: 502
   Topic: How Are Psychological Disorders Classified?
   Skill: Applied

74) If Jerome often thinks that he suffers from several ailments from many illnesses to which he could not possibly be suffering, he may have

   A) hypochondriasis.

   B) obsessive–compulsive disorder.

   C) panic attacks.

   D) a personality disorder.

   E) schizophrenia.

   Answer: A
   Diff: 2   Page Ref: 502
   Topic: How Are Psychological Disorders Classified?
   Skill: Applied

75) If an individual becomes 'detached' from themselves, they may be suffering from (a)

   A) panic attack.

   B) personality disorder.

   C) bipolar disorder.

   D) dissociative disorder.

   E) schizophrenia.

   Answer: D
   Diff: 2   Page Ref: 503
   Topic: How Are Psychological Disorders Classified?
   Skill: Factual

76) When one loses their memory, but there is no known reason for the memory loss the person may be suffering from _____.

    A) dissociative amnesia

    B) schizophrenia

    C) dissociative identity disorder

    D) depersonalization disorder

    E) bipolar disorder

Answer: A

Diff: 2   Page Ref: 503

Topic: How Are Psychological Disorders Classified?

Skill: Factual

77) _____ involves a persistent loss of memory as well as fleeing from one's family, home, and job.

    A) Dissociative fugue

    B) Fugue episodes

    C) Unconventionality

    D) Conversion disorder

    E) Dissociative identity disorder

Answer: A

Diff: 3   Page Ref: 503

Topic: How Are Psychological Disorders Classified?

Skill: Applied

78) The term fugue means

    A) confusion.

    B) to flee.

    C) a specific movement in music scores.

    D) a sense of disappointment.

    E) a splitting of the mind.

Answer: B

Diff: 2   Page Ref: 503

Topic: How Are Psychological Disorders Classified?

Skill: Factual

79) The feeling of observing one's own body and having an out-of-body experience are typical of

A) dissociative identity disorder.

B) anorexia nervosa.

C) fragmentation.

D) depersonalization disorder.

E) somatization.

Answer: D
Diff: 2   *Page Ref: 503*
Topic: How Are Psychological Disorders Classified?
Skill: Conceptual

80) After being abused throughout her childhood, Helen has three distinct personalities. One is aggressive, one is sexually promiscuous, and one is very timid. Helen most likely suffers from

A) dissociative identity disorder.

B) personality disorder.

C) psychogenic amnesia.

D) anxiety disorder.

E) conversion disorder.

Answer: A
Diff: 2   *Page Ref: 504*
Topic: How Are Psychological Disorders Classified?
Skill: Applied

81) A high percentage of persons suffering from dissociative identity disorder report

A) symptom fabrication.

B) somatoform complaints.

C) sexual abuse.

D) depression.

E) paranoia.

Answer: C
Diff: 2   *Page Ref: 504*
Topic: How Are Psychological Disorders Classified?
Skill: Factual

82) The major difference between dissociative identity disorder (DID) and schizophrenia is that
    A) schizophrenia is a true split personality.
    B) DID is a subclassification of schizophrenia.
    C) DID is not a psychotic disorder.
    D) schizophrenia is a subclassification of DID.
    E) they are two terms for the same problem.

Answer: C
Diff: 2   Page Ref: 505
Topic: How Are Psychological Disorders Classified?
Skill: Factual

83) Most people with eating disorders
    A) live in Eastern cultures.
    B) are living in poverty.
    C) are middle-aged.
    D) come from cultures in which hunger is wide-spread.
    E) are women.

Answer: E
Diff: 1   Page Ref: 505
Topic: How Are Psychological Disorders Classified?
Skill: Factual

84) _____ are the two best-known eating disorders.
    A) Anorexia nervosa and bulimia
    B) Bulimia and obsessive–compulsive eating disorder
    C) Obsessive–compulsive eating disorder and pica
    D) Dissociative nervosa and anorexia nervosa
    E) Binge eating syndrome and anorexia nervosa

Answer: A
Diff: 1   Page Ref: 505
Topic: How Are Psychological Disorders Classified?
Skill: Factual

85) A young woman who is dangerously thin after starving herself is most likely suffering from
   A) bulimia.
   B) a mood disorder.
   C) conversion disorder.
   D) bipolar disorder.
   E) anorexia nervosa.

Answer: E
Diff: 1   Page Ref: 505
Topic: How Are Psychological Disorders Classified?
Skill: Applied

86) _____ is characterized by a "binge-and-purge" syndrome.
   A) Unipolar depression
   B) Dissociative fugue
   C) Bulimia
   D) Bipolar disorder
   E) Obsessive-compulsive disorder

Answer: C
Diff: 1   Page Ref: 505
Topic: How Are Psychological Disorders Classified?
Skill: Factual

87) Which of the following individuals would be most likely to suffer from an eating disorder?
   A) Mary, whose family often times does not have enough to eat.
   B) Jeremy, who wants less fat and more muscle.
   C) Jennifer, who is 45 and trying to lose weight.
   D) Annie, who is 18 and gets good grades.
   E) Gloria, who has been in a car accident and has little appetite.

Answer: D
Diff: 2   Page Ref: 505
Topic: How Are Psychological Disorders Classified?
Skill: Applied

88) In a study conducted on women's body image, which of the following was found.

    A) Women often overpredicted what weight men would like best in a woman.

    B) Women underestimated their current body shape.

    C) Women underestimated what men would like best in a women.

    D) Men and women ranked what body shape they would like best as the same shape.

    E) A women's ideal body shape tended to be higher than men's ideal body shape.

Answer: C
Diff: 2   Page Ref: 506
Topic: How Are Psychological Disorders Classified?
Skill: Conceptual

89) A cognitive therapist would be most likely to treat a person with an eating disorder by

    A) checking family background.

    B) prescribing medicines to increase hunger.

    C) altering the person's self-perception.

    D) conducting a genetic screen.

    E) looking for the unconscious reasons why this occurred.

Answer: C
Diff: 2   Page Ref: 506
Topic: How Are Psychological Disorders Classified?
Skill: Applied

90) A person who is confused and experiencing hallucinations and who has bizarre thoughts and blunted emotions is most likely suffering from

    A) bipolar disorder.

    B) dissociative identity disorder.

    C) antisocial personality disorder.

    D) schizophrenia.

    E) seasonal affective disorder.

Answer: D
Diff: 2   Page Ref: 506
Topic: How Are Psychological Disorders Classified?
Skill: Applied

91) The term schizophrenia means

    A) a split of the mind from reality.

    B) multiple personality.

    C) a distortion of self-esteem.

    D) a split in personality.

    E) B and C are correct.

Answer: A

Diff: 2   Page Ref: 506

Topic: How Are Psychological Disorders Classified?

Skill: Factual

92) Which of the following statements is TRUE of schizophrenia?

    A) It accounts for about 40% of all admissions to public mental hospitals.

    B) It affects about one out of every 1000 Americans.

    C) Its first occurrence is usually when the person is about ten years old.

    D) Women tend to be diagnosed with schizophrenia at earlier ages than men.

    E) Only 1 of 2 of schizophrenia patients will fully recover.

Answer: A

Diff: 3   Page Ref: 506-507

Topic: How Are Psychological Disorders Classified?

Skill: Factual

93) A key feature of _____ is an odd motor state in which the individual may remain frozen in a stupor for long periods of time.

    A) obsessive-compulsive disorder

    B) undifferentiated schizophrenia

    C) residual schizophrenia

    D) catatonic schizophrenia

    E) paranoid schizophrenia

Answer: D

Diff: 2   Page Ref: 507

Topic: How Are Psychological Disorders Classified?

Skill: Applied

94) Disorganized, catatonic, paranoid, residual and undifferentiated are the five major types of

A) delusions.

B) affective disorders.

C) personality disorders.

D) schizophrenia.

E) bipolar disorder.

Answer: D

Diff: 2   Page Ref: 507

Topic: How Are Psychological Disorders Classified?

Skill: Factual

95) A diagnosis of _____ schizophrenia is reserved for persons whose symptoms do not clearly fall into other categories.

A) disorganized

B) undifferentiated

C) residual

D) dissociative

E) hebephrenic

Answer: B

Diff: 2   Page Ref: 507

Topic: How Are Psychological Disorders Classified?

Skill: Applied

96) _____ schizophrenia involves incoherent speech.

A) Undifferentiated

B) Disorganized

C) Residual

D) Catatonic

E) Paranoid

Answer: B

Diff: 2   Page Ref: 507

Topic: How Are Psychological Disorders Classified?

Skill: Factual

97) Hallucinations are

    A) often found n individuals with anxiety disorders.

    B) a positive symptom associated with schizophrenia.

    C) common in individuals with Dissociative Identity Disorder.

    D) a negative symptom associated with schizophrenia.

    E) always frightening to the individuals experiencing them.

Answer: B
Diff: 3   Page Ref: 508
Topic: How Are Psychological Disorders Classified?
Skill: Conceptual

98) Which of the following supports a biological basis for schizophrenia?

    A) You are not more likely to develop schizophrenia if you were mistakenly adopted at birth into a schizophrenic household.

    B) Positive schizophrenia symptoms are alleviated by dopamine receptor blocking drugs.

    C) Drugs that stimulate dopamine receptors induce schizophrenia symptoms.

    D) Brain abnormalities in schizophrenics have been found by imaging studies.

    E) All of the above are correct.

Answer: E
Diff: 3   Page Ref: 508
Topic: How Are Psychological Disorders Classified?
Skill: Conceptual

99) The diathesis–stress hypothesis of schizophrenia states that

    A) biological factors put someone at risk of schizophrenia, but environmental stressors are required to convert the potential.

    B) when psychic energy builds up, defense mechanisms take over.

    C) eating disorders will lead to major depression unless they are treated with cognitive–behavioral techniques.

    D) panic attacks can be prevented by limiting anticipatory anxiety.

    E) in chaotic environments, body chemistry will change to cause mood disorders.

Answer: A
Diff: 3   Page Ref: 509
Topic: How Are Psychological Disorders Classified?
Skill: Conceptual

100) The _____ refers to the notion that genetic factors put a person at risk for schizophrenia but environmental stress factors trigger the disorder itself.

   A) interactionist view

   B) double bind hypothesis

   C) environmental anxiety theory

   D) diathesis–stress hypothesis

   E) state–dependent view

Answer: D
Diff: 2   *Page Ref: 509*
Topic: How Are Psychological Disorders Classified?
Skill: Factual

101) _____ disorders are chronic, inflexible, pervasive, maladaptive patterns of thinking, emotions, or relationships.

   A) Anxiety

   B) Mood

   C) Dissociative

   D) Somatoform

   E) Personality

Answer: E
Diff: 2   *Page Ref: 510*
Topic: How Are Psychological Disorders Classified?
Skill: Factual

102) A person who has a grandiose sense of self-importance and a preoccupation with fantasies of success or power is most likely to suffer from

   A) dissociative identity disorder.

   B) antisocial personality disorder.

   C) narcissistic personality disorder.

   D) catatonic schizophrenia.

   E) conversion disorder.

Answer: C
Diff: 2   *Page Ref: 510*
Topic: How Are Psychological Disorders Classified?
Skill: Applied

103) Julie is extremely self-centered, even when she does not have a reservation she expects the best seat in any restaurant she thinks she deserves better treatment than anyone else and is upset of it is not forthcoming. Julie may have a

A) narcissistic personality disorder.

B) schizophrenia.

C) conversion disorder.

D) Alzheimer's disease.

E) hypochondriasis.

Answer: A

Diff: 2   Page Ref: 510

Topic: How Are Psychological Disorders Classified?

Skill: Applied

104) A key feature of _____ is a history of irresponsible behavior in a person who does not experience shame or intense emotion of any kind.

A) psychogenic amnesia

B) dissociative identity disorder

C) narcissistic personality disorder

D) antisocial personality disorder

E) seasonal affective disorder

Answer: D

Diff: 2   Page Ref: 510

Topic: How Are Psychological Disorders Classified?

Skill: Applied

105) A male student who disrupt class, gets into fights, and runs away from home during childhood is most likely to be diagnosed with _____ in adulthood.

A) antisocial personality disorder

B) narcissistic personality disorder

C) schizophrenia

D) hypochondriasis

E) dissociative fugue

Answer: A

Diff: 2   Page Ref: 510

Topic: How Are Psychological Disorders Classified?

Skill: Conceptual

106) Men are four times as likely to be diagnosed with _____ than are women., whereas women are more likely to suffer from _____.

    A) dissociative identity disorder; depression

    B) depression; borderline personality disorder

    C) anorexia nervosa; bulimia nervosa

    D) panic disorders; obsessive–compulsive disorders

    E) antisocial personality disorder; borderline personality disorder

Answer: E

Diff: 3   Page Ref: 510

Topic: How Are Psychological Disorders Classified?

Skill: Factual

107) Jenny cannot get along with anyone for an extended period of time. She moves through boyfriends quickly, but while she is dating them she is extremely demanding and manipulative. She is incredibly impulsive and often threatens to hurt herself if her current boyfriend does not do as she wants. Jenny may be diagnosed as having a

    A) borderline personality disorder.

    B) narcissistic personality disorder.

    C) schizophrenia.

    D) dissociative identity disorder.

    E) antisocial personality disorder.

Answer: A

Diff: 3   Page Ref: 510

Topic: How Are Psychological Disorders Classified?

Skill: Applied

108) A child with autism would be expected to

    A) achieve functional language.

    B) eventually develop the ability to interact socially.

    C) have above–normal intelligence scores.

    D) show evidence of strong musical talent.

    E) lack a theory of mind.

Answer: E

Diff: 3   Page Ref: 511

Topic: How Are Psychological Disorders Classified?

Skill: Conceptual

109) Jimmy cannot communicate well with there other children in his pre–school class. He tests well on IQ tests but has not begun talking, Jimmy may have

   A) savant syndrome.

   B) autism.

   C) ADHD.

   D) dyslexia.

   E) a social phobia.

Answer: B
Diff: 3   Page Ref: 511
Topic: How Are Psychological Disorders Classified?
Skill: Applied

110) Dyslexia usually involves

   A) the inability to communicate with others.

   B) an low score on IQ tests.

   C) a reading disability thought by some to involve a brain disorder.

   D) high school performance.

   E) the inability to concentrate in school.

Answer: C
Diff: 2   Page Ref: 512
Topic: How Are Psychological Disorders Classified?
Skill: Factual

111) ADHD affects about _____ percent of the population.

   A) 3-5   B) 10-12   C) 25-30   D) 15-20   E) 50-55

Answer: A
Diff: 2   Page Ref: 512
Topic: How Are Psychological Disorders Classified?
Skill: Recall

112) If Kurt has trouble concentrating on a given task for an extended period and cannot sit still in school he should be checked for

   A) ADHD.

   B) autism.

   C) panic disorder.

   D) savant syndrome.

   E) dyslexia.

Answer: A
Diff: 2   Page Ref: 512
Topic: How Are Psychological Disorders Classified?
Skill: Applied

113) Someone who is malingering is most likely to

    A) have pain without reason.

    B) hurt others without remorse.

    C) have fluctuating emotions.

    D) have an intense fear of being sick.

    E) fake an illness.

Answer: E
Diff: 2   *Page Ref: 513*
Topic: How Are Psychological Disorders Classified?
Skill: Conceptual

114) Frank has been a bit sad, but not clinically depressed, ever since his wife left him. Based on this limited information, in which of the following DSM-IV categories would Frank most likely be classified?

    A) Anxiety disorders

    B) Dissociative disorders

    C) Adjustment disorders

    D) Personality disorders

    E) Somatoform disorders

Answer: C
Diff: 3   *Page Ref: 513*
Topic: How Are Psychological Disorders Classified?
Skill: Applied

115) Shyness

    A) seems to be decreasing in the population.

    B) cannot be learned.

    C) is not defined as a disorder by the DSM-IV.

    D) is discouraged by Internet usage.

    E) is experienced by about one-tenth of the American population.

Answer: C
Diff: 2   *Page Ref: 513*
Topic: Shyness
Skill: Conceptual

116) Psychiatrist Thomas Szasz argues that mental illness
    A) is a serious form of illness that cannot be cured.
    B) is underdiagnosed.
    C) should lead to hospitalization.
    D) is actually caused by physical factors.
    E) is a myth.

Answer: E
Diff: 2   Page Ref: 515
Topic: What Are The Consequences of Labeling People?
Skill: Factual

117) The _____ model claims that cultural factors influence the prevalence of mental disorders.
    A) medical
    B) cognitive
    C) psychodynamic
    D) ecological
    E) humanistic

Answer: D
Diff: 2   Page Ref: 515–516
Topic: What Are The Consequences of Labeling People?
Skill: Conceptual

118) Cross-cultural studies of schizophrenia indicate that
    A) rates of schizophrenia are fairly constant across cultures.
    B) auditory hallucinations show variability across cultures.
    C) visual hallucinations do not show cultural variability.
    D) schizophrenic symptoms are learned behavior.
    E) schizophrenia is absent in some cultures.

Answer: B
Diff: 2   Page Ref: 516
Topic: What Are The Consequences of Labeling People?
Skill: Factual

119) The first person to be found innocent bt reason if insanity was

    A) Daniel M'Naughten.

    B) John Hinkley.

    C) John Wilkes Booth.

    D) Thomas Szasz.

    E) Robert Peel.

Answer: A
Diff: 3   *Page Ref: 516*
Topic: The Plea of Insanity
Skill: Factual

120) How frequently is the insanity plea used in criminal cases?

    A) 1 in 100   B) 2 in 1000   C) 1 in 50   D) 5 in 100   E) 10 in 100

Answer: B
Diff: 3   *Page Ref: 517*
Topic: The Plea of Insanity
Skill: Factual

121) _____ is a legal term, not a psychiatric or psychological term.

    A) Insanity

    B) Psychopathology

    C) Associative disorder

    D) General adaptation syndrome

    E) Split personality

Answer: A
Diff: 2   *Page Ref: 517*
Topic: The Plea of Insanity
Skill: Factual

122) Insanity pleas

    A) succeed about half the time.

    B) are used in about 20% of all court cases.

    C) are generally made in cases other than murder.

    D) mean that, if convicted, a person can never leave the mental hospital.

    E) can only be used after the psychologist has diagnosed insanity.

Answer: C
Diff: 2   *Page Ref: 517*
Topic: The Plea of Insanity
Skill: Factual

Check Your Understanding Questions

1) In Rosenhan's study, who discovered that the "pseudopatients" were faking mental illness?

A) psychiatrists

B) psychologists

C) nurses and aides working on the ward

D) other patients

E) other physicians

Answer: D
Diff: 2   Page Ref: 491
Topic: Check Your Understanding
Skill: Recall

2) Which of the following symptoms most clearly suggests the presence of abnormality?

A) hallucinations

B) worries

C) unusual behaviors

D) creativity

E) distraction

Answer: A
Diff: 2   Page Ref: 491
Topic: Check Your Understanding
Skill: Applied

3) Hippocrates proposed that mental disorder was caused by

A) possession by demons.

B) an imbalance in four bodily fluids.

C) a fungus growing on rye grain.

D) traumatic memories in the unconscious.

E) the taking of potions.

Answer: B
Diff: 2   Page Ref: 492
Topic: Check Your Understanding
Skill: Recall

4) The behavioral perspective emphasizes the influence of _____, while the cognitive perspective emphasizes _____.

    A) the environment; mental processes

    B) conscious processes; unconscious processes

    C) heredity; environment

    D) medical factors; psychological factors

    E) genetics; conscious processes

Answer: A
Diff: 3   Page Ref: 492
Topic: Check Your Understanding
Skill: Recall

5) Which of the following would be less likely to be noticed by a clinician using strictly the medical model of mental disorder?

    A) delusions

    B) severe disturbance in affect

    C) an unhealthy family environment

    D) a degenerative brain disease

    E) hallucinations

Answer: C
Diff: 2   Page Ref: 492
Topic: Check Your Understanding
Skill: Understanding the Core Concept

6) The DSM–IV classifies different disorders according to the individual's

    A) thoughts and perceptions.

    B) behaviors.

    C) medical background.

    D) childhood experiences.

    E) social interactions.

Answer: B
Diff: 2   Page Ref: 514
Topic: Check Your Understanding
Skill: Recall

7) Which disorder involves extreme swings of mood from elation to depression?

A) panic disorder

B) bipolar disorder

C) schizophrenia

D) unipolar depression

E) PTSD

Answer: B

Diff: 2   *Page Ref: 514*

Topic: Check Your Understanding

Skill: Recall

8) According to the preparedness hypothesis, which one of the following would you expect to be most common?

A) fear of snakes

B) fear of books

C) fear of horses

D) fear of the number 13

E) fear of water

Answer: A

Diff: 2   *Page Ref: 514*

Topic: Check Your Understanding

Skill: Applied

9) Which one of the following involves a deficiency in memory?

A) phobia

B) sntisocial personality

C) dissociative fugue

D) obsessive–compulsive disorder

E) schizophrenia

Answer: C

Diff: 2   *Page Ref: 514*

Topic: Check Your Understanding

Skill: Recall

10) Which of the following is a disorder in which the individual displays more than one distinct personality?
    A) schizophrenia
    B) depersonalization disorder
    C) bipolar disorder
    D) dissociative identity disorder
    E) phobia

Answer: D
Diff: 2   *Page Ref: 514*
Topic: Check Your Understanding
Skill: Recall

11) Which one of the following is primarily a disorder of young American women?
    A) bipolar disorder
    B) schizophrenia
    C) anorexia nervosa
    D) antisocial personality disorder
    E) phobias

Answer: C
Diff: 2   *Page Ref: 514*
Topic: Check Your Understanding
Skill: Recall

12) Hallucinations and delusions are symptoms of
    A) schizophrenia.
    B) somatoform disorders.
    C) anxiety disorders.
    D) depersonalization disorder.
    E) panic disorders.

Answer: A
Diff: 2   *Page Ref: 514*
Topic: Check Your Understanding
Skill: Recall

13) Which category of disorder is most common?

    A) schizophrenia

    B) dissociative disorders

    C) eating disorders

    D) the adjustment disorders and Other conditions that may be a focus of clinical attention

    E) mood disorders

Answer: D

Diff: 2   *Page Ref: 514*

Topic: Check Your Understanding

Skill: Recall

14) The DSM-IV groups most mental disorders by their

    A) treatments.

    B) causes.

    C) symptoms.

    D) theoretical basis.

    E) cures.

Answer: C

Diff: 2   *Page Ref: 514*

Topic: Check Your Understanding

Skill: Understanding the Core Concept

15) Which of the following statements is true?

    A) Mental disorders have a similar prevalence in all cultures.

    B) In general, biology creates mental disorder, while culture merely shapes the way a person experiences it.

    C) Culture-specific stressors occur primarily in developing countries.

    D) Cultures around the world seem to distinguish between people with mental disorders and people who are visionaries or prophets.

    E) Mental disorders are more prevalent in Eastern cultures.

Answer: D

Diff: 2   *Page Ref: 517*

Topic: Check Your Understanding

Skill: Recall

16) *Insanity* is a

    A) psychological term.

    B) psychiatric term, found in DSM-IV under "psychotic disorders."

    C) legal term.

    D) term that refers to "neurotic" or "psychotic" symptoms.

    E) a classification for those seeking treatment.

Answer: C
Diff: 2   *Page Ref: 517*
Topic: Check Your Understanding
Skill: Recall

17) Which unfortunate consequence of diagnosing mental disorders is emphasized in this section of the chapter?

    A) the inaccuracy of the diagnosis

    B) stigmatizing those with mental disorders

    C) adding to the already crowded conditions of in mental hospitals

    D) that some cultures do not recognize mental disorders

    E) the importance of the insanity defense

Answer: B
Diff: 2   *Page Ref: 517*
Topic: Check Your Understanding
Skill: Understanding the Core Concept

True/False Questions

1) In David Rosenhan's study of mental illness, the doctors immediately knew that the pseudopatients were not really ill.

Answer: FALSE
Diff: 2   *Page Ref: 483–484*
Topic: What is Psychological Disorder?
Skill: Factual

2) A delusion is a false sensory experience.

Answer: FALSE
Diff: 2   *Page Ref: 485*
Topic: What is Psychological Disorder?
Skill: Conceptual

3) Homosexuality is considered an illness according to the DSM-IV.

Answer: FALSE
Diff: 2   Page Ref: 486
Topic: What is Psychological Disorder?
Skill: Factual

4) Hippocrates believed that too much black bile would cause one to be cheerful.

Answer: FALSE
Diff: 2   Page Ref: 487
Topic: What is Psychological Disorder?
Skill: Recall

5) The medical model argues that mental disorders are diseases of the mind that require treatment.

Answer: TRUE
Diff: 2   Page Ref: 488
Topic: What is Psychological Disorder?
Skill: Conceptual

6) Genetic abnormalities to describe mental illness would fit the biopsychological model.

Answer: TRUE
Diff: 2   Page Ref: 489
Topic: What is Psychological Disorder?
Skill: Factual

7) Unpredictability is one of the potential signs of mental illness.

Answer: TRUE
Diff: 2   Page Ref: 490
Topic: What is Psychological Disorder?
Skill: Conceptual

8) The DSM-IV is organized by the causes of mental illness.

Answer: FALSE
Diff: 2   Page Ref: 492–493
Topic: How Are Psychological Disorders Classified?
Skill: Factual

9) Depression is the world's most prevalent mental disturbance.

Answer: TRUE
Diff: 2   Page Ref: 494
Topic: How Are Psychological Disorders Classified?
Skill: Factual

10) Seasonal Affective Disorder is a type of mood disorder.

Answer: TRUE
Diff: 2   Page Ref: 495
Topic: How Are Psychological Disorders Classified?
Skill: Factual

11) Neuroscience studies have shown a link between brain function and depression.

Answer: TRUE
Diff: 1   Page Ref: 495
Topic: What is Psychological Disorder?
Skill: Factual

12) Stress hormones have been found to adversely affect neurons in the hypothalamus–a part of the brain known to be a site of action for antidepressant drugs.

Answer: FALSE
Diff: 3   Page Ref: 496
Topic: How Are Psychological Disorders Classified?
Skill: Factual

13) Women are more likely than men to suffer from depression.

Answer: TRUE
Diff: 2   Page Ref: 497
Topic: How Are Psychological Disorders Classified?
Skill: Conceptual

14) Panic attacks are excruciating episodes of anxiety that can last for hours.

Answer: FALSE
Diff: 2   Page Ref: 498
Topic: How Are Psychological Disorders Classified?
Skill: Conceptual

15) According to Seligman's preparedness hypothesis, it is difficult to learn a fear of automobiles but easy to fear snakes.

Answer: TRUE
Diff: 2   Page Ref: 499
Topic: How Are Psychological Disorders Classified?
Skill: Factual

16) Compulsions are thoughts and obsessions are actions.

Answer: FALSE
Diff: 2   Page Ref: 500–501
Topic: How Are Psychological Disorders Classified?
Skill: Factual

17) The rate of appearance of conversion disorder has increased over the last century.

Answer: FALSE
Diff: 2   Page Ref: 502
Topic: How Are Psychological Disorders Classified?
Skill: Conceptual

18) Dissociate identity disorder and schizophrenia are essentially the dame disorder.

Answer: FALSE
Diff: 2   Page Ref: 502–503
Topic: How Are Psychological Disorders Classified?
Skill: Factual

19) Individuals with dissociative fugue may wake up and find them selves in a different place with a different identity and completely forget their past.

Answer: TRUE
Diff: 2   Page Ref: 503
Topic: How Are Psychological Disorders Classified?
Skill: Applied

20) Individuals who suffer from dissociative identity disorder commonly suffer from sexual abuse as children.

Answer: TRUE
Diff: 2   Page Ref: 504
Topic: How Are Psychological Disorders Classified?
Skill: Recall

21) Persons with anorexia nervosa have a distorted body image in that they view themselves as fat.

Answer: TRUE
Diff: 2   *Page Ref: 505*
Topic: How Are Psychological Disorders Classified?
Skill: Conceptual

22) A person experiencing hallucinations or delusions may well be suffering from schizophrenia.

Answer: TRUE
Diff: 2   *Page Ref: 507*
Topic: How Are Psychological Disorders Classified?
Skill: Applied

23) Disorganized schizophrenia often involves incoherent speech.

Answer: TRUE
Diff: 3   *Page Ref: 507*
Topic: How Are Psychological Disorders Classified?
Skill: Applied

24) Hallucinations and delusions are examples of positive symptoms of schizophrenia.

Answer: TRUE
Diff: 2   *Page Ref: 508*
Topic: How Are Psychological Disorders Classified?
Skill: Applied

25) If Lisa's identical twin, Nancy, has schizophrenia, Lisa's likelihood of developing schizophrenia is about 25%.

Answer: FALSE
Diff: 2   *Page Ref: 509*
Topic: How Are Psychological Disorders Classified?
Skill: Applied

26) A person diagnosed as having antisocial personality disorder would have no remorse.

Answer: TRUE
Diff: 2   *Page Ref: 510*
Topic: How Are Psychological Disorders Classified?
Skill: Conceptual

27) A individual with autism has a problem with reading.

Answer: FALSE
Diff: 2   Page Ref: 511
Topic: How Are Psychological Disorders Classified?
Skill: Factual

28) 3-5% of school age children are classified as having ADHD.

Answer: TRUE
Diff: 2   Page Ref: 512
Topic: How Are Psychological Disorders Classified?
Skill: Recall

29) Shyness is the most frequently diagnosed condition in the DSM-IV.

Answer: FALSE
Diff: 2   Page Ref: 513
Topic: Shyness
Skill: Factual

30) Ecological models of mental illness show that culture influences both the prevalence of psychological disorders and the symptoms that disturbed people display.

Answer: TRUE
Diff: 2   Page Ref: 516
Topic: What Are The Consequences of Labeling People?
Skill: Applied

31) The insanity plea is used in 1 of 1000 criminal cases and is successful most of the time it is used.

Answer: FALSE
Diff: 2   Page Ref: 517
Topic: The Plea of Insanity
Skill: Factual

Short Answer Questions

1) Distinguish between a hallucination and a delusion.

Answer: A hallucination is a perception that occurs in the absence of a stimulus; a delusion is a false belief system.
Diff: 2   Page Ref: 485
Topic: What is Psychological Disorder?
Skill: Applied

2) When a person makes people uncomfortable by making them feel threatened or distressed in some way, this indicator of abnormality is called what?

Answer: observer discomfort
Diff: 3   Page Ref: 489
Topic: What is Psychological Disorder?
Skill: Conceptual

3) Which book published by the APA classifies mental disorders by their symptoms?

Answer: DSM-IV (Diagnostic and Statistical Manual of Mental Disorders, 4th Edition); accept
      DSM as correct, too
Diff: 2   Page Ref: 492-493
Topic: How Are Psychological Disorders Classified?
Skill: Conceptual

4) Name the three mood disorders.

Answer: bipolar (disorder), major depression and seasonal affective disorder
Diff: 2   Page Ref: 493-494
Topic: How Are Psychological Disorders Classified?
Skill: Conceptual

5) What mood disorder often effects people in the winter and what is a biological explanation for the illness?

Answer: seasonal affective disorder (SAD), irregular levels of melatonin in the body
Diff: 3   Page Ref: 495
Topic: How Are Psychological Disorders Classified?
Skill: Conceptual

6) Briefly explain what happens when one is suffering from a panic disorder, and compare this to generalized anxiety disorder.

Answer: They have panic attacks with no connection to the present situation. eventually the
      panic attack subsides but with a generalized anxiety disorder the anxiety remains
      indefinitely.
Diff: 2   Page Ref: 498
Topic: How Are Psychological Disorders Classified?
Skill: Conceptual

7) The _____ hypothesis suggests that we carry around an evolutionary tendency to respond quickly to stimuli that our ancestors once feared.

Answer: preparedness
Diff: 3   Page Ref: 499
Topic: How Are Psychological Disorders Classified?
Skill: Conceptual

8) How are obsessions and compulsions different?

Answer: Obsessions are thoughts while compulsions are actions.
Diff: 2   Page Ref: 500

Topic: How Are Psychological Disorders Classified?

Skill: Factual

9) If someone believes they have every little bug that is going around even though there is no physical indication that they are sick they may suffer from

Answer: hypochondriasis.
Diff: 2   Page Ref: 502

Topic: How Are Psychological Disorders Classified?

Skill: Applied

10) The famous cases portrayed in the movies *Sybil* and *The Three Faces of Eve* depict patients with _____.

Answer: dissociative identity disorder
Diff: 2   Page Ref: 504

Topic: How Are Psychological Disorders Classified?

Skill: Conceptual

11) How do bulimics lose or maintain their body weight?

Answer: binge; purging
Diff: 1   Page Ref: 505–506

Topic: How Are Psychological Disorders Classified?

Skill: Conceptual

12) Describe two facts that support the notion that schizophrenia has a biological basis.

Answer: brain pathology; antipsychotic drugs block dopamine receptors; twin studies of schizophrenia
Diff: 3   Page Ref: 508–509

Topic: How Are Psychological Disorders Classified?

Skill: Applied

13) Briefly list three characteristics of an individual with an antisocial personality disorder.

Answer: irresponsible or harmful behavior, lack of conscience and lying
Diff: 3   Page Ref: 510

Topic: How Are Psychological Disorders Classified?

Skill: Conceptual

14) What is the main problem for those suffering from dyslexia?

Answer: They have trouble reading.
Diff: 2   Page Ref: 512
Topic: How Are Psychological Disorders Classified?
Skill: Factual

15) What does insanity actually mean?

Answer: It is a legal term referring to one who might not be able to control their own behavior.
Diff: 2   Page Ref: 516
Topic: What Are The Consequences of Labeling People?
Skill: Recall

Essay Questions

1) Describe the five indicators of abnormality.

Answer: The presence of these has been used to decide whether a behavior has reached the point of abnormality. The five are: distress, maladaptiveness, irrationality, unpredictability, and unconventionality / undesirable behavior.
Diff: 2   Page Ref: 490
Topic: What is Psychological Disorder?
Skill: Factual

2) Name, compare, and contrast two major types of mood disorders.

Answer: The two major types are major depression, which involves feelings of worthlessness, lack of appetite, sleep difficulty, withdrawal from friends and relatives, lethargy, and suicidal thought. One special type of depression is seasonal affective disorder, which occurs mainly in the dark months of winter. Bipolar disorder (or manic depression) involves depressive episodes as described above as well as manic episodes in which the person is talkative, energetic, euphoric, and hyperactive.
Diff: 2   Page Ref: 493–496
Topic: How Are Psychological Disorders Classified?
Skill: Conceptual

3) Provide a outline listing 2 disorders in each of the following categories
   Mood
   Dissociative
   Anxiety
   Types of schizophrenia

   Answer: (Answers will vary)
           Mood: Major Depression:; Bipolar
           Dissociative: Fugue; Dissociative Identity
           Anxiety: Obsessive-Compulsive; Panic disorder
           Types of Schizophrenia: Catatonic; Undifferentiated
   Diff: 3   *Page Ref: 495–510*
   Topic: How Are Psychological Disorders Classified?
   Skill: Conceptual

4) Discuss the symptoms of eating disorders, whom they impact most, and why.

   Answer: Anorexia nervosa involves loss of appetite and weight (starvation through dieting) coupled with a belief that one is overweight. Bulimia nervosa involves binges (overeating episodes) and purging (removing calories through vomiting, fasting, or excessive exercise). Both of these disorders primarily affect middle–class, young White American women.
   Diff: 2   *Page Ref: 505–506*
   Topic: How Are Psychological Disorders Classified?
   Skill: Conceptual

5) Discuss the symptoms and potential causes of schizophrenia. Name and describe the four most common types of schizophrenia and provide symptoms for each.

   Answer: The symptoms involve confusion, bleakness, hallucinations, delusions, blunted emotion, bizarre thought, and odd language. The four types are disorganized, catatonic, paranoid, and undifferentiated. (See the book for a discussion of the symptoms involved with each.) As for causes, biology, chemical toxins, stress, and other environmental factors have been implicated.
   Diff: 3   *Page Ref: 506–509*
   Topic: How Are Psychological Disorders Classified?
   Skill: Conceptual

6) Defend the position that schizophrenia has a biological basis.

   Answer: Sources of support for this position would include: adoption studies, twin studies, the fact that brain scans of schizophrenic patients show structural abnormalities, the fact that effective antipsychotic drugs block brain dopamine receptors, and the fact that dopamine-releasing drugs (e.g. amphetamine) can cause schizophrenia symptoms.
   Diff: 3   *Page Ref: 508–509*
   Topic: How Are Psychological Disorders Classified?
   Skill: Conceptual

Chapter 13 Therapies for Psychological Disorders

Multiple Choice Questions

1) A key common element among different forms of therapy such as psychoanalysis, behavioral therapy, and drug therapy is a relationship that focuses on
   A) improving behavior and mental processes.
   B) reinforcing existing behavioral patterns.
   C) removing the patient from existing social networks.
   D) discovering the unconscious reasons behind behaviors.
   E) There is no common element.

Answer: A
Diff: 2   *Page Ref: 525*
Topic: What is Therapy?
Skill: Conceptual

2) Practitioners who believe that mental illness is a psychological disorder that is not a mental illness but a problem in living typically refers to the individual they are working with as a
   A) subject.
   B) patient.
   C) client.
   D) participant.
   E) customer.

Answer: C
Diff: 2   *Page Ref: 526*
Topic: What is Therapy?
Skill: Factual

3) The group that is least likely to have access to adequate mental care is
   A) the poor.
   B) the middle class.
   C) adolescents.
   D) the elderly.
   E) college students.

Answer: A
Diff: 1   *Page Ref: 526*
Topic: What is Therapy?
Skill: Factual

4) All but _____ are a necessary part of the therapeutic process.

    A) accurate diagnosis of the problem

    B) determining the problem's cause

    C) determining the likelihood of improvement

    D) carrying out treatment

    E) uncovering unconscious memories

Answer: E
Diff: 2   *Page Ref: 527*
Topic: What is Therapy?
Skill: Conceptual

5) Before deciding on the particular form of treatment for an individual, a therapist needs to

    A) find out what medications the individual is taking to check for drug interactions.

    B) meet with close family members to apprise them of the situation.

    C) identify the problem and its causes.

    D) make a prognosis in consultation with a psychiatrist.

    E) explore the patients' repressed issues from childhood.

Answer: C
Diff: 2   *Page Ref: 527*
Topic: What is Therapy?
Skill: Conceptual

6) Which of the following are not allowed to prescribe drugs to clients?

    A) counseling psychologists

    B) psychiatric nurse practitioners

    C) psychiatrists

    D) psychoanalysts

    E) All are able to prescribe medication

Answer: A
Diff: 2   *Page Ref: 527*
Topic: What is Therapy?
Skill: Factual

7) A _____ is a specialist who often focuses on short-term assistance for a single problem.
   A) psychoanalyst
   B) psychiatric social worker
   C) clinical psychologist
   D) counseling psychologist
   E) psychiatrist

Answer: D
Diff: 2   Page Ref: 528
Topic: What is Therapy?
Skill: Factual

8) Based on the conditions in the London hospital of bethlehem, the word "Bedlam" came to be associated with
   A) good psychiatric treatment.
   B) a loss of touch with reality.
   C) any noisy, chaotic place.
   D) treating patients using medicine.
   E) neglecting patients.

Answer: C
Diff: 3   Page Ref: 528
Topic: What is Therapy?
Skill: Recall

9) Insight therapy and behavior therapy are collectively known as
   A) psychomania.
   B) psychopathology.
   C) psychophilia.
   D) psychotropism.
   E) psychotherapy.

Answer: E
Diff: 2   Page Ref: 529
Topic: What is Therapy?
Skill: Applied

10) If Diane is seeing a biomedical therapist to treat her depression, she is most likely to receive
   A) talking sessions.
   B) medication.
   C) group therapy.
   D) aversion therapy.
   E) psychoanalysis.

Answer: B
Diff: 2   Page Ref: 529
Topic: What is Therapy?
Skill: Applied

11) _____ cultures view mental disorder as to a disconnect between the person and their group.
   A) Western
   B) Medical
   C) Asian
   D) Eastern
   E) Third-world

Answer: C
Diff: 2   Page Ref: 529
Topic: What is Therapy?
Skill: Factual

12) _____ is considered to be one of the _____ therapies.
   A) Counter-conditioning; rational emotive
   B) Psychoanalysis; insight
   C) Talk radio; biomedical
   D) Counseling; aversion
   E) ECT; behavioral

Answer: B
Diff: 2   Page Ref: 529
Topic: What is Therapy?
Skill: Conceptual

13) _____ is considered a _____ therapy.

    A) Psychosurgery; insight

    B) Insight; behavioral

    C) ECT therapy; insight

    D) Psychosurgery; biomedical

    E) ECT; humanistic

Answer: D
Diff: 2   *Page Ref: 529*
Topic: What is Therapy?
Skill: Factual

14) Researchers have found that paraprofessionals

    A) are seldom effective.

    B) are more successful than professionals.

    C) have great ability with behavioral therapies.

    D) are about as effective as professionals.

    E) are ineffective with insight therapies.

Answer: D
Diff: 3   *Page Ref: 530*
Topic: Paraprofessionals Do Therapy, Too
Skill: Factual

15) _____ therapy tries to help patients understand the thoughts, emotions, and motives that underlie their difficulties.

    A) Insight

    B) Aversion

    C) psychosomatic

    D) Conditioning

    E) Token

Answer: A
Diff: 3   *Page Ref: 531*
Topic: What is Therapy?
Skill: Conceptual

16) The two main forms of treatment used by psychologists today are
    A) behavioral therapy and insight therapy.
    B) shock therapy and ECT.
    C) Rorschach tests and self-reporting data.
    D) eclectic therapies and personality theories.
    E) psychoanalysis and cognitive therapy.

Answer: A
Diff: 2   Page Ref: 531
Topic: What is Therapy?
Skill: Factual

17) This type of therapy focuses on communicating and verbalizing emotions and motives to understand their problems.
    A) behavioral therapy
    B) cognitive therapy
    C) insight therapy
    D) rational-Emotive therapy
    E) humanistic therapy

Answer: C
Diff: 2   Page Ref: 531
Topic: How Do Psychologists Treat Psychological Disorders?
Skill: Factual

18) Which approach views mental disorder as the visible symptom of unresolved childhood traumas and inner conflicts?
    A) cognitive
    B) humanistic
    C) behavioral
    D) psychoanalytic
    E) biomedical

Answer: D
Diff: 2   Page Ref: 532
Topic: How Do Psychologists Treat Psychological Disorders?
Skill: Conceptual

19) _____ are the typical practitioners of Freudian therapy.

    A) Counseling psychologists

    B) Social workers

    C) Psychiatrists

    D) Psychoanalysts

    E) Clinical psychologists

Answer: D

Diff: 1   *Page Ref: 532*

Topic: How Do Psychologists Treat Psychological Disorders?

Skill: Factual

20) In which of the following types of treatment would a patient relax and talk about whatever comes to mind while the therapist listens?

    A) behavioral

    B) cognitive

    C) psychoanalytic

    D) rational–emotive

    E) humanistic

Answer: C

Diff: 1   *Page Ref: 532*

Topic: How Do Psychologists Treat Psychological Disorders?

Skill: Conceptual

21) The technique of free association was intended to

    A) project the concerns of the therapist into the patients' thoughts.

    B) allow the therapist to listen to the client in order to gather clues about their unconscious impulses.

    C) suppress memory.

    D) interpret the symbolic meaning of dreams.

    E) allow the client to sublimate their impulses.

Answer: B

Diff: 3   *Page Ref: 532*

Topic: How Do Psychologists Treat Psychological Disorders?

Skill: Conceptual

22) The process of _____ refers to the situation in which a patients' feelings for his or her therapist reflect relationships with their parents.

    A) catharsis

    B) transference

    C) free association

    D) insight therapy

    E) systematic desensitization

Answer: B

Diff: 2   Page Ref: 533

Topic: How Do Psychologists Treat Psychological Disorders?

Skill: Conceptual

23) Freud believed that some of his patients were falling in love with him, he attributed this to recovered feelings they had towards their parents. This is called

    A) regression.

    B) projection.

    C) sublimation.

    D) transference.

    E) reaction formation.

Answer: D

Diff: 2   Page Ref: 533

Topic: How Do Psychologists Treat Psychological Disorders?

Skill: Applied

24) The modern day application of Freud's psychoanalytic theory is

    A) behavioral therapy.

    B) psychodynamic therapy.

    C) humanistic therapy.

    D) transference therapy.

    E) cognitive therapy.

Answer: B

Diff: 2   Page Ref: 533

Topic: How Do Psychologists Treat Psychological Disorders?

Skill: Factual

25) Post-Freudian analysts differ from classic psychoanalysts in that they emphasize
    A) learned relationships between behaviors and consequences.
    B) the relationship between physical and mental health.
    C) interpersonal relationships and self-concept.
    D) unconscious motivation and conflict.
    E) the influence of early childhood experiences.

Answer: C
Diff: 2   Page Ref: 533
Topic: How Do Psychologists Treat Psychological Disorders?
Skill: Factual

26) _____ therapy focuses on helping people with their existential crises.
    A) Cognitive
    B) Humanistic
    C) Behavioral
    D) Psychodynamic
    E) Dyadic

Answer: B
Diff: 2   Page Ref: 534
Topic: How Do Psychologists Treat Psychological Disorders?
Skill: Conceptual

27) _____ therapies are focused on the patients' self-concept, values, and needs.
    A) Social
    B) Systematic
    C) Behavioral
    D) Biomedical
    E) Humanistic

Answer: E
Diff: 2   Page Ref: 534
Topic: How Do Psychologists Treat Psychological Disorders?
Skill: Factual

28) An important emphasis of humanistic therapy is on

    A) hedonistic impulses.

    B) destructive tendencies.

    C) faulty thinking.

    D) problematic behaviors.

    E) the whole person is involved in a process of change.

Answer: E
Diff: 2   Page Ref: 534
Topic: How Do Psychologists Treat Psychological Disorders?
Skill: Conceptual

29) This type of therapy emphasizes an individual's free-will.

    A) humanistic

    B) behavioral

    C) cognitive

    D) psychodynamic

    E) social

Answer: A
Diff: 2   Page Ref: 534
Topic: How Do Psychologists Treat Psychological Disorders?
Skill: Conceptual

30) The cause of anxiety, according to Carl Rogers, lies in

    A) the inability of ego defense mechanisms to repress unconscious conflicts.

    B) social reinforcements of anxiety-related behaviors.

    C) realistic fears regarding the world and local crises.

    D) a conflict between a naturally positive self–image and negative external criticisms.

    E) chemical and structural features of the brain.

Answer: D
Diff: 2   Page Ref: 534
Topic: How Do Psychologists Treat Psychological Disorders?
Skill: Factual

31) Rogers well-kown type of therapy is considered

    A) systematic desensitization.

    B) rational-emotive therapy.

    C) client-centered therapy.

    D) aversive therapy.

    E) counterconditioning.

Answer: C

Diff: 2   Page Ref: 534

Topic: How Do Psychologists Treat Psychological Disorders?

Skill: Factual

32) A doting mother who loves her son despite his criminal past would be said by Rogers to show

    A) unconditional positive regard.

    B) reflection of feeling.

    C) systematic desensitization.

    D) aversion therapy.

    E) poor judgement.

Answer: A

Diff: 3   Page Ref: 535

Topic: How Do Psychologists Treat Psychological Disorders?

Skill: Applied

33) The focus of cognitive therapy is on

    A) concept formation.

    B) assimilation and accommodation.

    C) overcoming stereotypes.

    D) unconscious motives.

    E) rational thinking.

Answer: E

Diff: 2   Page Ref: 536

Topic: How Do Psychologists Treat Psychological Disorders?

Skill: Factual

34) Aaron Beck is known for developing a(n) _____ therapy for the treatment of _____.
   A) humanistic; schizophrenia
   B) cognitive; depression
   C) medical; phobias
   D) biological; addictions
   E) aversive; autism

   Answer: B
   Diff: 2   Page Ref: 536
   Topic: How Do Psychologists Treat Psychological Disorders?
   Skill: Factual

35) The cause of depression according to Aaron Beck is that depressed patients
   A) suffer from an imbalance of serotonin in their brains.
   B) are reinforced for their depressed behaviors.
   C) have low self-efficacy.
   D) use negative automatic thoughts they repeat about themselves.
   E) have had many childhood traumas.

   Answer: D
   Diff: 2   Page Ref: 536
   Topic: How Do Psychologists Treat Psychological Disorders?
   Skill: Factual

36) According to humanistic therapy, who has the ability to heal the client?
   A) loving friends
   B) a good therapist
   C) drug therapy
   D) themselves
   E) close family members

   Answer: D
   Diff: 2   Page Ref: 536
   Topic: How Do Psychologists Treat Psychological Disorders?
   Skill: Conceptual

37) The _____ approach to therapy would be most useful in aiding a person to change their belief that their life will never get better.

   A) biomedical

   B) cognitive

   C) psychoanalytic

   D) contingency management

   E) aversion

Answer: B

Diff: 2   Page Ref: 536

Topic: How Do Psychologists Treat Psychological Disorders?

Skill: Applied

38) The core methods of a _____ therapist are to challenge unrealistic, unjustified assumptions and to discuss alternative solutions.

   A) psychodynamic

   B) cognitive

   C) humanistic

   D) psychoanalytic

   E) systematic

Answer: B

Diff: 2   Page Ref: 536

Topic: How Do Psychologists Treat Psychological Disorders?

Skill: Conceptual

39) An advantage of _____ is that such therapy reassures people they are not alone in having a specific problem.

   A) psychoanalysis

   B) self-therapy

   C) ECT

   D) token economies

   E) group therapy

Answer: E

Diff: 2   Page Ref: 537

Topic: How Do Psychologists Treat Psychological Disorders?

Skill: Conceptual

40) A support group would be most likely to be useful in

    A) managing crises such as divorce or the death of a child.

    B) treating addictions such as alcohol or gambling.

    C) coping with mental and physical disorders.

    D) helping relatives or friends of addicts cope with the associated stresses.

    E) All of the above are correct.

Answer: E

Diff: 3   Page Ref: 537

Topic: How Do Psychologists Treat Psychological Disorders?

Skill: Conceptual

41) The first step in the path to recovery for an alcoholic person involved, according to the Alcoholics Anonymous program, is to

    A) take control of your life.

    B) apologize to those who you have hurt.

    C) tell the group that you do not plan to drink.

    D) ask relatives for their help.

    E) admit you are powerless in regard to alcohol.

Answer: E

Diff: 3   Page Ref: 537

Topic: How Do Psychologists Treat Psychological Disorders?

Skill: Factual

42) Which of the following individuals would be most likely to benefit from group therapy?

    A) Sally, who suffers for a narcissistic personality disorder

    B) Brad, who suffers from paranoid schizophrenia

    C) Gerry, who has an anti-social personality disorder

    D) Ellen, who is an alcoholic

    E) none of the above would benefit from group therapy

Answer: D

Diff: 2   Page Ref: 537

Topic: How Do Psychologists Treat Psychological Disorders?

Skill: Applied

43) Johanna and Stuart are seeing a couples therapist. The therapist is LEAST likely to help them figure out how they

    A) can use projection and transference to improve their relationship.

    B) dominate or confuse each other verbally and non–verbally.

    C) can reinforce desirable behavior in each other.

    D) can each help the other express his or her feelings and ideas.

    E) can develop nondirective listening skills.

Answer: A
Diff: 3   *Page Ref: 538*
Topic: How Do Psychologists Treat Psychological Disorders?
Skill: Applied

44) Which of the following would occur during a family therapy session?

    A) The therapist would remain objective.

    B) The family would work on improving it's functioning.

    C) The family would openly listen to one another.

    D) The therapist would work on altering "psychological spaces" between family members.

    E) All of the above

Answer: E
Diff: 2   *Page Ref: 538*
Topic: How Do Psychologists Treat Psychological Disorders?
Skill: Conceptual

45) The focus of couples therapy is on

    A) the processes of the relationship, not the personalities.

    B) the prior relationships of each member of the couple.

    C) dispositional tendencies of the individuals involved.

    D) maladaptive ego defense mechanisms.

    E) the sad childhoods of each partner.

Answer: A
Diff: 1   *Page Ref: 538*
Topic: How Do Psychologists Treat Psychological Disorders?
Skill: Conceptual

46) Behavioral therapists believe that both normal and abnormal behaviors develop

    A) through a learning process.

    B) due to traumatic childhood events.

    C) because of environmental influences.

    D) due to poor genetic makeup.

    E) as a result of unconscious forces.

Answer: A
Diff: 1   *Page Ref: 538*
Topic: How Do Psychologists Treat Psychological Disorders?
Skill: Conceptual

47) A Behavioral therapist is likely to focus on

    A) irrational thoughts.

    B) a positive self–image.

    C) outward actions.

    D) unconscious childhood trauma.

    E) the influence of culture on behavior.

Answer: C
Diff: 1   *Page Ref: 538*
Topic: How Do Psychologists Treat Psychological Disorders?
Skill: Conceptual

48) The first person to successfully implement behavioral therapy to eliminate young Peter's fear of a rabbit was

    A) Sigmund Freud.

    B) Albert bandura.

    C) Mary Cover Jones.

    D) John Watson.

    E) B.F. Skinner.

Answer: C
Diff: 3   *Page Ref: 538*
Topic: How Do Psychologists Treat Psychological Disorders?
Skill: Factual

49) Which is the correct sequence of steps in systematic desensitization?

    A) practice relaxation, develop anxiety hierarchy, associate relaxation with anxieties

    B) associate relaxation with anxieties, practice relaxation, develop anxiety hierarchy

    C) identify thinking flaws, change emotions, change faulty ways of thinking

    D) develop anxiety hierarchy, practice relaxation, associate relaxation with anxieties

    E) identify thinking flaws, change thinking flaws, experience more positive emotions

Answer: D
Diff: 2   Page Ref: 539
Topic: How Do Psychologists Treat Psychological Disorders?
Skill: Factual

50) Systematic desensitization is most often used to treat

    A) alcohol abuse.

    B) depression.

    C) schizophrenia.

    D) ADHD.

    E) anxiety disorders.

Answer: E
Diff: 2   Page Ref: 539
Topic: How Do Psychologists Treat Psychological Disorders?
Skill: Factual

51) The key to making systematic desensitization effective is

    A) to insure that the person demonstrates no anxiety during the treatment.

    B) to insure that the individuals is relaxed before moving on to the next step of the process.

    C) to introduce the individuals to the fear immediately.

    D) unconditional positive guard.

    E) to recover lost memories.

Answer: B
Diff: 2   Page Ref: 539
Topic: How Do Psychologists Treat Psychological Disorders?
Skill: Conceptual

52) Janet has a phobia for dogs, her therapist has her watch a film with dogs, then watch as others interact with dogs, then stay in the same room as a dog, and eventually pet the dog. her therapist is using what type of treatment to overcome Janet's phobia fo dogs?

   A) aversive therapy

   B) counterconditioning

   C) client–centered therapy

   D) cognitive therapy

   E) systematic desensitization

Answer: E
Diff: 2   *Page Ref: 540*
Topic: How Do Psychologists Treat Psychological Disorders?
Skill: Applied

53) Laura has an intense fear of spiders. Her therapist picks one up and lets it sit on her shoulder. The therapist is utilizing _____ therapy.

   A) contingency

   B) psychodynamic

   C) aversion

   D) post–Freudian

   E) exposure

Answer: E
Diff: 2   *Page Ref: 540*
Topic: How Do Psychologists Treat Psychological Disorders?
Skill: Applied

54) Aversion therapy is useful for the treatment of

   A) anxiety.

   B) a phobic fear.

   C) diminished self–esteem.

   D) fear of flying.

   E) drug addiction.

Answer: E
Diff: 2   *Page Ref: 540*
Topic: How Do Psychologists Treat Psychological Disorders?
Skill: Factual

55) A person who paints a foul-tasting polish on their fingernails is using _____ therapy to quit nail–biting.

    A) counterconditioning

    B) contingency management

    C) aversion

    D) participant modeling

    E) token economy

Answer: C

Diff: 2   Page Ref: 540

Topic: How Do Psychologists Treat Psychological Disorders?

Skill: Applied

56) The behavioral technique of _____, when used at its extreme, resembles torture.

    A) systematic desensitization

    B) aversion therapy

    C) participant modeling

    D) catharsis

    E) psychoanalysis

Answer: B

Diff: 2   Page Ref: 540

Topic: How Do Psychologists Treat Psychological Disorders?

Skill: Conceptual

57) Cindy's parents add 15 minutes to her bedtime, if she has completed all of her daily chores. Cindy's parents are using

    A) participant modeling.

    B) aversion therapy.

    C) contingency management.

    D) systematic desensitization.

    E) parent effectiveness training.

Answer: C

Diff: 2   Page Ref: 540–541

Topic: How Do Psychologists Treat Psychological Disorders?

Skill: Applied

58) The best therapy to rid individuals of bad habits is

    A) cognitive therapy.

    B) humanistic therapy.

    C) behavioral therapy.

    D) psychoanalytic therapy.

    E) group therapy.

Answer: C
Diff: 3   *Page Ref: 539-541*
Topic: How Do Psychologists Treat Psychological Disorders?
Skill: Conceptual

59) The type of behavioral therapy often used in institutional settings in order to have people exhibit desireable behaviors.

    A) aversive conditioning

    B) counterconditioning

    C) token economy

    D) systematic desensitization

    E) client-centered therapy

Answer: C
Diff: 2   *Page Ref: 541*
Topic: How Do Psychologists Treat Psychological Disorders?
Skill: Applied

60) What is the problem with using a token economy?

    A) It is not very effective at getting the individual to display given behaviors.

    B) It does not work anywhere except institutional settings.

    C) It can be addicting.

    D) Once the reward ends, the desired behavior often also ends.

    E) All of the following are problems with using a token economy.

Answer: D
Diff: 3   *Page Ref: 541*
Topic: How Do Psychologists Treat Psychological Disorders?
Skill: Conceptual

61) Young laboratory monkeys who saw their parents express fear to a live snake later showed fear themselves while viewing a live snake for the first time. This new fear would be the result of

    A) observational learning.

    B) behaviorism.

    C) situationism.

    D) exposure and response prevention.

    E) token economies.

Answer: A

Diff: 2   Page Ref: 542

Topic: How Do Psychologists Treat Psychological Disorders?

Skill: Conceptual

62) A company that awards vacations to salespeople who have made the most sales for the year are using _____ to modify sales behavior.

    A) participant modeling

    B) symbolic modeling

    C) token economy

    D) aversion therapy

    E) nondirective influence

Answer: C

Diff: 2   Page Ref: 542

Topic: How Do Psychologists Treat Psychological Disorders?

Skill: Applied

63) _____ tries to modify problematic behavior patterns by arranging conditions in which the client will observe role models being reinforced for the desired response.

    A) Social learning

    B) Aversion therapy

    C) Extinction strategy

    D) Humanistic existential

    E) Insight therapy

Answer: A

Diff: 2   Page Ref: 542

Topic: How Do Psychologists Treat Psychological Disorders?

Skill: Conceptual

64) Sheila suffers with obsessive–compulsive disorder. Her therapist has just placed his hands into dirt and is now encouraging Sheila to do likewise. Sheila's therapist is using

   A) live modeling.

   B) symbolic exposure.

   C) participant modeling.

   D) symbolic modeling.

   E) token economy.

Answer: C

Diff: 3   Page Ref: 542

Topic: How Do Psychologists Treat Psychological Disorders?

Skill: Applied

65) Veru fears snakes, so her therapist encourages her to watch a film containing people handling snakes. Veru's therapist is using

   A) symbolic modeling therapy.

   B) humanistic therapy.

   C) psychoanalysis.

   D) self–system therapy.

   E) insight therapy.

Answer: A

Diff: 2   Page Ref: 542

Topic: How Do Psychologists Treat Psychological Disorders?

Skill: Applied

66) _____ was a therapist who believed that unhappy patients need to rid themselves of ineffective, self–defeating ways of thinking.

   A) Rogers   B) Freud   C) Horney   D) Sullivan   E) Ellis

Answer: E

Diff: 3   Page Ref: 543

Topic: How Do Psychologists Treat Psychological Disorders?

Skill: Factual

67) Rational Emotive Therapy is a type of

    A) cognitive therapy.

    B) behavioral therapy.

    C) humanistic therapy.

    D) group therapy.

    E) family therapy.

Answer: A
Diff: 2   Page Ref: 544
Topic: How Do Psychologists Treat Psychological Disorders?
Skill: Factual

68) Which of the following would Albert Ellis identify as an irrational belief?

    A) I can succeed.

    B) I am honest.

    C) Other students are competent.

    D) I can change my beliefs.

    E) I should always be treated fairly.

Answer: E
Diff: 2   Page Ref: 544
Topic: How Do Psychologists Treat Psychological Disorders?
Skill: Conceptual

69) Positive emission tomography (PET) scans have shown that certain cognitive therapies can

    A) reduce brain activity related to fear.

    B) help form the union between mind and body.

    C) work, but only when drug therapy is also used.

    D) increase overall brain activity.

    E) increase the volume of some brain structures.

Answer: A
Diff: 3   Page Ref: 544
Topic: How Do Psychologists Treat Psychological Disorders?
Skill: Factual

70) The Consumer Reports study of personal experiences in therapy found that
   A) "passive shoppers" were just as successful as "active shoppers."
   B) most people sought the help of a mental health professional rather than that of friends and family.
   C) drug therapy along with psychotherapy was the most effective treatment.
   D) long-term therapy was better than short-term therapy.
   E) specific types of therapy were deemed to be most effective.

Answer: D
Diff: 3   Page Ref: 544–545
Topic: How Do Psychologists Treat Psychological Disorders?
Skill: Factual

71) _____ was the 1950s researcher who created a furor by claiming that psychotherapy does not work.
   A) Ellis   B) Sullivan   C) Eysenck   D) Beck   E) Freud

Answer: C
Diff: 2   Page Ref: 546
Topic: How Do Psychologists Treat Psychological Disorders?
Skill: Factual

72) Hans Eysenck believed that the odds of a person being helped by psychotherapy was
   A) no better than that of a person waiting for help.
   B) due to effective drug treatments.
   C) less than that of electroconvulsive therapy.
   D) similar to that achieved by witch–doctors and shamans.
   E) better than that of psychoanalysis.

Answer: A
Diff: 3   Page Ref: 546–547
Topic: How Do Psychologists Treat Psychological Disorders?
Skill: Factual

73) The legacy of the claims of Hans Eysenck about psychotherapy is that
   A) psychology restructured the DSM.
   B) schizophrenia was redefined.
   C) people began to abandon psychotherapy.
   D) HMOs were able to substitute placebos for therapy.
   E) subsequent research showed the effectiveness of psychotherapy.

Answer: E
Diff: 2   Page Ref: 546
Topic: How Do Psychologists Treat Psychological Disorders?
Skill: Conceptual

74) Insight therapies are effective for the treatment of

    A) autism.

    B) marital discord.

    C) mental retardation.

    D) depression.

    E) B and D are correct.

Answer: E
Diff: 3   Page Ref: 546
Topic: How Do Psychologists Treat Psychological Disorders?
Skill: Factual

75) Cognitive-behavioral therapy has been found to be particularly effective in treating _____ and _____.

    A) phobias; autism

    B) alcoholism; relationship problems

    C) phobias; relationship problems

    D) anorexia; depression

    E) depression; autism

Answer: D
Diff: 3   Page Ref: 546
Topic: How Do Psychologists Treat Psychological Disorders?
Skill: Factual

76) The American Psychological Association concluded that _____ therapy was demonstrably effective in treating _____.

    A) behavioral; bulimia

    B) cognitive–behavioral; bed wetting

    C) insight; generalized anxiety disorder

    D) cognitive–behavioral; OCD

    E) behavioral; specific phobias

Answer: E
Diff: 3   Page Ref: 547
Topic: How Do Psychologists Treat Psychological Disorders?
Skill: Factual

77) A recent survey of practitioners found that most practitioners
    A) use the type of therapy that seems most appropriate for the client.
    B) use cognitive therapy.
    C) use behavioral therapy.
    D) use humanistic therapy.
    E) use group therapy.

Answer: A
Diff: 3   Page Ref: 547
Topic: How Do Psychologists Treat Psychological Disorders?
Skill: Factual

78) A person who is suffering from mental problems is most likely to seek help from
    A) friends.
    B) a clinical psychologist.
    C) their doctor.
    D) a psychiatrist.
    E) a scientist.

Answer: A
Diff: 2   Page Ref: 547
Topic: Where Do Most People Get Help?
Skill: Factual

79) Linda's friend Allie comes to her because she is having marital problems. Linda should
    A) be an active listener.
    B) give her friend advice about what to do.
    C) show honest surprise or disgust, when she feels that way.
    D) tell Allie to accept things "as is."
    E) avoid using empathy — it is embarrassing to both parties.

Answer: A
Diff: 2   Page Ref: 548
Topic: Where Do Most People Get Help?
Skill: Applied

80) The introduction of drug therapy has done which of the following for the mentally ill?

    A) It has allowed all schizophrenics to remain symptom free throughout their lives.

    B) It has allowed many mentally ill individuals to live outside of institutional settings.

    C) It has eliminated the need for other types of therapy.

    D) It has created a solution to all of those suffering from obsessive–compulsive disorder.

    E) It has found the biological root of all mental disorders.

Answer: B
Diff: 3   Page Ref: 550
Topic: How Is the Biomedical Approach Used To Treat Disorders?
Skill: Conceptual

81) _____ alter the symptoms of delusions, hallucinations, social withdrawal, and occasional agitation.

    A) Antipsychotic

    B) Antidepressant

    C) Analgesic

    D) Anti–inflammatory

    E) Antianxiety

Answer: A
Diff: 2   Page Ref: 550
Topic: How Is the Biomedical Approach Used To Treat Disorders?
Skill: Conceptual

82) _____ treats psychotic symptoms by blocking _____ receptors.

    A) Benzodiazepine; gastric

    B) Haloperidol; dopamine

    C) Lithium; cortical

    D) Propanediol; GABA

    E) Valium; serotonin

Answer: B
Diff: 3   Page Ref: 550
Topic: How Is the Biomedical Approach Used To Treat Disorders?
Skill: Factual

83) Drugs such as Haldol are effective in treating the _____ associated with schizophrenia.

    A) social distance

    B) jumbled thoughts

    C) poor attention span

    D) lack of sleep

    E) hallucinations

Answer: E
Diff: 2   Page Ref: 550
Topic: How Is the Biomedical Approach Used To Treat Disorders?
Skill: Factual

84) Long term treatment with antipsychotic drugs can create a disturbance of motor control, especially facial muscles, that is termed

    A) aversion.

    B) TMS.

    C) tardive dyskinesia.

    D) participant modeling.

    E) psychoactivity.

Answer: C
Diff: 3   Page Ref: 550
Topic: How Is the Biomedical Approach Used To Treat Disorders?
Skill: Factual

85) What of the following is NOT a side effect found in some patients taking antipsychotic medication?

    A) uncontrollable bladder

    B) tartive dyskinesia

    C) agranulocytosis

    D) disturbance in motor control

    E) All of the above are potential side effects of antipsychotic drugs.

Answer: A
Diff: 3   Page Ref: 550
Topic: How Is the Biomedical Approach Used To Treat Disorders?
Skill: Factual

86) MAO inhibitors and tricyclics are two important types of

   A) antipsychotic medications.

   B) behavioral therapies.

   C) psychosurgeries.

   D) cognitive fear reduction techniques.

   E) antidepressant drugs.

Answer: E
Diff: 3   Page Ref: 551
Topic: How Is the Biomedical Approach Used To Treat Disorders?
Skill: Factual

87) _____ drugs work by increasing the activity of the neurotransmitters norepinephrine and serotonin.

   A) Antidepressant

   B) Antipsychotic

   C) Sleeping

   D) Analgesic

   E) Anti-anxiety

Answer: A
Diff: 2   Page Ref: 551
Topic: How Is the Biomedical Approach Used To Treat Disorders?
Skill: Factual

88) SSRI's work by

   A) depressing activity in the frontal lobe.

   B) preventing the reuptake of serotonin.

   C) aiding in the production of dopamine.

   D) increasing the reuptake of serotonin.

   E) inhibiting MAO.

Answer: B
Diff: 3   Page Ref: 551
Topic: How Is the Biomedical Approach Used To Treat Disorders?
Skill: Conceptual

89) Lithium carbonate is effective in treating

    A) dissociative disorder.

    B) schizophrenia.

    C) general anxiety

    D) bipolar disorder.

    E) antisocial personality disorder.

Answer: D
Diff: 2   Page Ref: 551
Topic: How Is the Biomedical Approach Used To Treat Disorders?
Skill: Factual

90) A serious side effect of lithium treatment is related to

    A) toxicity from high blood levels of lithium.

    B) gastric distress.

    C) a complaints of halitosis.

    D) the development of severe depression.

    E) a worsening of manic episodes.

Answer: A
Diff: 2   Page Ref: 551–552
Topic: How Is the Biomedical Approach Used To Treat Disorders?
Skill: Applied

91) Benzodiazepine drugs _____ by _____.

    A) increase anxiety; by promoting the release of serotonin in brain

    B) reduce anxiety; enhancing the inhibitory effects of GABA

    C) treat phobias; sedating the person

    D) treat alcoholism; creating feelings of euphoria

    E) promote sleep; increasing nervous system activity

Answer: B
Diff: 3   Page Ref: 552
Topic: How Is the Biomedical Approach Used To Treat Disorders?
Skill: Conceptual

92) Which drug was originally created to treat epilepsy, but now is often prescribed to patients suffering from bipolar disorder?

A) divalproex sodium

B) lithium carbonate

C) prozac

D) halodal

E) chlorpromazine

Answer: A

Diff: 3   Page Ref: 552

Topic: How Is the Biomedical Approach Used To Treat Disorders?

Skill: Factual

93) _____ are the most commonly prescribed anti-anxiety medications.

A) Prozac and Clozapine

B) Haldol and lithium

C) Thorazine and MAO inhibitors

D) Elavil and tricyclics

E) Barbiturates and benzodiazepines

Answer: E

Diff: 3   Page Ref: 552

Topic: How Is the Biomedical Approach Used To Treat Disorders?

Skill: Factual

94) Which of the following is NOT a concern when using anti-anxiety medications?

A) They should not be used for "everyday" stressors.

B) They should not be used for more than a week or two at a time.

C) They should not be abruptly stopped.

D) They may eliminate production of the neurotransmitter GABA.

E) They can impair ability to perform tasks requiring alertness, such as driving.

Answer: D

Diff: 2   Page Ref: 552

Topic: How Is the Biomedical Approach Used To Treat Disorders?

Skill: Conceptual

95) A patient suffering from attention–deficit/hyperactivity disorder (ADHD) may improve when treated with

    A) anti-anxiety medications.

    B) antidepressants.

    C) antipsychotic medications.

    D) Prozac and Valium.

    E) stimulants.

Answer: E
Diff: 2   Page Ref: 552
Topic: How Is the Biomedical Approach Used To Treat Disorders?
Skill: Factual

96) Which of the following is not a problem that has been raised in regard to prescribing stimulants to treat ADHD?

    A) It has not been shown to be effective in treating children who suffer from ADHD.

    B) Many behaviors in children could be described as the symptoms of ADHD but doe not necessarily mean that the child needs drug treatment.

    C) This may interfere with children's sleep patterns.

    D) There is some evidence that drug treatment can stunt children's growth.

    E) This may encourage drug use later on in life.

Answer: A
Diff: 2   Page Ref: 553
Topic: How Is the Biomedical Approach Used To Treat Disorders?
Skill: Conceptual

97) The technique of _____ involves severing the nerve fibers connecting the frontal lobes with deep brain structures including the thalamus and the hypothalamus.

    A) neurosurgery

    B) prefrontal lobotomy

    C) diencephalotomy

    D) electroconvulsive therapy

    E) TMS

Answer: B
Diff: 3   Page Ref: 554
Topic: How Is the Biomedical Approach Used To Treat Disorders?
Skill: Factual

98) A serious side effect of prefrontal lobotomy is related to
   A) the lifting of mood.
   B) major alterations of personality.
   C) memory disorder.
   D) a reduction in agitation and anxiety.
   E) improved sleep.

Answer: B
Diff: 2   Page Ref: 554
Topic: How Is the Biomedical Approach Used To Treat Disorders?
Skill: Factual

99) Psychosurgery is still performed today with some regularity in which of the following cases?
   A) to treat the criminally insane
   B) to cut the corpus callosum of individuals with epilepsy
   C) to lessen the effects of those experiencing hallucinations
   D) to dampen to severity of obsessive–compulsive disorder
   E) to eradicate phobias

Answer: B
Diff: 2   Page Ref: 554
Topic: How Is the Biomedical Approach Used To Treat Disorders?
Skill: Factual

100) Electroconvulsive therapy has proven successful in treating
   A) schizophrenia.
   B) general anxiety disorder.
   C) obsessive–compulsive disorder.
   D) severe depression.
   E) ADHD.

Answer: D
Diff: 2   Page Ref: 554
Topic: How Is the Biomedical Approach Used To Treat Disorders?
Skill: Factual

101) A serious side effect of electroconvulsive therapy is related to

    A) the lifting of mood.

    B) major alterations of personality.

    C) memory disorder.

    D) a reduction in agitation and anxiety.

    E) improved sleep.

Answer: C
Diff: 2   *Page Ref: 554*
Topic: How Is the Biomedical Approach Used To Treat Disorders?
Skill: Factual

102) Transcranial magnetic stimulation (TMS) may be superior to electroconvulsive therapy (ECT) in that

    A) TMS does not produce memory deficits.

    B) ECT produces temporary paralysis.

    C) white blood cells are not altered by TMS.

    D) grogginess in not an effect of TMS.

    E) TMS does not cause concentration difficulties.

Answer: A
Diff: 2   *Page Ref: 555*
Topic: How Is the Biomedical Approach Used To Treat Disorders?
Skill: Factual

103) The 1950s concept of therapeutic community was proposed by _____.

    A) Maxwell Jones

    B) Martin Seligman

    C) Timothy Leary

    D) James Randi

    E) Elliot Valenstein

Answer: A
Diff: 2   *Page Ref: 555*
Topic: How Is the Biomedical Approach Used To Treat Disorders?
Skill: Factual

104) The policy of removing patients, whenever possible, from mental hospitals.

A) institutionalization

B) mainstreaming

C) deinstitutionalization

D) tracking

E) None of the above

Answer: C

Diff: 2   Page Ref: 556

Topic: How Is the Biomedical Approach Used To Treat Disorders?

Skill: Factual

105) A person whose life is mostly stress-free would do well to avoid the use of

A) alcohol.

B) minor tranquilizers.

C) caffeine.

D) Prozac.

E) amphetamine.

Answer: B

Diff: 2   Page Ref: 559

Topic: What Sort of Therapy Would You Recommend?

Skill: Conceptual

Check Your Understanding Questions

1) People in collectivist cultures are likely view mental disorder as a symptom of something wrong in

A) the unconscious mind.

B) the person's behavior, rather than in the mind.

C) the person's relationship with family or community.

D) a person's character.

E) a person's attitude.

Answer: C

Diff: 2   Page Ref: 530

Topic: Check Your Understanding

Skill: Recall

2) A therapist, but not necessarily a friend, can be relied on to

   A) maintain confidentiality.

   B) give you good advice.

   C) offer sympathy when you are feeling depressed.

   D) be available when needed.

   E) All of the above

Answer: A
Diff: 2   Page Ref: 530
Topic: Check Your Understanding
Skill: Recall

3) Which of the following types of therapists would help clients with everyday problems such a troubled relationships?

   A) clinical psychologist

   B) counseling psychologist

   C) psychiatrist

   D) social worker

   E) psychoanalyst

Answer: B
Diff: 2   Page Ref: 531
Topic: Check Your Understanding
Skill: Factual

4) In what aspect are all therapies alike?

   A) All may be legally administered only by licensed, trained professionals.

   B) All make use of insight into a patients' problems.

   C) All involve the aim of altering the mind, behavior, or social relationships.

   D) All focus on discovering the underlying cause of the patients' problem, which is often in the unconscious mind.

   E) All involve a change in an individual's behavior.

Answer: C
Diff: 2   Page Ref: 531
Topic: Check Your Understanding
Skill: Understanding the Core Concept

5) Counterconditioning is based on the principles of
    A) operant conditioning.
    B) classical conditioning.
    C) social learning.
    D) cognitive learning.
    E) observational learning.

Answer: B
Diff: 2   Page Ref: 548
Topic: Check Your Understanding
Skill: Recall

6) You could use contingency management to change the behavior of a child who comes home late for dinner by
    A) pairing food with punishment.
    B) having the child observe someone else coming home on time and being rewarded.
    C) refusing to let the child have dinner.
    D) having the child relax and imagine being home on time for dinner.
    E) pairing food with rewards.

Answer: C
Diff: 2   Page Ref: 548
Topic: Check Your Understanding
Skill: Applied

7) Which of the following therapists would be most likely to treat an unwanted response, such as nail biting, as merely a bad habit, rather than as a symptom of underlying disorder?
    A) a psychoanalyst
    B) a psychiatrist
    C) an insight therapist
    D) a behavioral therapist
    E) a cognitive therapist

Answer: D
Diff: 2   Page Ref: 549
Topic: Check Your Understanding
Skill: Applied

8) A primary goal of psychoanalysis is to
   A) change behavior.
   B) reveal problems in the unconscious.
   C) overcome low self–esteem.
   D) learn how to get along with others.
   E) alter interior thought processes.

Answer: B
Diff: 2   Page Ref: 549
Topic: Check Your Understanding
Skill: Recall

9) Which form of therapy directly confronts a client's self-defeating thought patterns?
   A) humanistic therapy
   B) behavioral therapy
   C) participant modeling
   D) rational–emotive behavior therapy
   E) psychoanalytic therapy

Answer: D
Diff: 2   Page Ref: 549
Topic: Check Your Understanding
Skill: Recall

10) Eysenck caused a furor with his claim that people who receive psychotherapy
   A) are just looking for a paid friend.
   B) really should seek medical treatment for their disorders.
   C) are usually pampered rich people who have nothing better to do with their lives.
   D) get better no more often that people who receive no therapy at all.
   E) respond only to psychoanalysis.

Answer: D
Diff: 2   Page Ref: 549
Topic: Check Your Understanding
Skill: Recall

11) A phobia would be best treated by _____, while a problem choosing a major would be better suited for _____.

    A) behavioral therapy; insight therapy

    B) cognitive therapy; psychoanalysis

    C) insight therapy; behavioral therapy

    D) humanistic therapy; behavioral therapy

    E) psychoanalysis; humanistic therapy

Answer: A

Diff: 2   Page Ref: 549

Topic: Check Your Understanding

Skill: Understanding the Core Concept

12) Imagine that you are a psychiatrist. Which type of drug would you prescribe to a patient who has obsessive-compulsive disorder?

    A) an antipsychotic drug

    B) lithium

    C) an antianxiety drug

    D) a stimulant

    E) any of the above would be appropriate

Answer: C

Diff: 2   Page Ref: 558

Topic: Check Your Understanding

Skill: Recall

13) Which class of drugs blocks dopamine receptors in the brain?

    A) antipsychotics

    B) antidepressants

    C) antianxiety drugs

    D) stimulants

    E) depressants

Answer: A

Diff: 2   Page Ref: 558

Topic: Check Your Understanding

Skill: Recall

14) A controversial treatment for attention–deficit/hyperactivity disorder involves

   A) antipsychotic drugs.

   B) antidepressant drugs.

   C) antianxiety drugs.

   D) stimulants.

   E) depressants.

Answer: D
Diff: 2   Page Ref: 558
Topic: Check Your Understanding
Skill: Recall

15) Which of the following medical treatments for mental disorder has now been largely abandoned as ineffective and dangerous?

   A) electroconvulsive therapy

   B) lithium

   C) prefrontal lobotomy

   D) the "split–brain" operation

   E) antipsychotics

Answer: C
Diff: 2   Page Ref: 558
Topic: Check Your Understanding
Skill: Recall

16) The community mental health movement followed a deliberate plan of _____ mental patients.

   A) hospitalizing

   B) deinstitutionalizing

   C) administering insight therapy to

   D) removing stressful events in the lives of

   E) lobotomizing

Answer: B
Diff: 2   Page Ref: 558
Topic: Check Your Understanding
Skill: Recall

17) Drug therapies, psychosurgery, and ECT are all methods of treating mental disorder

    A) by changing the chemistry of the body.

    B) by removing the stress in the patients' life.

    C) by directly altering the function of the brain.

    D) that have no scientific basis.

    E) that have always been successful.

Answer: C
Diff: 2   *Page Ref: 558*
Topic: Check Your Understanding
Skill: Understanding the Core Concept

True/False Questions

1) The goal of psychotherapy is to improve the mental, behavioral or social functioning of a person.

Answer: TRUE
Diff: 2   *Page Ref: 525*
Topic: What is Therapy?
Skill: Factual

2) A key ingredient of successful therapy is a trusting relationship.

Answer: TRUE
Diff: 2   *Page Ref: 526–527*
Topic: What is Therapy?
Skill: Conceptual

3) Psychiatrists have earned their MD degrees and can prescribe drugs.

Answer: TRUE
Diff: 2   *Page Ref: 528*
Topic: What is Therapy?
Skill: Factual

4) Social workers often work with individuals with mental disorders especially from the viewpoint of the social and environmental context of the problem.

Answer: TRUE
Diff: 2   *Page Ref: 528*
Topic: What is Therapy?
Skill: Factual

5) Behavioral therapy would be said to be a type of Insight therapy.

Answer: TRUE
Diff: 2   Page Ref: 529
Topic: What is Therapy?
Skill: Factual

6) Professionals are consistently found to be more effective than paraprofessionals in treating mental disorder.

Answer: FALSE
Diff: 2   Page Ref: 530
Topic: Paraprofessionals Do Therapy, Too
Skill: Factual

7) Psychoanalytic therapy focuses specifically on modifying behaviors.

Answer: FALSE
Diff: 2   Page Ref: 532
Topic: How Do Psychologists Treat Psychological Disorders?
Skill: Factual

8) The process of transference may involve patients falling in love with their therapists.

Answer: TRUE
Diff: 2   Page Ref: 533
Topic: How Do Psychologists Treat Psychological Disorders?
Skill: Factual

9) Client-centered therapy is a type of humanistic therapy.

Answer: TRUE
Diff: 2   Page Ref: 534
Topic: How Do Psychologists Treat Psychological Disorders?
Skill: Factual

10) According to Beck, depression is the result of negative thought patterns.

Answer: TRUE
Diff: 1   Page Ref: 536
Topic: How Do Psychologists Treat Psychological Disorders?
Skill: Factual

11) Cognitive therapists help alleviate depression by helping clients attribute blame to situational factors rather than to their own incompetence.

Answer: TRUE
Diff: 2   *Page Ref: 536*
Topic: How Do Psychologists Treat Psychological Disorders?
Skill: Conceptual

12) Typically, couples therapy is more effective than individual therapy for resolving marital problems.

Answer: TRUE
Diff: 1   *Page Ref: 537*
Topic: How Do Psychologists Treat Psychological Disorders?
Skill: Factual

13) Systematic desensitization involves creating a hierarchy.

Answer: TRUE
Diff: 2   *Page Ref: 539*
Topic: How Do Psychologists Treat Psychological Disorders?
Skill: Factual

14) In aversion therapy, the therapist encourages the client to imitate the therapist's behavior.

Answer: FALSE
Diff: 2   *Page Ref: 540*
Topic: How Do Psychologists Treat Psychological Disorders?
Skill: Conceptual

15) A token economy involves rewarding patients for good behavior.

Answer: TRUE
Diff: 2   *Page Ref: 541*
Topic: How Do Psychologists Treat Psychological Disorders?
Skill: Factual

16) Aaron Beck is the founder of Rational–Emotive therapy.

Answer: FALSE
Diff: 2   *Page Ref: 543*
Topic: How Do Psychologists Treat Psychological Disorders?
Skill: Factual

17) Hans Eysenck found that most people with nonpsychotic problems spontaneously recover within two years of the onset of their problem.

Answer: TRUE
Diff: 3   *Page Ref: 545–546*
Topic: How Do Psychologists Treat Psychological Disorders?
Skill: Factual

18) Most people who suffer from a mental disorder do not seek professional therapy.

Answer: TRUE
Diff: 2   *Page Ref: 547*
Topic: Where Do Most People Get Help?
Skill: Conceptual

19) Active listening basically involves providing advice.

Answer: FALSE
Diff: 2   *Page Ref: 548*
Topic: Where Do Most People Get Help?
Skill: Conceptual

20) Antipsychotic drugs are used to treat symptoms of psychosis, including hallucinations and delusions.

Answer: TRUE
Diff: 2   *Page Ref: 550*
Topic: How Is the Biomedical Approach Used To Treat Disorders?
Skill: Factual

21) Tardive dyskinesia, an unusual disturbance of the facial muscles, is caused by prolonged use of antianxiety drugs.

Answer: FALSE
Diff: 2   *Page Ref: 550*
Topic: How Is the Biomedical Approach Used To Treat Disorders?
Skill: Factual

22) Antidepressant drugs generally act of the neurotransmitter dopamine.

Answer: FALSE
Diff: 2   *Page Ref: 551*
Topic: How Is the Biomedical Approach Used To Treat Disorders?
Skill: Factual

23) Lithium carbonate is a highly effective treatment for bipolar disorder.

Answer: TRUE
Diff: 2   Page Ref: 551
Topic: How Is the Biomedical Approach Used To Treat Disorders?
Skill: Factual

24) Use of an antianxiety drug can produce enough sedation to impair driving.

Answer: TRUE
Diff: 2   Page Ref: 552
Topic: How Is the Biomedical Approach Used To Treat Disorders?
Skill: Factual

25) Stimulants can treat disorders such as Attention–Deficit/Hyperactivity Disorder.

Answer: TRUE
Diff: 2   Page Ref: 552
Topic: How Is the Biomedical Approach Used To Treat Disorders?
Skill: Factual

26) Critics of drug therapies suggest that is is irresponsible to prescribe drugs to young people when the safety and effectiveness of that age group has yet to be determined.

Answer: TRUE
Diff: 2   Page Ref: 553
Topic: How Is the Biomedical Approach Used To Treat Disorders?
Skill: Conceptual

27) Psychosurgery is a therapy of last resort.

Answer: TRUE
Diff: 2   Page Ref: 553
Topic: How Is the Biomedical Approach Used To Treat Disorders?
Skill: Conceptual

28) Prefrontal lobotomies are often performed today.

Answer: FALSE
Diff: 2   Page Ref: 554
Topic: How Is the Biomedical Approach Used To Treat Disorders?
Skill: Factual

29) Mental hospitals almost exclusively use medication to treat patients and rarely engage in psychotherapy.

Answer: TRUE
Diff: 3   Page Ref: 556
Topic: How Is the Biomedical Approach Used To Treat Disorders?
Skill: Factual

30) The goal of de–institutionalization was to return mental patients to their community for treatment.

Answer: TRUE
Diff: 2   Page Ref: 556
Topic: How Is the Biomedical Approach Used To Treat Disorders?
Skill: Conceptual

31) A fear of flying would be best treated using either behavior therapy or cognitive-behavioral therapy.

Answer: TRUE
Diff: 2   Page Ref: 557
Topic: What Sort of Therapy Would You Recommend?
Skill: Factual

Short Answer Questions

1) What is the common element of all therapies?

Answer: The common element is to establish a relationship that focuses on improving mental function.
Diff: 2   Page Ref: 525
Topic: What is Therapy?
Skill: Applied

2) Name the four tasks of the therapeutic process.

Answer: identify the problem, determine the problem's cause, make a prognosis (prediction), choose and carry out treatment
Diff: 3   Page Ref: 527
Topic: What is Therapy?
Skill: Conceptual

3) Explain how a clinical psychologist and a psychiatrist would likely approach the same problem differently.

Answer: A clinical psychologist would be more likely to use behavioral or cognitive therapy and the psychiatrist would be more likely to prescribe medication.
Diff: 2   Page Ref: 528

Topic: What is Therapy?

Skill: Recall

4) Briefly explain the biomedical approach to treating mental illness, and provide two examples of this type of treatment.

Answer: The biomedical approach focuses on the brain, especially with drugs. Two types are psychosurgery and electroconvulsive therapy.
Diff: 2   Page Ref: 529

Topic: What is Therapy?

Skill: Factual

5) Psychodynamic therapy is a type of _____, because its goal is to help a patient understand the cause his or her problems.

Answer: insight therapy
Diff: 2   Page Ref: 531

Topic: How Do Psychologists Treat Psychological Disorders?

Skill: Conceptual

6) Briefly explain how psychoanalytic therapy works.

Answer: The patient relaxes and the therapists passively listens while the patients says anything that comes to mind.
Diff: 2   Page Ref: 532

Topic: How Do Psychologists Treat Psychological Disorders?

Skill: Applied

7) Briefly explain client-centered therapy.

Answer: A humanistic approach to treatment developed by Carl Rogers emphasizing an individual's tendency for healthy psychological growth through self-actualization.
Diff: 2   Page Ref: 534

Topic: How Do Psychologists Treat Psychological Disorders?

Skill: Conceptual

8) Name the qualities of therapy, as used by Carl Rogers, that have been found to produce successful results.

Answer: The qualities are empathy, positive regard, genuineness, and feedback.
Diff: 2   Page Ref: 534–535

Topic: How Do Psychologists Treat Psychological Disorders?

Skill: Conceptual

9) Which type of psychotherapist is most likely to use systematic desensitization and how does this work?

Answer: behavior(al) therapist, they create a hierarchy of the fear which they gradually address
Diff: 2   Page Ref: 539

Topic: How Do Psychologists Treat Psychological Disorders?

Skill: Conceptual

10) Taking a drug so that a patient becomes nauseous when consuming alcohol is an example of which therapy?

Answer: Aversion therapy is a classical conditioning therapy technique.
Diff: 2   Page Ref: 540

Topic: How Do Psychologists Treat Psychological Disorders?

Skill: Applied

11) Rational–emotive behavior therapy believes that the cause of psychological problems is what? Who is the founder of this type of therapy?

Answer: irrational beliefs, Albert Ellis
Diff: 2   Page Ref: 543

Topic: How Do Psychologists Treat Psychological Disorders?

Skill: Conceptual

12) How do anti–psychotic medications work?

Answer: they reduce the production of the neurotransmitter dopamine.
Diff: 2   Page Ref: 550

Topic: How Is the Biomedical Approach Used To Treat Disorders?

Skill: Applied

13) What drugs are commonly prescribed to treat bipolar disorder?

Answer: lithium (carbonate) or divalproex sodium (brand name Depakote)
Diff: 2   Page Ref: 551

Topic: How Is the Biomedical Approach Used To Treat Disorders?

Skill: Factual

14) What alternative strategy is being tested that may minimize the side–effects of electroconvulsive therapy?

Answer: transcranial magnetic stimulation, which can direct high–powered magnetic stimulation to specific brain areas.
Diff: 2   Page Ref: 555

Topic: How Is the Biomedical Approach Used To Treat Disorders?

Skill: Factual

15) _____ involves removing patients from mental hospitals, whenever possible.

Answer: Deinstitutionalization

Diff: 2   Page Ref: 556

Topic: How Is the Biomedical Approach Used To Treat Disorders?

Skill: Conceptual

Essay Questions

1) List four different types of professionals who treat mental disorders and how they are trained to treat someone who was ill.

Answer: (Answers will vary)

Clinical Psychiatrist: Trained to work with those who have severe disorders. Usually work in private practice or are employed as mental health agencies.

Counseling psychologists: Trained to work with individuals who are dealing with the problems of normal living such as relationship or family issues.

Psychiatrist: trained in medicine, usually work in private practice.

Psychoanalyst: practitioner of freudian theory, usually work in private practice.

Social worker: usually deal with mental disorders but look at them from the standpoint of the environmental or social context of the problem.

Diff: 3   Page Ref: 527

Topic: What is Therapy?

Skill: Applied

2) Contrast the psychodynamic approach to psychotherapy with the behavioral approach. Include discussion of their views on the nature of psychopathology and the role of the unconscious.

Answer: The behavioral therapies use the principles of conditioning to change behaviors. The focus is on how the behaviors have been learned, and more importantly, how the problematic behaviors can be replaced with healthy ones. This therapeutic perspective does not believe in examining the unconscious mind; only behaviors matter. The psychodynamic approach uses the principles of psychoanalysis to provide insight into the unconscious mind's conflicts and forces. The belief here is that ego defenses prevent problems from reaching consciousness.

Diff: 3   Page Ref: 531–542

Topic: How Do Psychologists Treat Psychological Disorders?

Skill: Applied

3) Give an example of how a cognitive-behaviorist would help an addicted smoker who claims that "One more cigarette won't hurt me." How might this same problem be approached using aversion therapy?

Answer: A cognitive-behaviorist would say that this type of thinking is irrational. The therapist would try to change these beliefs, as well as the unhealthy behavior (smoking) that accompanies it by rewarding desired behavior (not smoking) and punishing the smoking; this is contingency management. Aversion therapy would try to make smoking unappealing, perhaps by having the person chain smoke until they get sick.

Diff: 2   Page Ref: 542-543

Topic: How Do Psychologists Treat Psychological Disorders?

Skill: Applied

4) Discuss how psychologists have tested the efficacy of different therapies.

Answer: Efficacy asks whether a therapy is more successful than some control or placebo condition. In some studies, consumers haver reported greater satisfaction with most therapies. Meta-analytic studies have considered the average effect of published therapy experiments.

Diff: 2   Page Ref: 545-547

Topic: How Do Psychologists Treat Psychological Disorders?

Skill: Conceptual

5) Which drugs are most effective in treating which psychological problems? What are some of the advantages and disadvantages to using medication to treat such problems? Be sure to address antipsychotic drugs, antidepressants and anti-anxiety drugs and provide at least one example of each.

Answer: The student should discuss the antipsychotics (such as clozapine) to treat schizophrenia, the antidepressants (like Prozac) for treating depression, lithium for treating bipolar disorder, anti-anxiety medications (like the barbiturates) to treat anxiety, and the stimulants to treat ADHD and narcolepsy. The use of such medications has led to fewer people hospitalized for mental health problems and many are quite successful in their treatment of mental problems in a quick, cost-effective manner. However, the side effects may be risky, addiction or overdose may occur, people may not take their medicines, and medications for some problems have not yet been developed.

Diff: 3   Page Ref: 550-553

Topic: How Is the Biomedical Approach Used To Treat Disorders?

Skill: Conceptual

Chapter 14 Social Psychology

Multiple Choice Questions

1) An important lesson learned from the Stanford's prison is
   A) how passive prison guards can become.
   B) that prisoners tend to become violent.
   C) that stress can be prevented with relaxation.
   D) that criminals are difficult to detect.
   E) how stressful situations can rapidly affect personality.

   Answer: E
   Diff: 2   Page Ref: 566
   Topic: Introduction
   Skill: Conceptual

2) _____ is the field that studies human interactions and relationships.
   A) Psychobiology
   B) Social psychology
   C) Humanistic psychology
   D) Normative behavior
   E) Sociobiology

   Answer: B
   Diff: 1   Page Ref: 567
   Topic: Introduction
   Skill: Factual

3) _____ conducted the Stanford prison experiment.
   A) Philip Zimbardo
   B) Stanley Milgram
   C) Solomon Asch
   D) Tom Moriarity
   E) Robert Cialdini

   Answer: A
   Diff: 1   Page Ref: 566
   Topic: How Does the Social Situation Affect Our Behavior?
   Skill: Factual

4) The key determinant of individual behavior, according to social psychology, is the

    A) social situation.

    B) individual's personality.

    C) person's temperament.

    D) bystander effect.

    E) individual's upbringing.

Answer: A
Diff: 2   *Page Ref: 567*
Topic: Introduction
Skill: Conceptual

5) Social _____ refers to the real, imagined, or symbolic presence of other people.

    A) obedience

    B) conformity

    C) loafing

    D) context

    E) obligation

Answer: D
Diff: 1   *Page Ref: 567*
Topic: Introduction
Skill: Conceptual

6) A social psychologist would explain your behavior at a party with many people you do not know, as strongly determined by

    A) what you have had to eat and drink.

    B) your level of shyness.

    C) how you have behaved at other parties.

    D) the time and place of the party.

    E) how others are behaving.

Answer: E
Diff: 2   *Page Ref: 568*
Topic: How Does the Social Situation Affect Our Behavior?
Skill: Applied

7) Jenna is generally outgoing and talkative around her friends, but she is quest and reserved at work where everyone is older than her. According to social psychology, Jenna's changing behavior is different environments is due to

  A) disposition.

  B) norms.

  C) scripts.

  D) situationism.

  E) conformity.

Answer: D

Diff: 2   Page Ref: 568

Topic: How Does the Social Situation Affect Our Behavior?

Skill: Applied

8) Situationism assumes that _____ influences people's behavior, feelings, and thoughts to a greater degree than innate personality.

  A) the person's childhood

  B) past experience

  C) thinking patterns

  D) the environment

  E) a person's health

Answer: D

Diff: 1   Page Ref: 568

Topic: How Does the Social Situation Affect Our Behavior?

Skill: Conceptual

9) A(n) _____ refers to one of several socially defined behavior patterns expected of a person in a particular setting or group.

  A) self-fulfilling prophecy

  B) demand characteristic

  C) informational influence

  D) social role

  E) situational prophecy

Answer: D

Diff: 2   Page Ref: 569

Topic: How Does the Social Situation Affect Our Behavior?

Skill: Applied

10) The students in the Stanford prison experiment used _____ to guide their actions as guards; these were likely learned from film or literature depictions of guards.

A) their instincts

B) personal history

C) media–produced stereotypes

D) scripts

E) inventories

Answer: D

Diff: 2   Page Ref: 569

Topic: How Does the Social Situation Affect Our Behavior?

Skill: Conceptual

11) When you go the the mall, you know that you will look for whatever it is that you would like to buy, when you find it you will take it to a cashier and they will package your purchase and wish you a nice day. This sequence of events follows a

A) social norm.

B) groupthink.

C) script.

D) heuristic.

E) algorithm.

Answer: C

Diff: 2   Page Ref: 569

Topic: How Does the Social Situation Affect Our Behavior?

Skill: Applied

12) In Hawaii, few business meetings involve people wearing formal suits. To fit in, someone who is from the U.S. mainland who is used to wearing suits will have to

A) experience blind obedience.

B) learn norm crystallization.

C) adjust to new social norms.

D) experience the Milgram effect.

E) diffuse responsibility.

Answer: C

Diff: 1   Page Ref: 569

Topic: How Does the Social Situation Affect Our Behavior?

Skill: Applied

13) The fact that many Americans do not approve of public nudity is most likely due to

    A) mutual interdependence.

    B) social reality.

    C) social loafing.

    D) prevailing social norms.

    E) cognitive dissonance.

Answer: D
Diff: 2   Page Ref: 570
Topic: How Does the Social Situation Affect Our Behavior?
Skill: Applied

14) The Bennington College study involved students from conservative homes who attended a college with liberal faculty members. The students tended to

    A) become more liberal over time.

    B) have values that did not change.

    C) cling firmly to their conservative values.

    D) drop out of the school within one semester.

    E) initially adopt liberal values, but ultimately returned to their original beliefs.

Answer: A
Diff: 2   Page Ref: 570
Topic: How Does the Social Situation Affect Our Behavior?
Skill: Applied

15) A twenty year follow-up on the Bennington College study found that

    A) people eventually tend to stick with the same values as their parents.

    B) the attitudes adopted in college lasted for decades.

    C) conformity was part of role playing, but it never internalized.

    D) the conservative family upbringing of the students eventually changed the attitudes of the college.

    E) people tend to marry people with opposing political values.

Answer: B
Diff: 2   Page Ref: 570
Topic: How Does the Social Situation Affect Our Behavior?
Skill: Factual

16) Jason is from Chicago, he finds however that when he travels to the South for an extended period he takes on a slight southern accent in his voice. This tendency to mimic others is known as

    A) social norms.

    B) the chameleon effect.

    C) situationism.

    D) schemas.

    E) scripts.

Answer: B
Diff: 2   Page Ref: 571
Topic: How Does the Social Situation Affect Our Behavior?
Skill: Applied

17) Solomon Asch is best known for his studies involving

    A) length judgment and conformity.

    B) prisoners.

    C) teen–age camping groups.

    D) administering shocks to an elderly man.

    E) liberal and conservative attitudes.

Answer: A
Diff: 2   Page Ref: 571
Topic: How Does the Social Situation Affect Our Behavior?
Skill: Factual

18) In the Asch studies, most people

    A) continued administering shocks.

    B) acted independently.

    C) played the role of prisoner or guard.

    D) made accurate judgments every time.

    E) conformed at least once.

Answer: E
Diff: 2   Page Ref: 571
Topic: How Does the Social Situation Affect Our Behavior?
Skill: Factual

19) The _____ refers to the influence of a group majority on individuals' judgments is known as

    A) bystander effect

    B) Asch effect

    C) scapegoating scenario

    D) demand situation

    E) cognitive dissonance error

Answer: B
Diff: 2   Page Ref: 571
Topic: How Does the Social Situation Affect Our Behavior?
Skill: Conceptual

20) The Asch effect is known as the classic illustration of

    A) intelligence.

    B) conformity.

    C) confusion.

    D) obeying authority.

    E) diffusion of responsibility.

Answer: B
Diff: 1   Page Ref: 571
Topic: How Does the Social Situation Affect Our Behavior?
Skill: Factual

21) Drew is Jewish, but today he will attend a Lutheran church with his friend, Cheryl. If Drew were to _____ would be an example of the Asch effect.

    A) try to convert Cheryl to Judaism

    B) study the Lutheran religion before going there

    C) look for similarities between the religions

    D) find things to dislike about the Lutheran faith

    E) do what the other churchgoers are doing

Answer: E
Diff: 2   Page Ref: 571
Topic: How Does the Social Situation Affect Our Behavior?
Skill: Applied

22) Often times people conform to the will of the group because

    A) they do not want to be the only one who is "wrong".

    B) they do not want to look like a fool.

    C) they do not want the others to protest.

    D) they may fear the reactions of others in the group.

    E) All of the above

Answer: E
Diff: 2   *Page Ref: 572*
Topic: How Does the Social Situation Affect Our Behavior?
Skill: Conceptual

23) The Asch effect would be expected to operate in cases where

    A) there is secret balloting to decide the new class president.

    B) jurors discuss whether someone is guilty in a jury trial.

    C) an entire class is getting high grades on a psychology exam.

    D) people write responses to an essay contest on "Why I Love America."

    E) a doctor must determine her patient's diagnosis independently.

Answer: B
Diff: 3   *Page Ref: 571–572*
Topic: How Does the Social Situation Affect Our Behavior?
Skill: Applied

24) People are more likely to conform when

    A) a judgment task is easy.

    B) group members are perceived as biased.

    C) their responses are kept private.

    D) no one appears to agree with them.

    E) the group size is small.

Answer: D
Diff: 2   *Page Ref: 573*
Topic: How Does the Social Situation Affect Our Behavior?
Skill: Conceptual

25) People are least likely to conform when

    A) a judgment task is easy.

    B) the group has a divided opinion.

    C) their responses are public.

    D) they have at least one ally.

    E) the group size is small.

Answer: D
Diff: 2   Page Ref: 573
Topic: How Does the Social Situation Affect Our Behavior?
Skill: Conceptual

26) The decision to invade Iraq in 2003 may represent an instance of

    A) obedience.

    B) scapegoating.

    C) "group think."

    D) prejudice.

    E) A and D are correct.

Answer: C
Diff: 2   Page Ref: 573
Topic: How Does the Social Situation Affect Our Behavior?
Skill: Factual

27) The individual who proposed the concept of groupthink was

    A) Zimbardo.   B) Janis.   C) Migram.   D) Acsh.   E) Darley.

Answer: B
Diff: 2   Page Ref: 573
Topic: How Does the Social Situation Affect Our Behavior?
Skill: Factual

28) The mass deaths that occurred in Jonestown, Heaven's Gate, and the Branch Davidians examples of the power of

    A) scapegoating.

    B) the principle of proximity.

    C) cognitive dissonance.

    D) diffusion of responsibility.

    E) obedience.

Answer: E
Diff: 2   Page Ref: 574
Topic: How Does the Social Situation Affect Our Behavior?
Skill: Conceptual

29) When go along with a request from an authority figure without knowing who they are or what they represent, this is an example of

    A) conformity.

    B) groupthink.

    C) obedience.

    D) social loafing.

    E) role playing.

Answer: C

Diff: 2　　Page Ref: 574

Topic: How Does the Social Situation Affect Our Behavior?

Skill: Applied

30) A key implication of Stanley Milgram's research is that

    A) discrimination is widespread across the U.S.

    B) the bystander effect occurs in vague conditions.

    C) conformity is limited to laboratory studies.

    D) the similarity principle can explain the authoritarian personality.

    E) the power of the situation can induce an ordinary person to harm another.

Answer: E

Diff: 2　　Page Ref: 574–576

Topic: How Does the Social Situation Affect Our Behavior?

Skill: Factual

31) The experiments of _____ were powerful demonstration of obedience to authority.

    A) Freud　　　　B) Newcomb　　　C) Asch　　　　D) Milgram　　　E) Zimbardo

Answer: D

Diff: 1　　Page Ref: 575

Topic: How Does the Social Situation Affect Our Behavior?

Skill: Factual

32) Milgram led his subjects to believe that his obedience study was designed to measure

    A) memory and learning.

    B) how teachers maintain social roles.

    C) how authority figures command obedience.

    D) whether electric shock can be administered safely.

    E) the determinants of violence.

Answer: A

Diff: 2　　Page Ref: 575

Topic: How Does the Social Situation Affect Our Behavior?

Skill: Factual

33) Milgram was really studying _____ in his famous studies.

    A) conformity

    B) memory and learning

    C) bystander effect

    D) morality

    E) obedience to authority

Answer: E
Diff: 2   *Page Ref: 575*
Topic: How Does the Social Situation Affect Our Behavior?
Skill: Conceptual

34) Before the Obedience experiment began Milgram believed that

    A) all of the individuals would go to 450 volts of shock.

    B) none of the participants would give 450 volts of shock.

    C) only those who were sadistic would issue 450 volts of shock.

    D) only men would issue 450 volts of shock.

    E) only women would issue 450 volts of shock.

Answer: C
Diff: 2   *Page Ref: 575*
Topic: How Does the Social Situation Affect Our Behavior?
Skill: Factual

35) In the Milgram experiments, the study would end when

    A) the 'learner' stopped responding.

    B) the 'teacher' gave shocks too often.

    C) shocks reached the 100-volt level.

    D) the 'teacher' refused to continue or reached the maximum level of shock.

    E) the shocks were too intense for the 'learner.'

Answer: D
Diff: 2   *Page Ref: 575*
Topic: How Does the Social Situation Affect Our Behavior?
Skill: Factual

36) _____ of the experimental group continued administering the shocks in Stanley Milgram's experiments.

   A) Not one member
   B) Close to 10%
   C) Nearly two-thirds
   D) About 90%
   E) About half

Answer: C
Diff: 2   Page Ref: 577
Topic: How Does the Social Situation Affect Our Behavior?
Skill: Factual

37) The controversial aspect of Milgram's research was related to

   A) the ethics of inflicting potential mental harm on experimental subjects.
   B) his failure to debrief the subjects.
   C) the pain experienced by the teacher.
   D) authoritarian personality characteristics exhibited by the teacher.
   E) memory limitations of the learner.

Answer: A
Diff: 2   Page Ref: 577
Topic: How Does the Social Situation Affect Our Behavior?
Skill: Conceptual

38) Obedience to an authority figure in a Milgram study was most likely when

   A) they are the only ones obeying.
   B) the victim is nearby.
   C) the authority figure has low status.
   D) they have psychological problems.
   E) the authority figure is nearby to the teacher.

Answer: E
Diff: 2   Page Ref: 577
Topic: How Does the Social Situation Affect Our Behavior?
Skill: Conceptual

39) In Milgram's study, which of the following would not make an individual more likely to obey?

   A) The 'learner' was not able to be seen by the 'teacher'.

   B) The 'teacher' saw examples of disobedience.

   C) The experimenter was in the same room as the teacher.

   D) The experiment was affiliated with Yale university.

   E) The 'teacher' was told that the experiment must continue.

Answer: B
Diff: 2   Page Ref: 577
Topic: How Does the Social Situation Affect Our Behavior?
Skill: Factual

40) The results of Milgram's studies of obedience challenges the myth that

   A) bystanders rarely intervene.

   B) relative status has minimal influence on obedience.

   C) only certain people would blindly follow orders to harm another.

   D) women are more obedient as men.

   E) A and D are correct.

Answer: C
Diff: 2   Page Ref: 577
Topic: How Does the Social Situation Affect Our Behavior?
Skill: Conceptual

41) The murder of Kitty Genovese demonstrated the impact is an example of

   A) bystander apathy.

   B) the principle of proximity.

   C) social control.

   D) scapegoating.

   E) obedience to authority.

Answer: A
Diff: 2   Page Ref: 579
Topic: How Does the Social Situation Affect Our Behavior?
Skill: Conceptual

42) A contrived emergency was used by _____ to model the issue of bystander apathy

   A) Stanley Milgram

   B) Robert Sternberg

   C) Solomon Asch and Robert Stradlater

   D) Bibb Latane and John Darley

   E) Kitty Genovese

Answer: D

Diff: 2   Page Ref: 579

Topic: How Does the Social Situation Affect Our Behavior?

Skill: Factual

43) It is now assumed that none of the 38 bystanders did anything to help Kitty genovese when she was being attacked was because

   A) they did not want to get involved.

   B) they might put themselves at rick if they intervened.

   C) they did not know if Kitty knew her attacker.

   D) they all thought someone else would help.

   E) All of the above are potential reasons that they did not help.

Answer: E

Diff: 2   Page Ref: 579

Topic: How Does the Social Situation Affect Our Behavior?

Skill: Conceptual

44) When there is a large group of bystanders, individuals are likely to experience

   A) diffusion of responsibility.

   B) peer pressure.

   C) blind obedience.

   D) situationism.

   E) the similarity principle.

Answer: A

Diff: 2   Page Ref: 579

Topic: How Does the Social Situation Affect Our Behavior?

Skill: Conceptual

45) According to the theories on bystander intervention, as group size _____ the likely hood for intervention _____.

A) increases; stays the same

B) increases; decreases

C) increases; increases

D) decreases; stays the same

E) decreases; increases

Answer: B

Diff: 2   Page Ref: 579

Topic: How Does the Social Situation Affect Our Behavior?

Skill: Factual

46) As a result of diffusion of responsibility, people in a bystander situation tend to

A) obey authority figures.

B) do what others do.

C) be attracted to those similar to themselves.

D) be less likely to help others.

E) try to control others' behavior.

Answer: D

Diff: 2   Page Ref: 579

Topic: How Does the Social Situation Affect Our Behavior?

Skill: Conceptual

47) People are most likely to help out soon in an emergency situation if

A) they believe others are available to help.

B) they have an outgoing personality.

C) they have an unusual personality.

D) others are doing nothing.

E) there are few others who can help.

Answer: E

Diff: 3   Page Ref: 580

Topic: How Does the Social Situation Affect Our Behavior?

Skill: Conceptual

48) Which of these strangers is most likely to help a woman who has fainted at the mall?

    A) Erika, who has had CPR training

    B) Leah, who is late for piano practice

    C) Sara, who is delivering pizza

    D) Matt, who is homeless

    E) Zeb, who is a famous actor

Answer: A

Diff: 2   Page Ref: 580

Topic: How Does the Social Situation Affect Our Behavior?

Skill: Applied

49) Moriarity's research suggests that if we need help from others we should

    A) give them something.

    B) force them to obey.

    C) ask.

    D) have low expectations.

    E) None of the above

Answer: C

Diff: 1   Page Ref: 580

Topic: How Does the Social Situation Affect Our Behavior?

Skill: Factual

50) Subjects in Moriarity's theft studies were more likely to intervene if

    A) they had been attracted to the victim.

    B) the victim had never spoken to them.

    C) the victim had asked them "Do you have the time?"

    D) they had been asked to watch the victim's property.

    E) they had enough time to help out.

Answer: D

Diff: 2   Page Ref: 580

Topic: How Does the Social Situation Affect Our Behavior?

Skill: Factual

51) _____ determine whether bystanders will offer help in crises.

    A) Personality traits

    B) Situational factors

    C) The Asch effect

    D) Demand characteristics

    E) The chameleon effect

Answer: B

Diff: 2   Page Ref: 581

Topic: How Does the Social Situation Affect Our Behavior?

Skill: Conceptual

52) If Tess has lost her contact lens, she is most likely to get help from others if she

    A) says aloud, "Will someone please help me?"

    B) specifically asks one person for help.

    C) stays quiet and starts searching.

    D) begins crying loudly.

    E) is obviously in a hurry.

Answer: B

Diff: 2   Page Ref: 582

Topic: How Does the Social Situation Affect Our Behavior?

Skill: Applied

53) Which of the following is not likely to increase your chances of getting help in an emergency situation?

    A) identify a specific individual who can help you

    B) remain totally quiet

    C) let people know you need help

    D) stay away from large crowds of people

    E) make your situation clear

Answer: B

Diff: 2   Page Ref: 582

Topic: How Does the Social Situation Affect Our Behavior?

Skill: Conceptual

54) In the best relationships, we tend to

    A) give more than we receive.

    B) create a social reality.

    C) demand more than we receive.

    D) avoid social exchange.

    E) both give and receive rewards.

Answer: E

Diff: 2   Page Ref: 584

Topic: What Influences Our Judgments of Others?

Skill: Conceptual

55) _____ claims that we like those best who give us maximum rewards at minimum cost.

    A) Social reality theory

    B) Reward theory of attraction

    C) Peripheral action theory

    D) The law of proximity

    E) Expectancy-value theory

Answer: B

Diff: 2   Page Ref: 584

Topic: What Influences Our Judgments of Others?

Skill: Conceptual

56) Which of the following is NOT considered to be a major source of reward that predict interpersonal attraction?

    A) proximity

    B) similarity

    C) self-disclosure

    D) physical attractiveness

    E) personality

Answer: E

Diff: 2   Page Ref: 584-585

Topic: What Influences Our Judgments of Others?

Skill: Factual

57) College students tendency to date and be friends with those in their residence hall supports this theory of attraction.

   A) proximity
   B) similarity
   C) self-disclosure
   D) physical attractiveness
   E) closure

Answer: A
Diff: 2   Page Ref: 584-585
Topic: What Influences Our Judgments of Others?
Skill: Applied

58) The _____ would predict that Theo is more likely to want to date Aneesa, who sits next to him each day in his psychology class, than Cara, who he sees once every other week at choir practice.

   A) theory of social reality
   B) principle of closure
   C) principle of proximity
   D) rule of self-disclosure
   E) cognitive dissonance theory

Answer: C
Diff: 2   Page Ref: 584-585
Topic: What Influences Our Judgments of Others?
Skill: Applied

59) Two persons decide to marry after years of corresponding through the mail, but have never met one another. This situation reflects the attraction exerted by

   A) self-disclosure.
   B) proximity.
   C) conformity.
   D) in-grouping.
   E) cognitive dissonance.

Answer: A
Diff: 3   Page Ref: 585
Topic: What Influences Our Judgments of Others?
Skill: Applied

60) Rhonda and Gilmer both live in Chicago and like riding bikes and reading poetry, which of the following theories of attraction would best explain why Rhonda and Gilmer may start dating?

    A) proximity principle; similarity principle

    B) attribution theory; similarity principle

    C) similarity principle; self-disclosure principle

    D) Asch effect; self-disclosure principle

    E) oppositional theory; proximity principle

Answer: C
Diff: 2   *Page Ref: 585*
Topic: What Influences Our Judgments of Others?
Skill: Applied

61) The strongest predictor of how much we will like a person on meeting them for the first time is

    A) their level of intelligence.

    B) their level of physical attractiveness.

    C) their gender.

    D) whether we judge them to be sincere.

    E) the setting in which you meet.

Answer: B
Diff: 2   *Page Ref: 585*
Topic: What Influences Our Judgments of Others?
Skill: Factual

62) A person who is _____ is likely to be perceived as being cold and indifferent.

    A) poised and indifferent

    B) shy and average in looks

    C) an attractive female politician

    D) an attractive male politician

    E) shy and physically attractive

Answer: E
Diff: 2   *Page Ref: 586*
Topic: What Influences Our Judgments of Others?
Skill: Factual

63) In an experiment on physical attractiveness, which of the following faces did students report 'liking the best'?

    A) extremely attractive faces

    B) extremely unattractive faces

    C) average faces

    D) All of the faces were ranked the same

    E) None of the above are correct

Answer: C
Diff: 2   *Page Ref: 586*
Topic: What Influences Our Judgments of Others?
Skill: Factual

64) The _____ hypothesis argues that we are likely to end up with friends and mates that are at our level of attractiveness.

    A) proximity   B) familiarity   C) matching   D) reward   E) similarity

Answer: C
Diff: 1   *Page Ref: 586*
Topic: What Influences Our Judgments of Others?
Skill: Applied

65) If Calvin is average in terms of his looks, he may not ask the gorgeous Giselle to go on a date with him, because he believes that he will be rejected or that eventually the relationship would not work out. Thus, the _____ affected Calvin's decision to not ask Giselle to go out with him.

    A) diffusion of responsibility theory

    B) principle of proximity

    C) fundamental attribution error

    D) expectancy–value theory

    E) Asch effect

Answer: D
Diff: 3   *Page Ref: 586*
Topic: What Influences Our Judgments of Others?
Skill: Applied

66) A person with low self-esteem would tend to gravitate toward

    A) authoritarian personalities.

    B) a physically attractive person.

    C) persons who are approved of by their parents.

    D) people who see them as they see themselves.

    E) people who will boost their self-esteem.

Answer: D
Diff: 2   Page Ref: 587
Topic: What Influences Our Judgments of Others?
Skill: Conceptual

67) The fact that Vincent has _____ may account for his marriage to Amy who verbally abuses him.

    A) oodles of sex-appeal

    B) high self-esteem

    C) cognitive dissonance

    D) low self-esteem

    E) a self-serving bias

Answer: D
Diff: 2   Page Ref: 587
Topic: What Influences Our Judgments of Others?
Skill: Applied

68) The process of cognitive dissonance motivates people to try and match their _____ and _____.

    A) attitudes; beliefs

    B) actions; behaviors

    C) actions; attitudes

    D) unconscious; conscious

    E) ideas; thoughts

Answer: C
Diff: 2   Page Ref: 587
Topic: What Influences Our Judgments of Others?
Skill: Conceptual

69) _____ refers to the state of conflict someone experiences after making a decision that is contrary to prior beliefs, feelings, or values.

   A) Closure

   B) Cognitive dissonance

   C) The self-fulfilling prophecy

   D) The Pygmalion effect

   E) The fundamental attribution error

Answer: B
Diff: 2   Page Ref: 587
Topic: What Influences Our Judgments of Others?
Skill: Conceptual

70) If a person a saved up all of their money for the past three years to buy a car, they may be reluctant to believe that is not a god car because of

   A) attributional guilt.

   B) cognitive dissonance.

   C) situationism.

   D) diffusion of responsibility.

   E) prejudice.

Answer: B
Diff: 3   Page Ref: 588
Topic: What Influences Our Judgments of Others?
Skill: Applied

71) To reduce cognitive dissonance, people must

   A) admit to others that they are wrong.

   B) completely leave the situation.

   C) understand themselves better.

   D) improve their own self-esteem.

   E) change their behaviors or thoughts.

Answer: E
Diff: 2   Page Ref: 588
Topic: What Influences Our Judgments of Others?
Skill: Conceptual

72) A smoker illustrates the process of _____ when he claims that the evidence that smoking causes lung cancer is not very convincing.

   A) cognitive dissonance

   B) diffusion of responsibility

   C) disbelief

   D) normative influence

   E) cohesiveness

Answer: A
Diff: 2   Page Ref: 588
Topic: What Influences Our Judgments of Others?
Skill: Applied

73) Glinda does not believe in divorce, even though her husband is mean to her and treats her badly, she makes excuses for his behavior and tells everyone he is really a 'good guy'. _____ may explain Glinda's behavior.

   A) scapegoating

   B) prejudice

   C) discrimination

   D) a self–serving bias

   E) cognitive dissonance

Answer: E
Diff: 2   Page Ref: 588
Topic: What Influences Our Judgments of Others?
Skill: Applied

74) We tend to believe that other people's mistakes are due to

   A) situational factors.

   B) their personal traits.

   C) the situations they are in.

   D) random chance and luck.

   E) what is on that person's mind.

Answer: B
Diff: 2   Page Ref: 588
Topic: What Influences Our Judgments of Others?
Skill: Conceptual

75) The tendency to emphasize internal causes and ignore external pressures when describing others behavior is known as

A) cognitive dissonance.

B) social loafing.

C) self-serving bias.

D) groupthink.

E) fundamental attribution error.

Answer: E

Diff: 2   Page Ref: 589

Topic: What Influences Our Judgments of Others?

Skill: Factual

76) Tad gets an A in his psychology finals. When he tells his mother, she praises him for his brilliance. Tad's mother has committed which error?

A) parental myopia

B) fundamental attribution error

C) authoritarian error

D) self-serving bias

E) cognitive dissonance error

Answer: B

Diff: 2   Page Ref: 588

Topic: What Influences Our Judgments of Others?

Skill: Applied

77) A person who labels another another driver as an "idiot" after that driver cut them off during rush hour would be said to show

A) cognitive dissonance.

B) a self-fulfilling prophecy.

C) social norm validation.

D) the fundamental attribution error.

E) prejudice.

Answer: D

Diff: 2   Page Ref: 588

Topic: What Influences Our Judgments of Others?

Skill: Applied

78) People with a self-serving bias attribute their success to _____ factors and their failures to _____ factors.

    A) informative; normative

    B) normative; informative

    C) internal; external

    D) situational; dispositional

    E) prejudicial; discriminatory

Answer: C

Diff: 2   *Page Ref: 589–590*

Topic: What Influences Our Judgments of Others?

Skill: Conceptual

79) Mary is a superb golfer, she has hired the best and most expensive coach around, when she wins a big tournament she is likely to credit her own talent. When she loses however she is likely to blame her coach for, 'not doing enough to help her'. This explanatory style demonstrates the

    A) self-serving bias.

    B) fundamental attribution error.

    C) groupthink.

    D) social loafing.

    E) discrimination.

Answer: A

Diff: 2   *Page Ref: 590*

Topic: What Influences Our Judgments of Others?

Skill: Applied

80) When Ramon uses a self-serving bias, he is likely to believe that

    A) Kristin will go out on a date with him.

    B) he will not beat Kevin in racquetball.

    C) his friend, Emma, got an A in her anatomy class, because she is brilliant.

    D) other people will agree with his political views.

    E) it is his teacher's fault that he failed his chemistry test.

Answer: E

Diff: 2   *Page Ref: 589–590*

Topic: What Influences Our Judgments of Others?

Skill: Applied

81) _____ refers to a learned negative attitude toward a person based on that person's membership in a particular group.

   A) The Asch effect

   B) Discrimination

   C) Prejudice

   D) Normative justice

   E) Conformity

Answer: C
Diff: 2   *Page Ref: 590*
Topic: What Influences Our Judgments of Others?
Skill: Factual

82) Prejudice is to discrimination as

   A) social norms are to social rules.

   B) unpredictability is to cognitive dissonance.

   C) anger is to hate.

   D) thought is to action.

   E) hitting is to punching.

Answer: D
Diff: 3   *Page Ref: 590–591*
Topic: What Influences Our Judgments of Others?
Skill: Conceptual

83) Discrimination relates to _____, while prejudice relates to _____.

   A) unconscious forces; behavior

   B) behavior; cognition

   C) affect; behavior

   D) affect; cognition

   E) cognition; behavior

Answer: B
Diff: 2   *Page Ref: 590*
Topic: What Influences Our Judgments of Others?
Skill: Factual

84) A landlord who refuses to rent an apartment to a homosexual is

    A) conforming to prevailing social attitudes.

    B) discriminating.

    C) a compassionate conservative.

    D) not a good samaritan.

    E) scapegoating.

Answer: B
Diff: 2   *Page Ref: 590*
Topic: What Influences Our Judgments of Others?
Skill: Conceptual

85) Which of the following is TRUE about social distance?

    A) Prejudice increases social distance.

    B) The in-group serves to decrease social distance toward newcomers.

    C) As the social distance increases, the probability of prejudice increases.

    D) Social distance can only be bridged by scapegoating.

    E) Social distance leads to the prevention of discrimination.

Answer: C
Diff: 3   *Page Ref: 590-591*
Topic: What Influences Our Judgments of Others?
Skill: Conceptual

86) _____ refers to a situation in which an innocent group receives blame from a group that feels threatened.

    A) The bystander effect

    B) The fundamental attribution error

    C) Scapegoating

    D) Discrimination

    E) Proximity

Answer: C
Diff: 3   *Page Ref: 591*
Topic: What Influences Our Judgments of Others?
Skill: Conceptual

87) In families with multiple siblings, the youngest child who is often blamed for everything easily falls prey to

    A) out–group.

    B) prejudice.

    C) scapegoating.

    D) discrimination.

    E) self–serving bias.

Answer: C
Diff: 2   *Page Ref: 591*
Topic: What Influences Our Judgments of Others?
Skill: Applied

88) Which of the following violates a common social norm?

    A) a woman secretary

    B) a maternal older woman

    C) a handsome leading man

    D) a child being raised by 2 fathers

    E) a wise professor

Answer: D
Diff: 1   *Page Ref: 591–592*
Topic: What Influences Our Judgments of Others?
Skill: Conceptual

89) Research suggests that _____ and _____ can diminish prejudice in a person who do not wish to hear another point of view.

    A) education; contact

    B) equal status contact; new role models

    C) seminars; workshops

    D) cohabitation; rewards

    E) forced time spent together; lectures

Answer: B
Diff: 3   *Page Ref: 593*
Topic: What Influences Our Judgments of Others?
Skill: Conceptual

90) When people of various races are playing on the same soccer team, they are involved in
    A) equal status contact.
    B) general adaptation syndrome.
    C) mutual conformity.
    D) equal context conflict.
    E) contextual ambiguity.

Answer: A
Diff: 3   Page Ref: 593
Topic: What Influences Our Judgments of Others?
Skill: Applied

91) One of the most effective ways to eliminate prejudice towards groups unlike one's self is to
    A) force them together.
    B) have them spend time with one another.
    C) explain to each of the groups that prejudice and discrimination is bad.
    D) have them compete against one another in a given task.
    E) None of the above will work to reduce prejudice and discrimination.

Answer: B
Diff: 3   Page Ref: 593
Topic: What Influences Our Judgments of Others?
Skill: Applied

92) When one increases their performance while other people are watching they are demonstrating
    A) social facilitation.
    B) social loafing.
    C) discrimination.
    D) deindividuation.
    E) social interference.

Answer: A
Diff: 2   Page Ref: 593
Topic: What Influences Our Judgments of Others?
Skill: Factual

93) You have practice for weeks to perform in the fall play at school. In practice on occasion you have messed up your lines or forgotten a movement, however on the evening of the performance you are flawless. Which of the following phenomena did you likely experience?

  A) social loafing

  B) deindividuation

  C) fundamental attribution error

  D) social facilitation

  E) self–serving bias

  Answer: D

  Diff: 2   Page Ref: 593

  Topic: What Influences Our Judgments of Others?

  Skill: Applied

94) At the homecoming assembly at school, you take part in harassing the other grades in your school, and activity that you would not be likely to engage in by yourself. Which of the following best explains your behavior?

  A) social loafing

  B) deindividuation

  C) social facilitation

  D) fundamental attribution error

  E) self–serving bias

  Answer: B

  Diff: 2   Page Ref: 591

  Topic: What Influences Our Judgments of Others?

  Skill: Applied

95) You are working on a group project in class with four other people, it turns out that yourself and two others are the only one's doing any work. What best explains why the other two members of your group are not working?

  A) social loafing

  B) scapegoating

  C) social facilitation

  D) self–serving bias

  E) deindivuation

  Answer: A

  Diff: 2   Page Ref: 593

  Topic: What Influences Our Judgments of Others?

  Skill: Applied

96) A decrease in performance because f being in a group is

   A) social interference.

   B) social facilitation.

   C) social loafing.

   D) self–serving bias.

   E) the bystander effect.

Answer: C
Diff: 1   Page Ref: 594
Topic: What Influences Our Judgments of Others?
Skill: Factual

97) When individuals opinion become more extreme it is considered

   A) groupthink.

   B) group polarization.

   C) social loafing.

   D) fundamental attribution error.

   E) None of the above

Answer: B
Diff: 1   Page Ref: 594
Topic: What Influences Our Judgments of Others?
Skill: Factual

98) When you talk to your parents about extending your curfew beyond 12:00 you both become irate and wind up at an even more extreme position towards one another, this is an example of

   A) groupthink.

   B) fundamental attribution error.

   C) deindividuation.

   D) group polarization.

   E) social loafing.

Answer: D
Diff: 1   Page Ref: 594
Topic: What Influences Our Judgments of Others?
Skill: Applied

99) Often times in congressional sessions, republicans will present and issue and rather than listening, Democrats will become even more opposed to the idea. this is an example of

    A) group polarization.

    B) self-serving bias.

    C) self-fulfilling prophecy.

    D) groupthink.

    E) deindividuation.

Answer: A

Diff: 3   *Page Ref: 594*

Topic: What Influences Our Judgments of Others?

Skill: Applied

100) The excessive tendency to seek concurrence among group members is known as

    A) self-serving bias.

    B) groupthink.

    C) self-fulfilling prophecy.

    D) group polarization.

    E) prejudice.

Answer: B

Diff: 2   *Page Ref: 594*

Topic: What Influences Our Judgments of Others?

Skill: Factual

101) When your boss at work encourages all of the employees to go along with his ideas without questions he is encouraging

    A) deindividuation.

    B) groupthink.

    C) group polarization.

    D) self-serving bias.

    E) self-fulfilling prophecy.

Answer: B

Diff: 2   *Page Ref: 594*

Topic: What Influences Our Judgments of Others?

Skill: Applied

102) The key components of love, according to Robert Sternberg, are

    A) peace, love, and understanding.

    B) romance, kindness, and honesty.

    C) shared values, sense of humor, and selflessness.

    D) physical attraction, mutual concern, and compromise.

    E) passion, intimacy, and commitment.

Answer: E
Diff: 3   Page Ref: 594–595
Topic: Loving Relationships
Skill: Factual

103) According to Sternberg, the category of love known as _____ has much passion and intimacy, but little commitment.

    A) friendship

    B) infatuation

    C) romantic love

    D) self–love

    E) consummate love

Answer: C
Diff: 2   Page Ref: 594
Topic: Loving Relationships
Skill: Factual

104) Sternberg's theory regarding relationships is known as

    A) the theory of romantic love.

    B) the triangular theory of love.

    C) the companionate theory of love.

    D) reward model of love.

    E) physical attraction model of love.

Answer: B
Diff: 2   Page Ref: 595
Topic: Loving Relationships
Skill: Factual

105) Which of the following is true of aggression?

    A) Aggression is clearly different than simple violence.

    B) Violence involves purely psychological motives.

    C) An act is defined as aggression only if it harms the other person.

    D) Aggression is any behavior that is intended to harm another.

    E) Accidentally running over another person is an act of aggression.

Answer: D
Diff: 2   Page Ref: 596
Topic: What Are the Roots of Violence and Terrorism?
Skill: Factual

106) _____ and colleagues set up a Boy Scout Camp, known as the Robbers' Cave, to measure conflict.

    A) Solomon Asch

    B) Muzafer Sherif

    C) Robert Sternberg

    D) Stanley Milgram

    E) Philip Zimbardo

Answer: B
Diff: 1   Page Ref: 597
Topic: What Are the Roots of Violence and Terrorism?
Skill: Factual

107) In Sherif's 'Robber's Cave' study, the boys from the different group would work together when

    A) they were told they were just playing a game (such as tug-o-war).

    B) they were each given separate tasks to accomplish.

    C) they was a common task for the boys to achieve.

    D) they had friends on the other team.

    E) they were compting against one another.

Answer: C
Diff: 2   Page Ref: 597
Topic: What Are the Roots of Violence and Terrorism?
Skill: Conceptual

108) In the Robbers' Cave study, group _____ was increased within a single group by separating the two groups of boys.

A) cognition

B) cooperation

C) cohesiveness

D) conformity

E) civility

Answer: C

Diff: 2   Page Ref: 597

Topic: What Are the Roots of Violence and Terrorism?

Skill: Factual

109) By creating situations that demanded _____ between groups, the conflict between the Eagles and the Rattlers was eventually decreased in the Robbers' Cave experiment.

A) cooperation

B) socialization

C) competition

D) time spent

E) diversity

Answer: A

Diff: 1   Page Ref: 597

Topic: What Are the Roots of Violence and Terrorism?

Skill: Factual

110) According to your text, _____ acts as a fuel for global terrorism.

A) poverty

B) hopelessness

C) depleted resources

D) joblessness

E) All of the above are correct.

Answer: E

Diff: 2   Page Ref: 598

Topic: What Are the Roots of Violence and Terrorism?

Skill: Factual

111) _____ has applied theories about competition and common goals to help break down hostilities between the Israelis and the Palestinians.

   A) Robert Sternberg

   B) Muzafer Sherif

   C) Herbert Kelman

   D) Stanley Milgram

   E) Jonathan Lash

Answer: C
Diff: 2   Page Ref: 599
Topic: What Are the Roots of Violence and Terrorism?
Skill: Factual

112) An antismoking ad that shows the "Marlboro Man" as sickly, coughing, and needing a respirator would make use of

   A) the power of authority.

   B) conformity.

   C) scapegoating.

   D) social validation.

   E) the poison parasite argument.

Answer: E
Diff: 2   Page Ref: 602
Topic: Social Psychology: The State of the Art
Skill: Applied

Check Your Understanding Questions

1) The Stanford prison experiment illustrates the power of _____ to influence people's behavior.

   A) personality

   B) heredity

   C) childhood experiences

   D) the situation

   E) habituation

Answer: D
Diff: 2   Page Ref: 583
Topic: Check Your Understanding
Skill: Recall

2) Which of the following would be a social role?

A) prisoner

B) student

C) professor

D) All of the above are correct.

E) None of the above are correct.

Answer: D
Diff: 2   Page Ref: 583
Topic: Check Your Understanding
Skill: Recall

3) In the Asch studies, which of the following produced a decrease in conformity?

A) The task was seen as difficult or ambiguous.

B) The subject had to respond publicly, rather than privately.

C) The majority was not unanimous in its judgment.

D) The group was very large.

E) The group was very small.

Answer: C
Diff: 2   Page Ref: 583
Topic: Check Your Understanding
Skill: Recall

4) In Milgram's original study, about what proportion of the teachers gave the maximum shock?

A) about two–thirds

B) about 10%

C) about 3%

D) nearly all

E) about 50%

Answer: A
Diff: 2   Page Ref: 583
Topic: Check Your Understanding
Skill: Recall

5) In an emergency situation, you would have the best chance of getting help from a

    A) lone bystander.

    B) large group of people.

    C) group of people who are friends of each other.

    D) group of six people.

    E) group of strangers.

Answer: A
Diff: 2   *Page Ref: 583*
Topic: Check Your Understanding
Skill: Applied

6) Which of the following best illustrates people in ambiguous situations taking their cues from others?

    A) the majority of participants who expressed false judgments in the Asch experiments

    B) those who disobeyed Milgram

    C) helpers who has CPR training

    D) the experiments in the Latane & Darley study of bystander intervention

    E) those who obeyed Milgram

Answer: A
Diff: 2   *Page Ref: 583*
Topic: Check Your Understanding
Skill: Understanding the Core Concept

7) According to Aronson, we can explain almost everything about interpersonal attraction with a theory of

    A) love.

    B) rewards.

    C) genetics.

    D) gender.

    E) environmental influences.

Answer: B
Diff: 2   *Page Ref: 596*
Topic: Check Your Understanding
Skill: Recall

8) Which of the following does the research suggest os most important in predicting initial attraction?

A) physical attractiveness

B) money

C) personality

D) nurturing qualities

E) sense of humor

Answer: A

Diff: 2   *Page Ref: 596*

Topic: Check Your Understanding

Skill: Recall

9) Which theory of attraction best explains why people who are considered extremely competent are often not the people we are most attracted to?

A) reward theory

B) expectancy–value theory

C) cognitive dissonance theory

D) psychoanalytic theory

E) conformity theory

Answer: B

Diff: 3   *Page Ref: 596*

Topic: Check Your Understanding

Skill: Recall

10) According to the cognitive dissonance theory, why would people support a candidate who might potentially be corrupt?

A) because they may have put much money and time into campaigning for the candidate

B) because they want to benefit financially from being close to the candidate

C) because they want to have some influence over the candidate

D) because he(she) may still be the best alternative

E) According to the cognitive dissonance theory, we would never support a candidate who we thought might be corrupt.

Answer: A

Diff: 3   *Page Ref: 596*

Topic: Check Your Understanding

Skill: Applied

11) Prejudice is a(n)_____, while discrimination is a(n) _____.

    A) behavior; attitude

    B) instinct; choice

    C) attitude; behavior

    D) stimulus; response

    E) choice; ethic

Answer: C

Diff: 1   *Page Ref: 596*

Topic: Check Your Understanding

Skill: Recall

12) The evidence that one of the most effective techniques for eliminating racial prejudice has been

    A) education.

    B) threat and force.

    C) legislation.

    D) tax incentives.

    E) choice.

Answer: C

Diff: 3   *Page Ref: 596*

Topic: Check Your Understanding

Skill: Recall

13) Reward theory, expectancy–theory, cognitive dissonance, and attribution theory all tell us that we respond not just to situations but also to

    A) our cognitive interpretations of them.

    B) our social instincts.

    C) the intensity of the stimuli.

    D) our biological needs and drives.

    E) our unconscious needs.

Answer: A

Diff: 2   *Page Ref: 596*

Topic: Check Your Understanding

Skill: Understanding the Core Concept

14) Conflict between the groups in the Robbers Cave experiment was encouraged by
   A) punishing aggressive boys.
   B) showing movies featuring hostile role models.
   C) competitive games.
   D) putting a particularly aggressive boy in charge of each group.
   E) encouraging competition.

Answer: C
Diff: 2   Page Ref: 600
Topic: Check Your Understanding
Skill: Recall

15) In Kelman's work in the Middle East, he removed much of the incentive for competitive responses by
   A) punishing those who responded competitively.
   B) holding the meetings in private.
   C) taking hostages from both sides.
   D) publicly denouncing those who responded competitively.
   E) encouraging competition.

Answer: B
Diff: 2   Page Ref: 601
Topic: Check Your Understanding
Skill: Recall

16) In both the Robbers Cave experiment and Kelman's work in the Middle East, helping people to build a sense of mutual interdependence encouraged them to
   A) alter their perceptions of each other.
   B) punish those who had encouraged hostilities.
   C) become more creative.
   D) adopt new personality traits.
   E) become more aggressive.

Answer: A
Diff: 2   Page Ref: 601
Topic: Check Your Understanding
Skill: Understanding the Core Concept

True/False Questions

1) The situation we are in can be just as persuasive as our disposition in determining how we behave.

   Answer: TRUE
   Diff: 1   Page Ref: 566
   Topic: How Does the Social Situation Affect Our Behavior?
   Skill: Factual

2) We always see the world in a totally objective light.

   Answer: FALSE
   Diff: 1   Page Ref: 567
   Topic: How Does the Social Situation Affect Our Behavior?
   Skill: Factual

3) The fact that you behave differently in church than you do at a football game is an example of your different social roles.

   Answer: TRUE
   Diff: 1   Page Ref: 568
   Topic: How Does the Social Situation Affect Our Behavior?
   Skill: Applied

4) A script can influence our perception of what 'should' happen in a given situation.

   Answer: TRUE
   Diff: 2   Page Ref: 569
   Topic: How Does the Social Situation Affect Our Behavior?
   Skill: Factual

5) An emergent norm is one that has been well established over a long period of time.

   Answer: FALSE
   Diff: 2   Page Ref: 570
   Topic: How Does the Social Situation Affect Our Behavior?
   Skill: Factual

6) Solomon Asch found that about one-third of the subjects conformed with the majority's wrong perceptual judgments at least once.

   Answer: FALSE
   Diff: 2   Page Ref: 571
   Topic: How Does the Social Situation Affect Our Behavior?
   Skill: Factual

7) You are most likely to conform in the Asch task when the judgement task is easy.

Answer: FALSE
Diff: 2   Page Ref: 571–572
Topic: How Does the Social Situation Affect Our Behavior?
Skill: Conceptual

8) Groupthink tends to occur when there are many non-conforming individualists in the group.

Answer: FALSE
Diff: 2   Page Ref: 573
Topic: How Does the Social Situation Affect Our Behavior?
Skill: Conceptual

9) Milgram found that most people obeyed the order of the authority figure to purposely harm another person.

Answer: TRUE
Diff: 2   Page Ref: 574
Topic: How Does the Social Situation Affect Our Behavior?
Skill: Conceptual

10) People in Milgram's study were likely to resist obedience if they saw someone else doing this first.

Answer: TRUE
Diff: 2   Page Ref: 575
Topic: How Does the Social Situation Affect Our Behavior?
Skill: Conceptual

11) Before the study began, Milgram expected that about 50% of participants would go all the way to 450 volts on the shock plate.

Answer: FALSE
Diff: 2   Page Ref: 576
Topic: How Does the Social Situation Affect Our Behavior?
Skill: Factual

12) In Milgram's study, the participants was more likely to defy the experimenter if the experimenter gave instructions from another room.

Answer: TRUE
Diff: 2   Page Ref: 577
Topic: How Does the Social Situation Affect Our Behavior?
Skill: Factual

13) As the size of the group increases, your chances of getting help (should you need it) also increase.

Answer: FALSE
Diff: 2   Page Ref: 579
Topic: How Does the Social Situation Affect Our Behavior?
Skill: Factual

14) You can increase your chances of getting it by asking specific individuals to help you rather than just calling out, "Help me!"

Answer: TRUE
Diff: 2   Page Ref: 581
Topic: How Does the Social Situation Affect Our Behavior?
Skill: Factual

15) When Sally winds up dating her next door neighbor, this is an example of the proximity principle.

Answer: TRUE
Diff: 2   Page Ref: 585
Topic: What Influences Our Judgments of Others?
Skill: Factual

16) According to the proximity principle, the more we see someone, the more likely we are to like him or her.

Answer: TRUE
Diff: 2   Page Ref: 585
Topic: What Influences Our Judgments of Others?
Skill: Conceptual

17) Men are more influenced by physical attractiveness than are women.

Answer: TRUE
Diff: 2   Page Ref: 586
Topic: What Influences Our Judgments of Others?
Skill: Conceptual

18) Someone who believes in the matching hypothesis would not be surprised to find that two attractive people with different interests are dating each other.

Answer: TRUE
Diff: 2   Page Ref: 586-587
Topic: What Influences Our Judgments of Others?
Skill: Applied

19) You may experience cognitive dissonance if you find that a friend you have been sticking up for has been dishonest with you.

Answer: TRUE
Diff: 2   *Page Ref: 587*
Topic: What Influences Our Judgments of Others?
Skill: Applied

20) To alleviate cognitive dissonance from our lives we try to act consistently with our beliefs.

Answer: TRUE
Diff: 2   *Page Ref: 587–588*
Topic: What Influences Our Judgments of Others?
Skill: Factual

21) If you are late for class and your teacher attributes this to your laziness, she is using the self–serving bias.

Answer: FALSE
Diff: 2   *Page Ref: 589*
Topic: What Influences Our Judgments of Others?
Skill: Conceptual

22) If Donovan is typical, he would believe that the main reason he scored no points in a basketball game is that he has no basketball talent.

Answer: FALSE
Diff: 2   *Page Ref: 589*
Topic: What Influences Our Judgments of Others?
Skill: Applied

23) We are likely to use scapegoating to individuals who are in a subservient position to our own (even if this position is only perceived).

Answer: TRUE
Diff: 2   *Page Ref: 591*
Topic: What Influences Our Judgments of Others?
Skill: Conceptual

24) Romantic love is a temporary emotional state.

Answer: TRUE
Diff: 2   *Page Ref: 594*
Topic: Loving Relationships
Skill: Factual

25) Having "dumb jocks' in television shows reinforces stereotypes.

Answer: TRUE
Diff: 2   Page Ref: 592
Topic: What Influences Our Judgments of Others?
Skill: Conceptual

26) If George hits three home runs in the playoffs in front of a huge crowd, it could be said that social facilitation influenced his play.

Answer: TRUE
Diff: 2   Page Ref: 593
Topic: What Influences Our Judgments of Others?
Skill: Applied

27) Encouraging individuals to voice their opinions in a safe environment should discourage groupthink.

Answer: TRUE
Diff: 2   Page Ref: 594
Topic: What Influences Our Judgments of Others?
Skill: Conceptual

28) Half of all first marriages end in divorce.

Answer: TRUE
Diff: 1   Page Ref: 594
Topic: Loving Relationships
Skill: Factual

29) The three components to Robert Sternberg's triangular theory of love are intimacy, passion and romance.

Answer: FALSE
Diff: 3   Page Ref: 595
Topic: Loving Relationships
Skill: Factual

30) The Rattlers and Eagles of the Robbers' Cave study were bonded after listening to a series of lectures discussing cooperation.

Answer: FALSE
Diff: 2   Page Ref: 597
Topic: What Are the Roots of Violence and Terrorism?
Skill: Applied

31) In the 'Robber's Cave' experiment, they boys would not work together under any circumstances.

Answer: FALSE
Diff: 2   Page Ref: 597-598
Topic: What Are the Roots of Violence and Terrorism?
Skill: Factual

32) Global terrorism is fueled by conditions of poverty, helplessness, and powerlessness.

Answer: TRUE
Diff: 2   Page Ref: 598
Topic: Multiple Perspectives on Terrorism
Skill: Factual

Short Answer Questions

1) Provide a brief script for attending a birthday party.

Answer: You should arrive with a gift, the person of honor will eventually open the gifts, everyone will then sing happy birthday, the person will blow out the candles and everyone will enjoy cake.
Diff: 2   Page Ref: 569
Topic: How Does the Social Situation Affect Our Behavior?
Skill: Conceptual

2) What did Solomon Asch attempt to measure in his studies involving lines of differing lengths?

Answer: conformity to social norms
Diff: 1   Page Ref: 571
Topic: How Does the Social Situation Affect Our Behavior?
Skill: Factual

3) What was the rationale for Stanley Milgram's study of obedience?

Answer: To determine whether a person who would follow orders to harm another does so because they have some unique feature of personality.
Diff: 3   Page Ref: 574
Topic: How Does the Social Situation Affect Our Behavior?
Skill: Conceptual

4) _____ conducted the line study on conformity. _____ conducted the 'teacher/learner' obedience study and _____ conducted the Stanford Prison Experiment.

Answer: Asch; Milgram; Zimbardo
Diff: 3   Page Ref: 565-575
Topic: How Does the Social Situation Affect Our Behavior?
Skill: Factual

5) Some commentators on the Kitty Genovese murder blamed flaws in those people rather than social circumstances. This is an example of the _____ error.

Answer: fundamental attribution
Diff: 2   *Page Ref: 579*
Topic: What Influences Our Judgments of Others?
Skill: Conceptual

6) As a result of _____, people in larger groups feel less obligated to help someone in need.

Answer: diffusion of responsibility
Diff: 2   *Page Ref: 580*
Topic: How Does the Social Situation Affect Our Behavior?
Skill: Conceptual

7) What are the factors that dictate whom we like, according to the reward theory of attraction?

Answer: physical appearance, proximity, similarity, and self-disclosure
Diff: 3   *Page Ref: 584–585*
Topic: What Influences Our Judgments of Others?
Skill: Applied

8) _____ theory accounts for the self-justification that people engage in when they behave in ways that are not consistent with their internal state. how do we attempt to eliminate this in our lives?

Answer: Cognitive dissonance; we try to change our actions to match our beliefs or our beliefs to match our actions. We try to be congruent in our behavior and our beliefs.
Diff: 2   *Page Ref: 587–588*
Topic: What Influences Our Judgments of Others?
Skill: Conceptual

9) When you take credit for your success while denying responsibility for your failure, you are showing

Answer: self-serving bias
Diff: 2   *Page Ref: 589*
Topic: What Influences Our Judgments of Others?
Skill: Conceptual

10) Give an example of how prejudice and discrimination had been show to change.

Answer: Exposure to groups other than our own tends to be the best way to see member of different groups as individuals rather than as just, 'part of the crowd'. This interaction keeps us from making overgeneralizations.
Diff: 2   *Page Ref: 592*
Topic: What Influences Our Judgments of Others?
Skill: Conceptual

11) Why when working on a group project do some people work less hard, how can this be combatted?

Answer: social loafing, give everyone an individual role to play and a piece of the project for which they are responsibly this will hold them responsible for at least ding some of the work

Diff: 2   Page Ref: 593

Topic: What Influences Our Judgments of Others?

Skill: Conceptual

12) The Bay of Pigs invasion was ill advised, but there was not anyone to stand up and offer another solution, this is an example of _____.

Answer: groupthink

Diff: 2   Page Ref: 594

Topic: What Influences Our Judgments of Others?

Skill: Applied

13) Name the three components of love as emphasized by Sternberg's triangular theory of love.

Answer: passion, intimacy, and commitment

Diff: 3   Page Ref: 593

Topic: Loving Relationships

Skill: Applied

14) In Sherif's 'Robber's Cave' study under what conditions would the boys from the two different groups work together?

Answer: when they were given a common goal to achieve

Diff: 2   Page Ref: 597

Topic: What Are the Roots of Violence and Terrorism?

Skill: Factual

Essay Questions

1) Discuss the Asch effect and the factors that affect the conformity behaviors in his experiments.

Answer: The Asch effect means that the majority influences individuals' judgments. People are more likely to conform when: the group size is bigger, there are no dissenters, the size of the discrepancy is small, the task is difficult or ambiguous, group members are seen as equally competent, and when responses are given publicly.

Diff: 2   Page Ref: 571–573

Topic: How Does the Social Situation Affect Our Behavior?

Skill: Conceptual

2) Explain the larger implications of both the Stanford Prison experiment and Milgram's Obedience experiment. What good can from from the findings of these experiments.

   Answer: Both suggest that if given the right situation everyone has the capacity for good or evil. By making people aware of this as well as one's likelihood to role play (Prison experiment) or obey figures of authority (Milgram's experiment) we can make them question their behavior and perhaps behave better. Both studies also examine why the results turned out as they did, while we cannot replicate them because of ethical reasons, we can insure that certain environments, be that school or work environments do to exhibit the same characteristics.

   Diff: 2   Page Ref: 565-577

   Topic: How Does the Social Situation Affect Our Behavior?

   Skill: Applied

3) Describe the methods and results of the Milgram studies of obedience. Specifically, include the immediate findings, and the larger implications of the study.

   Answer: Milgram asked people to give increasingly higher voltage shocks to 'learners' who gave incorrect answers. Learners could be heard, but not seen. Milgram found that two-thirds of all subjects gave the maximum (450 volts) shocks, despite the fact that the learner stopped responding at some point. People tend to obey authority figures because: the authority figure had a higher status than the subjects, the authority figure was monitoring the person's behavior at all times, and the victim was remote. The power of the situation often determines behavior more so than personality traits. Even the nicest of all people may be capable of evil if the power of the situation is powerful enough.

   Diff: 2   Page Ref: 575-578

   Topic: How Does the Social Situation Affect Our Behavior?

   Skill: Conceptual

4) Describe the four factors that underlie interpersonal attraction.

   Answer: The factors include proximity (living in the same block), similarity, physical attractiveness, and the degree to which the person engages in self-disclosure.

   Diff: 1   Page Ref: 584-586

   Topic: What Influences Our Judgments of Others?

   Skill: Factual

5) Identify the five causes of prejudice discussed in the text, and discuss them in detail. How can prejudice be combatted?

   Answer: The five main factors are dissimilarity, economic competition, scapegoating, conformity to social norms, and media stereotypes. To combat prejudice, new role models, equal status contact, and legislation have all proven to be effective.

   Diff: 2   Page Ref: 590-592

   Topic: What Influences Our Judgments of Others?

   Skill: Applied

6) Give an example of hoe each of the following may be seen in a corporate setting in which e number of individuals are working on an advertising campaign.
groupthink
social loafing
self-serving bias
social facilitation

Answer: Groupthink: if the leader of the group has an idea about the advertisement and wants to use their idea without encouraging other ideas this may lead to groupthink.
Social Loafing: If there are eight people assigned t the project and nobody has specific roles to play, there may be people who decide they are not going to work very hard.
Self-Serving Bias: If they get the job, each member of the team is likely to take credit for their role in the project.
Social facilitation: As the team present their project to the buyer, they may put on a flawless front even if there are rough edges behind the scenes.

Diff: 2   *Page Ref: 589/593–594*

Topic: What Influences Our Judgments of Others?

Skill: Conceptual

7) Describe Sternberg's triangular theory of love.

Answer: Sternberg argued that three components of love combine to form different types of love. The factors are passion (erotic attraction), commitment (one's dedication to the relationship), and intimacy (shared feelings).

Diff: 2   *Page Ref: 594–595*

Topic: Loving Relationships

Skill: Factual

8) What can we learn from Sherif's 'Robber's Cave' study that can help us in getting groups to cooperate with one another?

Answer: When the boys were given a task in which they had to work together to accomplish, they put aside their personal disagreements with one another for the good of the group. herbert Kelman suggest that in the middle east for example, community leaders come together to work with one another to solve their regions problems rather than their own.

Diff: 2   *Page Ref: 597–599*

Topic: What Are the Roots of Violence and Terrorism?

Skill: Applied

NOTES

NOTES